# China's Exchange Rate System Reform

## Lessons for Macroeconomic Policy Management

# China's Exchange Rate System Reform

## Lessons for Macroeconomic Policy Management

## PAUL YIP Sau Leung

*Nanyang Technological University, Singapore*

 **World Scientific**

NEW JERSEY · LONDON · SINGAPORE · BEIJING · SHANGHAI · HONG KONG · TAIPEI · CHENNAI

*Published by*

World Scientific Publishing Co. Pte. Ltd.

5 Toh Tuck Link, Singapore 596224

*USA office:* 27 Warren Street, Suite 401-402, Hackensack, NJ 07601

*UK office:* 57 Shelton Street, Covent Garden, London WC2H 9HE

**British Library Cataloguing-in-Publication Data**
A catalogue record for this book is available from the British Library.

**CHINA'S EXCHANGE RATE SYSTEM REFORM**
**Lessons for Macroeconomic Policy Management**

ISBN-13 978-981-4289-10-8
ISBN-10 981-4289-10-8

Typeset by Stallion Press
Email: enquiries@stallionpress.com

Printed in Singapore.

*To my parents,*
*my wife,*
*my son, and*
*my daughter*

# Preface

In this book, the author would like to share his knowledge on macroeconomic policy management accumulated over the past thirty five years. The knowledge enabled him to help China

- avoid disastrous outcomes in its exchange rate system reform;
- correctly adopt a medium-term exchange rate arrangement with capital control so that it could better monitor its monetary growth and pace of appreciation;
- correctly freeze the development of the renminbi futures market in China and Hong Kong, which could lead to disastrous results on the Chinese economy;
- implement its banking reform along the right direction;
- correctly allow a trade surplus to finance China's outward investment until China's private and public holdings of overseas assets could match China's future status as a major economic power in the world;
- squeeze its stock market bubble before the global financial tsunami started to exert its substantial negative impacts on the Chinese economy;
- correctly adopt the ultra fiscal expansion and then substantial quantity easing during the global financial tsunami; and
- adopt enormous supply of public housing in its Twelfth Five-Year Plan as the long-term solution of property inflation in China.

The knowledge also enabled him to sell all his shares before the global financial tsunami, buy substantial amount of shares at extremely attractive prices during the lows in November 2008 and March–June

2009, and most importantly keep the same exposure to shares and avoid pre-mature profit taking for a few years until the expected overheated phase of the global economic recovery[1] (see also Chapter 12 on the importance of switching from high PE shares to good-quality low PE shares while keeping the same exposure to shares during the huge rally).

## I. The Risk of Severe Asset and CPI Inflation, Huge Exchange Rate Cycle and Then a Crisis in Economies Outside the US

If policy makers, economic officials and general readers believe that the author's knowledge and judgment during the above events are of any indication of usefulness of his accumulated knowledge, insights and talent on macroeconomic policy management, the author wants to warn them on

(1) the risk of severe global asset inflation, CPI inflation and exchange rate cycle during the global economic recovery from the financial tsunami; and
(2) the likelihood of an asset bubble and then a crisis in economies outside the US during the overheated phase of the recovery.

To avoid the above economic pains or disasters, the related governments should make every effort to mitigate the severity of the first problem and pre-empt the second problem from happening. The related governments should note that the economic pains or disasters could trigger social and political instability in their economies. For example, the rampant asset and CPI inflation could result in substantial accumulation of social dissatisfaction and hence political instability, especially in economies with high income inequality. The crisis, if ever happened, could also trigger political changes in the crisis-hit economies. For countries with internal social and

---

[1] Note, the most difficult part for most investors here is in fact the last step, i.e., keep the same exposure to shares and avoid pre-mature profit taking for a few years until reaching the expected overheated phase of the business cycle.

political weakness such as corruption, cronyism and improper political power structure, the political changes could be in the form of collapses of the governments.

Nevertheless, as explained in this book, containing the asset inflation era and pre-empting the crisis are never easy. To avoid the above from happening, the related governments are urged to read this book thoroughly and then do serious research on their internal and external economic conditions as well as the appropriate choice, dose and timing of the required policies.

## II. Three Prerequisites

Young readers who are interested in such kind of knowledge should note that there are at least three prerequisites behind such knowledge accumulation:

(a) solid theoretical foundation in economics;
(b) ability to observe and indentify important characteristics of various economic systems or major economic events; and most importantly,
(c) devotion to help people in their own economies or the global economy.

## IIa. *Importance of Solid Theorectial Training*

Very often in China's media and sometimes in the US media, the author has seen quite a large number of media discussants pretending to be experts when making their comments and suggestions on the macroeconomic policies in their countries. Nevertheless, if one has a reasonably solid training in economics, he can easily identify that many discussants' theoretical foundation is rather weak, and many of their comments or suggestions were made without deep, proper and serious enough thought. In some cases, their policy recommendations, if ever implemented, can result in disastrous outcomes in their countries.

For example, as explained in this book, those who recommended a once-and-for-all major revaluation of the renminbi, faster appreciation of the renminbi, or establishment of the renminbi futures market did not even know that their recommendations reflected their weak training in international macroeconomics and could cause disasters to their countries. Those who recommended to use policies to clear the trade surplus in China also did not know that their recommendation could deprive their country from the chance of accumulating sufficient private (and public) holdings of overseas asset until it matches China's growing economic status in the world. Even in the US or Japan, those who rejected the potential effectiveness of quantity easing because of their very limited understanding of the liquidity trap argument and their ignorance on other transmission mechanisms of monetary policy did not know that their recommendation could mean a much slower recovery of the US employment, and similar policy choice had contributed to the two-decade of economic stagnation in Japan.

To avoid similar mistakes, the author hopes that young readers with intention of helping their economies could make effort to strengthen their theoretical foundation in economics and keep updating themselves on new developments in economic theories. Meanwhile, he also hopes that academic economists could make appropriate arrangements so that new theoretical developments could be disseminated to policy makers in more readable and less technical form. In particular, it is the hope of the author to see the eventual establishment of macroeconomic policy management as a new discipline in economics.

## IIb. *Importance of Devotion*

In addition to solid theoretical training, devotion to help people is an even more important prerequisite for young readers to grow overtime as well-respected experts in macroeconomic policy management. Here, I would like to draw an analogy between devoted doctors and devoted economists. Consider a medical doctor who devotes his life-time effort to help people. Even if he cannot achieve much on the frontier of medicines because of his limitations in training or talent, he can still be a good general practitioner. Next, consider a doctor who is well-trained and talented enough to become a specialist in a certain field. If his major aim is to earn money, he cannot go far from there as most of his subsequent time and effort are used to earn money. In some cases, we can even see this type of doctors recommending people to do unnecessary operations. In fact, in Hong Kong and some other Asian economies, the author has seen a lot of private practitioners recommending, or more correctly, misleading pregnant women to give birth through operation instead of natural delivery. The author also saw a case in which a Hong Kong doctor recommended, or more correctly, misled the daughter of a 93-year old woman by saying that the old woman could live beyond 100 years if she took a recommended operation. Otherwise, the old woman could only live another few years. The end result was that the old women died within a few months after the operation.[2]

On the other hand, if the above mentioned specialist's original aim was to help people while having a decent income, he would very likely choose to work in a well-equipped public hospital, medical institute or university. After years of devotion and effort, he should be able to accumulate enough knowledge, experiences and even innovations that make him a well-respected expert in that field. If we look back to history, those who devoted their life-time efforts in the pursuance of medicine, such as the well-respected Li Shizhen (李时珍) in Chinese medicine in the Ming Dynasty, would get their well-respected status in history.

Similarly, devotion is also important in macroeconomic policy management. Even an economic official cannot achieve much in the frontier of economics because of the limitations of his training or talent. With devotion to do the job properly and readiness to consult experts when deemed necessary, he can still contribute a lot by helping his country to choose the right economic policy or the right expert. On the other hand, if an economist's only aim is to earn money, he can mislead his country to adopt a policy that is only favorable to his self-interest, which can be harmful to his country. For example, as discussed in Chapter 8, there were some economists in China's think-tank who recommended the government to support the stock market boom, or more correctly, fuel the stock market bubble in 2007, mainly because they had invested heavily in the stock market. Similarly, some property developers in China had also supported some

---

[2] While one major underlying reason for all these immoral medical recommendations is the property inflation in Hong Kong (i.e., these medical doctors purchase too many properties and need immoral medical recommendations to earn enough money to pay for the huge amount of monthly mortgage installment), the lack of devotion when these people choose their occupation is another major reason behind such immoral activities.

economists or research institutes so that their interest could be taken care through the biased reports by these economists.

Two common but important distractions among Chinese economists are:

(a) some are just interested in earning money in the stock market, property market and other asset markets; and
(b) some spend too much time to build up connections (guang-xi), which is extremely important to one's career in China.

As a result, only a very few percentage of economists has put most of their effort and time on the accumulation of the necessary knowledge that could enable them to deal with tough major economic problems.

## IIc. *Ability to Identify Important Characteristics*

In addition to solid theoretical foundation and devotion, ability to identify important characteristics of major economic events or economic systems is also important to macroeconomic policy management. This is so because on and off we might encounter some tough major economic problems that are new to us. By then, what we can rely on are:

(i) our devotion as an economist, i.e., the willingness to hear the complains of our people, find out the sources of their pains and accept potential limitations of existing models or analytical framework;
(ii) the ability to identify important characteristics of the tough economic problem; and
(iii) our theoretical foundation to rebuild the appropriate model or analytical framework for that economic problem.

One example of such tough major economic problems is the property inflation in China and some other Asian economies. As explained in Chapters 9–10, the Chinese (and East Asian) property markets have quite a few important characteristics that are very different from those in the Western world. As a result, there is not yet well-developed theory in the economic literature that one can use to analyze China's property market. Instead, some not that well-trained economists used the simple supply and demand analysis to analyze China's property market and made their policy recommendations. As explained in Chapters 9–10, this resulted in some predictions or diagnosis that seriously missed the actual outcomes. More importantly, it also resulted in very misleading and disastrous policy conclusions. However, as explained in Chapters 9–10, with the devotion to help his people, solid theoretical foundation as well as trained and in-born ability to identify important characteristics of the Chinese property market and income distribution, the author was able to discard the irrelevant part of the standard supply and demand analysis, rebuild the necessary analytical framework from first principle and come out with the appropriate solution to property inflation in China and some other Asian economies.

Another example of tough major economic problems is China's exchange rate system reform. As explained in Chapters 1–6, the exchange rate system reform is a very sophisticated exercise that requires consistency among various major dimensions of an economic system. If China adopted the proposals made by some Chinese economists at that time, the Chinese economy would be in deep trouble. Behind such misleading recommendations was the fact that these economists were not international macroeconomists by training (i.e., over 99% of the Chinese discussants do not have the formal training and hence solid theoretical foundation in international macroeconomics). Compared with the dogmatic market believers such as those who believed that free market force could do the allocation job in China's property market, these economists were at least better in the sense that they did read some books or articles while sorting out their recommendations on the exchange rate system reform. In fact, if these economists were asked to solve a standard macroeconomic problem, their efforts to look for the relevant references would usually be able to help them come out with the right policy, or at least not too bad a policy.

However, for the exchange rate system reform that requires consistency among various major dimensions of the economic system, such type of short-cut approach to problem solving is obviously insufficient. Instead, deep theoretical foundation and knowledge accumulation in international macroeconomics, devotion, and ability to identify important characteristics of the economic system are the keys for a proper design of the exchange rate system reform.

Another interesting phenomenon the author observed was that the top leaders in the Party, the State Council and the Chinese central bank at that time were able to appreciate the viability of the author's proposed design on the exchange rate system reform, while some of the above mentioned economists were not. One possible reason for the failure of the latter to appreciate the potential disasters of their recommendations was that their intention to defend their recommendations was greater than their concern on the potential disasters to the Chinese people (i.e., their devotion to help the people of their country was not strong enough). For example, when the author discussed with a *talented and knowledgeable* economic official in the State Administration of Foreign Exchange during his seminar at that authority, the economic official was more interested in convincing the author to accept his recommendation of an once-and-for-all revaluation of renminbi, which in turn stopped him from listening to potential disasters of his recommendation.

On the other hand, the top political leaders, Mr. Hu Jiantao and Mr. Wen Jiaobao, had the devotion to help their people. As a result, despite the fact that they were not economists by training, their devotion and their wisdom in political judgment enabled them to appreciate the viability of the author's proposal and the potential disasters of other recommendations. Similarly, the then Governor of the Chinese central bank at that time, Mr. Zhou Xiaochuan, was able to appreciate the viability of the author's proposal and the potential disasters of other recommendations, partly because he had the required economics training and partly because he had desire and need to pick up a viable proposal to safeguard his job.

## III. Devotion as an Important Safeguard Against Potential Misjudgment

Here, the author would like to further highlight the importance of devotion. After reading this book, readers might wonder why the author manages to make the right judgments and policy recommendations in most of the major economic events. The author's short answer is devotion. Throughout the past thirty five years of knowledge and experience accumulation on macroeconomic policy management, the author has been aware of the potential harm of making a misleading policy recommendation. Thus, he has put in a lot of efforts to ensure zero mistake, or at least close-to-zero mistake in major economic judgments and policy recommendations. In addition, whenever the author takes the time and trouble to write a policy article, there must be a reason (related to the well being of Chinese people). Thus, his devotion to help the people in his country gives him the right incentive behind each policy article, which will in turn provide some kind of safeguard on the importance and relevance of the policy article. Along with that, because of the above concern on the potential consequence of a misleading policy recommendation, the author will (i) only make policy comments and recommendations that he is very sure about; and (ii) always double-check the potential implications by asking himself whether the policy comments and recommendations will turn out to hurt the people of his country.

Finally, devotion also means willingness to hear and investigate people's complaints. This will in turn safeguard the economist from deviating far away from the people's needs. For example, during the property inflation in China in 2006–2010, the Chinese citizens had been yelling for their pains caused by the property inflation. However, some dogmatic market believers (usually with only elementary economics trainings)[3] still used the standard supply and demand analysis to insist that market force would do a good allocation job in China's property market. However,

---

[3] One major reason for some people to become dogmatic market believers is in fact their elementary and poor trainings in economics. As well-trained economists should have gone through many models and cases in which the market force would work reasonably well or poorly. Thus, even if some of them might be strong supporters of free market, they would never end up as dogmatic market believers. For example, Milton Friedman would not disagree that excessive monetary growth in a free market economy could cause a lot of problems. Neither would he disagree that the US's unintentional tight monetary conditions in the 1930s was one of the contributing (or at least assisting) causes of the Great Depression in the 1930s. On the other hand, many dogmatic market believers, because of their poor trainings in economics, had naturally chosen to memorize the result, such as "*one should always leave everything to the market*". As discussed in this book, there were in fact quite a number of cases that free market gave highly undesirable results (e.g., in the property market in China and in the generation of stock market bubble). Thus, for the dogmatic market believers, there was in fact a vicious cycle between their poor economics trainings and their tendency to memorize the result. In other words, it was their poor economics trainings that made them dogmatic market believers. On the other hand, their dogmatic belief was in fact a reflection of their poor economic trainings.

willingness to hear the pains of the Chinese people had induced the author to start investigating the characteristics of China's property market and reviewing the adequacy of the supply and demand analysis as an analytical framework on China's property market. As explained in Chapters 9–10, with the help of reasonably solid economic trainings, the author was able to come out with the right framework of and appropriate solution to China's property inflation. If the author had no such devotion, he would never start investigating and reconstructing the analytical framework.

After that, the author has kept telling his students, and would here like to tell readers, a good policy economist should be ready to hear and understand the needs and pains of people. The mistake of the above dogmatic market believers is that they are more interested in defending their belief rather than fulfilling the needs of the people in their country. In fact, their mistake is so ridiculous that it is equivalent to a medical doctor refusing to accept that his patients have pain by saying that "*according to my model, you (the patient) should not feel painful*". Of course, one can argue that the insufficient economic trainings of these dogmatic market believers stop them from realizing that supply and demand analysis is not the appropriate analytical framework for China's property market. However, the Chinese leader Mr. Hu Jiantao and the Chinese premier Mr. Wen Jiaobao are not even economists by training. How come they could hear the complaints and the pains of Chinese citizens, but the above dogmatic market believers could not? The author's answer is simple. It is because of their devotion and willingness to learn the needs and feelings of the people.[4] Once one can hear that, he can always find an expert to solve the problem.

---

[4] Here, the author would like to highlight that the Chinese translation of "*economics*", 经济 (Jing Ji), was actually extracted from the term 经世济民 (Jing Shi Ji Min), where the first two words 经世 (Jing Shi) mean "*running the society or economy*" and the last two words 济民 (Ji Min) mean "helping the people". Thus, the author hopes that young readers of this book would also bear this meaning in mind. Parallel with this, the author would like to include here one of his Chinese poems that is related to the above Chinese translation of economics:

泰河望舟

沧舟一叶御洪澜，漂泊江湖浩海间；
才气疏闲潇洒落，为磨经智济河山。

The poem was written at River Thames when he was doing his Ph.D. at the London School of Economics.

## IV. Avoid Over-Predicting, and Predict Only What Could Be Predicted

Thus, based on the above experience and thirty five years of making hard efforts, the author would like to inform young readers that it is possible to train themselves with the ability of close-to-zero mistakes at least in major economic judgments, provided they have the devotion to do so.[5] One more important point here is that one need to distinguish

(a) what can be predicted; and
(b) what cannot be predicted (i.e., not because you do not know, but because you *know* that it cannot be predicted).

For example, during the financial tsunami, there was a famous finance professor in the US who had given a series of warnings on the US economy. Despite the fact that he was a professor in finance, most of his comments were in fact based on his trainings in economics. While his accumulated knowledge in economics might not be as good as some other well-established economics professors, he did make very good judgments at the early stage of the financial tsunami. During that time, the author saw him as one of his favorite discussants on the US economy and the global economy. Nevertheless, in his subsequent comments, especially those after the stock market rebound from March–April 2009, he had committed a very serious mistake of over-predicting, i.e., he was trying to predict something that could not be precisely predicted, or trying to predict in a way that a prudent academia would avoid.

Throughout this book, the author organizes the chapters in the format that illustrates what a good economist can predict, and what a good economist cannot predict at a certain time. For example, as explained in Chapter 11,

---

[5] Of course, this would require many years of devoted effort on knowledge and experience accumulation. However, the key here is again devotion. In fact, in the first lecture of almost all his economics courses, the author would encourage his students to sort out their aspirations by saying that devoted effort on a difficult aspiration for 2–3 years might not be enough, but devoted effort on the same aspiration for 10 years would be quite something, devoted effort for 20 years would mean a lot, and devoted effort for 30 years could make them one the leading persons on that aspiration.

with the outbreak of the financial tsunami in the US, a good economist should be able to judge that that it would be just a matter of time that the effect would be spilled over to the export and hence GDP growth of China. Similarly, as explained in Chapters 9–10, with the market structure problem and other important characteristics in China's property market, a good economist should be able to judge that standard curbing measures of normal scale could at most reduce the property transaction volume with little change in the property price. Again, as explained in Chapter 8, if the Chinese government let the stock market bubble in 2007 continue to grow, a good economist should be able to judge that (i) it would be just a matter of time that some large enough negative shock in the future would trigger a bursting of the bubble; and (ii) by then, the Chinese economy would have to go through a very severe recession. Nevertheless, the exact timing of the bursting of bubble would depend on the pace that the bubble was growing, and when a large enough negative shock arrived. Thus, a good economist should know that, in the absence of extra relevant information, it would not be possible to predict the exact timing of the bursting of a bubble. However, a good economist should also know that, the later the arrival of the negative triggering shock, the greater the bubble and hence the greater the recession and crisis after the bursting of the bubble.

## V. Solving the Adverse Selection Problem in Macroeconomic Policy Management

While encouraging young readers to have aspiration to become great pioneers in macroeconomic policy management, the author wants to highlight important roles of economic officials and central bankers in China and other developing economies. Firstly, for standard economic problems, reasonably trained central bankers and economic officials should have knowledge and experience to solve the problems by themselves. Nevertheless, they should be humble enough to allow for the possibility that their theoretical foundations, experience and exposure might not be enough to enable them to solve tough major economic problems by themselves. Thus, they should make themselves more ready to seek for the help of experts.

Having said that, they can still play a very important role in helping their government solving the adverse selection problem in macroeconomic policy management. That is, given the huge amount of low-quality economic comments and policy recommendations in China and other developing economies, they can still use their knowledge of economics to help screen out the good quality economic comments and policy recommendations. Given that there are a lot of people in China trying to use ill-intention policy recommendations to pursue their personal interests, these officials should also use their economics knowledge to help screen out policy recommendations that could be harmful to their country. In fact, central bank and economic officials in China did make significant contribution along such direction, such as helping their country select a viable proposal on the exchange rate system reform, accept the proposal of freezing the renminbi futures market until the conditions of a liberalization are satisfied, adopt the proposal of huge supply of public housing as the appropriate long-term solution of China's housing problems, and so on.

Thus, despite occasional disagreements with the Chinese central bank on some major sophisticated economic issues, the author strongly believes that the Chinese government should try to utilize the economics knowledge of these central bank and economic officials by promoting them to various positions in the government.

## VI. Need to Have Macroeconomic Policy Management as a New Discipline of Economics

As explained above, solid theoretical foundation is important to good macroeconomic policy management. Nevertheless, as illustrated in this book, not all techniques in, and lessons from, macroeconomic policy management involve big and new theories in economics, i.e., they are not publishable in major economics journals. However, these techniques or lessons can affect the well being of millions or even billions of people. It is thus important to collect these techniques and lessons in a systematic way, which will facilitate further developments and evolution along this direction. Thus, it is particular useful to develop macroeconomic policy management as a new discipline in economics. It is the hope of the author that some established readers of this book will share the author's vision and strive along that direction. Parallel with this, the authors also hope that in the future there will be new specialized academic journals in the proposed discipline.

# About the Author

 Dr. Yip is currently employed as an Associate Professor in Economics at the Nanyang Technological University in Singapore. He was born in China and grew up in Hong Kong. He obtained his first degree from the University of Hong Kong, and his Master and Ph.D. degrees from the London School of Economics. He gained extensive central banking, financial and commercial experiences through senior positions with the Hong Kong Monetary Authority, the Bank of China and the Bank of East Asia. In addition to substantial publications in high-ranking economics, finance and management journals, he has made numerous important exchange rate and macroeconomic policy recommendations in China, Hong Kong and Singapore.

In particular, Dr. Yip is the original proponent of China's exchange rate system reform. His policy articles have also made substantial impacts on China's banking reform, choice of maintaining a trade surplus to finance outward investment, gradual squeezing of the stock market bubble before the global financial tsunami, use of ultra expansionary fiscal policy and substantial quantity easing to offset the impacts of the global financial tsunami, plan of using substantial public housing supply as a long-term solution of its property inflation. Dr. Yip has also published extensively on the exchange rate systems in China, Hong Kong and Singapore. In 2010–2011, he was selected as one of the 2000 intellectuals in the 21st Century by the International Biographical Centre and member of the Presidential Who's Who in the World by Marguis Who's Who.

# Brief Contents

# Contents

# Acknowledgements

The author would like to express his thanks to the *Hong Kong Economic Journal* for publishing more than one hundred of his policy articles on China's exchange rate system reform and macroeconomic policies, and the *Lianhe Zaobao*, the *China Securities Journal* and the *21ˢᵗ Century Business Herald* for publishing his remaining policy articles on China. He is also grateful to the *Xinhua News Agency* for reporting these policy articles as internal reports to the Chinese leaders, and Dr. Liu Guangxi for reporting these policy articles to the *People's Bank of China* and the *State Administration of Foreign Exchange*. Without their help and the support of the related authorities, the policy articles would not be able to exert so much influence on China's exchange rate system reform and macroeconomic policies. He would also like to thank the *State Administration of Foreign Exchange* for inviting him to deliver one internal seminar, two keynote speeches and some internal reports for the authority. Finally, he is grateful to the *People's Bank of China* and the *Hong Kong Exchange* for allowing him to express his disagreement on the setting up of the renminbi futures market in Hong Kong.

# Part I:

# China's Exchange Rate System Reform

# Chapter 1

# Macroeconomic Conditions and Debates Before the Reform

This chapter first briefly reviews China's macroeconomic condition before (and after) the transitional exchange rate system reform announced on 21 July 2005. It then outlines the debate before the transitional reform. By highlighting the risk of other proposals in the debate, this chapter will provide a better understanding on why China will eventually choose the transitional reform proposed by the author. The readers can also better appreciate that the exchange rate system reform is a highly sophisticated exercise that involves the right and mutually-consistent decisions in all relevant and inter-related dimensions of an economic system. By emphasizing this point, the author hopes that other developing or emerging economies can learn from China's experience, and be extremely careful whenever they want to reform or change their exchange rate systems.

## 1.1 Macroeconomic Conditions Before the Reform

### 1.1.1 *The Beginning of China's Persistent Trade Surplus*

As shown in Figure 1.1.1a, there was a major devaluation of the renminbi during the exchange rate system reform in January 1994 (i.e., the renminbi per US dollar rate rose 49.8% from the monthly average of 5.807 in December 1993 to 8.700 in January 1994). This resulted in a sudden surge in China's relative price competitiveness. For example, the inverse of China's CPI based real effective exchange rate (REER) rose 45% from 96.2 in December 1993 to 139.4 in January 1994.

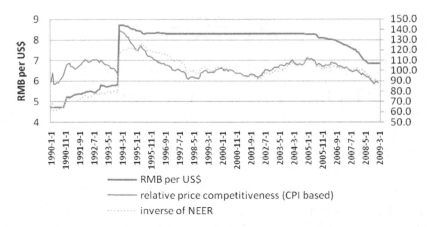

**Figure 1.1.1a.**   China's Exchange Rate

*Source*: Datastream

**Table 1.1.1.**   China's Trade Performance Before and After the Devaluation in 1994

| Schedule | 1991–1993 | 1994 | 1995 |
|---|---|---|---|
| Export Growth (%) | 12.8 | 36.3 | 23.1 |
| Import Growth (%) | 25.0 | 11.3 | 14.2 |
| Trade Balance (US$, billions) | -0.9 | 5.26 | 16.73 |

*Source*: Datastream

Such an increase in relative price competitiveness in turn caused a sudden surge of China's exports above the trend. For example, as shown in Table 1.1.1, China's total exports in US dollars grew by 36.3% in 1994 and 23.1% in 1995, much higher than the average growth of 12.8% during 1991–1993. Meanwhile, the import growth slowed down from the 1991–1993 average of 25% to 11.3% in 1994 and 14.2% in 1995. As a result, China's trade balance rose substantially from a slight deficit to a surplus of 5.26 billion US dollars in 1994 and then to a surplus of 16.73 billion US dollars in 1995.

Although the higher CPI inflation in China had thereafter caused a partial reversal in the rise of the relative price competitiveness, the competitiveness measure before the exchange rate system reform in July 2005 was still substantially above that before the major devaluation in 1994.[1] Meanwhile, with further upgrading of Chinese products, the continuation of the world's gradual acceptance of Chinese products, China's growing economic size and rising role in world trade, and other events such as China's entry into the WTO in December 2001 (i.e., lower tariff rate and less trade barriers for Chinese exports), China's trade surplus continued to grow between 1996 and 2005 (see Figure 1.1.1b). In addition, China's higher relative price competitiveness and growing internal market (due to growing economic size) had also attracted more and more FDI inflows.

Parallel with the persistent trade surplus and rising FDI inflows, China's foreign reserves also rose substantially during these years (see Figure 1.1.1c).

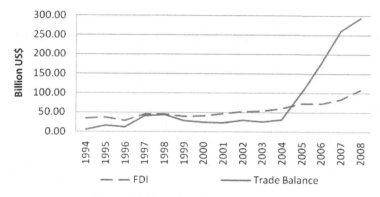

**Figure 1.1.1b.** Trade Surplus and FDIs

*Source*: CEIC

---

[1] As the renminbi did not vary much against the US dollar at that time, the 32.4% rise in the US's NEER between January 1994 and February 2002 had once wiped out most of China's gain in relative price competitiveness. However, with the subsequent reversal of the US's NEER since early 2002, China's relative price competitiveness rose back by some extent before the exchange rate system reform in July 2005 (see more detailed discussions in Section 1.1.2).

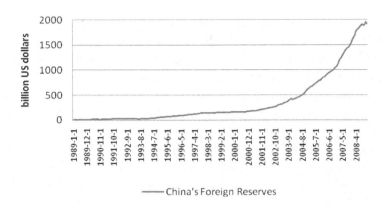

**Figure 1.1.1c.**   China's Foreign Reserves

*Source*: CEIC

## 1.1.2   *The Asian Financial Crisis: The Beginning of the Peg to US Dollar*

Figure 1.1.1a also shows that the renminbi per US dollar rate was not fixed, but gradually appreciating, between early 1994 and late 1997. However, with the outbreak of the Asian Financial Crisis (AFC) and China's announced international commitment to keep her currency stable during the AFC, the renminbi per US dollar rate had since then stayed around the level of 8.28 (i.e., within the narrow range of 8.276–8.280) between December 1997 and July 2005.

Thereafter, years of fixed rate had resulted in a widely accepted belief that China's exchange rate system at that time was a fixed one. While the economy was growing at a fast pace, the Chinese government did not seem to be able to anticipate the need to avoid being trapped in such a fixed rate system at the early stage. In particular, if China was to have a managed float or a very gradually appreciation right after the AFC, China might be able to avoid the fixed rate system and hence the need to exit from the peg in July 2005.

As explained in Footnote 1, the strengthening of the US dollar (and hence the renminbi) between 1994 and early 2002 had once helped to wipe out China's gain in relative price competitiveness originated from the major devaluation in 1994 (see Figure 1.1.2 and Figure 1.1.1a). However, with the substantial depreciation of the US dollar (and hence the renminbi) between

**Figure 1.1.2.** US's NEER

*Source*: Datastream.

early 2002 and June 2005 (see Section 1.1.3 for the reasons and impact of the weakening of the US dollar), China's relative price competitiveness rose back to a much higher level. This had to some extent contributed to a higher overall trade surplus during these years.

More importantly, there were some other major changes such as the continuation of the world's gradual acceptance of Chinese products, further upgrading of Chinese products, China's growing economic size and rising role in world trade, and China's entry into the WTO highlighted in Section 1.1.1. These changes had caused not only further rise in China's overall trade surplus but also a substantial rise in China's share of trade surplus in the world and the US.

As a result, there was enormous external political pressure for a major revaluation of the renminbi. While such external pressure was first initiated by Japan in early 2002, it was later more forcefully engineered by the US. For example, the US had on and off threatened to impose huge retaliatory tariff should it be determined that China had unfairly manipulated the exchange rate. While China was managing to resist or alleviate this type of pressure a few times, there were growing signs showing that China had to do something on her fixed rate system to provide changes that were not too costly and risky to the economy. However, as will be explained in Section 1.2, changes like these would never be as simple as what American politicians suggested.

In fact, without a well-thought plan with self-consistency in all relevant dimensions, chance of a disastrous outcome would be extremely high.

### 1.1.3 *The Weakening US Dollar Since Early 2002: Reasons and Impact*

Before we go to the debate on an appropriate design of the exchange rate system reform, let us first have a brief discussion of the reasons for, and impact of, the movements of the US dollar between 1995 and July 2005.

As shown in Figure 1.1.2, after a mild dip during the Mexican Crisis in 1994–1995, the US dollar started to rebound and build up an upward inertia before the Asian Financial Crisis. As many Asian currencies were quasi-fixed with the US dollar at that time, one could actually argue that, in addition to the internal financial weakness of Asian economies, the higher inflation rates in the Asain economies during the past decade and the strengthening of the US dollar since 1995 were at least the main assisting causes of the Asian Financial Crisis.[2]

Thereafter, the collapse of many Asian currencies and the rush to the US dollar as a safe-haven further pushed the US dollar to even higher level. By February 2002, the US nominal and real effective exchange rates were 24% and 16% higher than those in January 1995, respectively. The high US dollar had in turn contributed to a higher current account deficit in the US. Worse still, the substantial cut in the tax rate and the entry of the Iraqi war by the Bush Administration had caused a ballooning fiscal deficits and hence current account deficit (see Box 1.1.3a for the relation of the two deficits). As a result, there was renewed worry of a major correction of the

---

[2] While many of the crisis-hit Asian currencies had been quasi-fixed with the US dollar since the mid 1980s or early 1990s, substantial capital inflows at that time had caused rampant asset inflation and then general price and wage inflation in these economies. The much higher inflation than the US for such a sustained period had in turn caused a substantial deterioration of the relative price competitiveness of these economies. Thus, when the US nominal effective exchange rate made its substantial appreciation between January 1995 and August 1998, the crisis-hit economies were not able to convince the market that they could keep their quasi-peg with the US dollar.

---

**Box 1.1.3a:   Relationship Between Budget Deficit and Current Account Deficit**

The relationship between budget deficit and current account deficit (i.e., the twin deficits) can be seen with the help of the following equations first highlighted by William Branson:

$$Y = C + I + G + X - M \qquad (1.1)$$

$$Y \equiv C + S + T \qquad (1.2)$$

where Y is national income; G is government expenditure; T is tax; and C, I, S, X and M are the consumption, investment, saving, export and import functions, respectively. Equation (1.1) is the standard Keynesian equation of income determination, and identity (1.2) states that the income not consumed or taxed away will be saved.

Substitute equation (1.1) into identity (1.3) and simplify, we have:

$$(X - M) = (T - G) + (S - I) \qquad (1.3)$$

According to equation (1.3), if there is no major change in the saving and investment function, a substantial budget deficit (i.e., a very negative T – G due to, say, a substantial rise in G to finance a war or a substantial tax cut) will result in a large current account deficit (i.e., a very negative X – M).

---

US dollar. This had in turn caused enormous capital outflows from the US and portfolio shifts from US dollar assets.[3]

As the capital flows were enormous and the US dollar was a reserve currency, governments of other economies were facing a dilemma. If the

---

[3] Along with some major private funds betting heavily with a major correction of the US dollar, it was believed that some central banks had also shifted part of their portfolio away from US dollar assets. In fact, the capital flows and portfolio shifted away from US dollar assets had caused a more than 20% appreciation of the Euro *vis-à-vis* the US dollar between 2003 and early 2005.

related government let its currency rise against the US dollar (to some extent, the case in the EU), the appreciation would be substantial simply because the capital flows and portfolio shifts would be enormous. The sharp appreciation would then bring its output and employment below the full employment levels. Worse still, extrapolation of latest exchange rate trend and herding behavior could push the exchange rate far beyond the equilibrium level, thus enlarging the potential loss of output and employment as well as seeding painful correction or even crisis in the future.

On the other hand, if the related government tried to keep its exchange rate fixed against the US dollar (the case in China), it might not be able to sterilize all the potential rise in domestic money supply originated from the huge size of the capital inflows (see Box 1.1.3b for the meaning of sterilization). As a result, a significant portion of the capital inflows would be translated into a rise in domestic money supply, thus laying the seed of

---

**Box 1.1.3b:   Capital Flows and Sterilization Under the Fixed Exchange Rate System**

Under a fixed exchange rate system, capital inflows will imply appreciation pressure on the domestic currency. To keep the exchange rate fixed, the monetary authority has to buy foreign currency and sell domestic currency at the official rate. The purchase of foreign currency raises the government holdings of foreign reserve, while the sales of domestic currency are increasing domestic monetary base (i.e., a multiple increase of money supply), which will result in upward pressure on prices and wages. To stop the latter, the monetary authority can do sterilization, i.e., selling government bonds to mop up the increase in domestic money supply. By the same token, the government can also purchase government bonds to offset the reduction in monetary base due to capital outflows. However, if the capital flows is enormous (especially when the currency is substantially under-valued or over-valued), the government might not be able to sterilize all the changes in money supply induced by the capital flows.

higher asset inflation and then general price and wage inflation in the subsequent years. If left unattended or inappropriately managed, inertia of asset inflation could push the price and wage of the economy to uncompetitive levels and seed the possibility of painful corrections or crisis in the future.

### 1.1.4 *Other Macroeconomic Performance Before the Reform*

Let us now have a brief look on China's other macroeconomic aspects before the reform. Figure 1.1.4a shows that China's GDP growth was above 10% during the two years before the reform in July 2005.

For the monetary growth, after the excessive M1 growth in 1991–1993 and its substantial decline between 1993 and 1998, the growth rate had thereafter fluctuated within a narrower range during the few years before the reform in July 2005. Similarly, M2 growth during the year before July 2005 was at the healthy level of 15%.

Similarly, after the high CPI inflation in 1993–1994 and its substantial decline between 1994 and 1999, China's CPI inflation had been staying at reasonably low levels during the few years before the reform in July 2005 (see Figure 1.1.4c).

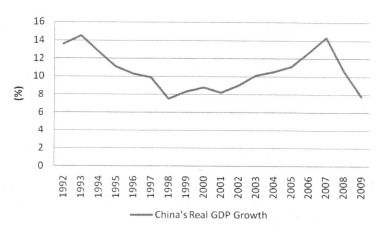

**Figure 1.1.4a.** China's Real GDP Growth

*Source*: Datastream

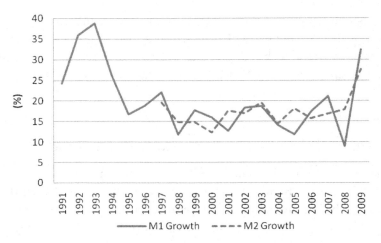

**Figure 1.1.4b.**   China's M1 and M2 Growth

*Source*: Datastream

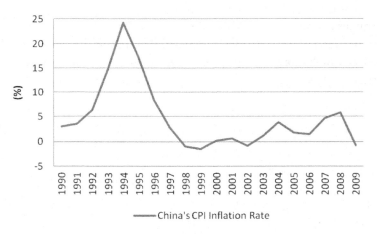

**Figure 1.1.4c.**   China's CPI Inflation Rate

Thus, before the reform in July 2005, China's monetary growth and CPI inflation were in general under control, although GDP growth was slightly on the high side and there was a reasonably large amount of trade surplus, FDI inflows and speculative inflows through the illegal channels or the abuse of legal channels.

## 1.2 Debate Before the Reform: Risk of Various Proposals

Before the transitional reform in July 2005, Chinese economists were debating on variants of a few sets of options on the exchange rate system.

The first set of options was to keep the peg, with some suggesting additional measures to mitigate the appreciation pressure on the renminbi.[4] Because of the existence of capital control in China, speculative funds could only flow into China through illegal channels or the abuse of legal channels.[5] As a result, speculative inflows at that time were still within the sterilization capacity of the People's Bank of China, the Chinese central bank (e.g., see Chapter 4 and Garton and Chang, 2005). That is, if China wanted to maintain the peg in the subsequent years and at the same time controlled her money supply, she could achieve the two targets with large enough issuance of central bank notes or government bonds. However, as noted by Eichengreen (2004) and Frankel (2005), the ability of the Chinese central bank to keep up the sterilization of this scale indefinitely was questionable.[6] Eichengreen and Frankel also highlighted that it would be advisable to exit a peg when time was good and the currency was strong, than to wait until time was bad and the currency was under attack. No doubt, the Chinese authority was aware that she might not be able to maintain the peg forever. Moreover, as highlighted in Section 1.1.2, there was substantial external political pressure, especially from the US, for an exit from the peg. Thus, as long as the exit would not involve too heavy a cost,

---

[4] Among the academia in the Western world, Mundell (2004) was the one very much in favor of keeping the peg. McKinnon (2005, 2006) also highlighted the costs of moving away from the peg, and emphasized the role of differential wage growth between China and the US as the major adjusting variable. Among the Chinese economists who preferred keeping the peg, some believed that it would be important to have additional measures to mitigate the appreciation pressure on the renminbi (see Chapter 4 for potential examples of the offsetting measures).

[5] One good example of illegal channels is huge amount of remittance through underground money changers. Examples of the abuse of legal channels are through over-invoicing of exports and over-claiming of FDI (i.e., the difference between the declared and actual amount would be the speculative inflows).

[6] As noted by Cheung, Chinn and Fujii (2003), Chinese capital control is declining in magnitude although it continues to bite. Thus, the required scale of sterilization will be bigger in the future.

the Chinese government would be interested in viable proposals, although the proposals could be quite far away from what the US was asking for.

The second set of options was a major revision (say, 15–25%) or medium revisions (say, 5%) of China's exchange rate.[7] The rationale behind the major revision was that a once-and-for-all unanticipated jump in exchange rate to the equilibrium level would avoid the possibility of a "one-way bet" for speculative inflows. Nevertheless, as will be explained in Chapter 2, a major revaluation of this magnitude would cause coordination failures, and hence enormous and relatively persistent economic costs to China. Besides, even under the case of relatively modest price elasticities of exports and imports, the effect of such a major revaluation to China's economic growth and unemployment could be too huge for China to bear. In particular, the unemployment situation in China was not as good as the high economic growth rates implied, the major revaluation could push the unemployment rate to politically and socially unbearable levels (see Box 1.2 for further explanations). Furthermore, as noted by Eichengreen, there

---

**Box 1.2:   China's Growth and Employment Conditions**

Although real economic growth rates in China at that time were in the impressive range of 8–10%, there was enormous amount of disguised unemployment and surplus labor. Thus, the employment situation in China was not as good as that implied by the high GDP growth figures. Moreover, because of the huge size of and great diversity within China, it would never be an easy job to maintain the political and social stability there. Thus, even if there was just a slowdown of economic growth to, say, 3–4%, the associate rise in unemployment could be large enough to invoke social instability, which might substantially weaken the ruling authority of the political leaders and hence invoke political instability.

---

[7] In this set of proposals, the Chinese authority could choose variants among a new peg, a managed float, a pure floating or even the two-stage reform recommended by Goldstein (2004).

would be difficulties in deciding the right amount of revaluation, and there would be serious costs if the authority got it wrong.

For the case of medium revaluation(s), the initial revaluation would reward speculators that had bet for a revaluation. The realized revaluation would encourage far greater speculative inflows through the excited expectation of further revaluation(s) or appreciation(s). If the then greater speculative inflows were too big (e.g., exceeded the sterilization capacity of the central bank), the associate monetary growth pressure would sooner or later force the central bank to accept further appreciations or revaluations. By then, there could be a development of herding behavior which would eventually push the Chinese currency well beyond the equilibrium level,[8] and seed a potential financial crisis or major correction in the distant future. Even if the greater speculative inflows were within the central bank's sterilization capacity, it would substantially increase the sterilization burden of the central bank. Thus, it would not be advisable for the Chinese government to accept any medium size revaluations or appreciations that exceeded the transaction costs and risk premium of speculative inflows.

The third set of options was the adoption of an exchange rate band, which could be adjustable or fixed, and with medium band (say, ±3% or ±5%) or wide band (say, ±10 or 15%). Proponents here normally favored an adjustable band, believing that such a band could be adjusted with changes in market fundamentals. No matter whether the band was adjustable or fixed, this set of options would encounter the same problem as those in the second set of options during the initial phase: Given the market's belief of a substantial under-valuation of the renminbi at that time,[9] the adoption of a medium or wide exchange rate band would only

---

[8] Along with the appreciations, it is likely that the greater speculative inflows would cause excessive monetary growth and hence higher inflation. For the effects of herding behavior, see Frankel and Froot (1986, 1987) and the related literature.

[9] There was a debate on whether the renminbi was under-valued, and if so, by how much (see for example Frankel, 2005; Goldstein, 2004; Funke and Rahn, 2005; Chang and Shao, 2004; and Cheung *et al.*, 2007). However, on the expectation side, the market did widely believe that the renminbi was substantially under-valued. As market expectation was the major cause of the flows of speculative funds into China, this book will focus on the effect of such market belief while leaving the estimation on the valuation of the renminbi for the ongoing academic debate.

result in an immediate appreciation of the renminbi to the upper edge of the band. Thus, the realized large appreciation in the wide-band design would imply high economic costs for China. On the other hand, the realized medium appreciation in the medium-band design would reward speculators and attract increased speculative inflows.

In addition to the above three sets of options, there was a proposal to peg the renminbi against a basket of currencies. Whether it would be *vis-à-vis* the US dollar or a basket of currencies, the author highlighted that there were other pertinent dimensions that should be considered. The whole reform should involve well-specified decisions on each relevant dimension or characteristic of the system. That is, in addition to the decision of focusing on a basket of currencies or the US dollar, one still has to make decisions on other dimensions such as (i) whether the exchange rate should be fixed, adjustable or highly flexible; (ii) whether there should be a major revision, or a few medium revisions, in the level of exchange rate; and (iii) whether there should be a narrow, medium or wide exchange rate band. As we will see in Chapter 2, the actual reform task is a more sophisticated exercise that requires right decisions in all relevant and inter-related dimensions. From this angle, the shift of focus to a basket of currencies is the most important dimension of the whole reform.

## ➤ Chapter 2 ◄

# Transitional and Medium-Term Designs of the Reform

In view of the risk and limitations of the various proposed reforms outlined in Section 1.2 of Chapter 1, the author had written a series of reform proposals[1] that could be classified into the following three areas of reforms: (a) the appropriate transitional arrangements; (b) the medium-term arrangements; and (c) the supplementary package of policies that could increase the chance of a successful reform as well as China's immunity and resilience against financial crises in the future. As we will see, the reforms implemented by the Chinese authority resembled closely to these proposals, which had far more sophisticated dimensions than previous proposals in the debate.

## 2.1 The Proposed Transitional Reform

This section will outline the proposed transitional reform which contains the following three important parts:

### 2.1.1 *Gradual Appreciation, No Major or Medium Jump in Exchange Rate and No Widening of Band*

The first part of the proposals highlighted that any widening of the exchange rate band at the initial stage was not advisable. Given the market's

---

[1] The proposals were sent to the appropriate authorities in China. They were also published in major Chinese newspapers in Hong Kong (*Hong Kong Economic Journal*) and Singapore (*Lianhe Zaobao*) between November 2004 and July 2005, followed by further post-reform comments and follow-up proposals. Yip (2005) also wrote a chapter that provided a summary discussion of the proposals.

belief of a substantial under-valuation of the renminbi (see Footnote 9 of Chapter 1), a widening of the band would only result in an immediate appreciation of the renminbi to the upper edge of the band, which would in turn induce more inflows of speculative funds, thus creating greater pressure for appreciation. Neither should there be any major or medium jump in the exchange rate. Instead, the Chinese government should at the initial stage engineer a very gradual appreciation of, say, 1–2% per annum with the precondition that speculative funds could not profit after the deduction of the transaction costs and risk premium of the (illegal) inflows.[2] If necessary, the Chinese government could raise the effort of inspection and penalty so as to increase the transaction costs and risk premium of this type of speculation.

Once the above gradual appreciation was sustained for a few years, the Chinese government could further refine its exchange rate policy based on the changing economic conditions. For example, it could raise the appreciation rate to, say, 2–3% if there was a rise in global inflation. It could also resort to depreciation in the case of extreme economic adversity. If there was no major change in the economic conditions, it could maintain the 1–2% appreciation target. These actions would gradually convince the market that the renminbi is no longer fixed *vis-à-vis* the US dollar, and could appreciate or depreciate. This in turn would lay the foundation for China to move towards its preferred exchange rate system in the longer term.

The benefit of a very gradual appreciation is that it can maintain a relatively low exchange value of renminbi for a reasonably long period, thus ensuring a strong economic growth and employment in the medium future.[3]

---

[2] Because of the capital control, the transaction costs and risk of speculating for an appreciation of the renminbi at that time were reasonably high (i.e., higher than 2%). Thus, the 1–2% target was just a tentative suggestion which had also taken care of the psychological effect. The Chinese government could make its judgment in striking a balance between the psychological effect and its estimation of the speculators' transaction costs and risk premium. Nevertheless, it should also be highlighted that, even when there was no appreciation of the renminbi, the speculators' gain in property and share price could be more than the transaction costs and risk premium. Thus, curbing of asset inflation would also play an important role in discouraging speculative inflows of funds (see Chapter 3 for more details).

[3] As explained in Box 1.2, the employment situation in China was not as good as that implied by the high economic growth rates of 8–10%. A major revaluation or appreciation could push the unemployment rate to politically and socially unbearable levels.

The cost is of course a less favorable term of trade. But given Chinese policy makers' strong preference for the former to the latter, the gradual appreciation would be the obvious choice. [In Chapter 7, we will highlight another powerful justification to avoid a sharp appreciation of the renminbi, i.e., China's private holdings of foreign assets was extremely low. Thus, it was dynamically more sensible to maintain a persistent trade surplus until China's public and private holdings of foreign assets reached their desired level. In other words, the proposal of a once-and-for-all major revaluation of renminbi was not optimal in the dynamic sense. As highlighted in Section 1.2, it was likely that such major revaluation would cause coordination failure in the economic system, severe recession and hence political and social instability in China. Thus, the proposal was not even optimal in the static sense.]

### 2.1.2 *A Basket of Currencies with Special Care to the Exchange Rate Against the US Dollar at the Early Stage*

The next part of the proposals was on whether the gradual appreciation should be monitored against a basket of currencies or against the US dollar during the transitional reform. While it recommended the Chinese government to declare a shift of the monitoring target towards a basket of currencies, it also highlighted the importance of maintaining at most a moderate appreciation against the US dollar at the early stage (e.g., the first 1–2 years) of the transitional period. This was because the renminbi was fixed against the US dollar before the reform. To avoid any profit from speculation, proper control on the appreciation of the renminbi against the US dollar was necessary. However, at the second stage (e.g., the later years) of the transitional arrangements, China should gradually bring market attention from just the rate against the US dollar back to that against a basket of currencies through speeches by officials. By then, the economy would be better equipped to deal with nominal swings in individual currencies.[4]

---

[4] For example, suppose there is a 10% depreciation of Euro against all other currencies, and the weight of Euro in China's basket of currencies is 25%. If China keeps her nominal effective exchange rate unchanged, the renminbi will appreciate against the Euro by 7.5% and

Again, Singapore's successful experience in this aspect was also used to support the argument.

### 2.1.3 *A Narrow Exchange Rate Band at the Early Stage*

The proposals also highlighted that any exchange rate band at the early stage should be as narrow as possible, mainly because market confidence at this stage would be of utmost importance. A widening of the band without any specific purpose would only weaken confidence and invite unnecessary speculation. However, once the gradual appreciation has been in practice for a few years, the Chinese government could consider a gradual expansion of the adjustable exchange rate band, and prepare itself for the next stage of the reform.

## 2.2 The Proposed Medium-Term Arrangements

### 2.2.1 *The Debating Process Before the Medium-Term Recommendation*

For the medium-term and long-term, the related part of the proposals first noted that a fixed exchange rate system might not be the best choice for China.[5] It also highlighted that the phenomena of herding behavior and exchange rate overshooting could result in undesirable outcomes if China adopted a pure floating regime.[6] Instead, it recommended more detailed studies of some interesting and desirable features in

---

depreciate against other currencies by 2.5%. The effect of the latter two will offset each other, leaving China's relative price competitiveness unchanged with the nominal swing of Euro. By automatically offsetting the effect of nominal swings in individual currency with a basket of currencies, the monetary authority's task will be greatly simplified, as the authority will only have to adjust her nominal effective exchange rate with changes in the real sector and the difference between domestic and global inflation rates.

[5] See Williamson (2007) and Yip (2005) for a summary of the disadvantages of the fixed exchange rate system.

[6] Frankel and Froot (1986, 1987) explained that herding behavior in the foreign exchange market could lead to huge cycles in foreign exchange rate. The development of exchange rate overshooting models (e.g., Dornbusch, 1976; Kouri, 1976; Calvo and Rodriguez, 1977; Dornbusch and Fischer, 1980; Rodriguez, 1980; Buiter and Miller, 1981 and 1982; and

(a) the monitoring band system in Singapore; and

(b) a floating exchange rate system with occasional interventions similar to, but more frequent than that of the US system.[7]

### 2.2.1.1 *A Spur of China's Interest in Singapore's Exchange Rate System*

The recommendation had resulted in a spur of official interest in Singapore's exchange rate system, and senior officials were sent to Singapore for further understandings of the system in March 2005. In May 2005, there was news reporting that the Chinese authority might adopt an exchange rate system similar to that of Singapore. Under this system, the renminbi would be monitored against a basket of currencies, with an exchange rate band within which the renminbi would be allowed to fluctuate. However, the exact band width and the weight of each currency in the basket would not be disclosed. The aim was to maintain a certain degree of confidentiality so as to increase speculators' difficulties in betting against the monetary authority. Along with this, the Chinese government could adjust the exchange rate band with changes in China's internal economic conditions and global trade environments.

In response to the above proposed design, the author wrote an article expressing his appreciation and concern on the design.[8] In particular, he emphasized that there were significant differences between Singapore and China. A mere adoption of Singapore's exchange rate system without due regard to these differences could be disastrous. More importantly, long-term arrangements should not dilute or distract the importance of the transitional arrangements. Even if the design was perfect in the long term, problems or mistakes in the transitional arrangements could result in failure of the whole reform.

---

Mussa (1982) also revealed that exchange rate had turned out to be far more volatile than that assumed by proponents of flexible exchange rate system in the late 1960s or early 1970s (e.g., Johnson, 1969 and Friedman, 1969).

[7] As explained in Yip (2005), the main purpose of the occasional interventions was to discourage herding behavior when deemed necessary.

[8] The article was sent to the related authorities. It was also published in major Chinese newspapers in Hong Kong (i.e., *Hong Kong Economic Journal* on 19 May 2005) and Singapore (i.e., *Lianhe Zaoboa* on 7 June 2005).

The article first elaborated the advantages of the proposed design, and then discussed its relative importance in the whole reform. It elaborated that the non-disclosure of the currency basket weights and band width had increased the market's information costs and uncertainty in going against the Monetary Authority of Singapore (MAS). Although institutional investors and speculators could roughly estimate the basket weights from Singapore's trade statistics so that the information cost was rather small for them, this information cost was large and even insurmountable for the general public. Meanwhile, MAS's non-disclosure of the band width and flexibility of revising the internal band target would increase the public's uncertainty in joining the speculation during normal circumstances. Even if institutional speculators attempted to mobilize the general public through market reports or rumors, the above information costs and risks to the general public would make it difficult to mobilize the general public under normal circumstances (see Yip, 2005 for more details on the advantages of Singapore's exchange rate system).

### 2.2.1.2 *The Risk of an Immediate Adoption of the Singapore System*

However, the situation would be different if the Singapore dollar or the renminbi was believed to be substantially under-valued or over-valued. Under this scenario, the general public's expected return from joining the speculation would easily overcome the hurdle due to the above information costs and uncertainty. Worse still, as long as the general public believed that the return would be greater, they would join the speculation without any need to pay for the information costs. Thus, the information costs and uncertainty for joining the speculation would fall substantially under this extreme condition.

In fact, this is the major difference between Singapore and China that needs to be addressed. As Singapore has adopted the adjustable band system for many years, her current exchange rate is unlikely to be far away from the equilibrium level. As a result, the above mentioned information costs and uncertainty for the general public would be sufficient to discourage speculators from mobilizing the general public to speculate against the monetary authority. However, China had adopted the fixed exchange rate system for many years. Market participants widely believed that its exchange rate was substantially under-valued. As a result, the expected gain from betting for the renminbi appreciation would be substantial, thus implying the above mentioned information costs and uncertainty would not be able to exert its influence under this extreme condition.

In other words, as the starting levels of exchange rate were different, the mere adoption of Singapore's exchange rate system in China would not be able to stop the renminbi from making substantial appreciation. Once there is a substantial appreciation, the Chinese government's credibility in this aspect will disappear. Under this circumstance, the proposed exchange rate band system would not be able to function properly. Worse still, because of herding behavior and the inclination of extrapolating past trend in the foreign exchange market, the renminbi could eventually over-appreciate, thus laying the seed for economic contraction or even a financial crisis in the future.

Thus, the advantages of the long-term design would not be sufficient to guarantee a successful reform. Appropriate transitional arrangements could sometimes be more important than long-term arrangements. It would also be dangerous for China to let the long-term design dilute the focus of the transitional arrangements and the whole reform.

After expressing the above concern, the article reiterated that the focus of the transitional arrangements should be a target of 1–2% annual appreciation of the renminbi during the early stage of the transitional period. In particular, China should not accept any appreciation that is greater than the transaction costs and risk premium of speculation so as to avoid increased inflows of speculative funds. Neither should China allow any wide or medium exchange rate band, whether disclosed or undisclosed. Otherwise, market force would push the exchange rate to the upper edge of the band, and hence attract enormous speculative inflows. In other words, during the transitional period, the one that could help the exit from a fixed exchange rate system would still be a variant of a fixed exchange rate system. The only difference is that the former would permanently stay at a fixed level of exchange rate (i.e., 8.28 renminbi per US dollar), while the latter would set the appreciation target to 1–2% per annum (with moderate variations along the appreciating path). Nevertheless, this small step would change the market expectation of a permanently fixed exchange rate. The small change would in fact be a big step in the whole exchange rate system reform.

Finally, the article clarified that the author's previous proposals did not recommend the mere adoption of Singapore's exchange rate system even in the long run. In fact, the difference in the degree of openness might imply a very different choice in the long run. For example, as a small open economy with high capital mobility, Singapore has found it more suitable to have an exchange rate targeting while giving up her independent control on money supply (see Teh and Shangmugaratnam, 1992; MAS, 1982/1983 and Yip, 2003). On the other hand, China is a large economy where internal demand can be more important than external demand. As a result, there are advantages for China to have independent control of her money supply. Thus, it is still debatable which long term exchange rate arrangement is most suitable to China.

### 2.2.1.3 *A Safe and Reversible Roadmap of Reform*

After the above warnings, the proposed design was shelved, or at least held up, for a while. In early July 2005, the author proposed the following roadmap of reform with particular emphasis on the *safety* and *reversibility* of the reform:

*Step 1*: Implement the transitional arrangement discussed in Section 2.1. If everything works well for some years, proceed to Step 2. In case of unexpected adverse developments, stay unchanged or go back to the fixed exchange rate system;

*Step 2*: Gradually widen the exchange rate band to achieve an exchange rate band system similar to that in Singapore.[9] If everything works well for some years, consider the advantages and disadvantages of proceeding to Step 3. In case of unexpected adverse developments, stay unchanged with the new arrangement or go back to the system in Step 1;

*Step 3*: Gradually widen the exchange rate band in Step 2 towards infinity and proceed towards a floating system with more occasional interventions than that in the US. If everything works well, stay

---

[9] As explained in Chapters 4 and 6, there should be a shift towards a NEER monitoring band before a gradual widening of the renminbi-US dollar band.

with this new system. In case of unexpected adverse developments, go back to the system in Step 2.

The transitional arrangement was chosen as the first step because it was the alternative that was most similar to the original fixed exchange rate system. It was the *safest choice* because the only recommended change was a shift from a horizontal path of exchange rate against time to an upward sloping path (i.e., it did not recommend a major or medium jump in exchange rate or widening of exchange rate band at the early stage). On the other hand, as explained earlier, a reasonably large or medium jump in exchange rate or widening of band would attract more speculative inflows, thus creating substantial upward pressure on the renminbi and raising the chance of a reform failure. Because of its similarities with the original fixed exchange rate system, the transitional arrangement was also the *most easily reversible choice.* For example, in case of unexpected adverse developments, it would be easier and less costly for the Chinese authority to retreat to a viable system (i.e., the original fixed exchange rate system) by announcing a change in the expected upward path of exchange rate back to a horizontal one.

The exchange rate band system in Step 2 was recommended because it is a viable system (i.e., exists in Singapore) with crucial features somewhere between the systems in Step 1 and Step 3 (i.e., its similarities with the system in Step 1 is much greater than that between the systems in Step 1 and Step 3). If the system in Step 1 works well for some years, the only major change towards Step 2 would be a gradual widening of the exchange rate band. Compared with the system in Step 3, it is also much more reversible to the system in Step 1 (which would be a viable system if the authority had chosen to move from Step 1 to Step 2). For example, in case of unexpected adverse developments, the Chinese authority could easily retreat to a viable system by narrowing the exchange rate band back to that in Step 1.

In view of external political pressure[10] for some changes away from the fixed exchange rate system at that time, the paper noted that the

---

[10] Senior officials had reflected that they were not that constrained by external political pressure if they believed that a certain change was risky or undesirable. However, as China might have made implicit agreements in the first half of 2005 for some exchange rate system reform later in the year, there seemed to be a pressure for some changes at that time.

implementation of Step 1 and then Step 2 would take at least a few years. This will give researchers sufficient time to sort out the appropriate long term direction of the exchange rate system reform (see the recommendation discussed in Section 2.2.2). If it is found that the system in Step 3 is the appropriate one for the long run, the Chinese authority can proceed to Step 3 by gradually widening the exchange rate band in Step 2 towards infinity. On the other hand, if it is found that the system in Step 3 will not be the appropriate system for China in the long run, the Chinese authority can stick with the system in Step 2 or move towards a modified system that will be most appropriate for China in the long run.

To further convince the Chinese authority to adopt the above view and proposal, the article drew an analogy between the proposal and the Chinese traditional wisdom of military strategy. According to the traditional military wisdom, moving an army forward or retreating an army is never a simple forward or backward movement of the army. Detailed plans on how to move the army forward or backward step by step, and group by group, are important. This analogy seemed to have raised the authority's trust on the viability of the proposal. On 21 July 2005, a first stage reform package was announced although the long run choice of China's exchange rate system was yet to be sorted out.

### 2.2.2 *The Medium-Term Recommendation*

To address the above question on the longer term direction of the reform, the author finally solved the problem by publishing a recommendation on 12 September 2005 (i.e., almost two months after the reform on 21 July 2005).[11] The article first used the doctrine of Impossible Trinity (e.g., see Krugman and Obstfeld, 2009) to highlight that an economy could only achieve any two goals of the following three: (a) free mobility of capital; (b) stability in exchange rate; and (c) independence in monetary policy. It also used examples of Hong Kong, Singapore and the US to illustrate the issue. For example, with free capital mobility and a fixed exchange rate implicit in its currency board system, Hong Kong has given up the choice of using independent

---

[11] The recommendation was published in the *Hong Kong Economic Journal* on 12 September 2005 and the *Lianhe Zaobao* (Singapore) on 20 October 2005.

monetary policy to fine tune her output (i.e., her quantity of money supply is determined by market demand,[12] and her interest rate has to follow the US rate under normal circumstance, no matter she likes it or not). Another example is Singapore. As capital is also freely mobile, Singapore has to choose between an independent exchange rate policy and an independent monetary policy. As a small open economy, Singapore has chosen to target her exchange rate.[13] For the US, capital mobility is also high. Meanwhile, the importance of her huge domestic market has dictated the use of independent monetary (or interest rate) policy for the fine tuning of her internal balance.[14] As a result, the US government has chosen to let her exchange rate be determined by market force (i.e., a flexible exchange rate system).

After the elaboration of the doctrine of Impossible Trinity, the article recommended China to opt for an independent monetary policy and independent control of the renminbi along a gradually appreciating path, while maintaining her current level of capital control. This is so because China, similar to the US, is a large economy in which a huge domestic market is crucial to her output determination. Thus, an independent monetary policy is important. Meanwhile, as the renminbi has been widely believed by market participants to be substantially under-valued, a release of the current control on the exchange value of the renminbi can result in substantial appreciation, which can result in severe recession in the Chinese and neighborhood economies.[15] In the worst scenario, this can in turn affect the

---

[12] With a currency board system, Hong Kong's money supply is demand determined.

[13] As highlighted in Yip (2005), Singapore has opted for the use of exchange rate policy to influence her internal balance while leaving the external balance as a residual balance. It first explained that the net Central Provident Fund (CPF) contribution in Singapore had resulted in persistent and huge current account (and balance of payment) surplus by ensuring Singapore residents spending less than what they earn. It then noted that the Singapore government was not particularly concerned with the variations in the external balance because the variation was only between a bigger and a smaller surplus.

[14] As a large economy, the US's interest rate decision also influences the world interest rate. This implies an additional advantage for the US to opt for an independent interest rate policy.

[15] If the renminbi were substantially under-valued, it could be dangerous to lift the control and let the market force to search for the equilibrium value of exchange rate. In particular, the economic outcomes of a gradual appreciation to the equilibrium value could be very

political status of the leaders and hence the stability of China. Once the political stability is endangered, it can result in endless turmoil. Thus, avoiding the sharp appreciation of the renminbi and the possibility of political instability are of utmost importance.

If China prefers maintaining an independent monetary policy and avoiding sharp appreciation of the renminbi, she has no choice but to maintain the degree of capital control at that time. Failure to do so will destroy or weaken her ability in achieving the first two objectives.[16] The capital control will of course imply costs such as efficiency loss. However, as there were substantial problems in China's financial system, such as the huge amount of non-performing bank loans and extensive moral hazard activities at that time, further liberalization of the capital control would provide a more lax environment for more extensive moral hazard activities. Furthermore, capital control could be the last defense against the outbreak of financial crises in China in the longer future.[17] Removing the control before a proper clearing of the non-performing bank loans and proper establishment of internal control against the extensive moral hazard activities might not be a wise choice. On the other hand, if China could

---

different from a substantial appreciation towards the "equilibrium". In the former case, the economic structure and market behavior will have sufficient time to make the required adjustments. On the other hand, a large appreciation in a short period can on one hand cause immediate destructions (say, on exports), and on another hand fail to achieve the substituting expansion (say, on import-substituting production or high value-added exports). In addition, a pre-condition for market force to work is the absence of coordination failure so that market (e.g., price and demand) signals can be transmitted through each sub-market of the economic chains. If agents in one particular part of a chain fail because of a sharp appreciation, agents in the subsequent part of the chain will not receive the right market signals. In such case, the market will not work in the way it is hoped for. In fact, failure of the shock therapy in the Russian economic reform is one good example of the coordination failure.

[16] As there are capital flows through the illegal channels or the abuse of legal channels, China normally needs the help of sterilization to achieve the two objectives. As long as there are sufficient controls on these capital flows so that they lie within the central bank's sterilization capacity, China will be able to monitor her exchange rate and money supply.

[17] Even if there is a plunge in asset price, an effective control will ensure that funds getting out of the related asset will still stay in the economy, thus alleviating the impacts of the plunge in the asset price.

maintain the degree of capital control at that time, she could still continue to develop at the fast growth rate at that time.

In short, if China cannot clear the problems of huge non-performing bank loans and extensive moral hazard activities, she is not qualified to enjoy the benefit of free capital mobility. Rushing for liberalization without the right environment only destroys the growth prospect of China. On the other hand, with a reasonable degree of capital control, China can still grow at relatively fast and stable pace.

Although China has not officially announced the medium- to long-term direction of reform, feedback from senior officials suggests that the Chinese authority has found the above arguments convincing. Baring out unexpected developments in the future, China will probably opt for an independent control of her money supply and good monitoring of her exchange rate along a gradually appreciating path in the medium future (say, next ten years). By then, if the problems of huge non-performing bank loans and extensive moral hazard activities are cleared, China can consider the costs and benefits of moving towards a flexible exchange rate system with occasional interventions.

# > Chapter 3 <

# Supplementary Measures

In addition to the proposed transitional and medium-term arrangements summarized in Chapter 2, the author's original series of proposals also recommended some important supplementary measures and stressed their role in increasing a chance of a successful reform. More importantly, they highlighted that these supplementary measures could also increase China's *immunity* and *resilience* against potential financial crises in the future. To see the importance of this, the author will first summarize the argument on why prolonged asset inflation can be one of the biggest and most likely threat to China's development into a major economic power in the world. This is then followed by a summary of the proposed supplementary measures.

## 3.1 Prolonged Asset Inflation and Then Economic Crisis: A Major Potential Threat to China's Economic Development

This part of the proposals first noted the following point: With China's current economic size and growth momentum, if there is no economic crisis in the next 1–2 decade(s), it will be just a matter of time that China will become a major economic power in the world. On the other hand, if there is an economic crisis such as that in Indonesia in 1997–1998, the severe recession and economic pains can seriously damage Chinese leaders' authority and credibility of ruling. If this triggers off further political and social instability (i.e., the country can be fragmented in an implicit or explicit sense), it is possible that China can never come back to stability and growth. Thus, pre-empting the emergence of financial or economic crisis is of utmost importance to China's macroeconomic management.

The complication is that the occurrence of an economic crisis at a particular time can actually be due to poor economic policies at least 8–10 years before the crisis. Take the Asian Financial Crisis in 1997 as an example, one of its major causes can be dated back to the capital account and financial liberalization in the crisis-hit economies in the mid-1980s or early 1990s.

In general, the chance of a financial crisis is low during the first decade of capital account liberalization. This is so because there is not yet significant amount of hot money to be flowed out. On the contrary, capital will only keep flowing in, thus causing sustained rise in exchange rate and asset prices (e.g., share prices and property prices) in the host economy. The latter and the booming economy will in turn cause sustained rise in wages and general price level. After sustained rise in these prices for a few years, people will gradually form an expectation that these prices could only rise. The expectation and then the behaviors based on this expectation will push these prices further up. With such accumulated rise for more than one decade, the asset price, exchange rate, wage and general price level of the host country will rise from a very competitive level to a highly uncompetitive or over-valued level. Meanwhile, with excessive consumption and investment caused by the excessive capital inflows (i.e., could be reflected as a huge current account deficit), corruption and deterioration of bank asset quality due to insufficient bank supervision, the host economy will reach a stage that any moderate negative shock can trigger off a financial crisis.

## 3.2 Supplementary Measures

Of course, it might be a little too demanding to expect the crisis-hit Asian economies to anticipate the risk right at the beginning (i.e., more than 10 years before the crisis). However, after seeing this important lesson from the crisis-hit economies, it will be stupid for China not to prevent or pre-empt such possibility. As such, the series of proposals recommended some supplementary measures that will increase not only the chance of a successful exchange rate system reform, but also China's immunity and resilience against financial crisis.

### 3.2.1 *Banking Reform*

Firstly, the proposals emphasized the importance of reforms in the banking sector in achieving the above two goals. By highlighting that the outbreak of the Asian Financial Crisis in 1997–1998 was very much related to the non-performing loans in Thailand and other Asian economies, the proposals pointed out that the huge amount of non-performing loans in China at that time could be a source of problems in the future. The banking sector is a particularly important sector because the related flows of funds are analogous to blood flows in the human body. If an event (e.g., bank run) causes a malfunctioning of the heart (banking sector) such that the blood (funds) cannot flow to various parts of the body (industries), the person will collapse or even die. On the other hand, the loss of another industry is analogous to the loss of an arm or a leg; the person (economy) can still survive, albeit in more unpleasant ways. Thus, clearing the non-performing bank loans to make sure that the banking sector will function properly, and free of bank runs or speculative attacks, is of utmost importance. In view of this, the author proposed to allow foreign banks to own a sufficient stake of domestic banks so as to improve internal control and reduce moral hazard activities in the banking industry. The author also recommended the recruitment of less corruption-inclined chief and senior bank executives from foreign countries so as to facilitate the establishment of proper internal control within domestic banks.[1]

When the author made the proposal, he thought that this could only alleviate the problem, mainly because the amount of non-performing bank loans in the four major state-owned commercial banks were too huge to be absorbed by major banks in the international market. He believed that foreign banks would only be interested in, and capable of, acquiring small and medium-size domestic banks (i.e., buy the right of doing banking business in China by absorbing the non-performing loans). However, as will be explained in Chapter 5, the subsequent development was much better than originally anticipated, mainly because of the possibility of Initial Public Offerings (IPOs) of the "reformed" domestic banks had offered potential

---

[1] This could also change the banks' mode of operation.

profit as well as exit for these foreign investors. In fact, the three-step injections by the government, the strategic partners and the IPOs had substantially increased the capital adequacy ratio of the Chinese banks. As the government's injection was done through the sales of banks' non-performing loans to the asset management corporation set up by the government, the absolute size of the non-performing loans was also reduced by a reasonably large amount (i.e., at least nine hundred billion renminbi). More importantly,

(i)   a booming economy with rapid loan growth in 2006–2007 had substantially reduced the relative size of the remaining non-performing loans; and

(ii)  there were less problems with the substantial amount of new loans after the injections by the strategic partners and the IPOs, as better loan management, lending criteria and internal control were adopted (i.e., bank executives would also need to take care of the interest of the strategic partners and the shareholders in order to avoid potential sackings in the future).

In Chapter 5, we will further discuss how China's successful experience here can be a valuable lesson, if not a role model, for other emerging economies with the aspiration to eliminate the huge amount of non-performing loans in their banking sector.

### 3.2.2 *Control of Asset Inflation*

The series of proposals also highlighted the importance of controlling asset inflation. It first noted that what eventually matters was the real exchange rate appreciation, which could be done by a nominal exchange rate appreciation, a surge in domestic inflation, or both. For example, even if the Chinese authority manages to keep a gradual appreciation of the renminbi, sustained and rapid asset inflation can still push domestic rentals, wages and prices to uncompetitive levels and seed the possibility of a financial crisis in the distant future. The proposals also highlighted the importance of curbing any potential rampant asset inflation era at the early stage, i.e., before the asset inflation is incorporated in people's expectation. Otherwise, the expectation would cause changes in people's behavior which would in turn fuel the asset inflation (see Chapter 8 for more details).

For example, as documented in Yip (2005) on Southeast Asia's experience on the asset inflation era before the financial crisis in 1997, the formation of the expected asset inflation had caused a surge in people's asset demand and their gearing in asset investment. In the property market, the expected property inflation had induced many existing property owners shifting to bigger properties or investing in additional properties. For those without properties, their relatives' and friends' investment gains had created enormous peer pressure and temptation for them to consider investing in properties. Even for those who were originally not inclined to get rich through property investment or those who did not have a strong need to own a property, the persistent rise in property price eventually pressurized many of them to join the herd for property investments. As a result, the demand for property surged with the expected property inflation. Similarly, the expected share price inflation had caused a substantial rise in the demand for shares.

In addition, Yip's book noted that the expected rise in asset prices had induced (i) the public to reduce their cash to deposit ratios; and (ii) the banks to reduce their desired excess reserve to deposit ratios. Thus, the change in behavior would increase the money multiplier, which would cause a surge in money supply even if the central bank managed to control the monetary base (see Box 8.2.1 for detailed discussions). Worse still, with expected asset inflation, banks and enterprises had strong incentives to borrow foreign currency loans and converted them into domestic currency for domestic usage.[2] This in turn raised the money supply through a rise in monetary base. Thus, all these changes in behavior arising from the expectation of asset inflation tend to offset any government's curbing measures

---

[2] In case of a solid expectation of high asset inflation, the impact of this could be beyond the sterilization capacity of the central bank. In such case, banks and loan officers would be under enormous competition and performance pressure to increase their loan growth. For example, suppose a Chief Executive Officer (CEO) sees a surge in another bank's loan growth from 20% to 25%. To justify his survival and "value" perceived by the Board of Director, he has to raise his bank's loan growth to 25% or more, even though he knows that this is done at the cost of a much higher credit risk. Similarly, when a loan officer sees some of his colleagues being rewarded or promoted because of the achievement of higher loan growth during the asset inflation period, he will be under performance and peer pressure to increase his own loan growth even though he knows that some of the borrowers could be over-leveraging in their investments.

and fuel the asset inflation. Hence, two conclusions could be drawn from the above discussion:

(i) It is always better to curb any potential rampant asset inflation era at the early stage, i.e., before the asset inflation is built into people's expectation;

(ii) If an expectation of rampant asset inflation is formed or established, the government has to raise the curbing measures substantially before the asset inflation could be properly controlled. That is, in addition to the original amount of curbing, extra curbing is required to offset the effect of the above changes in economic behaviors induced by the expected asset inflation.

In fact, because of the failure to recognize the above changes in economic behaviors induced by asset inflation, most market participants and Asian central banks had mistakenly believed that the curbing measures were not effective. Because of this misjudgment, the related central banks did not recognize that they could, and should, raise the curbing measures to offset the impacts of the changes in economic behaviors on asset inflation. Meanwhile, market participants continued, or even escalated, their asset investment. As a result, there were far from sufficient curbing measures, giving people the wrong impression that the cubing measures could only have minor and short-lived effects on the asset inflation. In Chapters 8 and 9, we will discuss the application of the above discussion on China's curbing of asset inflation in 2006 and 2007.

### 3.2.3 *Variable Wage Component*

Thirdly, the proposals recommended the Chinese government to establish the Singapore type of variable wage component (VWC) in the current wage structure.[3] This could be done by allocating a certain percentage (e.g., 80%

---

[3] The government could first introduce the variable wage component in the government and semi-government bodies, and then encourage the private sector to follow the same practice. Alternatively, it could pass a law requiring every employer to allocate a certain percentage of subsequent wage increment into the variable wage component until the latter reaches the target ratio of the total wage bill. The author is in favor of the second alternative.

or 100%) of subsequent wage increments into the variable wage component until the latter forms 25–30% of employees' total wage bill. During the normal period, the employees will receive the full amount of the variable wage component. In fact, the variable wage component can only be reduced through proper government procedures during the crisis period (e.g., proposed by the national wage board, and approved by the Premier or the State Council).[4] For example, suppose that sustained asset inflation and exchange rate appreciation over the next ten years make China's wage and currency no longer competitive, and there is a speculative attack on the renminbi thereafter.[5] In response to this speculative attack, the Chinese government can announce, say, a 10% nation-wide reduction in wage through a cut in the variable wage component. Such a reduction in wage, along with the depreciation of the renminbi triggered by the speculative attack, will help restoring China's competitiveness and hence increase her resilience from the crisis.

In addition, if speculators know in advance that the Chinese government has this powerful policy weapon (i.e., the VWC) that can influence the equilibrium level of China's exchange rate, their inclination of engineering a speculative attack can be greatly reduced. At the very least, a wage cut can reduce the required downward adjustment (and hence the instability) of the renminbi. Because of this, speculators will not dare to push the Chinese currency too far as an announced wage cut amid a medium-size depreciation can seriously hurt these speculators. Thus, China's immunity against a potential crisis will be increased. In addition, the chance of a failed reform, in terms of an eventual collapse of exchange rate in the longer future, will be reduced. Unfortunately, as the establishment of a variable wage component is outside the authority of the central bank and the Ministry of Labor does not have qualified economists to

---

[4] If private employers want to maintain another variable wage component as a buffer against firm-specific shocks or moderate business cycles, they can set up another variable wage component (e.g., variable bonus component) that can be varied by the employers.

[5] Note that the greatest danger of China's exchange rate system reform is not now, but in the longer future (e.g., when sustained asset inflation and exchange rate appreciation allows speculative attack to trigger a financial crisis, especially when the non-performing bank loans remain substantial).

appreciate the proposal, reforms along this direction have not yet been seriously explored.

### 3.2.4 *Capital Control*

Fourthly, the proposals re-iterated the importance of maintaining a sufficient degree of capital control (i.e., inconvertibility of capital account) until (i) the problems of non-performing bank loans and extensive moral hazard activities are cleared, and (ii) the real exchange rate has gradually adjusted to levels reasonably close to its equilibrium level. That is, removing capital control should be the last step of the reform.

In Chapter 5, we will further explain that it is necessary, at least in the next 8–10 years, for China to limit the development of the renminbi forward and futures markets until the above two conditions are satisfied. Otherwise, this will substantially weaken, or completely remove, the capital control — an important safeguard of the exchange rate system reform and financial stability — in China. In particular, given the market's belief that the renminbi is substantially undervalued, the existence of a free and liquid renminbi forward or futures market will invite enormous speculation for rennmibi appreciation in the forward or futures market which will through covered interest arbitrage or other transmission channels, result in enormous appreciation pressures in the renminbi spot market and enormous monetary growth pressure in China's money market (see the details of the transmission mechanism in Chapter 5). Furthermore, from the experiences of some crisis-hit economies during the Asian Financial Crisis, the existence of a free and liquid renminbi forward or futures market will make China vulnerable to speculative attacks in the future (see Chapter 5 for further discussions).

> Chapter 4 ◁

# The Transitional Reform in 2005

In this chapter, we will review China's transitional exchange rate system reform announced in July 2005, and the immediate market response to such announcement. We will also discuss the reasons for its relative success in the first year, and the moderate mistake committed by the Chinese Central Bank thereafter.

## 4.1 The Reform Announced in July 2005

On 21 July 2005, the People's Bank of China finally announced a reform of which timing was unanticipated by the market. In the reform,

(i)   the renminbi was revalued against the US dollar by 2.1% (i.e., from 8.28 renminbi per US dollar to 8.11 renminbi per US dollar);

(ii)  the renminbi-US dollar rate would only be allowed to fluctuate within a very narrow band of ±0.3% around the closing rate of the previous working day;[1] and

(iii) the renminbi would be monitored against an undisclosed basket of currencies instead of against the US dollar.

The interesting point here is that the renminbi was only revalued by 2.1% instead of a medium revaluation (e.g., 5%) expected by some market participants. As explained in Chapter 2, the main reason behind this more moderate appreciation was the concern of increased inflows of speculative fund if there was a medium size revaluation. That is, if the realized revaluation were greater than the transaction costs and risk premium of the speculation, it would

---

[1] The band against other major currencies such as Euro or Yen was ±1.5%, which was subsequently widened to ±3% from 25 September 2005.

attract more (illegal) inflows of speculative fund. A major revision was also ruled out because of its potential harmful impact on the unemployment problem as well as the economic growth of the Chinese economy. On the other hand, the 2.1% appreciation was made to deal with external political pressure for the renminbi appreciation: According to feedback from senior officials, China did have a bargaining power to resist external pressure for exchange rate appreciation. However, if the change was within the acceptable limit, the Chinese government would not mind making the concession if it could allow the other government to better deal with the internal political pressure on the same issue. Thus, the 2.1% revaluation could be regarded as a good compromise between internal and external needs.

Another interesting point is related to (ii), i.e., a narrow exchange rate band against the US dollar. As explained in Chapter 2, a widening of exchange rate band at the early stage of the reform without any specific purpose would only weaken confidence and invite unnecessary speculation. Thus, the measure was meant to avoid unnecessary speculation or other complications at the early stage of the transitional period.[2]

---

[2] Although the mean of the exchange rate band against the US dollar could vary so that the movements of the Chinese currency over a reasonable period of time could be quite different from that of the US dollar, it should be noted that the narrow exchange rate band *vis-à-vis* the US dollar would also mean that short-term movements of the Chinese currency could not deviate too much from the US dollar. In fact, should there be a sharp enough short term rise or fall in the US dollar so that there was a conflict between announcements (ii) and (iii), announcement (ii) would be a more binding constraint on the short term movements of the renminbi. However, this kind of conflict might not be observable or could be overcome because

(a) The widening of exchange rate band between the renminbi and other foreign currencies (e.g., Euro and Yen) from ±1.5% to ±3% since 25 September 2005 had substantially reduced the likelihood of a conflict between the two announcements. Together with the adjustable means of the bands (for the renminbi *vis-à-vis* the US dollar rate as well as the renminbi *vis-à-vis* other foreign currency rates), this would mean that there had to be very sharp rise or fall in US dollar before such conflict could arise.

(b) The non-disclosure of the weights of each currency in the currency basket had made the conflict less observable.

(c) In the extremely case of a very sharp rise or fall in the US dollar (say, one year after the reform in July 2005), the Chinese government would be justified to relax the exchange rate band between the renminbi and the US dollar.

## 4.2 Market Response at the Early Stage

After the announcement on 21 July 2005, the immediate market response was more moderate than originally expected. No doubt, the People's Bank of China's professional performance on the administrative aspect contributed to the better than expected result. More importantly, there was sufficient debate and discussion before the reform, thus resulting in the correct choice of a very moderate appreciation at the first stage of the reform and avoidance of inappropriate choices, such as a medium-size revaluation or a medium-size exchange rate band. As a result, many market participants found that the transitional reform had its own logic, viability and credibility. Supplemented by the government reputation and the likelihood that the transaction costs and risk premium[3] of the (illegal) speculation could be greater than the expected gain from the gradual appreciation, many market participants chose to believe the Chinese government and gave up the choice of joining the speculation.

Of course, there were also some speculators who still believed in a chance of further sharp appreciation(s) or revaluation(s) in the future. Furthermore, those who had connections with potentially profitable targets (such as Chinese property) and underground money changers (lower transaction costs) chose to join the speculation. As a result, there were still some inflows of speculative funds through the illegal channels or the abuse of legal channels. Nevertheless, the amount of inflows during the first year seemed to be within the sterilization capacity of the central bank.

In fact, in the two following-up articles published in mid-August, the author used the above observation to conclude that "*the overall condition*

---

Bearing in mind that announcement (ii) was only a transitional arrangement which should be relaxed at the second stage of the transitional reform and monitoring the NEER should be one of eventual aims of the reform, it was important to include announcement (iii).

[3] For normal investors in foreign countries, the transaction costs would include the inconvenience costs and time costs in understanding the regulations, market practice and culture in China. The unfamiliarity with the Chinese market and regulations would also mean a very high risk premium for these investors. Thus, the transaction costs and risk premium for these normal investors were rather high.

*was basically under control, although there were still moderate currents of speculative inflows*" (大局初定, 暗涌仍在). It then proposed measures that could

(i)  reduce the amount of speculative inflows; or
(ii)  offset the monetary impacts of the speculative inflows

so as to change the situation to "*despite minor currents of speculative inflows, the overall condition was under control*" (暗涌虽在, 大局已定) (see Section 4.4 for the list of proposed measures).

The articles also highlighted that, immediately after the transitional reform, the number of participants who chose not to join the speculation (i.e., the believers) should be far greater than those who chose to join (i.e., the non-believers). Otherwise, the size of the speculative inflows would exceed the limit that the central bank of China could deal with. Thus, the Chinese government should by all means keep the trust of these believers by honoring this implicit promise of at most a very gradual appreciation in the next few years. Failure to honor the implicit promise would invite the believers to think otherwise, which could result in enormous inflows and hence disastrous outcomes. Once the Chinese government manage to do so, the next step was to convert the non-believers into believers through subsequent result of very gradual appreciation as well as enhanced publicity of the government's intention.

Because of the initial success of the transitional reform, the author had written the following Chinese poem:

《贺汇改》
贺中国汇改初成, 并冀引入
可变动工资以定长治久安之局

艰难汇改伏波澜,
汇率微调破险关;
可变工资从此定,
风波难动秀河山。

The first half of the poem highlighted the enormous danger hidden behind the exchange rate system reform, and the use of gradual appreciation to overcome the problem. The second half of the poem was meant to remind the Chinese government to set up the variable wage component so as to increase China's immunity and resilience against potential crisis in the future (see Chapter 3 for more detailed discussion). Unfortunately, the suggestion was outside the authority of the Chinese central bank and there was no referral to the related authorities (e.g., the State Council or the Ministry of Labor) for the importance of such a proposal.

## 4.3  Two Important Characteristics That Contribute to the Initial Success

Unlike the prediction of Goldstein (2004) who believed that the "go-slow approach" would create a "one-way bet" for speculators and thereby increase speculation on the renminbi appreciation, the transitional exchange rate system reform explicitly took into account an important economic characteristic in China: speculative inflows into China, whether through the illegal channels or the abuse of legal channels, were in principle illegal by nature. The illegal nature in turn implied non-negligible transaction costs and risk premium for the speculative inflows, which further resulted in a corridor, or range of exchange rate appreciation through which the exchange rate system reform could go. Beyond this corridor, speculators would profit from the speculation which could in turn attract increased speculative inflows. However, within this corridor, the gain from appreciation would be less than the transaction costs and risk premium. More importantly, the illegal nature of the speculative inflows also implied that China would be well justified to widen the corridor through greater effort of inspection and heavier penalty when deemed necessary. As a result, many market analysts and participants found that the transitional reform had its own logic, viability and credibility.[4] Comments by these analysts in the second half of 2005 had in turn induced more market

---

[4] For example, many commercial bank economists, such as those in Hong Kong, had bought the argument and were: (a) projecting a very gradual appreciation; and (b) indicating that the potential gain from the appreciation could be more than offset by the lower renminbi deposit rates in Hong Kong. Even for those foreign investment banks which needed to attract business by exaggerating the potential appreciation, many of them had gradually reduced their projected appreciation so as to ensure that their forecast would not be too far away from the realized appreciation.

participants believing in the viability and credibility of the transitional reform.

Another important characteristic of the transitional reform was that it tried to work on market expectation. By portraying a logically viable reform, it managed to bring the market expectation towards its target path. This had in turn convinced many potential investors that the gain from appreciation could be lower than the associate transaction costs and risk premium.[5]

## 4.4 Proposed Measures to Deal With the Speculative Inflows

Despite the success of the reform at the early stage, there were moderate inflows of speculative funds through the illegal channels or the abuse of legal channels. If not curbed or sterilized, this could add to the monetary growth and inflation pressure in China. Thus, in the two articles published in mid August 2005 (see Sections 4.4.1 and 4.4.2) and two more following-up articles published in April and May 2006 (see Section 4.5), the author proposed a set of measures along the following two directions:

(a) measures that could reduce the incentives of speculative inflows; and
(b) measures that could offset the impacts of the speculative inflows on domestic monetary growth.

These proposals were important not only because they could reduce the central bank's sterilization burden but also because they could sustain the success of the reform.[6]

---

[5] Unfortunately, as will be discussed in Section 4.8, the Chinese central bank's subsequent failure to appreciate the importance of expectation management since the second year of the transitional reform had resulted in their moderate mistake of allowing too high a renminbi appreciation rate, which had in turn contributed to enormous speculative inflows and a severe asset inflation in 2007.

[6] For example, if there were other considerations that constrained the Chinese government from issuing too much central bank notes or government bonds for sterilization, or there were some other reasons that caused a bigger surge in speculative inflows beyond the central bank's sterilization capacity in the future, the proposed measures would mitigate the burden of sterilization.

### 4.4.1 *Measures That Discourage Speculative Inflows*

Among the two sets of proposals published in August 2005, the first set of proposed measures was to reduce the incentives of speculative inflows through (i) the increase in the transaction costs and risk premium of speculative inflows; (ii) the control of investment returns of speculative inflows; and (iii) the management of market expectation.

#### 4.4.1.1 *Raise the Transaction Costs and Risk Premium of Speculative Inflows*

To discourage speculative inflows, one viable way was to increase the transaction costs and risk premium of the (illegal) speculative inflows. For example, if part of the inflows was conducted through underground money changers, the Chinese government could raise the effort of inspection and penalty against these money changers. The articles did note that it would be impossible to eliminate all the underground money changers. However, the aim of the proposal was not an elimination of these money changers, but a reduction in speculative inflows through a rise in the transaction costs and risk premium of speculative inflows at least at the transitional stage of the reform.

#### 4.4.1.2 *Control the Investment Returns of Speculative Inflows*

To reduce the incentives of speculative inflows, it would also be important to contain the expected investment returns of these inflows in the domestic market. As speculators could invest their funds in the asset market in China, it would be important to avoid a *sharp* and *sustained* rise in asset price during the transitional reform. Note that what China needed to avoid here was sharp and sustained asset inflation. Gradual asset inflation comparable to international rates after risk adjustment would have relatively little effect on speculative inflows. For example, if part of the speculative inflows were invested in properties in China, it would be important for China to maintain or further strengthen its curbing measures on the property market at that time so as to ensure that there would not be too much rise in property price in the subsequent five years. Otherwise, the high investment return in the property market could attract enormous inflows.[7] Similarly, it would be important to avoid a sharp and sustained rise in share price during the transitional reform. As the stock market in 2005 was still weak after the crash a few years ago, the articles did not find it necessary to recommend any curbing measures on the stock market.[8] Nevertheless, in the following-up articles published in 2006, the author started to urge China to curb the stock market before it was too late (see Chapter 8 for more details).

### 4.4.1.3 *Further Works on Market Expectation*

To further discourage speculative inflows, the Chinese government could work on market expectation through enhanced publicity of the government's intention and viability of the reform. In addition to official clarifications, informal channels such as comments by market analysts with good relations with the government or spreading of those views in the market would help a lot.

## 4.4.2 *Measures That Offset the Impacts of Speculative Inflows*

The aim of the second set of measures was to offset the impact of speculative inflows on domestic money supply. The articles first explained that the problem created by the speculative inflows was *"not the associate rise in foreign reserves"* as highlighted in the media, *"but the associate rise in money supply"* which could imply asset and CPI inflation pressure. Thus, the key here should not be spending away of the precious foreign reserves, but mopping up of excess money supply which might or might not involve a reduction in foreign reserves.[9]

---

[7] Although the rise in property price at that time was moderate when compared with those after mid-2006, the articles had already noted that the subsequent rise could be dangerous.

[8] In addition to the avoidance of sustained and excessive returns in the property and share markets, it would also be important to keep a reasonable differential between domestic deposit rate and foreign borrowing rate so that the expected exchange rate appreciation gain of speculative inflows will not exceed the sum of the interest differential, the transaction costs and the risk premium.

[9] For example, sterilization will reduce money supply without any reduction in foreign reserves.

### 4.4.2.1 *Outward Foreign Investment and Purchase of Productive Assets*

One way to offset the impacts of the moderate inflows would be an increase in outward foreign direct investments and purchases of foreign productive assets. Examples of the former include investments in oil fields in Africa and South America, mines in resource-abundant countries and high-technology companies in developed economies. Examples of the latter include purchases of airplanes to support the expansions of Chinese airlines. The articles stressed the importance for the Chinese government to *"avoid financing state-owned enterprises' investments and purchases through a direct transfer of government's foreign reserves to the related enterprises"*. Instead, *"all enterprises should first raise the funds from the domestic market and then convert them to the foreign currencies through the foreign exchange market"*. Otherwise, the investments and purchases would not help mopping up the excess money supply. To convince the policy makers, the author quoted the successful experience of Singapore, which had substantially expanded her foreign outward investments after the Asian Financial Crisis. The foreign investments and the implied capital outflows had helped to keep the Singapore dollar low which had in turn facilitated Singapore's recovery during the post-Asian Financial Crisis period (see Section 4.5.5.1 for more details).

### 4.4.2.2 *Sterilization and Other Offsetting Measures*

While indicating that developing investment outflow channels would help, the articles also highlighted that sterilization would continue to be the most direct and effective measures to offset the monetary growth pressure in the near future. That is, China must issue sufficient amount of central bank notes or government bonds to ensure that its monetary growth would be within the target growth rate. In the next few sections, we will discuss the author's following-up discussions on other offsetting measures, such as

(a) the securitization of part of the rise in foreign reserves;
(b) the establishment of foreign index funds in China;
(c) the QDII; and
(d) the change in the reserve requirement ratio for banks.

## 4.5 Further Discussions on the Offsetting Measures

In April and May 2006, the author published two articles on further measures to offset the monetary growth pressure in China. The set of articles first reiterated that

(a) capital control should be kept as the last defense against financial crisis; and
(b) capital control was an important part of the medium-term exchange rate arrangement.

Thus, in designing measures to offset the monetary growth pressure, effort should be made to avoid weakening the capital control in China. It then discussed the appropriate direction of various offsetting measures, including the new Qualified Domestic Institutional Investors (QDII) scheme adopted by the Chinese government at that time (see Section 4.5.5 for more details).

### 4.5.1 *Importance of Maintaining Capital Control at That Time*

As explained in the author's previous articles (see Section 2.2.2), although maintaining capital control would involve a certain cost, China could continue to grow at the rapid pace at that time. On the other hand, if removing the capital control resulted in a financial crisis in the subsequent future, the loss to China would be far much greater. In case the crisis triggered off further social and political instability, China might not be able to come back to normal economic development. Thus, before the non-performing loans and the culture of moral hazard activities in the banking industries were properly cleared, China should keep her capital control as the last defense against financial crisis.

Furthermore, according to the medium term exchange rate design (see Section 2.2.2), China would still need to control the pace of appreciation in the subsequent 8–10 years so as to avoid a substantial decline in its GDP growth and employment. Meanwhile, China's central bank should maintain her control on money supply so that it could continue to use monetary policy to achieve internal balance and pre-empt asset inflation.

However, according to the doctrine of Impossible Trinity, China could only control both the money supply and the pace of appreciation if she could maintain a sufficient degree of capital control (i.e., as long as the porous part of the capital control was not too big, the impact of the illegal inflows could be offset by sterilization). Given the importance of maintaining independent control on the money supply and the pace of appreciation, maintaining capital control would be the best choice at that time.

### 4.5.2 *The Moderate Speculative Inflows Was Still within the Central Bank's Sterilization Capacity*

Nevertheless, because of changes in economic environment and numerous reforms made in the past decades, China's capital control had weakened substantially. For example, speculative funds could at that time flow into China through the illegal channels, such as huge amount of remittance through the underground money changers. It could also flow into China through the abuse of legal channels, such as over-invoicing the amount of exports or foreign direct investments. In fact, a moderately large amount of speculative inflows was done through these channels at that time, and had made it more difficult for the PBoC to control the monetary growth and the pace of appreciation. Fortunately, the PBoC at that time still had sufficient sterilization capacity to offset the impacts of these speculative inflows on monetary growth (see Section 4.8 for more details). Thus, as long as the amount of inflows was not too enormous, the PBoC could still control the money supply and the pace of appreciation.

### 4.5.3 *Two Other Important Sources of Inflows*

Nevertheless, in addition to the speculative inflows, there were two other importance sources of inflows that had substantially increased the monetary growth pressure at that time. The first one was the trade surplus and the second one was the FDI inflows. For example, according to the statistic available at that time, the trade surplus surged to 102 billion US dollars in 2005 from 32 billion US dollars in 2004. Meanwhile, FDI inflows rose to 72 billion US dollars in 2005 from 61 billion US dollars in 2004. In addition, a less precise estimate on the speculative inflows in 2005 suggested that it could be around 50 billion US dollars. All these had contributed to a sharp rise in China's foreign reserves by about 200 billion US dollars, and hence the same amount of pressure on China's monetary base.

With the monetary growth pressure due to these inflows, China was considering additional investment outflow channels, such as the QDII, to mitigate the monetary growth pressure (see Section 4.5.5 for more details).

### 4.5.4 *Some Basic Principles to Guide the Direction of the Offsetting Measures*

While developing QDII and other investment outflow channels was very important, it was however necessary to ensure that these measures would not weaken the capital control in China. Otherwise, this would seed the possibility of financial crisis, and then disastrous economic, social and political instability. In view of these, the articles provided some conceptual analysis to help guiding the design of the QDII and other offsetting measures on the right direction. After clarifying the related concept and the additional proposals outlined in Section 4.5.5, it would become clear that there might not be a conflict between the two goals of maintaining capital control and offsetting the monetary growth pressure. That is, there were some policy measures that could simultaneously address the two goals.

#### 4.5.4.1 *The Aim Should Be Offsetting of Monetary Growth Pressure Instead of Spending Away the Precious Foreign Reserves*

Firstly, as explained in Section 4.4.2.1, China's major aim at that time should be offsetting the monetary growth pressure generated by the inflows, instead of spending away the foreign reserves. That is, foreign reserve is a precious asset that should be used and invested appropriately. The rise in foreign reserves was not the source of the problem. It was at most a phenomenon created by the original source of problems (i.e., the inflows of funds). If the government followed some researchers' mistake of mis-identifying the rise in foreign reserves as the source of the problem, and followed the advice of spending away the foreign reserves, it would not only result in a relatively wasteful spending of the precious asset but would also substantially weaken China's ability to cope with reversal of flows in the future.

### 4.5.4.2 *Sterilization Would Continue to Be the Most Important Offsetting Instrument in the Intermediate Future*

Secondly, sterilization through issuance of central bank notes or government bonds would still be the most effective and controllable instrument to offset the monetary growth pressure at that time. In the near future, the pilot experiments on the offsetting measures could at most play a supplementary role in offsetting the monetary growth pressure. Thus, China still needed to rely on substantial issuance of central bank notes or government bonds to offset the monetary growth pressure.

Even in the intermediate future, sterilization would still have a certain role that could not be replaced by the relaxation of investment outflow regulation at that time. For example, as

(a) many of the regulation relaxations might not be reversible; and
(b) the amount of funds involved in the regulation relaxation would also be highly volatile and unpredictable,

it would be more appropriate for China to opt for a prudent pace of regulation relaxation. During this period of prudent relaxation, the inflows of fund would continue to be bigger than the outflows, and the implied monetary growth pressure would have to be sterilized by substantial issuance of central bank notes or government bonds. In other words, the existence of the sterilization tool would allow China to opt for a more prudent and safer pace of regulation relaxation.

### 4.5.4.3 *Distinguish the Once-and-for-all Flows from the Permanent Flows*

Thirdly and most importantly, among the various types of inflows, one should distinguish what type of flows would be once-and-for-all and what type of flows would be more long lasting. Similarly, among the various offsetting outflow measures, one should identify whether the measures would result in once-and-for-all outflows or persistent outflows. Failure to match the inflows and outflows in this dimension could mean disastrous outcome in the future.

For example, when dealing with once-and-for-all or temporary speculative inflows, it would be dangerous to use offsetting measures that could result in persistent outflows. When the speculative inflows stopped in the subsequent future, the related offsetting measures would continue to result in further outflows and reduction in foreign reserves. The latter would over time put China in a weak balance of payment position and make it vulnerable to speculative attack in the future.

### 4.5.4.4 *Distinguish Highly Reversible Flows from Less Reversible Flows*

Furthermore, it would be important to distinguish those easily reversible inflows and offsetting measures from those less reversible flows. For example, speculative inflows could be easily reversible. On the other hand, some of the new consumption and import habit due to the offsetting measures could be more difficult to reverse. If the offsetting measures did not have a good match with the speculative inflows in the reversibility dimension, it could also make China vulnerable to a reversal of speculative flows in the future.

### 4.5.4.5 *Be Cautious with Inflows That Could Increase Outflow Pressure in the Future*

In addition, some of the inflows of funds will increase China's liability and pressure of outflows in the future, while some will not. Generally speaking, speculative inflows usually belong to flows that are short-term, easily reversible and will increase national liability. They are in fact the most unreliable inflows, and one can even argue that they create more harms than benefits to China. Net exports and current account surplus are usually more long-lasting, less reversible and will not increase national liability. Among the three types of inflows, they should be the most reliable one. Foreign direct investment are somewhere in between the above two categories. When the economy is good, FDI will continue to flow in. On the other hand, when there is a perceived risk of financial crisis or currency depreciation, the inflows will fall substantially.

In fact, during the Asian Financial Crisis, the market's perceived risk of a moderate depreciation of renminbi had in 1998 caused a moderate decline in FDI inflows into China. Thus, although FDI inflows would not be reversed to a large negative number such as the case of speculative inflows,[10] a substantial reduction in FDI inflows during the adverse time could still have substantial impact on the Chinese economy.

Moreover, according to China's FDI regulation, foreign direct investors could remit their profit home. Thus, the FDI inflows at that time could increase the outflow pressure in the subsequent future. If some day in the future, foreign direct investors stop re-investing their earned profit in China, the outflow pressure during the peak of profit remittance will be substantial.

### 4.5.4.6 *A Prudent Pace of Regulation Relaxation*

Thus, when designing the offsetting regulation relaxation, China should take into account of the reliability of the three types of inflows. For example, if China believes that

(a) speculative inflows are highly unreliable;
(b) China should keep a sufficient amount of foreign reserves to meet any principal withdrawal and profit remittance due to FDIs in the future; and
(c) current account surplus is the most reliable inflow,

then, in designing or choosing the regulation relaxation, a relatively safe guideline is to ensure that the maximum amount of average annual outflows due to the regulation relaxation will not exceed the average annual current account surplus.[11]

It should however be noted that even such simple guideline can be debatable and not perfectly safe. For example, as explained in previous

---

[10] As foreign investors need to sell their plants or fixed assets at a big discount before they can repatriate the divestment proceeds home, they usually prefer to keep their investments in the host country unless the situation is really bad.

[11] If China believes that it is not necessary to keep foreign reserves for the principal withdrawal of FDIs, then it can go further to opt for a design in which the maximum amount of average annual outflows due to the regulation relaxation will not exceed the sum of average annual current account surplus and FDI inflows. Of course, such guideline is based on the stronger assumption that foreign direct investors will not, during the adverse time, sell their assets at a big discount and then repatriate the proceeds home.

chapters, not all the trade surplus recorded at that time was real trade surplus. Part of it could be speculative inflows through the over-invoicing of exports and under-invoicing of imports.[12] Thus, the related guideline should allow some rooms for such loopholes. In addition, among the trade surplus at that time and the subsequent future, quite some portion of it was actually profit of FDI, which could be remitted out in the future. Thus, the related guideline should also allow some rooms for potential remittance in the future.

In short, which guideline China should choose still is a subject of further studies and debate. However, the above discussion did suggest that making a choice without sufficient studies and debate could be disastrous. In view of the potential risk, the articles recommended the Chinese government to opt for a more prudent pace of regulation relaxation while waiting for more studies and findings on this issue. This would still be optimal and feasible because the existence of the sterilization tool: during the period of prudent regulation relaxation, the gap between the outflows and inflows could still be offset by sterilization.

### 4.5.5 *Ways to Build in More Controllability and Adjustability on Potential Outflows*

As explained in the previous section, if we believed

(a) speculative flows could be reversed at any time;
(b) part of the trade surplus and FDI inflows at that time could be speculative inflows;
(c) FDI could fall to a very low level when there is a perceived risk of crisis, economic downturn, political instability or exchange rate depreciation; and
(d) the time gap between the investment period and the profit remittance period of FDIs suggested that China should keep a sufficient amount of foreign reserves to meet the potential profit remittance,

then China should opt for a prudent pace of regulation relaxation.

---

[12] Similarly, among the FDIs recorded at that time, part of them could be speculative inflows through the over-claiming of the actual investment.

Of course, China should also avoid being over-cautious, which could result in too little offsetting investment outflows. In view of the *trade-off* between being "*not prudent enough*" and being "*over-cautious*", the articles proposed to add a certain degree of *controllability* and *adjustability* in the design of offsetting measures. Thus, when it was subsequently found that the actual outflows or inflows were much greater than the anticipated amount, the design would allow the Chinese government to adjust the amount of outflows and hence reduce the actual trade-off to a much lower level. On the other hand, if there were too little built-in controllability and adjustability in the offsetting outflow measures, even one simple mistake, such as underestimation of structural outflows created by the offsetting measures or underestimation of the speculative inflows through the abuse of legal channels, could result in serious outcome.

After highlighting the importance of building in some kind of controllability and adjustability on the offsetting measures, the articles made a few proposals along this line.

### 4.5.5.1 *Increase the Ratio of Once-and-for-all Overseas Investment*

One simple and effective way to increase the level of controllability and adjustability was to increase the proportion of once-and-for-all investment outflows. As explained in Section 4.4.2.1, the government could encourage the state and private enterprises to raise funds in the domestic market, and then use the funds to purchase foreign exchange from the central bank for overseas investments. Recommended examples of such overseas investments were direct investments in oilfields or mines in Africa, South America and other resource abundant economies, purchases of foreign airplanes to support the expansion of Chinese airlines, and investments in high-tech and medium-tech firms in the Western world.

As these once-and-for-all investments could be adjusted every year, the Chinese government would have high controllability and adjustability on the amount of outflows through this channel. For example, it could

(a) suspend all these overseas investments in case of extreme economic adversity; or
(b) increase these overseas investments during time with substantial inflows.

In fact, during the recession period just after the Asian Financial Crisis, the Singapore government was able to use large-scale overseas investment, such as asking its government-linked companies to purchase a bank in Hong Kong and a telecommunication firm in Australia, to keep the Singapore dollar down so as to facilitate the recovery of the economy during the post-crisis recession.[13]

It should however be emphasized that, in order to offset the monetary growth pressure, oversea investment had to be done through fund-raising in the domestic market. Otherwise, it would not offset the monetary growth pressure. Take the case of building China's national strategic reserve of petroleum as an example, although the purchase involved important national strategic considerations, there was no fund-raising in the domestic market. Thus, the purchase of foreign petroleum would not help offset the monetary growth pressure.

### 4.5.5.2 *Securitizing Part of the Government Holdings of Foreign Bonds*

Another effective measure was to (a) use the additional foreign reserves created by the inflows to purchase foreign bonds; and then (b) securitize the foreign bonds and sold the securitized asset to Chinese citizens. When the government sold the securitized assets to Chinese citizens, it would mop up money supply in the economy, and therefore offset the monetary growth pressure. If the government did not want to take any exchange rate risk, it could specify that the principal and interest of the securitized assets would be paid in foreign currency. The advantage of such arrangement would be as follows: the amount of assets to be securitized (and hence the amount of funds mopped up) would be under the control of the government. Thus, in case of a substantial increase in inflows, the government

---

[13] During the first half year of the Asian Financial Crisis, Singapore had let the Singapore dollar fell by about 10% *vis-à-vis* the US dollar (and about 2% depreciation in its NEER) so as to mitigate the speculation pressure triggered by the collapse of other crisis-hit currencies. In 1998–1999, the Government's encouragement of outward foreign direct investment (and further deepening of the Asian Financial Crisis) had result in a further deprecation of the Singapore's NEER by another 4%. As a result of the deprecations in these two episodes, Singapore's NEER had declined by about 6%, which was believed to have helped restore Singapore's export price competitiveness.

could offset it by a parallel increase in the amount of the securitized assets. On the other hand, in the case of a substantial reversal of speculative flows, the government could freeze the securitization or even redeemed some of the securitized assets. The latter would in turn help prevent a liquidity crunch due to the reversal of speculative flows.

Of course, as the foreign bond was already securitized as an asset of Chinese citizens, the related amount of foreign bonds held by the Chinese government as the back-up asset of the securitized asset should not be counted as China's foreign reserves.[14]

### 4.5.5.3 *Foreign Index Funds and the QDII Scheme*

The third way was to (a) use additional foreign reserves created by the inflows of funds to buy index component shares in foreign countries; (b) use the foreign shares to set up index funds (managed by a semi-government body); and (c) sell the index funds to Chinese citizens with a reasonable management fee. Alternatively, the government could give a certain quota limit to Chinese financial institutions so that they could purchase foreign shares, bonds and foreign exchanges on behalf of Chinese citizens. [Note that the second choice was in fact quite similar to the QDII scheme adopted by the Chinese government.]

One important advantage of the first choice was again the built-in controllability and adjustability: In case of a substantial increase in inflows, the government could offset it by a parallel increase in the scale and number of the index funds. In the case of a substantial reversal of speculative flows, the

---

[14] The article also noted that the Chinese government could choose to add a clause in the securitization document stating that the government-related securitizing agent could, when deemed necessary, choose to redeem the securitized asset in renminbi at a reasonable compensation interest rate. This would mean that China could change the collaterals of the securitized assets back as its foreign reserves, thus increasing China's capacity in defending against speculative attack. Of course, it would be important to choose an appropriate level of compensation interest rate which would on one hand keep the public interest in the securitized asset, and on the other hand would not excessively increase the government's interest burden during the speculative attack. Nevertheless, as the clause only meant an addition option to the government, the government could always choose not to exercise it if she found the compensation interest rate too high.

government could freeze the scale and number of the index funds, or even re-inject liquidity back into the economy by buying back part of the index funds. As the value of the index funds is linked with the value of the back-up share holdings, there would not be any capital gain or loss in the initial sales and the subsequent buy-back of the index funds.

There would also be some controllability and adjustability in the QDII scheme, but the government influence would be somewhat weaker here. For example, in the case of a moderate reversal of speculative flows, the government could freeze the amount of quota in the QDII. However, in the case of a substantial reversal of speculative flows, it could be quite difficult to reduce the quota previous granted to the qualified domestic institutional investors (see Box 4.5.5 for the differences between the proposed design of index funds and the QDII scheme).[15]

---

**Box 4.5.5: Other Differences Between the Proposed Design of Index Funds and the QDII Scheme**

Among the two choices, the author was slightly more inclined to first work on the index funds, mainly because

(a) the management fee for the index funds would be much lower than that of the QDII;
(b) the first choice would not suffer from the principal-agent problem while there could be such a risk in the QDII scheme;
(c) the establishment of index funds for various foreign stock markets would enrich the financial markets in China and provide a foundation for further financial developments based on these index funds.

*(Continued)*

---

[15] Another problem with such regulation relaxation was that the amount of actual outflows would very much depend on the decisions of the qualified domestic institutional investors, i.e., they might in some cases decide not to use up the quota. Thus, unlike the author's proposals, the government's controllability and adjustability here were weaker simply because the regulation relaxation would provide the government only an indirect control, instead of a direct control, on the amount of funds to be flowed out.

> *(Continued)*
>
> Of course, there was an argument that the QDII scheme could give the fund managers more investment flexibility and hence greater chance of higher returns to the investors. This could be true if the fund managers could identify which shares could give higher returns than the others. Nevertheless, this kind of potential gain could be more than offset by the problem of principal-agent problem. That is, the agent (fund managers) could use the assets of the principal (the investors) to pursue his personal interest instead of the principal's interest, e.g., use the investors' money to buy some bad shares in exchange for bribery. Moreover, the fund managers would be inclined to choose a high management fee so as maximize his return instead of the investors' return. While the author was slightly more skeptical to the latter because of the principal-agent problem and the much higher management fee, he did not have strong objection of having both so that (i) there would be at least a healthy competition between the two; and (ii) investors could at least make their own choice between the two.

### 4.5.5.4 *Bank Reserve Requirement Ratio*

Despite the author's recommendation of using huge amount of central bank notes to offset the monetary growth pressure, the People's Bank of China had, from June 2006 onwards, chosen to raise the bank reserve requirement ratio, i.e., the required ratio of cash or monetary base that banks have to keep per dollar of deposit. One reason for such choice was that it could avoid the interest expense due to the substantial issuance of central banks notes (see Section 4.6.2 for more detailed discussion).

Whatever, as will be explained in Box 8.2.1, a rise in the bank reserve requirement ratio ($r$) would reduce the money multiplier ($m$):

$$M = m \times MB$$

Thus, even though the inflows would cause a rise in the monetary base (MB), the central could use this method to reduce $m$ and hence keep the money supply (M) within its target.

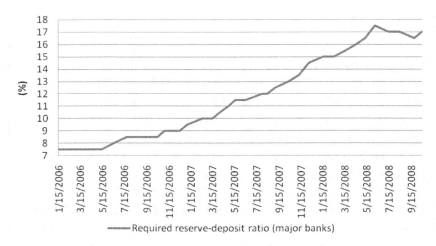

**Figure 4.5.5.**    Required Reserve-Deposit Ratio

*Soruce*: www.sina.com.cn

In fact, as shown in Figure 4.5.5, while the cumulated increase in bank reserve requirements was only moderate (i.e., 1.5 percentage points) in 2006, the cumulated rise between early 2007 and mid-2008 was substantial (i.e., 8.5 percentage points). Thus, unlike many other economies, bank reserve requirement ratio had turned out to be a very often used and powerful tool to offset the monetary growth pressure in China since mid-2006. Unfortunately, as will be explained in the subsequent sections, this was only used after the PBoC had mistakenly allowed the renminbi appreciation exceeding the recommended rate of 1–2% (see Section 4.8 for more detailed discussion), and after the stock market reached its second development stage of bubble (see Chapter 8 for more detailed discussion).

## 4.6   More Following-Up Comments on the Offsetting Measures

### 4.6.1   *Need to Scale Up the Offsetting Measures and Maintain a Trade Surplus*

In the keynote speech paper for a policy conference organized by the State Administration of Foreign Exchange in August 2006, the author further recommended the Chinese government to gradually scale up outward foreign investment and use it as a long-term solution against monetary growth pressure arising from the trade surplus, net FDI inflows and speculative inflows. While China's foreign reserve at that time could be considered as huge, the paper also highlighted that the amount of foreign assets held by China's private sector were extremely low. Thus, outward foreign investment will serve not only as a good long-term solution against the monetary growth pressure, but also as a good way to increase China's private and public holdings of foreign assets until it reaches a level and ratio that is consistent with China's growing status as a large country in the global economy (see Chapter 7 for more detailed discussion). The paper also pointed out that the offsetting measures discussed in Section 4.5 could take a long time to reach its full scale and become an effective tool to offset the effect of the three types of inflows. During the interim, the issuance of central banks notes or government bonds should still be the main tool to offset the monetary growth pressure. In particular, the Chinese government should completely sterilize all the inflows to avoid unnecessary asset and CPI inflation.

### 4.6.2 *An Accounting Hurdle on the Recommended Sterilization*

When the People's Bank of China started to issue more central bank notes in 2005H2 and 2006H1, the amount of issuance was still not enough to offset the monetary impacts of the moderate inflows at that time. For example, the average year-on-year M2 growth rate between end August 2005 and end May 2006 was 17.7%, about 1.7–3.7 percentage points above the recommended target rate of 14%.[16] Thus, during one of his visit to Beijing in June 2006, the author asked some Chinese officials why the PBoC did not appear to be active

---

[16] In one policy article, the author noted that, given China's real GDP growth was in the range of 8–10%, a M2 target growth of 16% might be too high. The article also recommended a gradual reduction of the M2 target growth to 15% and then 14%. In fact, with an actual M2 growth of about 2% higher than the already high target growth of 16%, it should not be surprising to see a CPI inflation much higher than the 3% CPI inflation target at that time, i.e., the actual (and target) M2 growth was in fact inconsistent with the 3% CPI inflation target at that time.

and determined enough to use substantial issuance of central bank notes to offset the monetary growth pressure. After hearing the feedbacks from various officials, the author found that there was in fact an obstacle in the accounting system that needed to be cleared. As such, he published an article on 6 September 2006 on this issue. The article first explained that

(a) The rise in foreign reserves due to the inflows would mean interest earnings for the China. On the other hand, the interest rate of central bank notes at that time was only slightly more than 2%. Even if one incorporated the anticipated appreciation of the renminbi, the interest earnings from the foreign reserves holdings at that time should be sufficient to offset the interest cost of the issuance of central bank notes; and

(b) Whether an economy is strong or weak is related to its productivity rather than the amount of domestic currency the government is holding. As the government has the right to print any amount of domestic currency, its monetary job should be the provision of a sufficient but not excessive amount of domestic money supply so as to ensure (i) its real economy could fully utilize its productivity (i.e., produce at its potential output); and (ii) its CPI and asset inflation could be kept at a low level. In other words, the focus of the government's monetary policy should be the utilization rate of the production capacity of the economy and the control of inflation. On the other hand, the interest cost involved in the sterilization should not be the core issue unless it is so big that will require the central bank to print domestic currency at a rate faster than that can be absorbed by real economic growth.

Thus, given the monetary growth pressure due to various types of inflows at that time, it would be important for the central bank to issue sufficient amount of central bank notes (or make large enough rise in the bank reserve requirement ratio) so as to ensure the M2 growth would be within the recommended target rate of 14%. The word "sufficient" here would refer to a large enough amount that could offset the impacts of inflows, even if this could mean 100 billion, 200 billion or even 300 billion US dollars.

Why was it necessary to issue so much central bank notes? That was because any monetary growth exceeding the recommended target rate could result in severe asset inflation and formation of asset bubble (see Chapters 8 and 9 for more detailed discussion). If one did not do sufficient curbing at the early stage, the formation of asset bubble could be unavoidable. This would in turn seed the possibility of a financial crisis and then a severe recession in the more distant future.

Nevertheless, from the feedbacks of various Chinese officials, there was an accounting hurdle on the use of the sterilization tool. That is, the interest receipts from the foreign reserves were not counted as the central bank's income, while the interest expense on the central banks notes would be counted as the central bank's expense. In other words, because of the initial accounting arrangement did not anticipate the subsequent amount of inflows and hence the implied needs to sterilize the monetary growth pressure, it had created a constraint on the central bank's capacity and determination to offset the monetary growth pressure. However, as explained in point (a) above, foreign reserves' interest receipts due to the inflows should not be separated from the central bank notes' interest payments. Thus, the article urged the Chinese government to clear the hurdle so as to ensure that the PBoC would not have to worry about using the sterilization tool to offset the monetary growth pressure.

Since then, there were re-arrangements between the central bank and the Treasury. In 2007, the China Investment Corporate Limited (CIC), similar to the Government Investment Corporation in Singapore, was formally established with the dual task of (i) issuing long term bonds to mop up the excess money supply in the economy; and (ii) using the proceeds to purchase foreign reserves from the government for its, and China's, oversea investment purposes.

## 4.7 Actions Taken by the Chinese Government

Some of the recommendations outlined in Sections 4.4–4.6 were very well-received by the Chinese government. For example, in 2005–2006, the Chinese government had used two one-off purchases of the US planes to mitigate the US pressure for the renminbi appreciation. Thereafter, more state enterprises had started to make overseas investments in mines and oilfields in resources rich places such Africa, South America and Australia. Meanwhile, state and private enterprises started to buy up plants or companies in the Western world. While the scale of these overseas investments was still at its infant stage, the author believe this would keep growing and would in the future play an important role in (i) acquiring sufficient overseas assets to augment China's economic influence and status in the global economy; and (ii) offsetting the monetary growth pressure due to the inflows discussed in the previous sections.

While the QDII scheme was not that popular at the early stage, the Chinese Central Bank did grant a reasonably large quota to qualified domestic institutional investors during the stock market boom in 2007. Unfortunately, this was done after China entered the vicious cycle of higher currency appreciation, higher speculative inflows, higher monetary growth and higher asset inflation. Thus, when the QDII helped offset part of the monetary growth pressure, it turned out to be far from sufficient when compared with the much higher inflows during the rampant asset inflation period between late 2006 and early 2008. Moreover, the Chinese government did not take up the proposal of securitizing part of government holdings of foreign bonds and the setting up of index funds. One possible reason for the choice was that Chinese economic officials did not like to have too many semi-government bodies playing active role in the market for a long time. While there was certain logic behind that choice, it did unnecessarily chop away a potentially very important and powerful offsetting channel at that time.

On the issuance of central bank notes and government bonds, the Treasury did issue a substantial amount of bonds ($\approx$ 200 billion US dollars) in 2007 on behalf of the China Investment Corporate Limited. Meanwhile, People's Bank of China did raise the bank reserve requirement ratio by a substantial percentage points in 2007 (see Figure 4.5.5).

While these had offset a lot of monetary growth pressure and helped avoiding the M2 growth from going too far from the PBoC's 16% target rate (see Figure 4.7), they were still much higher than the recommended target rate of 14%. More importantly, they were done only after the stock market bubble and the rampant property inflation had entered their development stage (see Chapter 8 for more details). If similar scale of offsetting measures were done at the early stage, it could have helped avoid the stock market bubble and rampant rise in property price in 2007. Worse still, as explained in the next section, the PBoC had mistakenly allowed relatively high appreciation rate between mid-2006 and early 2008. Such failure in

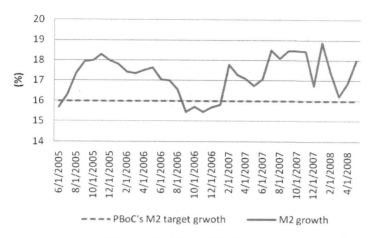

**Figure 4.7.** China's M2 Growth

*Source*: Datastream

the expectation management had in turn attracted substantial speculative inflows, thus fueling the monetary growth pressure and rise in asset prices. Fortunately, as explained in Chapter 8, China was able to achieve a gradually squeezing of the stock market bubble from late 2007, thus help pre-empting a crisis before it was too late.

## 4.8 The Moderate Mistake Committed by China's Central Bank Between Mid-2006 and Early 2008

Figures 4.8a and 4.8b show the renminbi–US dollar monthly average exchange rate and year-on-year appreciation rate since 21 July 2005.

As we can see from the figures, the renminbi's appreciation rate during the first year of the reform was basically in line with the recommendation of gradual appreciation, e.g., it appreciated by only 1.29% between 21 July 2005 and 30 June 2006, thanks to the People's Bank of China's cautious attitude during the first year of the reform.

Unfortunately, possibly because of not deep-enough understanding of the author's design (i.e., the role of a very gradual appreciation in the management of expectation and in the discouragement of speculative

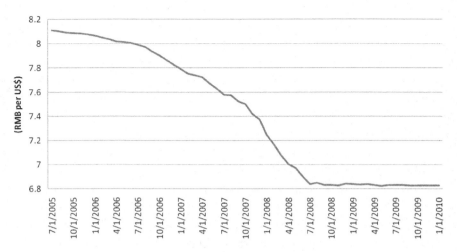

**Figure 4.8a.**   RMB per US$

*Source*: Datastream

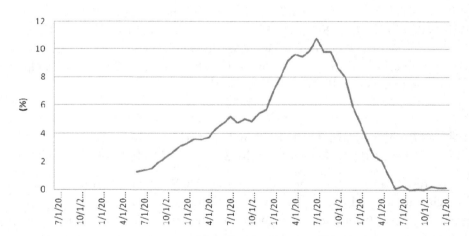

**Figure 4.8b.**   Renminbi Appreciation Rate (RMB-US$)

*Source*: Datastream

inflows),[17] and partly because of the US pressure for faster renminbi appreciation, the People's Bank of China mistakenly allowed a much higher appreciation rate of renminbi *vis-à-vis* the US dollar thereafter. For example, it allowed a 3.09% year-on-year appreciation by December 2006, a 4.69% year-on-year appreciation by June 2007 and then a 5.67% year-on-year appreciation by December 2007. The higher appreciation rates had not only rewarded speculators but also normal participants such as exporters and foreign direct investors. Since the second year of the reform, it was widely believed among market participants that renminbi would continue to rise at least at the concurrent appreciation rate (i.e., ≥ 3–5% per annum).[18] Worse still, some foreign investment banks, because of their vested interest in their investments in Chinese assets, had disseminated forecasts and research reports that the renminbi would appreciate at a rate much higher the appreciation rate recorded at that time.

As a result, there were much greater speculative inflows, and repatriation of foreign assets back into renminbi assets by Chinese residents through the illegal channels (e.g., money changers) and the abuse of the legal channels (e.g., the trade and foreign direct investment channels). Meanwhile, China's entry into the WTO, growing acceptance of Chinese products in the global economy, China's growing attractiveness to foreign direct investors and other factors had contributed to a substantial rise in trade surplus and further rise in foreign direct investment inflows. Such surge in speculative inflows, trade surplus and foreign direct investment inflows had in turn contributed to an enormous monetary

---

[17] As explained in Chapter 2, the gradual appreciation design was meant to discourage speculative inflows by ensuring no gain in the renminbi appreciation speculation after the deduction of transaction costs and risk premium. During the first year of the reform, the Chinese-US interest discount was more than 2%. As a result, the moderate 1.29% annual appreciation could be more than offset by the interest discount.

[18] During the second year of the reform, the three-month interbank rates in the US and China were 5.38% and 3.09%, respectively. Adding the 2.29% interest differentials and at least 3% expected appreciation of renminbi *vis-à-vis* the US dollar, there was at least an 5.29% expected gain ($i_{US} - i_{CH}$ + expected appreciation = 5.38% − 3.09% + 3% = 5.29%) for speculators doing uncovered interest arbitrage. The expected gain would be even higher for speculators doing dollar-carry trade (e.g., borrowing from the US interbank market and investing in China's share or property market).

growth pressure in China. As these inflows amounted to a huge size (i.e., around 250 billion US dollars in 2006 and 460 billion US dollars in 2007), China's money supply grew rapidly, even though the People's Bank of China tried very hard to offset the monetary growth pressure through substantial rises in the bank reserve requirement ratio (see Figures 4.5.5 and 4.7).

As will be discussed in Chapters 8 and 9, such rise in money supply had to some extent contributed to the rampant rise in China's share price and property price between mid-2006 and early 2008. Worse still, such rampant rise in Chinese asset price had in turn rewarded speculators who invested their renminbi in Chinese shares and properties. This in turn attracted more speculative inflows and then more renminbi appreciation pressure, more monetary growth pressure, more asset inflation pressure and even more general price and wage inflation pressure. As will be discussed in Chapters 8 and 9, the situation had become almost out of control, with the formation of a stock market bubble and property price bubble between 2007 and 2008. For the exchange rate, the year-on-year renminbi appreciation rate continued to rise to the peak of 10.8% in May 2008!

So, what we could learn from the above experience? The author believed that the situation could be much better if the People's Bank of China at the very beginning (i) continued to managed the renminbi appreciation rare at a much gradual pace; and (ii) was very determined to keep the monetary growth within the recommended target of 14% through sterilization (or increase in the reverse requirement ratio). If these were also done during the second year of the reform, then China might have been able to dampen the speculative inflows and Chinese residents' repatriation of the foreign assets into the renminbi assets. Without the support of these speculative inflows and repatriation, the trade surplus and net FDI inflows at that time would not be able to cause the excessive monetary growth and then rampant asset inflation for the following two reasons:

(a) China's real GDP growth could support a 10% monetary growth without causing extra inflation pressure; and

(b) China should have the sterilization capacity to offset the monetary growth pressure through (i) substantial issuance of central banknotes and government bonds; and (ii) substantial increase in banks' required reserve-deposit ratio.[19]

In such case, China could avoid the above vicious cycle between excessive appreciation and speculative inflows, and hence the formation of a stock market bubble and a rampant property price inflation between late 2006 and early 2008.

The incidence also tells us that central bankers' apparently *"minor"* negligence on events or factors with effect on market expectation may not be that minor. That is, central bank should never underestimate the impact of expectation, and factors or events that have effects on expectation. Pushing the argument a bit further, management of expectation is an area that central banks should strive to explore and learn.

Furthermore, similar to the remarks in Section 3.2.2, it is always better (and less costly) to pre-empt the emergence of undesirable expectation (e.g., asset inflation expectation or expected profits from undesirable currency speculation) at the beginning. Once the undesirable expectation is formed, much more powerful policies are required to keep the situation under control. We will come back to this discussion in Chapters 8 and 9.

---

[19] Unlike other developed economies, change in banks' required reserve-deposit ratio is a very often used (and powerful) tool in China.

## ➤ Chapter 5 ◀

# Further Proposals on Supplementary Measures After the Transitional Reform

This chapter will first explain why it could be disastrous to develop the renminbi forward or futures market when the renminbi was widely believed to be substantially undervalued. The second part would discuss the following-up proposals on the supplementary measures that could on one hand increase the chance of a successful exchange rate system reform, and on the other hand increase China's immunity and resilience against financial crisis. The last part would discuss the banking reform implemented in 2005–2006 and its role as a supplementary measure for the above two goals.

## 5.1 The Potential Disaster of Developing the Renminbi Forward or Futures Market at That Time

### 5.1.1 *The Chinese Central Bank's Initial Proposal to Develop the Renminbi Forward Market*

After the initial success of the transitional reform, there was a proposal within the Chinese Central Bank to develop the renminbi forward market. The intuition behind that proposal was as followed: With greater flexibility (and volatility) of exchange rate after the exit from the peg with the US dollar, the Chinese exporters and importers needed the renminbi forward market to hedge against their exchange rate risk. In view of the potential damage of the proposal, the author had published a few articles between August 2005 and November 2005, highlighting that the establishment of the liquid renminbi forward or futures market at that time would destroy the exchange rate system reform and bring financial chaos to China. In particular, the proposal would invite enormous speculation for the renminbi appreciation in the forward or futures market which would, through covered interest arbitrage or other transmission channels, result in enormous appreciation pressure in the renminbi spot market and enormous monetary growth pressure in China's money market (see the details of the transmission mechanism in Box 5.1.2). Furthermore, the proposal would mean a complete removal of the capital control in China and make China vulnerable to speculative attacks in the future (see further discussions in Section 5.2.2).

## 5.1.2 *The Potential Damage*

The articles first noted that without the renminbi forward or futures market, even if market participants widely believed that the renminbi was substantially undervalued, it would not be that easy for them to engage in the speculative activity in a very large scale at that time. This was so because speculators had to use 100% of their foreign currencies and convert all of them into renminbi, or renminbi assets such as Chinese shares or properties. As the conversion had to be done through the illegal channels or the abuse of legal channels, the whole process would involve a relatively high risk and a certain transaction cost, which in turn helped avoid a substantial amount of speculative inflows.[1]

On the other hand, if China had established the renminbi forward or futures market that allowed any participant to buy or sell the renminbi forward, a lot of speculators and even normal Chinese citizens would be induced to buy the renminbi forward. This was so because the renminbi was widely believed to be substantially undervalued. The establishment of the renminbi forward market would mean that it would no longer be illegal for anyone to speculate for the renminbi appreciation or depreciation. Worse still, as one only had to pay a small percentage of deposit, instead of 100% cash, for the forward transaction, the high gearing ratio would substantially augment the size of funds speculating for the renminbi appreciation.

---

[1] Chinese firms interested in hedging their exchange rate risk at that time could only buy and sell the renminbi forward through forward contracts with a limited number of Chinese banks. However, such kind of transactions was subjected to regulatory constraints. For example, the Chinese firms had to produce export and import documents before the transactions could be approved.

With the huge amount of funds speculating for the renminbi appreciation, the renmibi forward rate would be pushed up and rise well beyond the spot rate at that time. Once the difference in the forward and spot rates exceeded the US-Chinese interest differential and the related transaction costs, arbitragers such as banks would find it profitable to conduct covered interest arbitrage (see the operation details in Box 5.1.2). Through the covered interest arbitrage or other transmission channels, the enormous speculation pressure in the renminbi forward or futures market would be transmitted into enormous appreciation pressure in the renminbi spot market and enormous monetary growth pressure in China's money market. As explained in Box 5.1.2, the Chinese central bank would not be able to fend off the huge amount of speculation pressure and speculative inflows. The end result would be:

(a)    a substantial appreciation of both the renminbi forward and spot rates; and

(b)    a substantial increases in domestic money supply.

The process would only stop when both the renminbi forward and spot rates rose to a *no-longer-perceived-to-be-undervalued* level. In other words, they would rise by at least 15–20%, if not 15–40%. Such substantial exchange rate appreciation would naturally mean substantial downward pressure on China's export, GDP and employment, which could in turn imply substantial social pains and political dissatisfaction for a country like China (see the discussion in Chapter 2). Worse still, with the possibility of herding behaviors (discussed in Chapter 8), it would be likely that the spot and forward rates to over-appreciate beyond the long run equilibrium level. As China's money supply would also rise substantially during the process, it would probably (a) create financial chaos in the short run; and (b) seed the outcome of an economic and financial crisis in the distant future (see Chapter 2 on how countries like China might no longer be able to come back to normal political and economic stability in the case of a severe financial crisis).

The articles also noted that the above discussion has not yet included the potential role of hedge funds in speculating against the renminbi in the distant future. With the high leverage in currency forward or futures market, the market would be an ideal tool for international speculators or hedge funds to speculate against the renminbi in the distant future (see further discussions in Section 5.2.2). In fact, during the Asian Financial Crisis in 1997–1998, hedge funds had used the forward or futures market to trigger a collapse of many Asian currencies. In the case of Hong Kong, they had also used the futures and swap markets to engineer a speculative attack on Hong Kong's financial market (see more discussions in the Appendix 5.1). Thus, if China were to establish the renminbi forward or futures market, the action would be analogous to the *"opening of the city gate to invite invasion by foreign armies"*.

---

**Box 5.1.2:   Why the Establishment of a Renminbi Forward or Futures Market at That Time Could Be Disastrous**

*A.   Two groups of participants: The speculators and the arbitragers*

To understand the details of the mechanism, first note that there would in fact be two groups of market participants here. The first group of participants would be those who believed that the renminbi was substantially undervalued, and if ever allowed by law, would like to take the risk of speculating for the renminbi appreciation in the forward or futures market. These participants could be speculators, firms in other businesses or even normal Chinese citizens. The second group of market participants would be the arbitragers, who would like to earn profit without taking any exchange rate or interest rate risk by conducting covered interest arbitrage between the renminbi forward rate ($f_t$), the renminbi spot rate ($s_t$), and the interest rates in China and the US ($i_t^{CH}$ and $i_t^{US}$). These participants could be the banks or large Chinese enterprises.

*B.   People would be legally allowed to speculate for the renminbi appreciation with a high leverage ratio*

Without the renminbi forward or futures market, the first group of participants would need to use or borrow 100% of the foreign currencies (e.g., US dollar), covert them into renminbi at the sport rate at that time, lend the renminbi in the Chinese money market (or

*(Continued)*

**Box 5.1.2:**   (*Continued*)

use it to invest in other Chinese asset market) for one or a few quarters, and hope that the renminbi appreciation at the end of the lending (or investment) period would exceed the difference between their US dollar borrowing rate and their renminbi lending rate (or investment return in other Chinese asset market). As this would involve a certain exchange rate risk as well as the transaction costs and risk premium discussed in Chapter 2, not everybody would be interested in doing such kind of speculation, or *uncovered* interest arbitrage with the additional risk of being caught illegal.

However, once there was a free and liquid renminbi forward or futures market, the first group of participants would be legally allowed to speculate for renminbi appreciation with the high leverage ratio in the forward or futures market (e.g., use one hundred thousand dollars of deposit to enter into a two million dollars forward or futures contract if the required deposit of the contract is 5%).

*C.   Would invite huge speculate demand in the forward market*

As the renminbi at that time was widely believed to be undervalued by 15–40%, it would be a very good bet to speculate for the renminbi appreciation in the forward or futures market. Thus, with the establishment of the renminbi forward or futures market, numerous amount of speculators, firms and Chinese citizens would be interested in buying huge amount of renminbi in the forward or futures market.

Because of the huge size of such speculative demand, the equilibrium forward rate would be at least a few hundred basis points above the spot rate (i.e., the equilibrium forward-spot differential could be 3–5% or even higher).

*D.   Arbitrager would transmit the speculation pressure to the spot market and the money market*

If there were only the first group but not the second group of participants, the renminbi futures and spot markets would be two

(*Continued*)

**Box 5.1.2:** *(Continued)*

segmented markets. Unfortunately, once there was the first group of participants speculating the renminbi appreciation in the forward or futures market, there would definitely be the second group of participants conducting the covered interest arbitrage between the renminbi futures and spot markets. Such arbitrage activities would then transmit the enormous appreciation pressure in the futures market into enormous appreciation pressure in the spot market and enormous monetary growth pressure in China's money market. The transmission mechanism could be illustrated by the following example:

*The mechanism*

Suppose the US interest rate $(i_t^{US})$ was 4%, Chinese interest rate $(i_t^{CH})$ was 2%, and the spot renminbi–US dollar rate $s_t$ was 7.81. In addition, there were numerous first-group participants who believed that the renmibi appreciation would be greater than 2%. They would therefore buy huge amount of renminbi in the forward or futures market, thus making the forward–spot rate differential higher than 2% per annum. Even if such differential was not big (e.g., 3.2% when the forward rate $f_t$ was 7.57), arbitragers would be able to use the following operations to earn a decent profit:

*Chart: Operating Details of the Covered Interest Arbitrage*

*borrow 1 billion US$*　　　　$s_t = 7.81$　　*covert to 7.81 billion RMB*
　*(pay 4% interest)*　　　⟶　　　*(lend out to earn 2% interest)*

*one year later,*　　　　　　　　　*simultaneously use the current*
*receive 1.052 billion US$,*　$f_t = 7.57$　*forward rate ($f_t$), sell 7.81×1.02*
*repay 1.04 billion US$,*　　⟵　　*billion RMB forward (buy 7.81×*
*profit ≈ 1.2%*　　　　　　　　*1.02/7.57≈1.052 billion US$)*

*Process:*
*The arbitrager will first do all the following four steps on the same day:*
*(1) borrow 1 billion US$ in the overseas market at 4% interest rate ($i_t^{US}$);*

*(Continued)*

---

### Box 5.1.2:    (*Continued*)

(2) *convert it into 7.81 billion RMB at the current spot rate ($s_t$=7.81);*

(3) *lend the 7.81 billion RMB in the Chinese money market at 2% interest rate ($i_t^{CH}$); and*

(4) *at the current forward rate ($f_t$) of 7.57, sell 7.81 × 1.02 billion RMB forward (and buy 7.81 × 1.02/7.57≈1.052 billion US$ forward).*

One year later, the arbitrager can receive the US$1.052 billion. After repaying the principal and interest of US$1.04 billion, she will have a profit of US$1.2 million.

### E.    *Enormous pressure in the spot market and money market*

As the interest rates and the exchange rates (i.e., $i_t^{US}$, $i_t^{CH}$, $s_t$, $f_t$) would be fixed at the same day, there would be no exchange rate or interest rate risk in the arbitrage activities. In other words, as long as there was a huge number of first-group participants willing to speculate for the renminbi appreciation, the arbitragers could do 10 billion US dollars, 100 billion US dollars or even more covered interest arbitrage. As shown in the chart, the arbitragers' action of:

(a) borrowing huge amount of US dollars and converting the huge amount of US dollars into renminbi at the spot rate $s_t$ would substantially increase the appreciation pressure of renminbi in the spot market; and

(b) lending the huge amount of the converted renminbi at the Chinese interest rate ($i_t^{CH}$) would substantially increase China's monetary base, thus creating even greater increase in money supply through the money multiplier.

In other words, as long as there was a sufficient number of first-group participants speculating for the renminbi appreciation through the high leverage ratio in the forward or futures market, there would be a sufficient number of second-group participants to conduct covered interest arbitrages. Their arbitrage action would then transmit the

(*Continued*)

**Box 5.1.2:** *(Continued)*

huge renminbi appreciation pressure in the forward or futures market into huge renminbi appreciation pressure in the spot market and huge monetary growth pressure in China's money market.

As the renminbi was widely believed by the market to be undervalued by 15–40% and speculation in the forward or futures market could be done with a high leverage ratio, the amount of speculation by the first-group participants would be enormous. Thus, the appreciation pressure transmitted to the spot market and the monetary growth pressure transmitted to China's money market would be enormous and far much greater than that could be taken by any central bank, including the Chinese central bank. As a result, the Chinese central bank would be forced to allow the renminbi spot rate to rise beyond the recommended 1–2% appreciation target at that time, say by 3–5% or more.[2]

*F. The higher forward rate would keep pulling up the spot rate*

Nevertheless, this would only be the first step of the whole process. When the spot rate rose (say, by 3–5%), as the renminbi was widely believed by the market to be substantially undervalued, the speculation pressure in the forward or futures market would remain enormous (actually more enormous as early speculators were rewarded). As a result, the new forward rate $f_t$ had to be higher than the new spot rate $s_t$ to ensure an equilibrium in the forward or futures market. Through the covered interest arbitrage discussed above, the speculation pressure in the forward or futures market would once again be transmitted into appreciation pressure in the spot market. As a result, the every time higher forward rate would keep pulling the spot rate up. In fact, the spot rate would be pulled up in a very short

*(Continued)*

---

[2] Note that the higher appreciation would also induce more people speculating for the renminbi appreciation and more speculative inflows.

---

**Box 5.1.2:** (*Continued*)

time through the above "step-by-step" pulling. The process will go on until the spot rate rose to a relatively high and *no–longer–perceived–to–be–undervalued* level. Unfortunately, this *no–longer–perceived–to–be–undervalued* level would also mean the renminbi had already appreciated by 15–40%. Such substantial exchange rate appreciation would naturally mean a substantial decline in China's export, GDP and employment, which could trigger the political and social instability discussed in Chapter 2.[3]

In short, among the four markets discussed in the above chart, i.e., the US dollar money market ($i_t^{US}$), the domestic renminbi money market ($i_t^{CH}$), the spot currency market between the renminbi and the US dollar ($s_t$), and the currency forward or futures market between renminbi and the US dollar ($f_t$), the first three were already well-developed with high transaction volume. Once there was a *liquid enough* renminbi forward or futures market *in any part of the world*, there would be enormous speculators, firms and even normal Chinese citizens speculating for renminbi appreciation with the high leverage ratio permitted in the forward or futures. This would very soon ensure a financial and economic disaster through the above transmission mechanism.

---

[3] Even if the Chinese government used administrative measures to stop the Chinese and foreign banks from conducting the covered interest arbitrage, other foreign and Chinese enterprises could still use more primitive methods to do the arbitrage. For example, the related enterprise could issue debts or borrow syndicated loans at an interest rate slightly higher than the 4% US interbank rate. It could then convert US dollar into renminbi through the abuse of legal channels (e.g., abuse of the export channel, the foreign direct investment channel, or other legal remittance channel). Once there was such kind of activities, there would be rapid development in the related US dollar borrowing market and Chinese lending market until the US dollar borrowing rate $i_t^{US}$ and the Chinese lending rate $i_t^{CH}$ for the enterprise was not much different from the 4% and 2% discussed above. Even in this more primitive case, the amount of arbitrage done by these enterprises would be much greater than that could be taken by the Chinese central bank.

### 5.1.3 *The Central Bank's Decision to Freeze the Development of the Renminbi Futures Market*

Fortunately, with the help of the author's reputation among China's policy makers at that time, the Chinese central bank had finally decided to freeze the development of the renminbi forward market at that time. That is, Chinese firms had to produce documents of real transactions (e.g., export or import invoices) before they could buy and sell renminbi forward through forward contracts with banks in China. Meanwhile, banks in China would try to match the forward buying and selling between exporters and importers. Because of the need to provide supporting documents and unusually large forward transaction could easily catch the attention of the regulating authority, the frozen forward market had on one hand helped meet the hedging needs of exporters and importers, and on the other hand avoided the emergence of the potential disaster discussed in Section 5.1.2 and Box 5.1.2.

### 5.1.4 *Hong Kong's Intention to Establish the Renminbi Futures Market*

While the Chinese central bank had frozen the development of the renminbi forward market, the Chicago Mercantile Exchange in the US had thereafter established its renminbi futures market. Similar to the Non-delivery forward (NDF) services provided by foreign investment banks in overseas market, the transaction volume was relatively small. Moreover, part of the operation discussed in Box 5.2.1 (i.e., the covered interest arbitrage) was still classified as illegal in China. As a result, these offshore renminbi futures market were both thin and segmented from the renminbi spot market in China. Thus, even if the forward rate in these futures markets were very different from the spot rate in China, the very small transaction in these futures market had almost no impact (other than short-lived psychological effect caused by misleading media reports) on the renminbi spot market and money market in China.

Nevertheless, in 2006, the Hong Kong Stock Exchange announced a plan to launch the renminbi futures market in Hong Kong in a year thereafter. As Hong Kong is geographically and culturally much closer to China, it is possible that Hong Kong could develop a reasonably liquid renminbi futures market. In view of the potential damage of this, the author had written the more detailed discussions as shown in Box 5.1.2, and sent the article to the Hong Kong Stock Exchange, the Secretary of the Financial Services of the Hong Kong Government, the Peoples' Bank of China and the Chinese leaders through the Xinhua's News Agency. He also published the article in the newspapers in China and Hong Kong, and made visits to the Hong Kong Stock Exchange and the Peoples' Bank of China. In May 2007, he was personally informed by the then CEO of the Hong Kong Stock Exchange that the plan to establish the renminbi futures market in Hong Kong would be shelved.

## 5.2 Further Proposals to Increase China's Immunity and Resilience Against Financial Crisis

After the recommendation to freeze the development of the renminbi forward or futures market in China, the author published another set of following-up proposals in November–December 2005 on how to increase China's immunity and resilience against a financial crisis.

The article first highlighted the following point in Section 3.1: With China's current economic size and growth momentum, if there is no economic crisis in the next 1–2 decade(s), it will be just a matter of time that China will become a major economic power in the world. On the other hand, if there is an economic crisis such as that in Indonesia in 1997–1998, the severe recession and economic pains can seriously damage Chinese leaders' authority and credibility of ruling. If this triggers off further political and social instability (i.e., the country could be fragmented in an implicit or explicit sense), it is possible that China never comes back to stability and growth. Thus, pre-empting the emergence of financial or economic crisis is of utmost importance to China's macroeconomic management. It then made further proposals to increase China's immunity and resilience against financial crisis (see also the discussions in Chapter 3).

## 5.2.1 *Law to Increase Speculators' Non-Economic Risk*

The first proposal was on the use of law to increase international speculators' non-economic risk. From the author's observation on the behaviors
of speculators and their implementation agents or executives during the
Asian Financial Crisis in 1997–1998, he found that many of them did not
mind being immoral. However, they did mind being caught and imprisoned for conducting illegal activities. Thus, one effective way to pre-empt
international speculative attack on China's economy is to pass a law ille-
galizing very large dollar amount of foreign exchange speculation that
could threaten the economic and political stability of China. The passing
of such a law would substantially increase the non-economic risk of major
international speculators or hedge funds. Once these well-dressed and
probably immoral speculators know that they could be imprisoned for the
large scale speculation activities, their incentives to engage in it would
greatly diminish, i.e., if they were imprisoned for the excessively large
scale (and bad-intention) speculation, they would not be able to enjoy their
wealth accumulated in the past, they could even lose the "social status"
built up in the past.

Of course, to avoid such a law from disturbing the normal functioning
of the economy and punishing the wrong people, the dollar amount of
speculation defined as illegal bad-intention speculation (i.e., the illegal
threshold) should be very high. The coverage should be as narrow as possible (e.g., only for foreign exchange speculation of extremely large
amount). There should also be transparency and check-and-balance in the
prosecution process. For example, it has to be proposed by the Chinese central bank and approved by the premier before these people can be
prosecuted by the Chinese legal department. When these speculators or
their executives are prosecuted, they should be given sufficient right to
defend and appeal in the court. As long as the illegal threshold is set well
beyond normal investment behavior, it is unlikely that the law will affect
normal investment behavior and the normal functioning of the economy.
Of course, passing of the law itself could still have some negative effect on
market sentiment at that particular time. To contain or minimize the effect
of this, the Chinese government could (a) prepare in advance some policies
that would have positive effects to market sentiment; and (b) make such
policy announcement at the time the law is passed.

Once the law is passed, it will help discourage speculative attack in the future. Thereafter, as the law is already there before the speculation, it will be fair and reasonable to prosecute the misconducts of these international speculators, their executives and their implementing investment banks during speculative attacks in the distant future. That is, if in the future international speculators and their executing agents try to speculate heavily and excessively against China's foreign exchange market, it will be reasonable to prosecute them as the law is already there. If the bosses or senior executives of the speculative funds know the consequence of their speculating activity in advance (e.g., they might never be able to visit or pass by China for their whole life), their incentives to go into such speculative attack will greatly diminish. More importantly, the law can be an effective deterrent for senior executives assigned to, or recruited from, China for the implementation of the speculation: If they know that they can be caught into a long and exhausting court defense with the possibility of being imprisoned, they will no longer be eager to participate and execute such speculative activities. Instead, they will rather use their "talent or ability" to earn money elsewhere.

If there is nobody implementing the speculative attack for the owners or the CEOs of the speculative funds (or charges by the implementing agents are extremely high), they will not be able to get the speculation done even if they want to do this very much. On top of potential prosecution, the Chinese government can establish another useful deterrent by developing the practice of sending tax officers to the Chinese office of the hedge funds and the implementing investment banks to check the possibility of tax evasion of these Chinese offices.

The articles also recommended the following arrangements. When the law was set at the beginning, it might be better to set the "illegal threshold" at a very high level (e.g., many times more than the maximum normal transaction), but with a clause allowing the Chinese central bank to seek for the government's approval of reducing the threshold to lower level when deemed necessary. The advantages of such arrangement are as follows: The high threshold will help ensure that normal investment activities and normal running of the economy will not be affected. It will also help contain the effect on market sentiment at the time the law is passed. However, once there is a speculative attack, reducing the threshold can be sufficient to induce most speculators (and other market participants) to unwind their investment position, thus resulting in an immediate rebound in the renminbi exchange rate. While there is no big economic theory behind such an arrangement, the power of the policy in the emergency case is something not to be underestimated. In fact, it can be much more powerful than most intervention policies discussed in mainstream economics.

In terms of implementation, the author highlighted that it would be better not to use the law except at time of extremely heavy speculation. That is, even if there was moderately large selling pressure in the foreign exchange market, it would be better to let the market force help clearing some of the over-valuation of the exchange rate or asset price.

Finally, the articles highlighted that international speculators or hedge funds were not necessarily that omnipotent or "without weakness" as many market participants believed. The fear was mainly due to their failure to understand the hedge funds' strength and weakness. However, if one really spend time to study their characteristics and operation modes, (s)he will soon recognize that these international speculators and hedge funds do have a lot of weakness. In the next section, we will discuss other important characteristics and operation mode of hedge funds during a currency attack.

## 5.2.2 Development of the Renminbi Forward or Futures Market Should Be the Last Step of the Reform

### 5.2.2.1 Blocking the Crucial Channel through Which Speculators Could Launch Speculative Attacks on China

Another important characteristic observed by the author during the Asian Financial Crisis was that, before or even during the speculative attack, international speculators or hedge funds had no or very little holding of the attacked Asian currencies. One important part of the speculative attack was through substantial amount of sales of the Asian currencies in the forward or futures market. Without the forward or futures market, these hedge funds would not be able to launch the attack simply because they did not have the Asian currencies and did not have the credit limit to borrow that huge amount of the Asian currencies in the interbank market. However, with the existence of the forward or futures market, the hedge funds could do a lot of high-leverage selling in the forward or futures market, as domestic banks would use their credit limit in the interbank market to conduct covered interest arbitrage which would in turn transmit the high-leverage selling in the forward or futures market into (i) enormous selling pressure in the spot market until the related government gave up the defense; and (ii) substantial shrinkage in money supply and sharp surge in domestic interest rate (i.e., the mechanism is just the opposite of the case in Box 5.1.2). The result of the former would be a collapse of the spot exchange value of domestic currency, while the result of the latter would be a credit crunch, substantial plunges in asset prices and then a severe recession.

For the speculative attack on Hong Kong in 1997–1998 (see Appendix 5.1 for more details), in addition to the sales of Hong Kong dollar in the forward or futures market, the Hong Kong dollar sold in the spot market by international speculators was actually borrowed from a swap market before the attack. As a swap transaction is in fact a combination of a spot transaction plus a forward transaction, a pre-requisite of a liquid swap market is a liquid forward or futures market. Thus, one way to pre-empt international speculative attacks was to freeze the development of the renminbi forward and futures market and make the development as the last step of the whole reform. This would remove an important strategic tool or channel for international speculators to attack the Chinese economy. Without the renminbi forward or futures market, international speculators or hedge funds would not be able to borrow enough domestic currencies to launch any meaningful speculative attack on the exchange rate of renminbi.

Thus, even if China found it necessary to establish a renminbi forward market to allow exporters and importers to hedge their exchange rate risk, it should restrict the trading to only those with real exports and imports, e.g., only those exporting or importing firms with supporting export or import documents would be allowed to buy or sell the renminbi forward with banks in China up to the amount stated in the export and import documents. Meanwhile, the Chinese government should keep the regulation forbidding forward transaction based on capital account purposes.

In the article, the author also expressed his belief that in the medium-term future, it would be better to freeze the development of the renminbi forward market. One of the reasons was, as explained above, to avoid it from becoming a strategic tool and channel that international speculators could use to attack the Chinese economy. The second reason was that some people could use fake import and export documents to speculate for renminbi appreciation in the near and intermediate future, and speculation for the renminbi depreciation in the distant future (see Box 5.1.2 on how covered interest arbitrage would help transmitting the buying or selling pressure in the forward market to the spot market and domestic money market). Although the regulation to produce supporting export or import documents should be sufficient to contain speculative flows (through the abuse of the new legal channel) within a certain limit, it would still increase the Chinese central bank's costs and difficulties in monitoring her money supply and exchange rate. Moreover, further relaxation or expansion of the regulated forward market would require more government resources on the inspection of potential abuse, and allow the forward market to grow as a perfect place for corruption.

In addition, an expanded forward market with barrier of usage would increase the unfair treatment between those who would be allowed to trade in the forward market and those who would not be allowed to trade in the forward market: If the "allowed users" were able to abuse the permission to create a cycle or greater volatility of the spot rate, the normal Chinese citizens and those who were not allowed to trade in the forward market would have to bear the consequences and costs of the cycle or greater volatility of the spot rate. In the extreme case that the forward market had developed into such a size that international speculators could trigger off a currency or financial crisis in China, all normal and innocent Chinese citizens would have to bear the risk and consequences of the potential abuse by international speculators.

### 5.2.2.2 *Five Groups of People, not Just One Group*

Thus, in deciding the details, the scope and the tightness of the regulation on the renminbi forward market, the government should note that the analysis should include the interest of five groups of people, instead of the interest of only one group of people. That is, in addition to exporters' and importers' hedging need and the effect of the forward market on the total amount of international trade,[4] there would also be extra costs and benefits due to potential abuse of the forward market. In particular, the government should take into account of the extra risk and costs for those normal and innocent Chinese citizens who were not allowed to make forward trading. In addition, for those state and private enterprises with weak internal control, the owners or shareholders of these enterprises had to bear the risk and potential consequences of its senior executives using the expanded forward market to engage in risky and high-leverage speculation.

### 5.2.2.3 *Order of Development of the Derivatives Markets*

Finally, if China really wants to develop her finance industry, and to nuture enough professionals in the currency futures market, it is better to develop the forward or futures market between one foreign currency and another foreign currency (e.g., US dollar versus yen). As explained above, it was certainly not appropriate to expand the renminbi forward market in the near and intermediate future, simply because the risk and potential costs were too high.

On the orders of development of various markets of financial derivatives,[5] the articles noted that it would be better to first develop derivatives market on other domestic financial products instead of developing the renminbi forward or futures market.[6]

---

[4] An expanded forward market could also have some effects on the forward premium. However, the forward premium in the frozen forward market and hence its difference from that of the expanded market should be small, as the huge amount of international trade in China should be large enough to ensure sufficient competitions among banks.

[5] Note that from past experiences such as the global financial tsunami in 2008–2009, the costs (benefits) of having these financial derivatives could be much higher (lower) than what the market used to believe. Thus, if China ever intends to develop a certain derivative market, it is important to have rigorous debate on the potential costs and benefits of having such a derivative market in China.

[6] As highlighted in Section 5.1, developing the renminbi forward and futures market actually means working in the direction of a complete removal of capital control in China, which is equivalent to the removal of an important defence of China's exchange rate system reform and financial stability.

To see this, suppose a speculation in other domestic derivatives market has in the future caused a crisis in the related financial market (e.g., the stock market or a commodity market). As long as China has kept her capital control, most of the funds would still stay in China even if there is a crisis in one financial market. The existence of these funds in the economy would in turn ensure that China would sooner or later be able to recover from the light to moderate recession triggered by the crisis in that financial market.

While the author was more liberal on the development of other derivatives market in China, the articles also highlighted that there should be sufficient analysis and debate on (a) the costs and benefits of developing any particular derivatives market; (b) the details of the arrangement; and (c) the timing of having that particular establishment. With the substantial abuse, moral hazard activities and weak internal control within enterprises, liberalizing or establishing high-leverage derivatives market would not necessarily bring more benefits than costs. For example, the establishment of a domestic derivatives market could induce some senior executives of state or private enterprises to use the firm's money to make risky and high-leverage bet in the derivatives market. In some cases, the loss from these bets could be greater than the asset value of the firm, thus causing huge loss to the state or shareholders of the firm. Thus, before the establishment of proper internal control in state and private enterprises, the Chinese government should be more cautious in the development of other domestic derivatives markets, not to mention the more dangerous renminbi forward or futures market.

Finally, the articles highlighted that, without good detailed arrangements to stop the loopholes, the derivatives market could develop into something very different from the original aim. One such example was the stock option market in Hong Kong. In this highly speculative market, there were plenty of reports on how these issuers managed to abuse the mental or behavioral weakness of small investors (e.g., the in-born gambling inclination deep inside many Chinese) by using various types of tactics to squeeze money from these small and gambling-inclined investors. Thus, before the formal establishment of a certain derivatives market, the related regulating authority should spell out the detailed arrangements for further debate and external analysis. There should also be pilot experiment and formal external review before the formal launch of the derivatives market. Thereafter, there should also be regular external review on whether the derivatives market had developed into something very different from what was originally aimed.

Unfortunately, the related regulating authority on the stock option market in China had not gone through the proper procedure of sufficient debate and external review. As a result, the stock option market in China had become a highly speculative venue for people interested in gambling instead of hedging. Issuers of these stock options were also able to earn huge amount of money by exploiting the mental and behavior weakness of small investors. It is the author's hope that the Chinese (and Hong Kong) government could one day do a thorough study of this and other malfunctioned derivatives market.

## 5.3 Further Proposals on the Banking Reform

Further to the state's injection of capital into state-owned commercial banks and then the invitation of foreign banks' strategic investment in the state-owned commercial banks (see the author's proposal in Section 3.2.1), China had finally started its Initial Public Offerings (IPOs) of the state-owned commercial banks in Hong Kong from late 2005. While Chinese media and share investors were concentrating their attention on whether the IPOs was a cheap sales of state assets to foreign strategic partners and whether the IPOs would be a "feast or trap", the author wrote another two policy articles in December 2005, clarifying that the original and most important aim of the banking reform was to *introduce sufficient internal control in Chinese banks, and therefore help pre-empting economically and politically destructive financial crisis from happening in China in the future.*

To understand that, it would be necessary to explain the role and characteristic of the banking system in the whole banking system: As highlighted in Section 3.2.1, the banking system is related to flows of funds in the whole economy and the flows of funds are pretty similar to the flows of blood inside a human body. If there are events that stop the blood (funds) from flowing through the whole body (economy), the whole body (economy) will fail to function. Thus, it is of utmost importance to ensure the banking system can function properly so that funds can continue to flow through the various industries of the economic system. Furthermore, huge non-performing loans of banks and bank runs are in fact the triggering cause (and one of the underlying causes) of the Asian Financial Crisis. Thus, finding ways to clear the non-performing loans and to improve the internal control of new bank loans is a very important step to pre-empt financial crisis in the future.

### 5.3.1 *Non-Performing Loans in Chinese Banks Were Huge*

Nevertheless, as the non-performing loans in the state-owned commercial banks have kept on accumulating over the past few decades, even if we use the lowest non-performing ratio reported by the government, the total amount of non-performing loans will be trillions of renminbi. Worse still, the non-performing loans are inter-related with state-owned enterprise (SoE) problem and corruption, which makes it extremely difficult to solve.

To reduce the severity of the problem, the authors' policy articles in late 2004 has recommended China to use foreign banks' strategic participation to (a) strengthen the internal control of Chinese banks; and (b) change the banks' operation modes. When the author made the proposals, he did not believe that it could be sufficient to solve the non-performing loans problem in China's banking industry. The rationale was that foreign strategic partners would only be interested in investing in small and medium banks, i.e., to pay the cost of absorbing the non-performing loans in the small and medium banks in exchange for the right to do banking business in China. In fact, that was what the Hong Kong and Shanghai Banking Corporation (HSBC) trying to do when they bought the China Communication Bank.

### 5.3.2 *The Three-Step Injections Had Strengthened the Capital Adequacy Ratio of the Chinese Banks*

To the author's surprise, foreign strategic partners had turned out to be very interested in taking up the 20–25% shares offered by three of four state commercial banks.[7]

---

[7] Non-performing loans of the fourth state commercial bank, China Agricultural Bank, was so high at that time that the Chinese government postponed the invitation of strategic partner and IPOs to a much later year. In 2010, the China Agricultural Bank finally had their shares listed in the stock exchange in both Hong Kong and China.

Of course, the better than expected result could be attributed to the hard works of the related government bodies, and the related Chinese banks' "ability to hide" their problems. Nevertheless, the foreign strategic partners were not idiot (otherwise it would not make sense to invite them to help establish proper internal control in the Chinese banks). While recognizing that there could be another yet-to-be-known black hole of non-performing loans in the related Chinese banks, the foreign strategic partners insisted in (a) their purchasing price of shares could be adjusted down to reflect any extra discovery of non-performing loans in the related Chinese banks; and (b) a three-year repurchase guarantee which would allow the foreign strategic partners to sell the shares back to the related Chinese banks under certain pre-specified conditions. However, one of the most important factors that convinced the foreign strategic partners to take up the share offer was actually the planned IPOs of these state-owned commercial banks which would mean potentially huge investment profits and possibility of exit for the foreign strategic partners.

Thus, even though most of these strategic partners were concerned with the possibility of an unknown black hole of non-performing loans inside each state-owned commercial bank, all of the foreign strategic partners, the Chinese state-owned commercial banks, the underwriting investment banks and the brokerage houses that helped allocate the new shares to investors had been making rosy comments on the future profitability of these state-owned commercial banks. This had in turn created enormous individual share investor interest. Thus, it turned out that all these IPOs were substantially oversubscribed.

As a result, the three-step injections — first by the government, then by the foreign strategic partners and then through the IPOs — had substantially augmented the capital adequacy ratios of these state-owned commercial banks, thus making them able to deal with the non-performing loans accumulated in the past few decades.

### 5.3.3 *The Keys Would Still Be Proper Internal Control, Proper Lending Criteria and Proper Lending Behaviors*

While the three-step injections had substantially augmented the capitals of the related Chinese banks, it should be noted that they were still small when compared with the trillion yuans of non-performing loans. The key to the clearance of the non-performing loans would be the establishment of proper internal control, proper lending criteria and proper lending behaviors inside the Chinese banks. If these were properly done, the related Chinese banks could then use future profits to gradually write off the huge amount of non-performing loans accumulated in the past. Given the rapid GDP growth in China and the existence of substantial rooms for further development in the Chinese banking industry, the chance was good as long as the new loans were made properly. On the other hand, if the Chinese banks failed to establish proper internal control and proper lending behaviors in this round, the non-performing loans problem (and hence the potential damage of a subsequent crisis) would be even greater.

Thus, the core of the whole banking reform and the Chinese government's major operating target here were to use foreign banks' strategic participation to help establish proper internal control, proper lending criteria and proper lending behaviors in China's banking industry. In fact, this should be the first and most important criteria in assessing whether the banking reform in China would be successful or not. That is, while bringing in more efficient ways of operation, better services and new products from foreign strategic partners was also important, the core here should still be the establishment of proper internal control and proper lending behaviors in the Chinese banks.

### 5.3.4 *The Strategy of Inviting Foreign Strategic Participation Had Helped Avoid an Immediate Crisis*

The article also highlighted that China's strategy of inviting foreign strategic participation had in fact helped avoid a crisis in the years thereafter. Suppose China did not invite the foreign banks to invest their stakes in the Chinese banks. According to the financial service liberalization schedule that China had committed to during her entrance into the World Trade Organization (WTO) in 2001, foreign banks would be gradually allowed to open their branches in various cities in China, and most of the restrictions had to be lifted by the end of 2006. If foreign banks were not invited to invest in the major state-owned commercial banks, they would probably set up their own subsidiaries or branches in China through either greenfield investment or acquisition of some small- and medium-sized

Chinese banks. In case of greenfield investment, there would not be any non-performing loans from the beginning, and most of the products, services and operation routines would be copied from the parent companies with only the necessary modifications. Even in the case of acquisition, the foreign banks would still gradually write off the non-performing loans of the acquired subsidiaries and transformed it into one similar to the parent companies.

While such slow-way of expansion could take quite some time, the impacts of this type of expansion to the state-owned commercial banks could be disastrous: When compared with the foreign banks' greenfield branches or acquired subsidiaries, the high ratios of non-performing loans and poor services in the state-owned commercial banks could mean a sustained shift of deposits from the state-owned commercial banks to foreign banks in China. Since the ratios of non-performing loans in the state-owned commercial banks was already at the range of 20–40%, further loss of deposits could push them into a vicious cycle. That is, with a 20–40% non-performing loan ratio, the gradual reduction of performing loans (along with the shrinkage of deposit base) would mean that sooner or later the total net return from the shrinking performing loans would one day be lower than the interest expenses of total deposits and the normal operating expenses. Once the state-owned commercial banks reached that stage, it would be just a matter of time that there would be a bank run in one of the state-owned commercial banks. Such a bank run would in turn trigger concerns on the other state-owned commercial banks, and hence speed up the shift of deposits from these state-owned commercial banks to foreign banks.

Fortunately, China had wisely adopted the strategy of inviting foreign banks to engage in strategic investment in China's domestic banks, which had in turn diverted their effort and financial strength from

> *"hurting China's domestic banks through competition and hence deposit drain from domestic banks"*

to

> *"help improving the operation modes, lending behaviors and internal control of domestic banks"*.

**Box 5.3.4: Role of Inviting Foreign Strategic Participation Under Imperfect Settings: Another Illustration on the Harm of Dogmatic Market Belief**

In the main text, I have explained the great wisdom behind China's strategy of inviting foreign banks as strategic partners was to divert their effort from competing (and hurting) domestic banks to help improving domestic banks. In fact, the author has very often used this example to highlight to his students that a great wisdom of life is how to find ways to convert a potential competitor or enemy to a stakeholder.

It should also be noted that this strategy is not only unique to China's banking industry. In China's telecommunication industry, insurance industry and other industries where foreign firms' technology and management were better than domestic firms at that time, a simple opening up of China's domestic market to foreign firms according to the WTO agreement would simply mean that the foreign firms would eventually dominate China's domestic market. Thus, unlike the prediction of dogmatic market believers, a simple opening up of the domestic market under the imperfect settings would mean a total elimination of domestic firms in the industry, i.e., they would not be given any chance to improve and grow overtime. Thus, instead of allowing the foreign firms to replace the domestic firms, it would pay the host countries to explore other forms of foreign investor participation. From this angle, China's invitation for foreign strategic participation while at the same time requiring a minimum domestic ownership in these industries could be a better choice, and could be justified on theoretical grounds. In fact, after all these foreign strategic participations, and competitions among the joined-venture domestic firms, we have seen joined-venture domestic firms emerging strongly and continue growing in these industries. Sooner or later, we could see some of these joined-venture domestic firms making substantial investments overseas. While a formal modeling of this is beyond the scope of this book, it would be interesting to see such theoretical developments in the future.

## 5.3.5 *Not All the Products or Services in Foreign Banks Are Worth Importing*

The articles also highlighted that China should be selective in importing services or products from foreign banks, as some of them might not be beneficial to China. One such example was related to the credit card business. In the case in Hong Kong (and to a lesser extent in other places), the penalty interest charge for delayed card payment was at the "loan-shark" level of 36% per annum. On top of this, there were various types of "administrative charges" for the delayed card payment that made the banks' effective penalty yield from deferred card payment far much higher than the stated 36%. In fact, when the author was working as the head of the economic research department of a commercial bank in Hong Kong, the head of the credit card department personally told him what the bank most interested in was not customers who always paid the card payment on time, but customers who could only afford partial payment of the card bill, i.e., the "*card slaves*" who used most their monthly income to pay the penalty interest and penalty administrative charge until one day they could not even pay the penalty charges. By then, family members (e.g., parents or wife) of the card slaves would be aware of the card debt. In most cases, the family members would choose to use their savings (or other source of finance such as selling assets or re-mortgaging their flat) to clear the card debt for the card slaves as the penalty charges were really high. However, there were still cases that the card slaves had to declare bankruptcy or committ suicide.

While the banks would on average be able to profit a lot from the above social problems that they had created, the author was of the view that the government should not allow this to happen in the first place. The articles therefore suggested that the supervisory body in China should have proper regulation on imported financial services and products. For the case of credit card, the articles highlighted the penalty interest rate should not be higher than the base lending rate plus 6–8% risk premium, and there should also be restrictions on the administrative charges. Once the penalty interest rate is caped at the recommended level, the bank would adjust their criteria in card issuance and credit limit of each applicant. After all, credit card should be a mean to facilitate the system of payment instead of a mean for banks to profit from the "loan-shark" level of penalty interest rate by exploiting the weakness of human nature. This is particularly important for China, as the bankruptcy law in China is not as well-established as in Hong Kong. Unfortunately, as senior government officials were not aware of the potential damage of this apparently minor issue, Chinese banks were able to quietly establish the practice of having the "loan-shark" level of penalty interest rate of at least 0.05% per day (i.e., 19.7% per annum).[8] During the stock market bubble in 2007 (see Chapter 8 for more details), there were quite a lot of cases in which university students used the credit cards cash withdrawal facility to speculate in shares. During the crash, many of these students' parents had to clear the credit card debts for their children. To some extent, China was a bit fortunate because credit card issuance in China has not yet penetrated deep into the lower income earning groups. However, if China continues to neglect this problem, it will be just a matter of time that the card slave problem will emerge as a widespread social problem in China.

### 5.3.6 *Why Foreign Strategic Partners Have Strong Incentives to Help Establish Internal Control within the Banks*

In the first article (i.e., the previous sections), the author highlighted that China could make use of the foreign banks' strategic participation to help establish proper internal control and remove the non-performing loans in China's banking sector, thus pre-empt an important cause of a politically destructive financial crisis in the future. In this section (i.e., the second article), the author will explain why a simple IPO without the participation of strategic partner would not help establish proper internal control and monitor moral hazard activities in China's banking industry.

#### 5.3.6.1 *Individual Shareholders' Ownership Too Diffused to Play the Role*

According to the monetary theory on moral hazard, a sufficient share of ownership will provide the investor sufficient incentives to overcome the

---

[8] Worse still, there were various types of tricks that would increase the effective penalty interest rate. For example, for the case of partial repayment, the penalty interest charge was based on the original amount of credit instead of the remaining debt. On top of this, there were various types of administrative charge for those who could not repay the credit within the first month.

reasonably large cost of establishing internal control and monitoring moral hazard activities inside the invested (Chinese) bank, as failure to do so could result in substantial losses to them. On the other hand, as each individual shareholder's share of ownership is too dilute and hence relatively too small when compared with the above "monitoring costs", individual shareholders will not have sufficient incentives to initiate the establishment of proper internal control and monitor hazard activities inside the (Chinese) banks. Thus, to achieve the goal, it is important to invite foreign banks to make a sizable investment (e.g., 10–25%) in the Chinese banks.

The foreign strategic partners' relatively large amount of share holdings also explained why, during the bargaining stage of the strategic investment, strategic partners were particularly eager to have their officers being posted to the Board of Director and some other departments in the invested Chinese banks. In some cases, they even offered such posting or provision of expertise free of charge (i.e., at their own expense). Based on the "no free lunch" argument, behind the free of charge offer was the need to have their own people looking after their interest, including monitoring of moral hazard activities, building up of proper internal control and upgrading of the efficiencies, products and services of the invested Chinese banks.

Based on the above observation, the article therefore recommended the Chinese government to make use of foreign strategic partner to help the establishment of proper internal control in the Chinese banking industry. In particular, the Chinese government should (a) try to support foreign strategic partners' proposed measures on strengthening the internal control of Chinese banks; and (b) take supportive attitude to foreign strategic partners' complaint(s) of specific moral hazard activities inside the Chinese banks.

### 5.3.6.2 *Employment of a Clean Management Team*

On the employment of the CEO and senior executives, the article first highlighted the fact that "*culture could influence behaviors; and behaviors over a sustained period could also influence the culture*".

Before the economic reform in 1978, China's culture was one of the cleanest in the world. Although the economic reform had transformed the Chinese economy to a far more productive one, the low salary of Chinese officials and senior executives of banks, and the lack of check and balance to the power of the department chief had also nurtured a severe and sophisticated culture of corruption. With the already established corruption culture, even if we gave an annual salary of 10–20 million renminbi to the CEO of a bank, his inclination to corruption would still be strong, because his behaviors would be very much influenced by the culture surrounding him. For example, a representative senior executive in China at that time might have to pay for the overseas education expenses of his children, support some close relatives' purchase of property, luxurious living expenses and even "corruption investment" in careers. Those who took up the bad habits might even have to pay for huge gambling losses and substantial expenses on the mistresses and the mistresses' close relatives. With these huge expenses, the established corruption culture and the lack of check and balance to the power of the CEO of the bank, even if China paid the bank CEO with an annual salary of 10–20 million renminbi, the chance that he would get rid of his corruption habit would still be slim.

On the other hand, if China used the same salary to employ a CEO from Singapore, Hong Kong or other economies with a relatively clean banking culture, the corruption inclination of the executive would be small.[9] This was so because the culture in his original country or economy had told them that the salary was in fact more than sufficient for a comfortable living. There was no point taking the risk that could eventually put them into jail. Such decision would then influence their spending habit and economic behavior, which would further reduce their inclination to take up bribe. Thus, the article also recommended the Chinese government to consider recruiting banks CEOs from economies with a clean banking culture.[10]

---

[9] Even for those who did take up some bribe, it would at most be occasional, i.e., not pervasive.

[10] The proposal did result in the experiment of the recruitment of a foreign CEO (albeit not from Hong Kong or Singapore as preferred by the author) in a medium sized bank in Shenzhen. On the other hand, senior officers with knowledge on the banking industry, such as former deputy governors of the central bank, were posted as the Chairman of the major state-owned commercial banks. Meanwhile, in all the state-owned commercial banks, the positions of the Chairman and the CEO were held by two different persons. It would be interesting to see whether these arrangements would help clean the corruption culture in China's banking industry.

### 5.3.7 Starting the Anti-Corruption from the Banking Industry

Finally, the article suggested that China could start cleaning the country-wide corruption culture from the banking industry. As the Chinese top leaders were aware that corruption could eventually lead to the collapse of the Communist Party and the Communist Government, they did put in a lot of efforts in investigating corruption cases. Nevertheless, if China continued the current way of anti-corruption, it would be almost certain to be a failure. The widespread corruption behavior was of course one of the main reasons for this, the lack of a well-thought and effective design of anti-corruption strategy was also a major reason for China's failure to curb corruption.

Thus, the article recommended the following strategy: make use of the banking reform and choose the banking industry as the first place to clean the corruption culture sectors by sectors. That is, the Chinese government should first use most of her efforts and resources to eliminate the corruption culture in the banking industry. In particular, she should use the proposals in the previous sections to gradually establish a clean banking culture that hate corruption. Once this is done, consolidation effort should be made to ensure that the fruit of clean culture has its root in the industry. Thereafter, the Chinese government could extend the same effort to a closely related industry (e.g., insurance), i.e., clean the corruption culture and consolidate the result until the culture in the industry dislike corruption. Thereafter, the Chinese government could extend the same effort to another related industry (e.g., stock market or the auditing industry), then other financial industries, and then other non-financial industries.

Why choose the banking sector as the first place for the strategy of cleaning corruption culture? As explained in the previous discussions, if China could not clean the non-performing loans in this banking reform, chance that it could be cleaned in the future would be rather slim. This would in turn imply a high chance of a politically destructive financial crisis sometime in the future. Thus, the Chinese government had no choice but to work hard to resolve the problem in the banking industry. Once China manage to clean the banking industry, it would be easier to extend the strategy to another industry. Even if China failed to extend it to another industry, China would still have a clean banking industry, which would be crucial to the stable development of the Chinese economy.

In the wordings of Chinese military strategy on the issue of cleaning non-performing loans, the Chinese government was already in the "*no-retreat but must-fight-to-survive position*" (绝地一战). Because of such a must-fight-to-survive position, the Chinese government would have the determination to implement the necessary measures to clean the banking industry. With sufficient determination, the chance of getting an eventually clean banking industry would be high.

The article also recommended the Chinese government to

   (i)   set up various types of reporting channels;
  (ii)   make more soft advertisements and hard propaganda; and
 (iii)   provide incentives

to encourage Chinese citizens to report suspected corruption cases in the banking industry until the gradual establishment of an anti-corruption culture in the banking industry. Actually, the establishment of an anti-corruption culture in a particular area is not as impossible as most people believe. One good existing example is the public high-level (i.e., university entrance) examination in China.[11] Thus, persistent effort and advertisements on the banking industry can gradually establish an anti-corruption culture here. Once an anti-corruption culture is firmly established in the banking industry, corrupted government officials will find that the risk and potential penalty of taking bribe in the banking industry will be much higher than those in other industries. Thus, whenever possible, they will prefer taking bribe elsewhere and avoid receiving bribe in the banking industry. This will in turn imply a substantial decline in corruption activities in the banking industry to manageable level.

Such a proposed strategy is actually borrowed from the Chinese military strategy of "*intentionally open an escaping exit to the surrounded enemy*" (围兵必阙). That is, it is less costly to take over the place and drastically weaken the surrounded enemy by intentionally leaving an escaping exit with hidden army near the exit. This is so because the aim of the escaping soldiers

---

[11] As this is related to the well being of the next generation of each Chinese citizens, the anti-corruption culture here in China is very strong. Of course, rich people could still send their children to overseas universities or profit-making universities in China. The public examination in China is still clean.

is to escape. Their weak intention to fight back means that one can use the hidden army to eliminate a certain portion of the enemy while leaving the remaining portion to escape. After that, it will be quite difficult for the escaped portion to regroup into a powerful fight team.

In other words, while surrounding the place (the banking industry), leaving an exit for part of the corrupted officials to escape to other places will reduce the resources and costs of eliminating corruption in the banking industry. It will also substantially reduce the resistance of corrupted officials whose connections should not be underestimated if they are ever forced to group together. Once the corruption culture is cleaned and an anti-corruption culture is firmly established in the banking industry, the government will only need to keep a small amount of army (resources) to maintain the anti-corruption culture there. The success in the banking industry will also mean that the government can recruit more army (resources) in its anti-corruption campaign. Thus, the government can use the remaining portion of old army (resources) plus the newly recruited army (resources) to repeat the same cleaning-and-consolidating procedure in another industry. Through such industry-by-industry strategy of concentrated effort of cleaning, consolidating, and then another concentrated effort of cleaning, the population of corrupted officials will keep falling over time until one day the Chinese economy is much less corrupted.

## Appendix 5.1 The Speculative Attack on Hong Kong's Financial Markets in 1997–1998

Hong Kong's financial market was under severe speculative attack in October 1997. Because of the Currency Board System in Hong Kong, tactics used by speculators were far more complex than those in other crisis-affected economies. Speculative selling of the Hong Kong dollar in the spot market was only moderate and psychological. The main speculative activities were the selling of the Hong Kong dollar in the forward market, the selling of stock futures and the short selling of shares. The strategy of the speculators was to bid up Hong Kong's interbank rate and subsequently benefit from the huge short positions they had built up in the stock futures market prior to the formal launch of their attack. The whole strategy would involve the following three steps (see also Chart 5.1):

**Chart 5.1:**   Speculators' Strategy used in HK in 1997–1998

## (A)  The Foreign Exchange Market

| Preparation | | Formal Attack | | Profit Taking |
|---|---|---|---|---|

| Preparation | Formal Attack | Profit Taking |
|---|---|---|
| • Borrow huge amount of Hong Kong dollars at normal interest rates through the swap market<br><br>• Sell huge amounts of forward Hong Kong dollars (extremely high gearing, no deposit required, credit limit is the only constraint) | • Sell part of the Hong Kong dollars in the relatively thin offshore spot market (to maximize the impact of the attack on market sentiment)<br><br>• Continue to sell huge amounts forward Hong Kong dollar Aims: create sentiment that Hong Kong dollar is under attack, attract other speculators and hedgers to follow, bid up the interbank rates. | • Close the short position in forward Hong Kong dollar (reasonable profit because of high gearing)<br><br>• Lend out any remaining Hong Kong dollars borrowed from the swap market |

Between Preparation and Formal Attack: *Take advantage of poor external news from Southeast Asia*

Between Formal Attack and Profit Taking: *Forward Hong Kong dollar was pushed down and interbank rates were pushed up (the latter allows speculators to trigger off a collapse in the Hang Seng index)*

## (B)  The Share Market

| Preparation | Formal Attack | Profit Taking |
|---|---|---|
| • Borrow Hang Seng Index component shares from custodians and trustees (for short selling)<br><br>• Sell huge amounts of Hang Seng futures (high gearing) | • Short sell those shares borrowed from the custodians and trustees<br><br>• Continue to sell huge amounts of Hang Seng futures<br><br>• Announce poor forecasts on share prices or spread rumours concerning stability of banks | • Buy back short sell shares at a much cheaper price, and return them to the custodians and trustees<br><br>• Close all short positions in Hang Seng futures |

Between Preparation and Formal Attack: *Take advantage of poor external news, sharp rise in Hong Kong interbank rates due to speculative attacks in the currency market*

Between Formal Attack and Profit Taking: *Manage to create panic selling: Hang Seng Index falls by a few thousand points*

## Step 1: Preparation

The speculators first borrowed, or pre-funded themselves with, substantial amount of medium-term (e.g., 6–12 months) Hong Kong dollar through the swap market (see Box 5.A1 for details). Some speculators also bought Hong Kong dollar (and sold US dollar) forward in the forward market. In

---

**Box 5.A1:  Relationship between The Swap Market and the Spot and Forward (Futures) Foreign Exchange Market**

A swap market is a market in which a participant can borrow domestic currency (or foreign currency) through a swap market operation. A swap market operation is in fact a spot market operation plus a corresponding forward market operation. For example, if somebody swap US dollar for Hong Kong dollar for six months, this would mean

(a)  a spot selling of US dollar (and buying of Hong Kong dollar); plus
(b)  a six-month forward buying of US dollar (and selling of Hong Kong dollar).

After six months from now, the forward market operation will offset the spot market operation, leaving the person neutral in his currency position. However, during the six months from now, the person has in fact borrowed Hong Kong dollar (and lent US dollar). As the forward exchange rate can be different from the spot exchange rate, there is an implicit interest differential in the operation. In Hong Kong, the swap market is rather developed with high turnover. Thus, in the preparation stage, speculators can borrow sufficient amount of Hong Kong dollar from the swap market with only moderate rise in the HK-US interest differential.[12] In Box 5.A3, we will explain how arbitrage activities between the swap market and interbank market allow speculators using forward operations to bid up the interbank rate.

---

[12] Here, the lower profile the borrowing, the lower the implicit interest differential and hence the pre-funding costs for the speculators.

the stock futures market, the speculators started to build up large short positions. To equip themselves with the ability to create panic selling in the stock market during the formal attack, the speculators also utilized a "loophole" in the stock custodian sector to borrow substantial amount of shares from the custodians (see Box 5.A2 for details).

---

### Box 5.A2:   Loophole in the Stock Custodian Sector in Hong Kong During the Crisis Period

During and before the crisis, customers' holdings of Hong Kong shares were normally not deposited in the central depository. Instead, many of these shares were deposited in the brokerage firms with custodian service. When these customers opened their account with the brokerage firms, they signed a contract that effectively allowed the custodians to lend their shares out to anybody (including the speculators).[13] Because of this loophole, speculators could short sell huge amount of Hong Kong shares and hence added downward pressure on the stock market. Meanwhile, these custodians were willing to lend their customers' shares to the speculators for a lucrative interest payment. Thus, it was extremely unfair to the share depositors who did not receive any interest on one hand and took the pain of a plunge in asset value of their shares on the other hand. Besides, they had to bear the risk, without being informed, of a possible bankruptcy of the custodians. In response to the bankruptcy of some brokerage firms during the crisis, the Hong Kong government had implemented central depository for shares in the cash account of brokerage firms.[14]

---

[13] As the contracts were written in tiny words with lengthy terms and conditions, many customers did not bother to read these contracts, not to mention the likelihood of a reasonable awareness of the risk, implications and interest foregone.

[14] Under the new system, brokerage firms can still lend out their customers' shares in the margin account.

## Step 2: Formal Attack

After the above preparation, the speculators sold their pre-funded Hong Kong dollar (and bought US dollar) in the spot market. To maximize the impact of their attack, they sold the Hong Kong dollar in the relatively thin offshore markets. When the HKMA attempted to support the Hong Kong dollar by purchasing the Hong Kong dollar in the spot market, the interbank liquidity was squeezed. This in turn caused a surge in the interbank rate. In addition to the selling in the spot market, the speculators also sold large amount of Hong Kong dollar (and bought US dollar) in the forward market. As banks in Hong Kong usually did arbitrage between the swap market and the interbank market (see Box 5.A3), the forward selling of Hong Kong dollar would also bid up Hong Kong's interbank rate.[15]

---

**Box 5.A3:  Arbitrage between the Swap Market and the Interbank Market**

It should first be noted that speculators did not have direct access to the interbank market.[16] However, many participant banks in the interbank market usually did arbitrage between the interbank market and the swap market. For example, if the implicit interest rate for Hong Kong dollar in the swap market was higher than that of the interbank market, the participant bank would borrow Hong Kong dollars from

*(Continued)*

---

[15] Consider the following covered interest parity $i_{HK} - i_{US} = (f\text{-}s)/s$, where $i_{HK}$ and $i_{US}$ are the interbank rates in Hong Kong and the US, respectively; $s$ and $f$ are the spot and forward (say, 12 months) Hong Kong dollar rate per US dollar, respectively. As the US interest rate ($i_{US}$) and the spot exchange rate ($s$) can be take as given due to the small size of the Hong Kong economy and the fixed exchange rate system, speculators can bid up $f$ (by substantial forward selling of Hong Kong dollar), and hence the swap rate, $(f\text{-}s)/s$. With the arbitrage activities between the swap market and the interbank market, the rise in the swap rate will cause a rise in the Hong Kong interbank rate ($i_{HK}$).

[16] Even if speculators attempted to get access to the interbank market through the investment banks that implemented their speculation, the amount they can borrow would be constrained by the investment banks' accessible credit limit in the interbank market.

**Box 5.A3:** (*Continued*)

the interbank market[17] and then lend these Hong Kong dollars at a higher interest rate in the swap market (i.e., they can earn the difference in the Hong Kong dollar interest rate between the two markets). Because of the existence of such risk-free arbitrage activities by commercial banks in Hong Kong, speculators were able to influence the interbank market through operations in the forward or swap market. For example, if they want to pre-fund themselves with Hong Kong dollar (in the preparation stage), they can swap US dollars for Hong Kong dollars for 6–12 months in a low profile. Similarly, in the stage of formal attack, if they want to bid up Hong Kong's interbank rate, they can sell Hong Kong dollar forward in a large amount with a high profile, which will in turn affect the swap rate and hence the interbank rate.

This would create a sentiment that the Hong Kong dollar was under attack, thus attracting more speculators (and even normal citizens) to follow.

Concurrently, the speculators attacked the stock market by (i) selling their shares originally borrowed from the custodians, and (ii) accelerating their selling in the stock futures market with a high profile (see Box 5.A4 for its effect on the spot index). These actions had created panic selling of shares. In fact, these strategies turned out to be very successful and there was substantial fall in HK's stock index during the attack.

## Step 3: Profit Taking

Having bid up the interbank rate and pushed down the spot and futures stock indices, the speculators took their profits by closing the short

---

[17] The main lenders of Hong Kong dollar in the interbank market are the large commercial banks such as HSBC, Standard Chartered Bank and Bank of China (Hong Kong).

> ### Box 5.A4:  Relationship Between the Stock Futures and Spot Market
>
> In Hong Kong, the stock futures market was developed with high turnover and high gearing (i.e., the deposit before the crisis was HK$75,000 per contract, which would mean a gearing of 11 times when the Hang Seng index was at 16500). Besides, stock futures contracts can be as short as the number of days between the trading day and the end of the corresponding month. Although risk consideration implies still differences between the futures index and the spot index, a large enough gap between the two indices will induce participants to buy the shares in one market and sell the shares in the other market. As a result, movements in the futures index can often influence the spot index and vice versa. During the crisis period, speculators' huge selling of futures index caused plunges in the spot index.

positions in the stock futures market. They also bought back the shares (at much lower prices) and returned them to the custodian. In the foreign exchange market, they closed their short position in forward Hong Kong dollar (and made profit from the lower forward rate), and lent out any surplus Hong Kong dollar (at a shorter maturity) borrowed from the swap market before the formal speculative attack.

## Appendix 5.2   Impacts of the Speculative Attack, the Proposed Solutions and the HKMA's Stock Market Intervention

### A5.2.1 *The Immediate Impacts of the Speculative Attack*

By taking advantage of the vulnerable sentiment associated with the contagion effect of the Asian Financial Crisis, speculators were able to bid up the forward premium of the Hong Kong dollar by a substantial amount, and through arbitrage, this was translated into a substantial rise in interbank interest rates. The situation was further aggravated by the HKMA's announcement that those banks needed to borrow Hong Kong dollars from the HKMA for clearing might be charged with an extremely high penalty interest rate.[18] As a result, the overnight interbank rate shot up to the unprecedented level of 280% on 23 October 1997. The three month interbank rate also shot up to 37%, and had been staying at high levels between 8.5% and 16% (on average 10.5%) until the next attack in January 1998. The sharp rise in interest rates allowed the speculators to amplify the impact of their short selling of shares and speculative selling of stock futures on the stock index. As a result, the Hang Seng Index fell 30% in just one week from 12,412 on 22 October 1997 to 8,776 on 28 October 1997.

While the speculative attack on the forward currency market was the prime mover of the turmoil, most of the profits came from the speculative selling in the stock futures market. For example, a fall of the Hang Seng Index by 1,000 points would mean a profit of half-a-billion Hong Kong dollars for every 10,000 contracts. If speculators altogether sold 50,000 contracts and gained 4,000 points in the future index, the profit would be 10 billion Hong Kong dollars ($\approx$ 1.29 billion US dollars). The second source of profit was generated from short selling of shares, with the selling of forward Hong Kong dollars being a distant third. It was believed that the speculative selling of Hong Kong dollars in the spot market only played the role of affecting market sentiment. The activity itself was unlikely to generate any visible profit or loss to the speculators.

By repeating the above strategy in January, April, June and August 1998, speculators were able to drive down the Hang Seng Index by 61% from the peak of 16,820 to the trough of 6,544 on 13 August 1998. While speculators profit was unlikely to exceed 30 billion Hong Kong dollars, the

---

[18] The aim of the announcement was to cut bank's support to speculators by penalizing those banks who were short of Hong Kong dollars because they had lent the Hong Kong dollars to speculators, whether intentionally or unintentionally. However, the announcement was too heavy and the whole banking sector went into a panic. On top of this, some market participants also believed that the HKMA has orchestrated an additional squeeze of interbank liquidity on the morning of 23 October 1997, thus leading to the excessive rise in interest rates.

disaster it created on the Hong Kong economy far exceeded the profit it had earned. For example, market capitalization of the Hong Kong stock market fell by 1,711 billion Hong Kong dollars between September 1997 and August 1998.[19] Coupled with an over-ambitious housing supply scheme, the high interest rates and the liquidity crunch generated by the speculative activities caused a slide in the property prices. In fact, one commercial bank in Hong Kong estimated that the loss of wealth during the crisis amounted to 5,000 billion Hong Kong dollars ($\approx$ 645 billion US dollars).

While part of the loss of wealth was eventually recovered, the losses in terms of output and social frustration were not. By triggering episodes of high interest rate, coupled with a liquidity crunch and a plunge in wealth as well as weak external demand (particularly from Southeast Asia), the speculative activities had caused a recession and surge in unemployment in Hong Kong. Real GDP product started to register consecutive negative year-on-year growth from the first quarter of 1998 and reached $-6.7\%$ in the third quarter of 1998. In 1998, the volume of the retail sales fell by 17% compared with a year ago. The unemployment rate and under-employment rate surged to 6.2% and 2.9%, respectively in 1999. Worse still, some of the retrenched employees, particularly those aged above 40, had permanently quit the labour force because of difficulty in finding another job. All these had led to enormous social frustration, which in some cases caused suicides committed by the unemployed as well as those experienced who lost in the stock and property markets. Therefore, while the pre-crisis asset bubble was no doubt an important loophole that attracted the speculative attack, the role of speculators in triggering a hard landing of the economy in the most catastrophic way should also be criticized.

### A5.2.2 *Source of the Problem: Interest Rate Hike and Absence of Covered Interest Arbitrage*

In view of the surge in interest rate, the plunge in asset prices and hence the harm done to the HK economy, Chen and Chan (1999),

---

[19] The stock market capitalization in September 1997 and August 1998 were 4,384 billion Hong Kong dollars and 2,673 billion Hong Kong dollars, respectively.

Tsang (1999),[20] Miller (1998) and Yip (1999)[21] had each made their own proposals in 1997–1998 to bring down domestic interest rate and hence the economic pain (see Appendix 5–3 for a brief summary of the proposals). Of particular interest are the proposals by Tsang (1999) and Yip (1999). Tsang first argued that because of institutional imperfection, cash arbitrage (between the market exchange rate and the official linked rate) was never operative in Hong Kong's linked exchange rate system. He proposed to modernize Hong Kong's Currency Board by adopting the "convertible reserves mechanism" of Argentina, Estonia and Lithuania (the AEL model), under which arbitrage could be done electronically without moving cash around. In the design, each bank will have an account with the central bank, in which deposit reserves as well as other balances are kept. The central bank guarantees the full convertibility of these bank balances at the official exchange rate. Tsang believed this would correct the institutional imperfection and make cash arbitrage operative. He also mentioned the possibility of interest arbitrage under this system. However, Tsang did not explicitly elaborate the mechanism to remove the exchange-rate risk of interest arbitrage, which was the main reason that stopped the Hong Kong interest rate from falling to the US level during the crisis. Yip (1999) on the hand provided a detailed discussion of this. First, he noted that if the market believed that the peg would continue, any speculative attack that bid up domestic interest rate would induce covered interest arbitrage activities until domestic interest fall back to the US level. Nevertheless, the speculative attack and the economic crisis had induced potential arbitragers to worry about a possibility of a collapse of the peg. Such expected chance of devaluation had in turn implied a substantial exchange rate risk[22] in conducting covered interest arbitrage. As a result, there were no such arbitrage activities

---

[20] The proposals included in Chen and Chan (1999) and Tsang (1999) were first made in late 1997.

[21] The proposal was first made as an internal report in the Bank of China (Hong Kong-Macau Regional Office) in late 1997, and was released in a local newspaper (Hong Kong Economic Journal) on 24 February 1998. It was subsequently included in Yip (1999).

[22] In addition to the rise in exchange rate risk, there was also a surge in expected depreciation. For example, if the market expected an 80% chance of no devaluation and 20% chance of a 30% devaluation in the coming year, the expected depreciation would be 6%.

despite an enormous gap between the domestic and US interest rate. Thus, on top of Tsang's suggested set-up, Yip proposed to use the electronic Certificate of Indebtedness as a guarantee to remove the exchange-rate risk of covered interest arbitrage (see Proposal D of Appendix 5.3 for more details). With the guarantee, banks would be interested in earning the interest differential by borrowing US dollar (from aboard) at the low US interest rate and lending Hong Kong dollar at the high Hong Kong interest rate. Thus, with the guarantee, covered interest arbitrage would continue until the Hong Kong interest rate falls back to the US level.

### A5.2.3 *The HKMA's Stock Market Intervention and the Subsequent Currency Board Reform*

In the speculative attack during August 1998, the HKMA had opted for stock market interventions. Nevertheless, with the weak market sentiment, traditional funds dumped about HK$100 billion Hong Kong shares during the first week after the announced intervention, and the HKMA had no choice but to purchase all these shares. To avoid the development in the stock market from deteriorating into a deeper crisis, the HKMA eventually modified the researchers' proposals and came up with its "own" reform package (or modern Currency Board Systems) on 5 September 1998, highlighted under the Seven Technical Measures. Of the seven measures, the most important measures were: (1) an exchange rate guarantee (convertibility undertaking) for the banks' net balance in the account with the HKMA, and (2) a modification of previous practice to a discount window which allows banks substantial freedom to use their holdings of Exchange Fund debts (and selected semi-government debt papers) as a collateral for over-night liquidity borrowing from the HKMA (see Yam, 1998).

Measure 1 removed the exchange-rate risk of banks' interest arbitrage and hence brought the Hong Kong interest rate down towards the US level. Measure 2 aimed at allowing an increase in interbank liquidity in case of speculative attack, so that the impacts of the attack on the interbank rate could be mitigated. Before this reform, Hong Kong banks' clearing balance and interbank liquidity were relatively small.[23] Thus, allowing the interbank liquidity to expand when deemed necessary may stop the speculators from squeezing the interbank liquidity (and hence interbank rate) with a relatively small amount of spot selling of the HK dollar. To justify this arrangement, the HKMA re-defined its monetary base to cover the currency issued, the banks' net clearing balance with the HKMA and the debts issued by the Exchange Fund. The HKMA justified their definition of monetary base by arguing that all the three components were fully backed up by their holdings of foreign reserve.[24]

After the introduction of the Seven Technical Measures, the interest rate in Hong Kong began to fall gradually towards the US level in the fourth quarter of 1998. By mid-October 1998, the three-month interbank rate was only 6%, as compared to 11.8% on 14 September 1998. With further cuts in the US interest rate and a continued reduction in the interest-rate differential, the Hong Kong three-month interbank rate fell further to 5.63% on 28 December 1998, which was only 0.4 percentage point higher than the US rate.

### A5.2.4  *Which Measure Had Saved Hong Kong from the Speculative Attack: The Stock Market Intervention or the Revitalization of Covered Interest Arbitrage?*

As a concluding remark, it should be clarified that many prominent economists outside Hong Kong, such as Alan Greenspan, were not fully aware of the above details of the speculative attack. As a result, they had mis-identified that it was the HKMA's stock market intervention that had saved Hong Kong from the speculative attack. As a matter of fact, after

---

[23] As a result, it took only US$1-2 billion spot selling of the Hong Kong dollar in the foreign exchange market to create a substantial shortage of interbank liquidity on 23 October 1997.
[24] No doubt, such definition and arrangement did help discourage speculative attacks. It is, however, interesting to note that Hong Kong is probably the only economy in the world that includes long-term bonds as a component of the monetary base.

the HKMA declared the stock market intervention at end August 1998, there was enormous selling pressure in the Hong Kong stock market between 31 August 1998 and 4 September 1998, and the HKMA had no choice but to buy up more than HK$100 billion of Hong Kong shares. In view of the risk of further selling pressure that could go beyond the HKMA's buying capacity, the HKMA had finally modified Proposal D in Appendix 5.3 and came up with the "convertibility undertaking" measure in its Seven Technical Measures announced on 5 September 1998 (Saturday). That is, instead of granting the electronic CIs that would guarantee covered interest arbitragers would not lose even if the linked exchange rate system collapsed (i.e., could get back the same amount of US dollars at the linked rate), the HKMA just simplified the proposal into just an announced guarantee.

Thus, from the next working day after the announcement (i.e., 7 September 1998), covered interest arbitrage was revitalized which in turn brought the Hong Kong interest rates down towards the US level. Meanwhile, the decline in the Hong Kong interest rate had caused a strong rebound of the stock market. Thus, it was in fact the convertibility under-taking and revitalization of covered interest arbitrage that had saved Hong Kong from the speculative attack. Without the revitalization of cov-ered interest arbitrage and hence the fall of Hong Kong's interest rate towards the US level, it was not clear that the stock market intervention could end up as a success. Without the revitalization of covered interest arbitrage, it would also be questionable that the stock market intervention could stop speculators from using the same strategy of bidding up Hong Kong interest rate and making another speculation at a later date. Seeing from this perspective, the stock market intervention could at best be an assisting measure that stopped the speculative attack.[25]

---

[25] Another assisting factor was that hedge funds had at that time suffered from a heavy loss in their bet in the Russian market. Another important development at that time was Malaysia's adoption of Paul Krugman's proposal of capital control on 1 September 1998. However, unlike the Russian event, it was not clear whether the capital control in Malaysia had to some extent hurt the speculators and hence contributed to the stabilization in the Hong Kong market.

**Box 5.A5:    Further Information and Personal Views on the Speculative Attack**

As the author was involved in the defense against the speculative attack and there were a lot of events and developments not known to the public. To enable historians to group pieces of information for a better picture for the whole event, the author would like to list down what he knows and what he thinks on this episode:

- Proposal D in Appendix 5.3 was sent to the Central Policy Unit of the Hong Kong Government in late 1997, and the Head of the Unit, Mr. Gordon Siu, had responsibly replied that he had forwarded the proposal to the then CEO of Hong Kong and the HKMA;

- Seeing no further action from the HKMA and the Hong Kong Government, the author published the proposal in the *Hong Kong Economic Journal*, a major financial newspaper in Hong Kong, on 24 February 1998. Meanwhile, the author was told that his boss at that time, the Deputy Head of the Hong Kong – Macau Regional Office of the Bank of China (Hong Kong), had submitted and discussed the proposal with Mr. Joseph Yam, the then CEO of the HKMA;

- Seeing no further action from the HKMA, the author had submitted the proposal as well as a detailed report on the speculative attack and the Hong Kong economy to the Chinese government through a Chinese official in Hong Kong, who was also the author's senior classmates at the London School of Economics;

- During the HKMA stock market intervention, the author was told by his colleagues in the Hong Kong – Macau Regional office that the PBoC had sent two of its senior officials to Shenzhen to help monitor the development;

- A few days before 5 September 1998, the author was requested by his boss in the Hong Kong – Macau Regional office to write a proposal on the following-up measures after the HKMA stock

*(Continued)*

**Box 5.A5:** (*Continued*)

market intervention. The author again submitted Proposal D in Appendix 5.3 as a measure to bring the Hong Kong interest rate down towards the US level.

- After the HKMA's announcement of the convertibility undertaking to bring the Hong Kong interest rate down towards the US level, a foreigner claiming to be the journalist of the South China Morning Post, the major English newpaper in Hong Kong, called into the author's office in the Bank of China (Hong Kong), saying that he would like to interview the author on the issue. Suspecting the person could be someone from the speculative funds, the author asked for his telephone number so that the author could call back and confirm his declared identity. When the author called back within a minute of that call, he found that the phone number given was invalid. During the speculative attack, the author had also received reports in the Hong Kong – Macau Regional office reporting that one of the major Chinese newspapers was supported by the Tiger Funds, one of the two most active speculative funds during the speculative attack. Even up to now (2010), that Chinese newspaper is still supported by the Tiger Funds, and is taking an anti-China and anti-Hong Kong Government stance when reporting news.

In addition to the above information known to the author, it might also help to spell out the author's view for historians to debate and write the history of this particular episode:

- Hedge Funds did use rumors, investment bank reports and other dirty means to help their speculative attack. While the governments of the attacked economies did have their own faults, it was misleading and immoral for the hedge funds to use this to justify their speculative attacks. The economic losses they caused to the Asian economies were far much higher than the profit they

(*Continued*)

**Box 5.A5:** ˙ (*Continued*)

earned from the speculative attack. Numerous innocent people in Asia were hurt by the mal-functioning of the financial system during the crisis and the recession during the post-crisis period. The author believed that it was just fair for Thai people to throw eggs to George Soro during his visit to Thailand a decade after his speculative attack in Asia. The author could not bar out the possibility of political motives behind the speculative attack in 1997–98;

- The way some Hong Kong finance professionals criticizing Joseph Yam, the then CEO of the HKMA, for the surge of overnight interbank rates to 280% on 23 October 1997 had made things worse. The fierce criticism had made Joseph Yam too defensive to accept external proposals in the subsequent periods. To some extent, Joseph Yam's mistake at that time was not unreasonable as the whole speculative strategy was very complicated and unknown to the HKMA at the beginning, i.e., the mistake was technical but not intentional. Nevertheless, the author did believe that Joseph Yam should also be responsible for the supsequent delay to deal with the speculative attack;

- It was Joseph Yam and the HKMA that fought with the speculators in August-September 1998. The then CEO and Finance secretary of Hong Kong, Mr. Tung Chee Hua and Mr. Donald Tsang, knew almost nothing about the speculative attack and the defense, not to mention the ability to monitor the defense. Some subsequent government reports had given credit to these two persons for the defense against the speculative attack. This type of claim would only weaken the credibility of the Hong Kong Government and the Chinese Government. It was not only unfair to Joseph Yam, but would also result in a culture that would not give sufficient credit to those who did the hard work. Nevertheless, Joseph Yam did owe a thank to those academia who made the proposals to bring Hong Kong interest rates down towards the US level.

# Appendix 5.3   Summary of Proposals to Deal With the Speculative Attack

As explained in Appendix 5.2, the major channel of destruction of the speculative attack was the sharp rise in interest rates for a prolonged period. If let unattended for a few months, these would lead to the development of various types of vicious cycles, such as plunge in asset prices and recession, falling consumption and rising unemployment, as well as tightening of credit and increasing amount of corporate failures and bad debts. To avoid these, academia had made various types of proposals in late 1997 and 1998 to minimize the impact of speculative attack on the real economy. The first category of proposals was the dollarization of the Hong Kong dollar while the second category was the Argentina-Estonia-Lithuania (AEL) version of currency board system which aimed at strengthening the mechanism of the system. The third category was the use of an option to remove the exchange rate risk of interest arbitrage. The last category was the use of electronic Certificate of Indebtedness (CI) as an exchange rate guarantee for arbitrage between the Hong Kong and US interest rates.[26] In this appendix, we will summarize these proposals.

## A.  Dollarization of Hong Kong dollar

According to the proposal, if Hong Kong could not maintain the linked exchange rate system or had to maintain it at an extremely high cost, one possible solution was to announce the replacement of the Hong Kong dollar by the US dollar as the circulating currency. This could completely eliminate the exchange rate risk, restore confidence and ensure that economic activities would not be affected by the speculative attack. Furthermore, if speculators knew that the best result of their speculation was only the dollarization of the Hong Kong dollar, there would be no interest in speculating against the Hong Kong dollar right from the beginning.[27]

---

[26] While classified as a separate category, the last category could also be classified as an extension of the second category (i.e., both involve electronic transfer) or the third category (i.e., the CI could also be seen as an option although the HKMA's exposure under the two designs are different).

[27] Note that the dollarization will not be able to solve the problem of over-valuation of Hong Kong dollar (or too high the relative price and wage in Hong Kong) during the post-crisis period.

## B. AEL Version of Currency Board System

The second proposal was the Argentina-Estonia-Lithuania (AEL) version of currency board system proposed by Tsang (1998). According to the proposal, banks would have a direct reserve account with the HKMA so as to avoid moving cash around for arbitrage. Arbitrage would then ensure that the spot exchange rate would always be around the official rate. *"Over time, the fixation of the spot rate should lead to a return of confidence, and convergence in domestic-foreign interest rates and spot-forward exchange rates would take place as people engage in interest arbitrage and capital inflow exceeded capital outflow"* (Tsang, 1998).

## C. Use of Option to Remove Exchange Rate Risk of Interest Arbitrage

Here, we will discuss two proposals that engage the idea of an option to remove the exchange rate risk of interest arbitrage so as to bring the high Hong Kong interest rate back to the US level, reducing the impact of the October 1997 attack on the Hong Kong economy and stopping further attack in the future. From the theoretical point of view, the second proposal could be considered as an improved or modified model of the first one.

### C.1 *US Dollar Liquidity Adjustment Facility*

To reduce the Hong Kong-US dollar interest rate premium and hence reduce the adverse impact of any speculative attack on the Hong Kong economy, Chen and Chan (1997) proposed to extend the usual Hong Kong dollar Liquidity Adjustment Facility (LAF) to a US dollar LAF. According to the proposal, banks would be allowed to use Exchange Fund bills as a collateral to borrow US dollars from the HKMA, but they would be given an option to return the borrowings in the form of US dollar or Hong Kong dollar (at the official rate). Such an option would remove the exchange rate risk for banks to conduct interest arbitrage between Hong Kong dollar and US dollar, thus ensuring that the Hong Kong dollar interest rate would fall to the US dollar rate.

While the proposals was extremely innovative, there was no limit[28] on the quantum of US dollars which banks could borrow from the HKMA and the quantum which the debt could be returned in the form of Hong Kong dollars, thus making the commitment of the HKMA too large to be borne in case of an extreme adversity (such as bank runs or other panics that would prevent the financial and economic system from function properly). Furthermore, once the system was implemented, there would be difficulties of removal if it was decided to change the exchange rate system in the future.

## C.2 *Merton Miller's Option Note*

The major contribution of the above proposal was that it introduced the idea of using an option to remove the exchange rate risk of interest arbitrage between the Hong Kong dollar and the US dollar. The problem was that there was no limit on the amount of the option, making HKMA's commitment excessively large. Theoretically, the proposal could be divided into two parts:

(a) an option that guaranteed a fixed exchange rate between the Hong Kong dollar and the US dollar, thus removing the exchange rate risk for banks to conduct interest arbitrage between the Hong Kong dollar and the US dollar interbank markets; and
(b) a facility that allowed banks to use US dollar bills as a collateral to borrow (and return) US dollars from (to) the HKMA.

While part (a) was our major concern, part b was totally irrelevant to the current issue. Seeing this, Merton Miller (1998) suggested the issuance of an option that would guarantee a fixed exchange rate between

---

[28] According to the proposal, a bank can keep repeating the following procedures: use the Exchange Fund bills as a collateral to borrow US dollars from the HKMA, and then repay the loans in terms of Hong Kong dollars and get the Exchange Fund bills for further borrowing. By doing so, the bank will have virturally no limit to borrow US dollars from the HKMA.

the Hong Kong dollar and the US dollar. The advantages of this proposal were:

(a) the amount of the option would be controlled, thus removing the problem of an unlimited commitment for HKMA;
(b) HKMA could charge a certain premium for the issuance of the option, thus generating a hefty income for the Hong Kong government; and
(c) The second part of the Chen and Chan proposal could be discarded, thus avoiding any possible complications.

Unfortunately, the suggestion was not adopted due to insufficient understanding of how the mechanism worked. The major argument behind the hesitation was as follows:

(a) if the amount of the option issued was too much, the contingent loss of the HKMA in the case of an extreme adversity could be too high; and
(b) if the amount of the option issued was too little, the premium could be too high which could worsen market sentiment.

The problem of the above arguments was that it failed to recognize that the price in the new option market would be linked with those in the futures (forward) currency and interbank market as a result of arbitrage activities. In other words, the three markets could be pooled together with the following two outcomes:

(a) the addition of the option note, no matter how small, would help to reduce the interbank rates and the forward premium of the Hong Kong dollar; and
(b) the premium of the option note could not exceed those in the interbank and future currency markets because of the arbitrage between these markets.

Recognizing these, the monetary authority could gradually increase the issuance of the option note until the interbank rates and Hong Kong dollar forward premium fall to a more desirable level.

## D. Electronic Certificate of Indebtedness

In view of the hesitation to adopt Merton Miller's proposal, Yip proposed to use the electronic Certificate of Indebtedness (CI) as a built-in option to remove the exchange rate risk of interest arbitrage. The mechanism of the proposal was as follows:

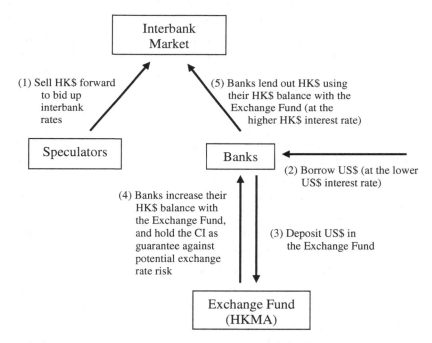

Note: In procedures 3 and 4, banks will hold the Certificate of Indebtedness (CI) which entitles them to convert the amount of HK$ balance with Exchange Fund back to US$ any time at the official rate for repayment. As a result, there will be no exchange rate risk for banks' interest arbitrage activity. On the other hand, the commitment of the Exchange Fund/HKMA is only limited to the amount of CIs issued which are fully supported by the amount of US$ deposited in the Exchange Fund in procedure 3.

Following the above chart, if speculators wanted to bid up the interbank rates by selling Hong Kong dollars forward (procedure 1), banks could conduct interest arbitrage according to procedures (2)–(5). That is, banks can borrow US dollars overseas at the lower US interest rate (procedure 2), and then deposit the US dollars with the Exchange Fund (procedure 3) in exchange for the Hong Kong dollars plus the electronic CIs from the Exchange Fund (procedure 4). The bank could then lend out the Hong Kong dollars at the higher interest rate (procedure 5). When the loans matured, the banks could always reverse the procedures at the official exchange rate (i.e., use the electronic CIs obtained in procedure 4 to convert the matured Hong Kong dollar principal back into the same amount of US dollar for repayment). As a result, there would not be any exchange rate risk for banks to conduct such a kind of interest arbitrage activity. Meanwhile, the arbitrage activity would increase the money supply of Hong Kong until Hong Kong interest rates converged to the lower US interest rate, thus solving the problems of a liquidity crunch and high interest rates simultaneously.

The advantages of the proposal were:

(a) HKMA's commitment was only the amount of CIs issued which were fully supported by the US dollars deposited in the Exchange Fund, and HKMA was only acting as a custodian for the US dollars deposited by the banks. There would be no exchange rate risk, even in case of extreme adversity;

(b) during the crisis, arbitrage activities would increase domestic money supply, thus alleviating the problems of a liquidity crunch;

(c) arbitrage would ensure that domestic interest rates eventually converged to the much lower US dollar interest rates, while the decline of interest rates in Merton Miller's proposals would depend on the amount of the option issued;

(d) the proposal is consistent with the mechanism of the currency board system.

As explained in Appendix 5.2, this proposal was eventually modified by the HKMA as the "convertibility taking" measure on 5 September 1998.

# Chapter 6

# The Second-Stage Transitional Reform and Potential Choices on the Long-Term System

After the first stage transitional reform implemented on 21 July 2005, the author had published four sets of following-up articles between November 2005 and May 2007 on the detailed arrangements of the second stage of the transitional reform. The proposed aim of the second stage reform was a shift from the monitoring of the renminbi-US dollar rate with a narrow band to the monitoring of the nominal effective exchange rate (NEER) with a moderate band width and an adjustable parity. The last two sets of article also provided further discussions on the medium-term and long-term exchange rate systems.

## 6.1 The First Following-Up Article on the Second Stage of the Transitional Reform

The first article was published on 10 November 2005. At that time, there was a proposal to widen the narrow exchange rate band between the renminbi and the US dollar.[1] In response to the proposal, the article recommended to solve the problem with the following Chinese military strategy: "*Some cities are not worth attacking, and some routes are not worth*

---

[1] According to the announcement on 21 July 2005, the renminbi-US dollar band was ±0.3% around the closing rate of the previous working day. While the band was narrow, the maximum appreciation (and depreciation) rate it could allow for was not that small. For example, suppose there were 250 working days per year, the maximum appreciation rate it could allow for would be $[(1.003)^{250} - 1] \times 100\% \approx 110\%$ per annum.

*taking*" (城有所不攻, 途有所不由). That is, it may not be worthy to use all the resources to attack a hard-to-conquer city (i.e., the widening of the renminbi-US dollar exchange rate band) if it is not crucial to the ultimate success of the war. Instead, one can on the one hand use part of the army to surround and monitor the hard-to-conquer city and on the other hand, use the remaining part of the army to occupy the other easy-to-conquer places that are crucial to the ultimate success of the war. When all the other places are occupied, the problem or resistance of the hard-to-conquer city will automatically weaken or disappear.

### 6.1.1 *The Monitoring Target Should Be the NEER Instead of the Renminbi-US Dollar Rate*

The suggestion to apply such strategy to the second-stage transitional reform was based on the following two considerations. Firstly, it was only slightly more than three months since the first stage transitional reform was implemented in July 2005. To announce a widening of the narrow exchange rate band between the renminbi and the US dollar in such a short period could be too much a shock to the market.

Secondly, what China should monitor was her exchange rate *vis-à-vis* a trade weighted basket of currencies (i.e., the NEER) instead of her exchange rate *vis-à-vis* the US dollar. The advantage of monitoring the former was that it could automatically deal with large nominal swings of any major currency. For example, suppose a major currency (e.g., the US dollar or the Euro) surges by 10% against all other currencies within a particular short period, and the weight of that currency in China's NEER is 30%. To keep China's competitiveness from being affected by the nominal swing of the major currency, what China has to do is to keep her NEER unchanged. That is, China could let renminbi depreciate 7% *vis-à-vis* the major currency and appreciate 3% *vsis-à-vis* all other currencies. By doing so, the gain is China's relative price competitiveness from the former (= 7% × 30% = 2.1%) would be able to offset the loss in China's relative price competitiveness from the latter (= −3% × 70% = −2.1%).

This would mean that the central bank's exchange rate monitoring job could be greatly simplified: What the central bank has to do is to change her NEER only when there is a change in the real factor or a change in the domestic-foreign inflation differential (i.e., even if there is a huge nominal swing in a major currency such as the US dollar, what the central bank has to do is to keep her NEER unchanged).

That is, if the Chinese Central Bank monitors her currency *vis-à-vis* the trade weighted basket of currencies, she only needs to change the NEER if she identifies a major permanent change in the real economy or change in the inflation differential. On the other hand, if China's monitoring target is the renminbi–US dollar rate instead of the NEER, a major nominal swing of the US dollar could push China into a very difficult position. Thus, monitoring the NEER, instead of the renminbi–US dollar rate, should be one of the ultimate aims of the second-stage transitional reform.

### 6.1.2 Complete the Reform on the NEER Before Shifting the Market Attention from the Renminbi–US Dollar Rate to the NEER

Meanwhile, as the market attention at that time was all the way biased towards the renminbi–US dollar rate instead of the NEER, China could take this chance to apply the military strategy of *"pretending to repair the Sichuan foot passage while secretly sending the army through Chen-Chang"* (明修栈道, 暗渡陈仓). That is, to take the opportunity that the market's attention is not yet on China's NEER, and to complete the remaining necessary reform related to the NEER (i.e., analogous to the strategy of occupying the easy-to-conquer places that are crucial to the success of the war). Once this is properly done, China can then start to shift the market attention from the renminbi–US dollar rate to the NEER.

One effective way to change the market attention is to keep reiterating that the central bank's monitoring target is the NEER, not the renminbi–US dollar rate. Such process can take at least 6–9 months of reiterations before it can have some effects on market attention. Nevertheless, the article highlighted that persistent effort along this line would eventually be successful. If *"repeating lies one thousand times could attract quite some believers, there is no reason that reiterating a to-be-realized plan would not be successful"*.

Meanwhile, one reason for the media's and market's biased attention to the renminbi–US dollar rate was in fact the absence of a widely available

NEER index for public reference. Thus, the People's Bank of China (PBoC) should encourage one of the state-owned commercial banks to publish its own index of NEER, in which the weight of each currency could be slightly different from that of the PBoC so as to maintain a moderate degree of confidentiality (see Section 2.2.1 for the advantage of this).[2] In addition, the PBoC could also (i) report her NEER index on an occasional basis; and (ii) reiterate in the monetary policy report that the previous and forthcoming NEER appreciation rate would only be gradual. In other words, the best arrangement would be that the appreciation rate shown by state-owned commercial bank's NEER index would be close to, but slightly different from, that reported by the PBoC.

### 6.1.3 *Still Need to Monitor the Renminbi-US Dollar Rate*

While reiterating that the NEER would be the monitoring target and waiting for the reiteration to take effect overtime, the PBoC should also continue to monitor the renminbi-US dollar rate (i.e., the hard-to-conquer city). If conditions allowed (e.g., the US dollar had not yet exhibited any major nominal swing so that the NEER appreciation rate would not be much different from the renminbi-US dollar appreciation rate), it would be the best to keep the renminbi-US dollar appreciation rate within 2% per annum for another one to two years. This was so because realizing this would strengthen the market's trust on the PBoC's future announcements on her exchange rate system reform, which would be an extremely valuable intangible asset to the central bank. In fact, one major reason for the market trust on Singapore's exchange rate policy was its good record in honoring her previous announcements. In some cases, such kind of intangible assets (market's trust on the government) could affect the success or failure of a policy announcement during the crisis period.

---

[2] As explained in Yip (2005) for the case of Singapore, it would be rather easy for professional investors and speculators to use China's external trade figures to obtain a rough estimate of the currency weights. However, maintaining some degree of confidentiality here could still make it more difficult for the speculators to use investment bank reports or rumors to mobilize the public to follow their speculation.

### 6.1.4 *Better to Complete the Reform on the NEER and Then Shift the Market Attention Before Any Major Nominal Swing in the US Dollar*

Why would it be important to complete the necessary reform on the NEER and then shift the market attention as soon as possible? Because it would be better to do these before the US dollar exhibited a major nominal swing, whose occurrence would be just a matter of time. In the lucky case that the US dollar only exhibited a mild or moderate nominal swing *vis-à-vis* the other currencies in the subsequent 1–2 years, it would still be possible for China to achieve a less than 2% appreciation rate in both the NEER and the renminbi-US dollar rate, thus allowing the PBoC to accumulate the above valuable intangible credibility.

However, in the unlucky case of a major nominal swing of the US dollar (e.g., 10% depreciation) in the year thereafter, it would not be possible for China to keep a less than 2% appreciation rate in both the NEER and the renminbi-US dollar rate. In such case, China should opt for the gradual appreciation of the NEER. Thus, on top of the previous reiteration, China should at that time further clarify and reiterate that China's monitoring target was her NEER, not the renminbi-US dollar rate. As the major swing of the US dollar would be considered as an extreme case, if the PBoC had already reiterated its position in the past, the clarification and the parallel re-centering, or temporary widening, of the renminbi-US dollar exchange rate band to allow for the necessary major movement in the renminbi-US dollar rate would still be acceptable to the market. Neither would the credibility of the central bank be much affected or weakened by this extreme case. Of course, this would still mean that the PBoC had missed the chance of accumulating the above intangible credibility. Once the major nominal swing of the US dollar was over, the PBoC could even take the chance to remove the renminbi-US dollar exchange rate band, and reiterate that its monitoring target was in fact the NEER.[3]

In short, the narrow renminbi-US dollar exchange rate band at that time was a hard-to-conquer city (or hurdle) and was not that related to the

---

[3] Here, there is still a choice of doing it by an announcement of an immediate removal, an announcement of a gradual removal, or removal by steps.

ultimate aim of the reform. On the other hand, the reform on the NEER was an easy-to-overcome hurdle that was more related to the ultimate aim of the reform. Thus, China should first complete the reform on the NEER before it gradually expand the narrow renminbi-US dollar band towards infinity.

### 6.1.5 *The Appropriate Arrangement in the Subsequent Years: Add a Bit Fluctuations Along a Gradually Appreciating Path*

The article further highlighted that the occurrence of a major nominal swing in the US dollar would be just a matter of time. In the unlucky case that the swing occurred in the first 1–2 year after the transitional reform, the above proposed measures should be sufficient to tackle the problem. On the other hand, in the lucky case that the nominal swing of the US dollar occurred at a much later time, China should be glad to see that the subsequent 1–2 year's appreciation rates in both the NEER and the renminbi-US dollar rate were less than 2%. This would give China more time to complete the necessary reform on the NEER, shift the market attention to the NEER through official reiterations and "private provision" of the NEER index, and accumulate the above mentioned intangible credibility.

Thereafter, if conditions allowed, the PBoC should monitor for a gradual appreciation of *just* the NEER. The PBoC should also allow the NEER to make moderate fluctuations around a gradually appreciating path with changes in economic conditions. This would allow the market to gradually accept that the renminbi exchange rate could go up or down. The article also emphasized that the fluctuation of exchange rate did not have to fully reflect changes in market conditions. The key here was to let the market accept, and get used to, the possibility that renminbi could go up and down with changes in market conditions. In fact, the exchange rate mechanism at that time would still be a variant of the fixed rate system, i.e., a fixed rate mechanism with the exchange rate making moderate fluctuations along a slightly upward sloping path instead of a horizontal path.

As the transitional reform in the first few months had already weakened the market's belief on the possibility of a substantial profit from the appreciation speculation and brought the market expectation down to a more gradual appreciation, if the PBoC continued its effort to honor a gradual appreciation, it would be relatively easy to establish a market expectation of occasional ups and downs along a gradually appreciating path.

The article also highlighted that changes in market expectation (i.e., from the expectation of a fixed rate to the expectation of a possible major revaluation) were in fact the major source of disturbance on the Chinese economy. Bringing the market expectation to an expectation of gradual appreciation had substantially helped stabilize the exchange rate market. On top of this, allowing moderate fluctuations in both the level of exchange rate and the slope of the appreciation path would also bring in moderate flexibility of exchange rate. Under such market expectation, if the PBoC could control the effect of other factors (such as the trade surplus and the net FDI inflows) on domestic money supply, such market expectation of gradual appreciation with moderate fluctuations could be sustained until one day in the future China would like to move from the appreciation path to its "perceived" equilibrium path.

### 6.1.6 *A Possible Arrangement in the Case of Diplomatic Need*

Meanwhile, if diplomatic need dictated some announced reform on the exchange rate system during the expected visit of the US President, China could announce the following changes:

(a) merge the various ±3% exchange rate bands of renminbi *vis-à-vis* the non-US dollar major currencies into a single ±3% exchange rate band of NEER (i.e., renminbi *vis-à-vis* the trade weighted basket of currencies); and then

(b) announce a very gradual widening of the ±0.3% exchange rate band between renminbi and the US dollar.

The rationale for the proposal of (b), i.e., a very gradual widening of the renminbi-US dollar band, was that an immediate widening of the exchange rate band to ±3% could result in an immediate appreciation of the renminbi-US dollar rate to the upper edge of the band. This would in turn imply the cumulated appreciation since 21 July 2005 would be 4–5% instead of 1–2%. As highlighted in Chapters 2 and 4, the 4–5% cumulated appreciation would push up the market's expected appreciation, eliminate the believers' trust on China's announced gradual appreciation, and invite enormous speculative inflows until the PBoC found it no longer possible to control the monetary growth and the appreciation rate. Thus, a gradual widening of the renminbi-US dollar exchange rate band was the maximum that China could compromise for at that time.

### 6.1.7 *China's Choice of No Widening of Exchange Rate Band at That Time*

Despite the pressure from the US, there was no widening of the renminbi-US dollar exchange rate band at that time. As explained in the previous sections, China should do its necessary reform on the NEER and make effort to shift the market attention to the NEER before a gradual widening of the renminbi-US dollar exchange rate band. A widening of the exchange rate band without the former two would not do anything good to China. While the above discussion had contributed to China's choice of no widening of the renminbi-US dollar exchange rate band at that time, a more important reason could be the incentives of China's economic officials to take risk to make another major move: It was just a few months after the "successful" transitional reform in July 2005 and the related Chinese economic officials were still enjoying the praise and credit of the success. If there was no urgent need to go into the second stage reform, at least some of them would found that it would be to their personal benefits to recommend no further change for the time being. By doing so, they could continue to enjoy the praise and credit for a longer time. On the other hand, if they took the risk of recommending another major move such as the second stage of the transitional reform, any failure could mean the end of the current praise and credit. As China had not done the first two parts of the second stage reform recommended by the author, China's choice of no widening of the renminbi-US dollar band at that time had actually benefited China.

## 6.2 The Second Following-Up Article

While China had chosen not to widen the exchange rate band between late 2005 and early 2006, there was greater US pressure for more renminbi appreciation in February 2006. In response to the US pressure, some Chinese researchers in the government-funded research bodies recommended the Chinese government to make more medium-size revaluations of 2–3% or 3–5%. In view of the potential consequences of the proposal, the author published the second following-up article on 2 March 2006.

### 6.2.1 No More "Unanticipated" Revaluation

The article first highlighted that the keys of the whole reform were *market expectation* and *government's credibility*. The former is important as change in market expectation can again invite enormous speculative inflows and severely increase the PBoC's costs and difficulties in controlling her monetary growth and monitoring the pace of appreciation. Moreover, as highlighted by the author in the previous discussions, one reason for China to achieve a gradual appreciation with only moderate fluctuations was the existence of a large number of believers on the announced gradual appreciation: Because the Chinese government had explicitly or implicitly indicated that the renminbi-US dollar rate would only appreciate gradually so that the potential speculation profit might not be high enough when compared with the transaction cost and risk premium of doing the speculation through the illegal channels or the abuse of legal channels, many market participants had chosen not to join the speculation for renminbi appreciation. Thus, the Chinese government at that time should consolidate the support and trust of these believers through official reiteration of the plan of gradual appreciation and subsequent realization of the plan. On the one hand, if the policy maker intentionally or unintentionally violated the implicit promise, thus inducing the believers to give up their initial trust, the consequence could be serious. Thus, making another unanticipated revaluation at that time could be disastrous. On the other hand, keep on honoring the announced plan and ensure the subsequent realization of the implicit promise would be the best choice.

Furthermore, according to the literature of rational expectation, the government could not fool the market forever. Take China's exchange rate system reform as an example, the 2.1% revaluation of the renminbi-US dollar rate on 21 July 2005 was unanticipated. If China could maintain a gradual appreciation of less than 2% and abstain from another moderate unanticipated revaluation, the market would not incorporate the initial 2.1% revaluation in her expectation. Under such circumstance, the Chinese government had honored her promise. On the other hand, if the Chinese government announced another 2–3% revaluation, the market would incorporate the 2.1% revaluation on 21 July 2005 into her expectation. Adding the 1% appreciation of the renminbi–US dollar over the past 7–8 months would be a cumulated appreciation of 5–6% within 7–8 months. Given that the stock market and property price had started rising at that time, incorporation of such cumulated appreciation into market expectation would mean another round of rampant speculative inflows, thus substantially increasing the PBoC's difficulty and cost in controlling the monetary growth and monitoring the pace of appreciation. Even in the very lucky case that the amount of speculative inflows was still not too big so that the PBoC could eventually offset the impacts of the speculative inflows, the cost and problem were absolutely unnecessary.

### 6.2.2 *Alternative Ways of Making Concession to the US*

Therefore, even if it was necessary for China to make some concessions to the US, it would be better to make them within the announced exchange rate framework. For example, the Chinese government could first merge the various ±3% exchange rate bands between the renminbi and other non-US dollar major currencies into a single ±3% NEER band, and then keep reiterating that its monitoring target was the NEER instead of the renminbi–US dollar rate. After sufficient effort to shift the market attention from the renminbi–US dollar rate to the NEER (see Section 6.1.2 on how this could be done), the Chinese government could announce a 2–3 month schedule in which the renminbi–US dollar exchange rate band would be widened a bit everyday until the exchange rate band reached, say, ±0.5% by the end of the schedule. [Note that during the widening of the band, the parity of the band should be kept unchanged.] After that, there should be a formal review and serious debate on whether China should continue to expand the exchange rate band.

When these were probably done, the PBoC could then make more gradual widening of the renminbi–US dollar band until it reached infinity, which was actually equivalent to the abolishment of the renminbi–US dollar band and the establishment of the NEER monitoring band. By doing so, China could on one hand make the necessary concession to the US and could on the other hand, complete the second stage transitional reform. On the contrary, the proposal of medium-size revaluation made by the government-funded research bodies would not only cause unnecessary speculative inflows and potential chaos, but would also change the exchange rate system reform from an initial success to an eventual failure.

While the author understood that China as a large economy had certain capacity to resist pressure from the US, he was not 100% sure whether some unknown developments had reduced China's capacity of resistance. Therefore, he gave the following list of potential concessions for the Chinese leaders to choose:

(a) If the Chinese government could resist the pressure from the US, it would be the best to keep the original plan, i.e., ensured that the renminbi–US dollar appreciation rate would not exceed 2% per annum, and then did the second stage transitional reform according to the recommended steps outlined in Section 6.1;

(b) If it was necessary to make some concessions to the US, a better choice would be making concessions in other areas, such as those related to the bi-lateral trade. Among the acceptable concessions in bi-lateral trade, a *once-and-for-all* concession would be better than a concession with *permanent* effect. Examples of the former would be a once-and-for-all purchase of airplanes, oil extraction equipments, and high-tech products manufactured by the US as well as oilfields or other assets in the US. Examples of the latter would be trade and non-trade policies that could cause a permanent increase in US exports to China; and

(c) If the US pressure was so great that some kind of concession on the exchange rate system reform was necessary, China could then adopt the proposal outlined at the beginning of this section. As there would not be another "unanticipated" revaluation, even if the renminbi–US dollar rate would be moving along the upper edge of the band, the cumulated appreciation would still be less than 2% per annum. With the additional design of possible freezing or postponement of the next widening schedule after each formal review, the concession made here would still be reasonably safe.

In the concluding section, the article rejected the proposal of more revaluations of medium or moderate size. Even for the case of 2% revaluation, the potential increase in speculative inflows and disturbance could still be too large. In the case of 3–5% revaluation, it could even cause chaos to the Chinese economy and change the exchange rate system reform from its initial success to an eventual failure. If it was really necessary to make a revaluation, 1% could be the maximum that China could afford. However, this would not be sufficient to satisfy the US. It would also invite speculations and rumors of further revaluations in the future. Obviously, this would not be a good choice for China. Thus, the choice was inferior to the proposed reform outlined at the beginning of this section.

Finally, the article also reminded China's top leaders on the following political trade-off: If it was not possible to come into an agreement with the US so that there would be a trade sanction or high tariff imposed on Chinese exports to the US, China citizens would perceive this as an unreasonable action from the US, i.e., it was the problem of unfavorable external environment, not a mistake of government policy. Thus, Chinese citizens would support Chinese leaders' decision. On the other hand, if a concession mistake in the exchange rate system reform caused a financial chaos and then recession in China, Chinese citizens would then perceive that Chinese leaders were not tough enough to the US and the concession was a policy mistake. These would in turn severely weaken the ruling authority and credibility of the Chinese government.

### 6.2.3 China's Announcement of No More "Unanticipated" Revaluation

After the publication of the article and its submission to China's top leaders through the *Xinhua News Agency*, China's premier, Mr. Wen Jiao Bao, announced in mid-March 2006 that there would not be any more "unanticipated" revaluation in the future. Instead, China would work to increase the "flexibility" of its exchange rate. The author believed that the announcement had actually pre-empted any speculation of another revaluation in the subsequent future.

## 6.3 The Third Set of Policy Articles

In July 2006, i.e., the anniversary of the exchange rate system reform, some Chinese economists had recommended the speeding up of the renminbi appreciation. In response to this, the author published three articles between late July and early August in 2006. The first article was on the undesirable consequences of a faster renminbi appreciation rate. It also encouraged the Chinese government and the market to be more confident with the design of the exchange rate system reform and be cautious with some of the misleading proposals. The second article then elaborated further details on the proposed second stage transitional reform. The third article first made some following-up comments on the offsetting measures to the monetary growth pressures, as failure to do so would turn the exchange rate system reform from its initial success to an eventual failure. The last part of the article then made further discussions on the medium-term arrangements of the exchange rate system reform.

### 6.3.1 *No Speeding Up of Appreciation*

The first article was published on 28 July 2006. It first noted that the first year of the exchange rate system reform was rather successful. While there was a slightly higher monetary and credit growth, they were still of manageable magnitude. As long as the PBoC did her job properly and did not commit any foolish mistake, China's exchange rate system reform would eventually turn out to be a successful one.

It also highlighted that the success of the exchange rate system reform was not only crucial to the peaceful uprising of China's status in global economy, it could also become a successful example or role model for other economies interested in getting out of a fixed exchange rate system in the future. The latter would in turn contribute to the soft power of China in the global economy. On the other hand, if China sped up the appreciation rate, say to 4–5%, it would only invite more speculative inflows, thus creating enormous monetary growth pressure in the economy. It could even turn the exchange rate system reform from its current success to an eventual failure. This would not only destroy China's current opportunity of peaceful uprising in the global economy. It could even become an example of failure that would be often cited, and even joked about, by the international community in the future.

It also explained that the success of the exchange rate system reform over the first year could at least be reflected by the following two facts:

(a) China had successfully exited from the fixed renminbi-US dollar rate of 8.28; and
(b) many market participants had believed in, accepted and gotten used to the implicit promise of gradual appreciation, and gradual appreciation had in a certain extent been incorporated into the market expectation.

Before the reform in July 2005, almost everybody could at any time recall the renminbi-US dollar rate was 8.28. However, over the year after the reform,[4] most people could not quite exactly recall the renminbi-US dollar rate in a particular day. The more informed one could at most roughly know that the rate was somewhat between 8 and 8.11. While such change did not appear to be great at first sight, it did open a range of possibilities of further major reform in the future as well as major but necessary exchange rate adjustments in case of extreme economic adversity.

In addition, the reform in July 2005 had successfully changed the market expectation from the expectation of "*a certain probability of major revaluation*" to the expectation of "*a probably very gradual appreciation*". This in turn convinced a lot of market participants that, after the deduction of the transaction costs and risk premium of the illegal speculative inflows, it might not be that worthy to join the speculation for renminbi appreciation. As market participants other than Mainland Chinese, such as those from the US, Europe, Japan, Hong Kong, Singapore and other Asian economies, were not particularly familiar with the conditions, law and risk of investing in China, the amount of participants not joining the speculation was actually the majority. Thus, even though there were some Mainland Chinese and international investors who were familiar with the related loopholes in China and got the channels to invest the speculative funds in the Chinese property and stock

---

[4] The only exception was perhaps the time it caught the media attention when the rate crossed the psychological barrier of 8.

markets, the amount of speculative inflows and hence the monetary growth pressure were still within the PBoC's sterilization capacity.

In other words, the transitional reform in July 2005 had actually stabilized the market expectation, thus reducing many market participants' incentives to speculate for renminbi appreciation. Even among the speculative inflows, the major source of incentive was the potential gain from China's stock and property market. With the Chinese-US interest discount as well as the transaction costs and risk premium of the speculative inflows at that time, just the gradual appreciation itself would not be sufficient to attract substantial speculative inflows.

Therefore, what China should do at that time would be further effort to (a) plug the loopholes of speculative inflows through the illegal channels and the abuse of legal channels; (b) control its monetary growth through sterilization and other methods (see Sections 4.4 and 4.5 for a list of these measures); (c) control the rise in asset price; and (d) increase the inspection and penalty against speculative inflows. Meanwhile, China should reject the proposal of speeding up the appreciation rate to 4–5% per annum, as this would attract more speculative inflows.

### 6.3.2 *Further Suggestions on the Details of the Second-Stage Reform*

The second article then proposed the more detailed arrangements on the second-stage reform. It first indicated that once the second stage of the transitional reform was completed, China's exchange rate system would enter a new phase. However, during most part of the second-stage reform, China should still monitor the appreciation rate at a gradual pace. To ensure a smooth transition, the widening of the renminbi-US dollar band should also be gradual. On the other hand, if China allowed a speeding up of appreciation at this stage, it would induce more speculative inflows and monetary growth pressure, which could turn the reform from its initial success to an eventual failure.

The core of the second-stage reform was to *"use two hands to grasp"* the following two rates: the renminbi-US dollar rate and the NEER rate. The first step was to take the chance that market attention still very much focused on the renminbi-US dollar rate, announced the merging of the various ±3% exchange rate bands between renminbi and the other non-US dollar major currencies (such as the Euro and the yen) into a single ±3% NEER band. Thereafter, the PBoC should make effort to shift the market attention from the renminbi-US dollar rate to the NEER by (i) re-iterating in the monetary policy reports and official speeches that the PBoC's monitoring target is the NEER instead of the renminbi-US dollar rate; and (ii) supporting the provision of a NEER index for public reference. During this period, the PBoC should continue its usual monitoring of the renminbi-US dollar rate, including the maintenance of the narrow ±0.3% renminbi-US dollar band.

As the renminbi-US dollar band at that time was still the effective binding constraint on the exchange value of renminbi, if the PBoC explicitly or implicitly indicated that the renminbi would at most appreciate gradually, the above announced merging of the non-binding exchange rate bands should have little effect on the exchange value of the renminbi. Nevertheless, such merging would lay the foundation of China's transition to the eventual aim of monitoring the NEER. In other words, the change was an important "hidden" move before the formal launching of the second-stage reform.

Meanwhile, as the NEER was a weighted average of the exchange value of the renminbi *vis-à-vis* a basket of currencies, merging the individual exchange rate bands into a single NEER band would effectively mean a widening of the exchange rate band against each major non-US dollar currencies: Suppose yen appreciated by 5% *vis-à-vis* other currencies so that it might not be economically worthy to keep the renminbi-yen rate within its ±3% band. As the US dollar and Euro did not appreciate, it would be relatively easy and economically appropriate to keep China's NEER within the ±3% NEER band.[5,6]

---

[5] According to the announced reform on 21 July 2005, the parity of the narrow ±0.3% renminbi-US dollar band would be set at the closing rate of the previous day. On the other hand, the usual practice of an NEER band would be that the parity of the ±3% NEER band that set and fixed by the central bank during the previous review and decision meeting. That was, there was no point to have a ±3% NEER band based on the previous closing rate, as the permitted annual appreciation rate of the renminbi would be too large.

[6] As the PBoC could recenter the exchange rate band in the future, there was in fact no need to have too wide an exchange rate band. Even in the unlikely case that the PBoC felt that the ±3% NEER was too narrow, they could in the future choose to gradually widen the band to their desire level.

During the above merging process, the narrow ±0.3% renminbi–US dollar band would still be the effective binding constraint on the exchange value of the renminbi. Thus, the Chinese government should at that time keep a tight and effective control on the narrow exchange rate band. Once the merging process was completed, the PBoC should make effort to shift the market attention from the renminbi–US dollar rate to the NEER. When these were properly done, the PBoC could start the gradual widening of the narrow renminbi–US dollar band. At the early stage of this part of reform, the gradual widening of the renminbi–US dollar band would directly affect the exchange value of the renminbi. Thus, the increase in the band had to be gradual, and should not exceed 2% per annum.

To achieve this, the article recommended a few schedules of gradual widening and formal review. For example, suppose the acceptable renminbi–US dollar appreciation rate was 2.3% and widening the exchange rate band at that time could mean a rise in the renminbi–US dollar rate from the band parity to the upper edge of the band. If the PBoC kept the parity of the band unchanged during the reform, she could in the subsequent year afford, on top of the original ±0.3% renminbi–US dollar band, a widening of the band by another ±2% (i.e., about 0.25% for every 45 days). Thus, she could widen the band with the following procedures:

First announced a 25-day schedule in which the renminbi–US dollar band would be gradually increased by ±8 points (≈±0.01%) per day. For example, if the upper edge of the renminbi–US dollar band at the announcement day was 7.97 renminbi per US dollar, the upper edge of the band in the subsequent days would be 7.9692, 7.9684, 7.9676 and so on. By the end of the 25 days, the upper and lower edges of the band should have been changed by ±0.25%. After that, there should be a review period of at least 20 days to assess the outcome, and decide whether China should proceed to the next schedule of gradual widening of band.[7]

That is, if the above procedure proceeded smoothly and successfully, the PBoC could

(a) further expand the band by another ±0.25% through another 45-day schedule of gradual expansion of band and formal review; and

---

[7] Thus, there would be at most a widening of band by ±0.25% in 45 days.

(b)  at the same time reiterate that her monitoring target was the NEER and its ±3% exchange rate band.

During this period, the renminbi–US dollar band would only be increased gradually (i.e., less than 2% per annum). With the onging widening of the renminbi–US dollar band, the announced ±3% NEER band would sooner or later become a more and more effective binding constraint on the exchange value of renminbi. On the other hand, the ongoing widening renminbi–US dollar band would gradually become a less and less effective binding constraint until such a stage that it would no longer be an effective binding constraint on the exchange value of renminbi. The article also emphasized that, during the whole process, the PBoC should keep reiterating that its monitoring target was the NEER instead of the renminbi–US dollar rate.

Of course, in the less likely case of unexpected adverse developments during the first schedule of band widening, the Chinese government could freeze, or even abolish, the subsequent schedules.[8] As the exchange rate band for the first schedule would at most involve a widening of band from ±0.3% to ±0.55%, the potential complications for further advancement or retreat of the reform should be controllable.

To further increase the chance of a successful reform, the Chinese government should, before the announcement of the above reform, prepare some *supplementary measures* that could be used to mitigate the appreciation pressure of renminbi after the announced widening of the renminbi–US dollar band. Examples of these would be further relaxation of the QDII or some major overseas acquisitions by Chinese state enterprises. In addition, the PBoC could also use the usual foreign exchange operation (i.e., buying US dollar and selling renminbi) to help keeping the renminbi–US dollar rate within the widened band. The article also indicated that the 25-day schedule was just an example, the Chinese government could appropriately adjust the length of the schedule and the magnitude of each widening. For example, if the Chinese government prefered to do each schedule quick in

---

[8] In the unlikely case of extreme adversity, the Chinese government could even announce a return to the renminbi–US dollar band back to the original ±0.3% band.

order to minimize the possibility of unexpected events in the relatively long schedule, she could choose to reduce the length of the schedule from 25 days to 10 days (or even 1 day).[9]

### 6.3.3 *Proper Control on Monetary Growth Was Crucial to the Success of the Exchange Rate System Reform*

The third article first made some following-up comments on the offsetting measures to the monetary growth pressure, as failure to do so would turn the exchange rate system reform from its initial success to an eventual failure. The last part of the article then discussed the medium-term arrangements of the exchange rate system reform.

#### 6.3.3.1 *Need to Scale Up the Offsetting Measures*

The article first re-iterated that, in addition to the speculative inflows, the current account surplus and the net FDI inflows were two other important sources of the monetary growth pressure at that time. Thus, in the search for measures to reduce the monetary growth pressure, the measures had to be strong enough to offset the impacts of the three sources of inflows. It then made some following-up comments on some of the offsetting measures outlined in Sections 4.4 and 4.5, i.e., the QDII scheme designed by the Chinese government, the author's proposal of securitizing part of foreign bonds and securities held by the government, and the increase in the ratio of once-and-for-all outward investment.

Meanwhile, as it would take quite some time for the QDII scheme and the other offsetting measures to exert large enough offsetting effect on China's monetary growth, the PBoC should, during the interim period, use

---

[9] To achieve the ±0.25% widening of band, the daily widening in the 10-day schedule would be ±20 points per day, which was still pretty small. The 10-day schedule would mean that the PBoC could afford even longer time (i.e., at least 35 days) for the formal review. Alternatively, the PBoC could opt for the 1-day schedule, i.e., a single announcement of ±0.25% widening of band on any particular day, followed by at least 44 days of formal review.

(a) substantial issuance of central bank notes and government bonds; and
(b) substantial increase in bank reserve requirement ratio,
to offset the monetary growth pressure.[10]

As the Chinese government at that time had already made effort in making some once-and-for-all overseas investments and the sterilization measures, the article therefore proceeded to elaborate more on the proposed securitization measures. The article highlighted that Chinese individuals and enterprises were not only interested in investments with high returns. Many of them were also interested in safe and stable foreign bonds with lower interest rates. In view of the huge city population and financial strength of domestic enterprises in China, the private sector's demand for foreign bonds would be enormous, and were at least comparable to the size of inflows into China. Thus, once such investment channel was properly established, even if the inflow of funds increased by a few times, the Chinese government could still use this method to offset the monetary growth pressure created by the increased inflows. This would in turn guarantee the Chinese monetary growth could be kept at the PBoC's target rate.

### 6.3.3.2 *Better to Curb the Overheating Before Proceeding to the Second Stage of the Transitional Reform*

As highlighted in the author's previous proposals, gradual appreciation was only the first step of the exchange rate system reform. The aim was to exit from the fixed rate of 8.28 with the minimum disturbance. As China had already achieved that aim, its next step would be the second-stage transitional reform as outlined in Sections 6.1 and 6.2. However, in view of the signs of an emerging overheating in the stock market and the property market at that time, it would be better to avoid unnecessary complications by first curbing the overheating. When it became clear that the overheating was properly curbed, the Chinese government could then proceed to the second-stage reform.

---

[10] In a closely related article, the author also disagreed with some economists' view that the Chinese economy would weaken at that time. The article also highlighted that the risk of overheating was much greater than the risk of economic softening. Thus, China should pre-empt the overheating by stepping up its effort to mop up the excess liquidity.

The article also highlighted that the proposed securitization measures, if implemented early enough, should be sufficient to help containing the M2 growth within the recommended target of 14–16%. The curbing of the M2 growth was in turn crucial to the control of the gradual overheating of the stock market and the property market before it was too late. In other words, the securitization measures should be implemented before the second-stage transitional reform.

In addition, to ensure that the property market would be under control, the Chinese government could start imposing a property tax on large and luxurious flats (e.g., those above 200 square meters) in major cities. The aim was to develop a policy weapon that could be expanded in the future. For example, if the overheated property market was thereafter properly curbed, the Chinese government could choose to keep the property tax rate unchanged. On the other hand, if the property market continued to be overheated, the Chinese government could further adopted the proposal of progressive property tax rate in the author's policy article published in May 2006 (see Chapter 9 for more details). The advantage of the proposed arrangement would be twofold. On one hand, it would send a very clear message to the market: The government would keep announcing new curbing measures until the overheated property market was properly curbed. On the other hand, it would help cool the sentiment with a very mild property tax imposed only on the rich but not normal Chinese citizens for the time being.

### 6.3.3.3 *Medium-Term Arrangements: Neither Necessary Nor Appropriate to Have a Trade Balance at That Time*

After curbing the overheated asset market and the successful implementation of the second-stage reform, China should have entered the medium-term exchange rate arrangements outlined in the previous sections. That is, China would maintain a certain degree of capital control so as to ensure that the PBoC could control

(i) the appreciation rate of its nominal effective exchange rate (NEER) at the recommended rate of 1–2%; and
(ii) its monetary growth rate to attain internal balance.

During this interim period, China would continue to have a substantial trade surplus. It was however neither necessary nor appropriate to rush to clear this trade surplus.

Firstly, as explained in Yip (2005), Singapore economy was also the economy with persistent trade surplus over the past three decades, and its exchange rate policy was meant for keeping internal balance. Thus, persistent trade surplus does not necessarily mean that it is a problem that must be cleared as soon as possible. The key here should be how to use the surplus to make good overseas investment that could generate good and safe returns for the country.

Secondly, one reason for the substantial inflows (including FDI) into China at that time was that China had a substantial trade surplus, which would mean a rather low risk of an unanticipated devaluation in the future. However, imagine China could really use some polices (e.g., a combination of a substantial increase in domestic demand and a substantial revaluation of the renminbi) to bring the trade surplus to a traded balance. What would that situation be like? Obviously, this would at least mean that the exchange rate risk of FDI into China would no longer be as low as it was. If this caused a reduction of annual FDI inflows from the US$60 billion at that time to, say, US$50 billion or even US$40 billion, just the reduction in FDI would be sufficient to trigger a recession and further vicious cycles, not to mention the impacts of other changes.

Furthermore, without a trade surplus, international speculators and their implementing investment banks could then use various excuses to portray that the renminbi was overvalued at that time (to some extent they could be right as the economy must have changed a lot before it could get rid of the trade surplus). This would in turn trigger substantial outflow of funds and stoppage of inflows, thus creating unnecessary disturbance to the economy. For example, they could say that because of the huge amount of FDI accumulated in the past few decades, the trade balance would mean that China would no longer be able to repay the principal and profit of FDI, should foreign investors decide to leave China. They could also say that the size of non-performing loans in China was enormous, and the risk of a substantial devaluation of renminbi in the future was high.

Unlike many other economists in China, the author believed that the gradual appreciation period could be the golden time of China's economic development. As long as China used the proposed measures to keep the monetary growth under control, there was really no need for China to make any urgent move to clear the trade surplus. As long as China could do the same as Singapore by investing its trade surplus and obtained a reasonable return from its foreign reserves holdings, China did not have to worry that its foreign reserve was too high.

It should also be noted that, in addition to the gradual appreciation, the higher wage increment in China could also result in a rise in China's real effective exchange rate (REER). As at least part of the high annual wage increment was due to China's higher inflation rate than the global average, there was really no urgent need for China to speed up the pace of appreciation.

The article also highlighted that, during the 8–10 year medium-term exchange rate arrangement, China must work hard to clear the non-performing loans and the culture of moral hazard activities in its banking industry. China should only consider the gradual removal of its capital control after she had cleared these problems. If in the meantime it was discovered that the progress in clearing the non-performing loans and culture of moral hazard activities was not as good as anticipated, China should

(a) continue to keep the capital control in order to pre-empt the possible financial crisis in the future;
(b) reduce the pace of renminbi appreciation until the above problems were properly cleared.

Of course, maintaining the capital control was a "buying time" measure to pre-empt the worst scenario of speculative attack and financial crisis. If China did not make sufficient effort to clear the non-performing loans, the eventual outcome would still be horrible enough. On the other hand, if China could clear the above problems as scheduled, then it could consider a gradual removal of the capital control.

### 6.3.3.4 *Maintaining a Trade Surplus Was in Fact a Dynamically Optimal Choice at That Time*

Parallel with the article discussed in the previous section, the author had delivered a keynote speech paper in a policy conference organized in August 2006 (see also the discussion in Section 4.6.1). In this paper, the author explained that it would be dynamically optimal to raise the overseas assets held by the Chinese private sector until it reached the level that could match the China's major economic power status in the global economy. Thus, maintaining a trade surplus was in fact a dynamically optimal choice for China at that time. We will come back to this discussion in Chapter 7.

## 6.4 Direction of the Reform in the Long Term

In May 2007, the author published another two articles on the exchange rate system reform. The first article was on the transitional, medium–term and long-term arrangements of the reform. The second was an re-iteration of the author's proposal on the second stage transitional reform, which had contributed to China's widening of the renminbi–US dollar band to ±0.5% in the same month.

The article first noted that there were three major stages of the reform: the transitional arrangements, the medium–term arrangements, and the long-term arrangements. The first part of the transitional reform was the exit from the fixed rate of 8.28 renminbi per US dollar. As explained in the previous sections, the author also recommended to keep the narrow renminbi–US dollar band at the first stage of the transitional reform. The second stage of the transitional reform had two aims; (i) a shift to the monitoring of the NEER with a ±3% NEER band; and (ii) a gradual widening of the narrow renminbi–US dollar band until the NEER band, instead of the renminbi–US dollar band, become the effective binding constraint on the exchange value of renminbi.

### 6.4.1 *Further Discussions on the Medium-Term Exchange Rate Arrangements*

By the time China completed the second stage of the transitional reform, China should have a NEER monitoring band system, which would in fact be China's medium-term exchange rate system for at least the subsequent 8–10 years. In such a system, China still had to maintain a certain degree of capital control so as to ensure that the PBoC could control her monetary growth and pace of renminbi appreciation (see Section 2.2.2 for the discussion on the doctrine of Impossible Trinity). During that period, the PBoC could adjust the pace of renminbi appreciation when deemed necessary, including a temporary adjustment to zero or even negative appreciation rate. During that time, China would register a relatively large current account surplus, and would be gradually developing controllable channels of overseas investments until it reached a stage that the overseas investment outflows could offset the monetary growth pressure and renminbi appreciation pressure originated from the current account surplus, FDI inflows and speculative inflows. Meanwhile, these overseas investments would mean continuous accumulation of overseas assets held by the Chinese public and private sectors (i.e., government enterprises and individuals) until they reached these participants' desired levels. Such size of overseas asset holdings would also be more consistent with China's growing economic status in the global economy (see Chapter 7 for more detailed discussions).

Before the overseas investment channels and its internal control were properly established, or when inflows of funds were still much higher than the overseas investment outflows, the PBoC should use substantial issuance of central banks notes (or rise in bank reserve requirement ratio) to ensure China's monetary growth be kept within its target. The State Administration of Foreign Exchange should also make effort to plug the loopholes in speculative inflows so as to ensure that the pressure of inflows would be within the PBoC sterilization capacity.

### 6.4.2 *Two Possible Long-Term Arrangements*

After the above medium-term arrangements for at least 8–10 years, the gradual appreciation of China's NEER and the relatively higher wage increments in China would probably bring China's real effective exchange rate (REER) to a level not too far away from its equilibrium level. At that time, China would be in a better position to gradually relax its capital control and proceed to its long-term exchange rate system. Before such a step, it would however be highlighted that China should at least satisfy a few pre-requisites. Two of these pre-requisites would be:

(a) The non-performing loans in China had been basically cleared within this 8–10 years; and
(b) China's REER would be relatively close to its equilibrium level.

If at that time China had not yet satisfied these pre-requisites, it should then stay in the medium-term system for more years until the pre-requisites were satisfied.

This is important as capital control should be the last defense against financial crisis and international speculative attacks. Unless the non-performing loans were properly cleared, it would be better not to take away the last defense. Meanwhile, waiting for the REER to be reasonably close to the equilibrium level would reduce the potential shock during the transition to the long-term system.

For the choice of long-term system, there would be two choices that worth further analysis and debate. The first choice would be one similar to the US system, probably with more occasional interventions (see Section 2.2.1 for the rationale). That is, capital would be freely mobile, the central bank would control its money supply (or interest rate) to attain internal balance, and the exchange rate would be determined by market force with only occasional government interventions (i.e., a relatively flexible exchange rate system in which the exchange rate would eventually adjust to ensure a balance of payment in the long-term).

The second choice is a modified version of the Singapore exchange rate system. In the Singapore exchange rate system, capital is freely mobile and the exchange rate is used to achieve internal balance (see Yip, 1995 on why the exchange rate in Singapore is used to achieve internal balance, not external balance). On the other hand, the current account balance in Singapore will become a residual account, i.e., the surplus can sometimes be bigger or smaller due to the need to adjust the exchange rate to achieve internal balance. Meanwhile, investment outflows by the public and private sector will on one hand be used to offset the effect of current account surplus on money supply, and on the other hand accumulate overseas assets for Singapore.

As Singapore is a small open economy, under the constraint implied by the doctrine of Impossible Trinity, the above system is obviously the best system for Singapore. However, as China is a large economy, it will need the following modifications before it can become one of the candidate of the long-term system for China: That is, with free capital mobility this time, the PBoC should use monetary policy to achieve internal balance while keeping a NEER monitoring band at which there will be a current account surplus. Under this system, the current account balance will be a residual balance (i.e., it can be bigger at some time and smaller at another time, depending on changes in economic conditions and the PBoC's choice on money supply for the internal balance). Oversea investments will pay a major role in (i) offsetting the effect of current account surplus on monetary growth; and (ii) accumulating oversea assets for China. That is, the overseas investments will follow the variations of the current account surplus, i.e., as long as the current account surplus and oversea investments are positive, the government does not mind them to be some time bigger and some time smaller due to the PBoC's needs to use monetary policy to achieve internal balance.

The article also highlighted that the medium-term arrangements discussed in the previous sections could be maintained forever. Whether China should progress from the medium-term system to one of the above two alternative long-term systems, or any other long-term system, should be subjected to further research and debate. That is, the two alternative long-term systems are only proposed for further research.

# Part II:

# Macroeconomic Policies, the Stock Market and the Property Market

> **Chapter 7** ◁

# China's Foreign Reserves, Trade Surplus, Outward Investments and Overseas Assets

While China's foreign reserves in recent years was large compared to international standard (see Table 7.1a), its private sector's holding of foreign assets was very small. The first part of this chapter will explain why it is dynamically optimal for China to continue to run a certain amount of trade and current account surplus until its private and public holdings of overseas assets reach a level that can match its desired large economy status in the global economy. The second part of the chapter will use the Swan Diagram to discuss some of the misleading proposals on China's external and internal balances.

## 7.1 Foreign Reserves and Holdings of Foreign Assets: Some Misconceptions and Policy Implications

As shown in Table 7.1a, there were (i) a substantial surge in China's trade surplus and current account surplus since 2005; and (ii) a sustained and reasonably large rise in FDI inflows, albeit less drastic than the rise in trade surplus. Meanwhile, various reports also suggested that there was a reasonably large amount of speculative inflows.[1] The rise in these inflows had in

---

[1] As noted in Section 4.5.3, one rough estimate of speculative inflows in 2005 was in the order of 50 billion US dollars. It should however be noted that some of the speculative inflows were done through the abuse of the legal trade and FDI channels, which would mean that the actual speculative inflows would be higher than the estimate while the actual trade surplus and FDIs would be lower than the corresponding trade and FDI statistics.

**Table 7.1a.**   Current Account Surplus, FDI Inflows and Foreign Reserves (billion US$)

| Year | Trade Surplus | C/A Surplus | FDI | Foreign Reserves (R) | ΔR |
|------|---------------|-------------|-----|----------------------|------|
| 2000 | 24.109  | 20.519  | 40.72  | 165.6  | 10.9  |
| 2001 | 22.545  | 17.405  | 46.88  | 212.2  | 46.6  |
| 2002 | 30.426  | 35.422  | 52.74  | 286.4  | 74.2  |
| 2003 | 25.468  | 45.875  | 53.51  | 403.3  | 116.8 |
| 2004 | 32.097  | 68.659  | 60.63  | 609.9  | 206.6 |
| 2005 | 102.001 | 160.818 | 72.41  | 818.9  | 209.0 |
| 2006 | 177.058 | 253.268 | 72.72  | 1066.3 | 247.4 |
| 2007 | 264.340 | 371.883 | 83.52  | 1528.2 | 461.9 |
| 2008 | 298.126 | 436.107 | 108.30 | 1946.0 | 417.8 |
| 2009 | 195.698 | 297.100 | 94.07  | 2399.2 | 453.2 |

*Source*: CEIC

turn resulted in a substantial jump in China's foreign reserves from 609.9 billion US dollars in 2004 to 818.9 billion US dollars in 2005 and then to 1.066 trillion US dollars in 2006:

Parallel with the rise in foreign reserves, there was enormous monetary growth pressure. Trying to solve the problem, some Chinese economists had recommended various ways, such as a once–and–for–all revaluation and/or a substantial stimulation of domestic demand, to reduce the rise in foreign reserves and monetary growth pressure in China.

In response to these proposals, the author had written a few articles, including a keynote speech paper for a conference organized by the State Administration of Foreign Exchange in August 2006, to clarify the misconceptions in these proposals. For example, while China's foreign reserves was large by international standard, its private sector's holding of overseas assets was very low. As a result, the sum of China's public and private holdings of foreign assets were still relatively low, i.e., not enough to match China's growing economic influence and status in the global economy.

In fact, if we compared the perceived international status of Singapore with most of its statistics such as population, geographical size, GDP or even external trade, one would find that the perceived international status would be much higher than what these statistics suggested. On important reason for this was the huge amount of its public and private holdings of overseas assets and investments. In fact, this was also to some extent the same for Japan, Germany and even the US.

Thus, if China wants to grow as a major participant in the global economy, one important way is to continue to accumulate overseas assets until it reaches China's desired level, i.e., a level that can match its growing status as a large country in the global economy. To achieve this, China has to keep making overseas investments in the next one to two decades, and this can only be possible if China continues to run a trade and current account surplus.[2]

Hence, it is not a good choice for China to follow these Chinese economists' advice of finding measures to bring the trade and current account back to a balance. In other words, keeping a certain amount of trade and current account surplus for the next one to two decades will be a dynamically optimal choice for China. On the other hand, using measures such as a substantial appreciation or substantial stimulation of domestic demand would be a dynamically sub-optimal choice for China at that time.

In addition to the issue on the dynamic optimality, the articles also highlighted the risk of removing the trade surplus at that time (see Section 6.3.3.3 on the possibility of a fall in FDI and a speculative attack in case the current account surplus was removed).

In Chapter 2, we have also explained that a once-and-for-all large revaluation of renminbi would at least cause a substantial plunge in the GDP growth and employment in China. It could also cause a serious coordination failure of the economic system, such as that created by the shock therapy in Russia during the Yeltsin's era. Thus, a sharp revaluation of renminbi would also be sub-optimal even in the static sense.

---

[2] Of course, it was still necessary to offset the monetary growth pressure while keeping the trade surplus. Thus, the articles recommended the Chinese government to (i) use outward foreign investment as a long term solution to the monetary growth pressure due to the inflows; and (ii) use the measures listed in Sections 4.4–4.6 to offset the monetary growth pressure in the interim.

**Table 7.1b.** China's Outward Investments (billion US$)

| Year | Outward Investment | Cumulated Investment (Ministry of Commerce) | Cumulated Investment (State Adm. of Foreign Exchange) |
|------|------|------|------|
| 2004 |       |       | 52.7  |
| 2005 |       |       | 64.5  |
| 2006 | 21.2  | 90.6  | 90.6  |
| 2007 | 26.5  | 117.9 | 116.0 |
| 2008 | 55.9  | 184.0 | 185.7 |
| 2009 | 56.5  | 245.8 | 229.6 |

*Source*: CEIC

Fortunately, the author's above advice had been well received and adopted by the Chinese government. In fact, the argument to maintain sufficient trade surplus until the public and private holdings of foreign assets reached the desired level was already adopted as one of China's national policy. Thus, at least in the next 8–10 years, we will probably see more and more overseas investments made by Chinese state and private enterprises (see Table 7.1b on the rising trend of China's outward investment since 2006). Meanwhile, China will continue to run a reasonable large current account surplus. In fact, as noted in Chapters 4 and 6, the author perceives this as the golden period of China's economic development.

The above discussion suggested that solid economics training and theoretical foundation were important. If China took the above Chinese economists' advice of adopting a once-and-for-all revaluation, it would first cause a disastrous result to China's output, employment and political stability. It would also mean that China would no longer be able to have a large and sustained trade surplus that could finance the private and public sectors' accumulation of foreign asset holdings until it matched China's big country status in the global economy. That is, a mistake in the policy choice would change the future perceived status of China from a strong and rich economy (with large amount of overseas assets) to a not that strong and rich economy (with very low private holdings of overseas assets). In case of a recession such as that triggered by the global financial tsunami (see Chapter 10 for more details), it would also mean that China would have much lower degree of freedom (i.e., constrained by the current account balance consideration) to stimulate its domestic demand. We will come back to such a discussion in Box 7.3.

## 7.2 Increasing Domestic Demand to Attain Trade Balance: A Misleading Proposal

After the author successfully convinced the Chinese government not to adopt the misleading proposal of a once-and-for-all revaluation until a trade balance, there came another misleading proposal in 2006–2007. In this proposal, some other Chinese economists recommended the Chinese government to stimulate domestic demand (and hence imports) as a way to remove the trade surplus and monetary growth pressure. As some central bank officers seemed to be supportive to the proposal, the author published an article on 5 February 2007 that used the Swan Diagram to explain that the proposal was in fact not a sensible or viable choice under China's economic conditions at that time.[3] Let us see why this was the case.

### 7.2.1 *The External Balance Curve*

In Diagram 7.2.1, the vertical axis is China's nominal effective exchange rate, E (i.e., higher value means appreciation), while the horizontal axis is the domestic demand instrument such as the government expenditure, G (higher value means greater fiscal stimulation). As explained in the explanatory box of the diagram, the external balance (EB) curve is a downward sloping curve. A point to the right hand side of the EB curve means trade deficit, while a point on the left hand side of the EB curve means trade surplus.

### 7.2.2 *The Internal Balance Curve*

Similarly, as explained in the explanatory box of Diagram 7.2.2, the internal balance (IB) curve is an upward sloping curve. A point on the right hand

---

[3] Note that we can use the Swan Diagram here because there is capital control in China. For economies with free capital mobility, the Swan Diagram is not the appropriate tool of analysis.

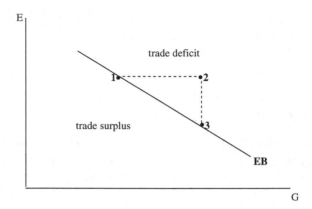

**Diagram 7.2.1:** The External Balance Curve

side of the IB curve represents economic overheating, while a point on the left hand side means unemployment.

---

### Why the EB curve is downward sloping ?

Suppose point 1 is a point of external balance. A horizontal movement from point 1 to point 2 represents an increase in G which will increase imports and hence put the economy into a trade deficit position. To re-establish external balance, we can increase net exports by depreciating the currency to, say, point 3. Joining the two external balance points (i.e., points 1 and 3), we get a downward sloping external balance curve.

### Points outside the EB curve

On the right hand side of the EB curve (e.g., point 2), the economy will have a trade deficit, as expenditure G is too high or exchange rate E is too strong. On the other hand, a point on the left hand side of the EB curve means a trade surplus, as expenditure G is lower than, or exchange rate E is weaker than, that required for external balance.

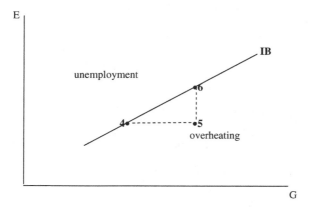

**Diagram 7.2.2**: The Internal Balance Curve

**Why the IB curve is upward sloping ?**

Suppose point 4 is a point of internal balance. A horizontal movement from point 4 to point 5 represents an increase in G which will increase aggregate demand and hence, put the economy into an overheated position. To re-establish internal balance, we can reduce demand for net exports by appreciating the currency to, say, point 6. Joining the two internal balance points (i.e., points 4 and 6), we get an upward sloping internal balance curve.

**Points outside the IB curve**

On the right hand side of the IB curve (e.g., point 5), the economy will be overheated, as expenditure G is too high or exchange rate E is too low. On the other hand, a point on the left hand side of the IB curve means unemployment, as expenditure G is lower than, or exchange rate E is stronger than, that required for internal balance.

## 7.2.3 *The Swan Diagram and Its Policy Implications in 2007*

Putting the external balance and internal balance curves in the same diagram, we get the Swan Diagram as shown in Diagram 7.2.3:

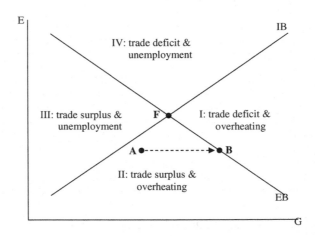

**Diagram 7.2.3:** The Swan Diagram

As we can see, there are four quadrants representing four different combinations of internal imbalance and external imbalance. As China in late 2006 was in mild overheating and had huge trade surplus, the situation of China at that time could be represented by point A at quadrant II of the diagram (i.e., slightly to the right of the IB curve, but on the far left of the EB curve). Now, consider the proposal of increasing domestic demand to clear the trade surplus, which could be represented by a horizontal movement from point A to point B. As we can see, although the proposed policy could help to remove the trade surplus, it would create another (and perhaps bigger) problem: substantial overheating of the Chinese economy, as point B is now on the far right of the IB curve.

Of course, even if the Chinese government attempted to move from point A to point B, it would very soon find that the economy became more and more overheated. Before it reached point B, the Chinese government would give up the domestic demand stimulation. Thus, the article concluded that proposal was neither a sensible nor a viable choice. Fortunately, some government and central bank officials were convinced by the author's argument, and the proposal was never implemented amid the aggravated overheating in 2007 (see Chapters 4 and 8 for more details).

**Box 7.2.3: Why Did the Above Misleading Proposal Miss the Very Important Implications to Internal Imbalance?**

As is well-known in the literature of internal and external balance, exchange rate policy (E) will have effect on not only external balance, but also on internal balance. Similarly, fiscal expenditure (G) will have effects on both internal and external balances. This wisdom accumulated in the olden day debate was also nicely incorporated in the Swan Diagram so that even good undergraduate students should be able to use the diagram to make a proper analysis on the Chinese issue at that time. Unfortunately, many of the often-cited policy discussants in China's media did not have good enough foundations in economic theory for more sophisticated policy analysis, partly because some did not have sufficient economics training right at the beginning and partly because strong incentives to chase for personal benefits had stopped many of them from making serious studies and updating thereafter. As a result, many of them had relied on their own "smart thinking" for a "quick meal" on policy comments, without recognizing the need of having sufficient knowledge on the wisdom accumulated in the economic literature.

As we will see here and there in this book, this is not a unique incidence in China's current policy discussion circle. For example, in Chapter 8, we will see how some of these policy discussants contributed to the building up of the stock market bubble in 2006–2007. In Chapter 9, we will see how some of them had inappropriately used the supply and demand analysis to discuss policies in China's property market, without recognizing (i) the developers' and home purchasers' *asymmetries in market power, holding power and information* on the related housing estates; (ii) the existence of *a large fixed development cost, static economies of scale and cumulative dynamic efficiency* in China's estate development would result in a reasonably large *barrier of entries, less than social optimal supply and developers' hoarding of*

*(Continued)*

**Box 7.2.3:** (*Continued*)

*land*; (iii) the market force described by supply and demand analysis will work well only if there is no *serious distortion arising from income inequality* which is obviously not the case in China; and (iv) barrier of entries, less than optimal supply, land hoarding, toothpaste-squeezing flat selling strategy and continued rise in property price has created *panic demand and speculative demand* for housings, which had further pushed the property price level even beyond middle-high income earners' affordability. As a result, failure to recognize these important characteristics in China had led to extremely misleading policy recommendations on China's property market. Based on the belief that China and other emerging economies need a better pool of policy discussants, the author decided to write this book to illustrate the importance of having a better pool of policy analysts in China and other emerging economies. In fact, the author believes that many of the crises in emerging economies could have been avoided if there were a better pool of policy analysts.

## 7.3 Another Application for the Case in 2008–2009

The Swan Diagram could also be used to analyze the case of China in 2008–2009 during which the global financial tsunami had pushed the Chinese economy to the edge of a recession. Yet, China would continue to have a huge trade surplus although the amount of surplus could be lower than that in 2007. Based on the above information, China at that time could be represented by point C in Diagram 7.3. To avoid the recession, China should increase its government expenditure G until it reaches the point D. At point D, the economy would be close to internal balance. Meanwhile, China would continue to run a trade surplus, albeit smaller than that in 2007. With the trade surplus, China could continue its national policy of making outward foreign investment and accumulating overseas assets until it reached the desired level in the distant future.

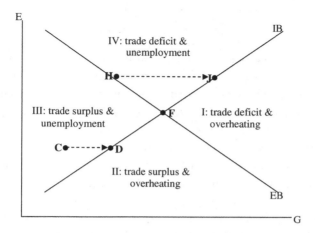

**Diagram 7.3:** Application to the Case of China in 2008–2009

**Box 7.3:   The Scenario in Which China Had No Trade Surplus Before the Global Financial Tsunami**

Next, consider the hypothetical case in which China had in the past adopted proposals that could bring its trade surplus back to a balance. Meanwhile, the global financial tsunami in 2008–2009 had pushed the Chinese economy to the edge of a recession. In such case, China would be at point H in Diagram 7.3. This time, if international economic and political environment did not allow China to engineer a substantial depreciation of its currency, the Chinese government would be constrained by the trade account to implement the ultra expansionary fiscal policy (see Chapter 10 for more details). For example, if it attempted to use ultra fiscal stimulation to bring the economy back to internal balance (e.g., point J), the fiscal stimulation would cause a substantial rise in trade deficit.

This would put China into a dilemma: If it wanted to avoid a huge trade deficit (i.e., external balance at point H), it would have to suffer a severe recession. On the other hand, if it wanted to avoid the recession

*(Continued)*

**Box 7.3:** *(Continued)*

(i.e., internal balance at point J), it would have to run a huge trade deficit. However, with huge deficits in both the trade account and the budget (due to ultra fiscal expansion), the market would eventually doubt about the healthiness of the Chinese government budget and the Chinese economy. The consequences could be disastrous if there were other major weaknesses in the economy. For example, before the global financial tsunami spread to Europe, some "weaker European economies" had already had a reasonably large property bubble and/or high fiscal deficit. With the plunge in property price during the financial tsunami, these economies had entered a recession which had also resulted in less tax revenue and higher fiscal deficit. To stop the recession from deepening further, these countries had adopted reasonably large fiscal stimulation which had in turn pushed the already high national debt to GDP ratio to even higher levels. As we now know, this was eventually followed by the European debt crisis in 2010.

The above discussion also suggests that it is important to keep the economy in a healthy position before the rainy days. Otherwise, the economy might be constrained to adopt appropriate policy to offset the impacts of an unexpected negative economic shock. For example, with a reasonably large trade surplus, a healthy budget and a low national debt to GDP ratio, China and Germany were free to use fiscal expansion to offset the impacts of global financial tsunami. On the other hand, with a huge national debt to GDP ratio, a persistent budget deficit, virtually no trade surplus and excessively high property price in some European economies, these economies were eventually plagued by the European debt crisis. To avoid a full blown crisis, these economies (a) had to seek the help of its wealthier neighbors, the European Central Bank (ECB) and the International Monetary Funds (IMF); and (b) were forced to make substantial cuts in its fiscal expenditure for a sustained period, which would in turn mean a relatively severe recession at least in the subsequent few years (e.g., 3–5 years if there is a strong global economic recovery, or 5–8 years without the support of a strong global economic recovery).

## 7.4 Limitation of the Swan Diagram: A Static Analysis

Readers familiar to the Swan Diagram might ask why the author did not recommend China to move from, say point A in Diagram 7.2.3 or point C in Diagram 7.3, to point F, where the economy would be at both internal and external balance. This is so because the Swan Diagram is only suitable for static or comparative static analysis. Choosing to move *immediately* from any point in the diagrams to the steady state (e.g., point F) will actually force us to neglect the choice of a dynamically optimal path towards the desired steady state. However, as explained in Section 7.1, determining China's optimal path of overseas asset accumulation over various periods in the future is a dynamic analysis. If China did move immediately from point A (or point C) to point F, China would lose the golden chance of accumulating its overseas asset holdings until its desired level.

## > Chapter 8 <

# China's Stock Market Bubble and Lessons from the Bubble Squeezing Strategy

This chapter will discuss (i) the formation of the stock market bubble in China between 2006Q3 and 2007Q4; (ii) the gradual squeezing of the bubble between late 2007 and mid-2008; and (iii) the avoidance of over-correction in the stock market in 2008H2. Although the process of China's bubble squeezing was far from perfect, some important lessons and insights could be drawn from this experience. The author believes that these lessons and insights can be very useful to other economies in the prevention stage and curbing stage of a stock market bubble.

## 8.1 Excessive Asset Inflation: The More Likely Cause of a Failed Reform

In Chapter 3, we explained that even if the Chinese authority managed to keep a gradual appreciation of the renminbi, sustained and rapid asset inflation could still push the rentals, wages and domestic prices to uncompetitive levels and seed the possibility of an economic crisis in the distant future. It also highlights that

(a) it is always better to curb any potential rampant asset inflation era (or asset bubble) at the early stage; and
(b) if an expectation of rampant asset inflation has been formed, much greater curbing measures are needed before the asset inflation can be properly controlled.

167

In fact, despite the relative success of the transitional reform at the early stage, the author had from November 2005 onwards written a series of articles warning the Chinese government that excessive and unchecked asset inflation, instead of exchange rate appreciation, could be the more likely cause of a crisis and hence, an eventual failure of the whole exchange rate system reform in the longer future.[1]

Unfortunately, as was the case in the crisis-hit economies during the more than ten years asset inflation era before the Asian Financial Crisis, the Chinese government had also underestimated the consequences of asset price inertia and expected asset inflation built up at the early stage of an asset inflation era. Down below, we will review the sequence of the events in the form that it can illustrate that the mistakes are in fact avoidable. It is hoped that readers in the future could learn from this history that such type of asset inflation could, and should, be avoided.

## 8.2 The Formation of a Stock Market Bubble in 2006–2007

### 8.2.1 *The Sharp Rise of Share Prices in 2006*

#### 8.2.1.1 *The Seeding Stage of a Bubble: Upward Inertia From a Trough, and Then the Formation of Asset Inflation Expectation*

On 5 June 2006, the author published an article warning that China's stock market could be at the early stage of a huge bubble (the Shanghai Composite Index at that time was still below 1700, see Figure 8.2.1). It first noted that Chinese share prices had accumulated an upward inertia from its trough in mid 2005[2] (e.g., the Shanghai Composite Index at end May 2006

---

[1] The first article was published in the *Hong Kong Economic Journal* on 16 November 2005 and in the *Lianhe Zaobao* on 24 November 2005. This was followed by a series of articles between May 2006 and September 2007.

[2] Before the rebound in 2005–2006, a significant portion of the majority shares held by the "legal entities" were not allowed to be traded in the market. This had created severe incentive problems. For example, controlling executives could not benefit from the improvement of company's performance as they were not allowed to sell the shares even if the price rose with the improved performance. On the other hand, senior executives had the incentive to exploit the company at the cost of the shareholders, thus resulting in quite a number of scandals. After a number of big scandals, the Chinese government had finally decided to

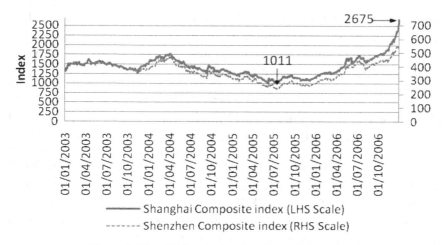

Figure 8.2.1.   2006 as the Seeding Stage of the Bubble

*Source*: Datastream

was 62% higher than its trough in 2005). It then used the experience of the US and Hong Kong to highlight the possibility of a sustained upward inertia, if unchecked, could result in an expectation of asset inflation in the stock market, which could in turn push the share price into an automatic path towards a huge bubble.[3] To stop the formation of such asset inflation expectation in the stock market, the article proposed to use the prosecution of those listed companies with fake accounting reports to

---

introduce a detailed reform that removed the restriction. As the reform would mean a much larger supply of shares in the market, it had resulted in a few years of bear stock market until the trough in mid-2005. The stock market reform did have a significant contribution in redirecting firm managers' effort towards profit maximization of the firm. Nevertheless, as we will see, the rebound plus the related authority's lack of knowledge on the consequence of an established upward inertia had contributed to the formation of a stock market bubble thereafter.

[3] Since the trough arising from the political incidence in China in 4 June 1989, Hong Kong share and property prices had rebounded and accumulated an upward inertia, which had further pushed the asset prices into a bubble path until the bubble burst in late 1997. Similarly, the Dow Jones Industrial Index had accumulated an upward inertia during its rebound from the trough of 1739 in October 1987 to 3169 at end 1991. During the subsequent years, this inertia had in turn pushed the index further up to the peak of 11722 in January 2000 before the index fell to the trough of 7286 in October 2002.

(i) improve the foundation of China's stock market for more healthy developments in the future; and

(ii) contain the rise in share prices and guide the share market to rise along a more gradual and sustainable path.

---

**Box 8.2.1a:   The Risk of a Subsequent Bubble After the Recovery From an Exceptionally Low Trough**

From the author's observation, such as the case of the US and Hong Kong discussed in Footnote 3 or the case of China discussed in this chapter, it is possible that the stock (and property) market could, after recovering from an exceptionally low trough, eventually go into a bubble in the subsequent years. While not every recovery from an exceptionally low through would eventually result in a bubble, the chance of such a outcome is however much greater than most people believe during the recovery stage. This is so because of the upward inertia built up during the recovery could result in an expectation of further rise in asset price (i.e., the seeding stage of the bubble), then changes in economic behaviors and formation of a few vicious cycles (see Section 8.2.1.2 on the development stage of a bubble), and then the formation of herding behaviors (see Section 8.2.1.3 on the final stage of the bubble). In fact, ceteris paribus, the lower the trough the market started from, the stronger the rebound and then the bigger the accumulated upward inertia and the higher the risk of a bubble.

Thus, it is hoped that policy makers and readers of this book could in the future pay special attention to the risk of a subsequent bubble when an asset market recovered from an exceptionally low trough. Bearing in mind that

(i)  it is very difficult to curb the rise in asset price during the development stage of the bubble; and

(ii) curbing the market too early could run the risk of destroying the recovery,

the author would recommend using curbing measures at the later part of the seeding stage of the bubble so as to reduce the upward inertia and guide the expected rise in the asset price to a sustainable rate.

Unfortunately, it was too early for the Chinese government to appreciate the importance of such warning and share the author's early anticipation of a potential stock market bubble. From November 2006 onwards, the upward inertia in share prices had finally resulted in an expectation of further rise in share prices, which had in turn caused sharper rises in share prices thereafter (see Figure 8.2.1).

By end December 2006, the Shanghai Composite index rose to 2675, which was 63% higher than that on end May 2006, and 165% higher than the trough in mid 2005. During a keynote speech in a policy conference organized in Beijing by the State Administration of Foreign Exchange in late December 2006, the author took the opportunity to warn the possibility of a stock market bubble. This had in turn resulted in an internal report in the same authority and three articles published in the *Hong Kong Economic Journal*. The latter was also summarized by a publication of the Xinhua News Agency, China's official news agency.

### 8.2.1.2 *The Development Stage of a Bubble: Changes in Economic Behaviors and Formation of Vicious Cycles*

In these publications, the author urged the Chinese government to curb the rising trend of the stock market. Otherwise, the Shanghai A-Share Index would go beyond the levels of three thousand, four thousand and then five thousand. By then, the only remaining question would be at which point (i.e., five thousand, seven thousand or nine thousand point) the bubble would burst.[4] Besides, the further the index rose, the more would be the pain after the bursting. To convince the Chinese authority of this possibility, the articles first highlighted that the expectation of asset inflation in the stock market was already firmly established by late 2006. Worse still, such expectation was beginning to cause some changes in economic behaviors, which would fuel the share prices further up and push China's stock market

---

[4] As the anticipation was too forward looking for the readers at that time to believe, the statement that the index could go beyond five thousand points were deleted from the above mentioned internal report by the officer in charge. Neither was it included in the Xinhua News Agency's publication. However, it was published in the *Hong Kong Economic Journal*. Whatever, seven months later, the index did rise beyond five thousand points.

into an automatic path towards a huge bubble. For example, more and more individuals and enterprises had started to invest in the stock market. Existing stock market participants had also started to increase their investments in the stock market by increasing their borrowings and/or by using funds originally meant for other purposes.[5] Sooner or later, individuals and enterprises would reduce their desired cash to deposit ratios, while banks would reduce their desired excess reserve to deposit ratios. Both of these would increase the money multiplier which would increase money supply even if there was no change in the monetary base (see the detail explanation in Box 8.2.1b). On top of this, banks would also try to meet the rising domestic demand for loans through overseas borrowings. Worse still, the rise in share (and property) price would, through the change in peoples' economic behaviors, induce more inflows of funds through the illegal channels or the abuse of legal channels. These inflows would tend to cause a substantial rise in the monetary base, and then a multiple expansion of money supply through the higher money multiplier. If the central bank failed to sterilize at least part of the inflows or the rise in money multiplier, the rise in money supply would fuel the rise in share (and property) price.

---

### Box 8.2.1b:  Why Is It Dangerous to Assume a Constant Money Multiplier During a Crisis or Asset Inflation Era?

In the standard textbook, it is usually assumed that the public's desired cash to deposit ratio ($k$) and the banks' desired excess reserve to deposit ratio ($e$) are constant, which implies that the money multiplier ($m$) is constant. While such an assumption is acceptable during the normal time, it is obviously not the case during a crisis or

*(Continued)*

---

[5] As huge amount of individual investors were investing most of their savings originally meant for future housing, marriage, education, retirement and other important purposes, the amount of additional funds was enormous. Nevertheless, the additional funds due to enterprises could be even bigger, where funds were diverted out, legally or illegally, from the working capital, savings and assets of private enterprises and public organizations. Thus, the ongoing injection of these additional funds into the stock market had resulted in persistent surges in the share prices.

**Box 8.2.1b:** (*Continued*)

a severe asset inflation era. This is so because a crisis or severe asset inflation will cause a change in people's economic behaviors. For example, during an asset inflation era, people will have incentives to invest more by economizing their cash or borrowing more, which will in turn cause a reduction in people's desired cash to deposit ratio. Meanwhile, banks will also try to lend more by reducing their desired excess reserve to deposit ratio. As a result, these changes in economic behaviors (i.e., fall in $k$ and $e$) can cause a rise in money multiplier trough a reduction in the leakage of the money creation process. In other words, even if there is no change in the monetary base (MB), a sustained asset inflation can cause a change in economic behaviors (i.e., a fall in $k$ and $e$ and hence a rise in $m$), which can raise the money supply by a substantial amount. Such surge in money supply will in turn fuel the asset inflation and cause further changes in economic behaviors. To see the argument mathematically, first let

$$k = C/D,$$
$$r = R/D,$$
$$e = ER/D,$$

where $k$ is the public's desired cash (C) to deposit (D) ratio, $r$ is the required ratio of bank reserve (R) to deposit, and $e$ is banks' desired excess reserve (ER) to deposit ratio.

Defining the money supply (M) as the sum of deposit and cash held by the public:

$$M \equiv C + D,$$

the monetary base as the sum of cash held by the public and the bank:

$$MB \equiv C + R + ER,$$

and the money multiplier as

$$m \equiv M/MB,$$

(*Continued*)

---

**Box 8.2.1b:**   (*Continued*)

it can be shown that the

$$m = (1 + k)/(k + r + e) \quad \text{or} \quad [1 - (1 - r - e)/(k + r + e)]$$

Thus, a fall in $k$ and/or $e$ will cause a rise in the money multiplier $m$.

So far, we have been assuming that the monetary base (MB) is constant. However, from the experience during the asset inflation era in most Asian economies before the 1997–1998 financial crisis and in China in 2006–2007, the asset inflation could induce (i) banks to borrow overseas; and (ii) speculative funds to flow into the economies. When the central banks fail to sterilize at least part of these inflows, the rise in money multiplier will be multiplied by a substantial rise in monetary base, thus causing an enormous rise in money supply.

While the above discussion focus on the rise in money supply through the rise in $m$ and MB during the asset inflation era, Chapter 11 will explain that an economic crisis or severe recession can also cause a fall in $m$ and MB and hence a severe plunge in money supply, which can significantly deepen the recession if the government fails to offset the impacts of these changes in economic behaviors on money supply.

**Lessons from the above discussion:** One important lesson is that, during a crisis or a sustained asset inflation era, one should not assume a constant money multiplier as there would be changes in economic behaviors. Failure to take into account of these changes in economic behaviors can lead to far from sufficient policies, and the emergence of a far more severe recession or asset inflation.

---

In addition to the above changes in economic behaviors, the articles also pointed out the possibility of a few forthcoming vicious cycles,[6] such as those

(i) between property price inflation and share price hike; and

---

[6] One vicious cycle is between share price hike and property price inflation. For example, rise in share price will increase share investors' demand for housing, while rise in property prices will increase listed property firms' profits, and allow property owners to use

(ii) between the stock market boom and rising consumption and investment, which would fuel the rise in share price.

### 8.2.1.3 *The Final Stage of a Bubble: Herding Behavior*

Finally, the articles highlighted that, along with the surge in share price, herding behavior would gradually develop which would further fuel the stock market towards a huge bubble. Once the herding behavior is established, more and more fund managers will be attracted, or forced by performance pressure, to join the herd by speculating for further rise in share prices, even if some of them are aware of the risk of an eventual bursting. Similarly, banks' chief executives and managers will be attracted, or forced by performance pressure, to increase loans to the stock (and property) market even if some of them are aware that some of the loans are not that secure and the lending boom is not sustainable. Once the stock market has entered the stage with herding behavior, there will be more and more people and funds joining the stock market, and fuel the rise in share price. At this stage, standard curbing measures such as moderate rise in interest rate will not be sufficient to stop the share price from rising. However, when the stock market enters the final stage of the bubble during which close to 100% of the potential participants and funds have already joined the market, the rise in share price will slow down and then stop. At this time, even a very mild change can cause a fall in share price, trigger herding behavior in the downward direction, and cause a reversal of the above changes in economic behaviors until the share price plunges to a level well below the normal equilibrium level.

### 8.2.2 *The Moderate Corrections in Early 2007*

The above warnings had attracted the attention of the Chinese government. From late January 2007 onwards, quite a number of senior Chinese

---

the properties as collaterals to borrow more money from the banks for greater investment in the stock market. Meanwhile, there could be a vicious cycle between the stock market boom and rising consumption and investment through the wealth effect and Tobin's $q$ effect (e.g., the rising share prices will increase individual consumption and firms' investment, which would in turn push the listed companies' profit further up).

officials had come out in an orderly manner to warn Chinese shareholders on the risk of share speculation. These had in turn caused a 10.9% correction in the Shanghai Composite Index (i.e., it fell from 3,097 on 30 January 2007 to 2612 on 5 February 2007).

Nevertheless, in an internal correspondence with a Chinese official and an article published on 2 February 2007, the author warned that this type of stock market boom (with an established upward inertia and expectation) was usually very stubborn. To prevent the stock market from resuming its surge after the moderate correction, the Chinese government should prepare a series of curbing measures so that they could be used one by one in case of an early sign of resumption of the upward momentum, such as a medium or major rebound. Unfortunately, no further curbing measure was planned. As a result, the index rebounded sharply in the next 11 days (i.e., by 14.8% to 2,998 on 16 February 2007, the eve before the long Chinese New Year holiday). After the holiday, the index shot further up to 3,041 in the first working day (i.e., 26 February 2007). However, concerns that there could be further curbing measures during the major national political meetings in March had thereafter caused an 8.4% correction of the index to 2,785 on 5 March 2007. Further to this correction, the author recommended the maintenance of market's perceived risk of further curbing measures so as to keep the index within a range for at least one year. Once

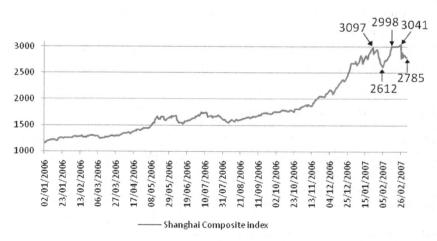

**Figure 8.2.2.** Stock Price Movements in 2007Q1

the upward momentum and the associate expectation were properly halted, the Chinese government could then allow the share prices to rise at the normal and sustainable pace.

### 8.2.3 *The Sharp Rise in March–May 2007*

However, because of reasons only known to the author at a later stage (see the later discussion in this section), the recommendation did not seem to have any effect on the Chinese government. Recognizing that further persuasion along this line would only result in negative consequences, and bearing in mind the need to concentrate effort to persuade the Hong Kong Exchanges to suspend the announced introduction of the renminbi futures market (see Chapter 5 for the detailed discussion),[7] the author had decided to temporarily suspend further persuasion on the stock market intervention until the share price rose to levels that would alarm the State Council to reconsider the risk and harm of an unchecked share price hike. During the above inaction period, the author eventually recognized that a government research institute and some think tanks had submitted reports and recommendations to the State Council stating that it was not easy to have the current stock market boom. The State Council should use this golden opportunity to push for further developments of China's stock market. As shown in Figure 8.2.3, the misleading reports and recommendations had contributed to the extremely sharp rise in the Shanghai Composite Index between 5 March and 29 May in 2007 [i.e., in less than 3 months, it rose by 56%, or 1,550 points, from 2,785 to 4,335, where the average price–earning (PE) ratio was close to 50]. Worse still, huge amount of individual investors were speculating heavily in penny stocks and shares with extremely poor fundamentals, thus resulting in huge bubbles in the latter.

---

[7] With a series of press articles and television interviews as well as letters and personal visits to the related Chinese authorities in Beijing, the Hong Kong Exchanges and the Hong Kong Government between December 2006 and May 2007, the author managed to convince the related authorities that the renminbi futures market could destroy the capital control and hence the exchange rate arrangements at that time. In May 2007, the Hong Kong Exchanges had finally suspended the introduction of the renminbi futures market. Nevertheless, during the lobby, the author had paid heavily in terms of personal health.

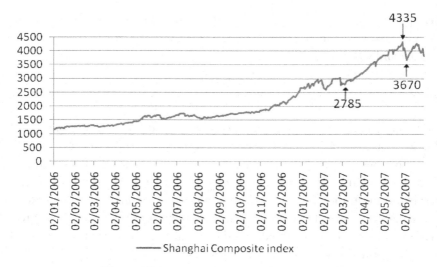

**Figure 8.2.3.**   Stock Price Movements in 2007H1

## 8.2.4 *The Correction in May–June 2007*

In the later stage of the share price hike (i.e., between 22 April and 23 May in 2007), the author judged that it was time to write a series of articles to convince the Chinese government on how misleading the above reports and recommendations were. The articles first noted that the stock market and economic boom as well as the greater amount of funds raised from the stock market were achieved through rises in share prices to higher and higher levels. If share prices continued to rise at such a rampant speed, then a collapse of the stock market would be just a matter of time. By then, China would pay heavily for the mistake. The articles then explained that the net economic losses during the subsequent bust period would be much greater than the net gains during the boom period.

With the rise in share prices seemed to be out of control at the later stage (i.e., huge amount of funds was flowing into the stock market, and share prices continued to rise even if the Chinese central bank raise the interest rate and the bank reserve requirement ratio), there were worries even among government officials that the Chinese government would not be able to contain the share price hike. To remove the worry and clarify the confusion, the second part of the article series explained that theoretically there existed strong enough curbing measures that could stop the share price hike. For example, if the bank reserve requirement ratio, an often used policy instrument in China, was raised to 100%, the money supply would be reduced to the amount of coins and notes issued. By then, there would be insufficient liquidity in the economy. While China would not be so silly to raise the ratio to 100%, the discussion did suggest that there existed a high enough bank reserve requirement ratio that could reverse the situation of excess liquidity (i.e., excess money supply) into a situation of just enough, or a slight shortage of, liquidity. Meanwhile, the Chinese government could always keep the monetary base unchanged by using the additional foreign reserves, whether arising from trade surplus, net FDI inflows or speculative inflows, to back up an equivalent amount of domestic bond issuance by the Ministry of Finance on behalf of the forthcoming China Investment Corporate Limited (CIC). So, the question was not whether the Chinese government could reverse the excess liquidity condition and stop the share price hike or not. Instead, the questions were whether the Chinese government would be willing to stop the hike, and be skillful enough to stop the hike in a not too costly way. Thereafter, the article series proposed a list of effective curbing measures. To search for the right dose of curbing measures and hence achieve a correction at a reasonably low cost, the series also suggested to implement the measures one by one (and bit by bit, if necessary). For more powerful measures such as using a significant part of the foreign reserves to back up the bond issuance by the proposed China Investment Corporation, which would imply a very strong effect at the beginning through anticipation of further changes in the future, the government could separate the initial impacts into two parts by first indicating the intended policy to the market before a formal implementation at the second stage. Thus, the indication of intention would first affect the market through the market's expectation of such a possibility. With the formal implementation at the second stage, the remaining impacts would take place as the expected probability of the policy would by that time rise from less than 1 to 100%.

After meeting with China's central bank governor in an international meeting in late May 2007, China's premier Wan Jiabao finally announced that the Chinese government would be determined, and able, to keep financial stability in China. On 30 May 2007, China's Ministry of

Finance announced a rise in the stock market stamp duty from 0.1% to 0.3%. As stamp duty was traditionally used to curb stock market bubble in China and the rise in stamp duty were historically followed by a significant plunge in China's stock market, the announcement, together with the high and vulnerable share price level at that time, had caused a significant correction of the Shanghai Composite Index. For example, it fell 6.5% from a local peak of 4335 on 29 May 2007 to 4053 on 30 May 2007. Thereafter, it fell another 9.4% to 3670 on 4 June 2007. On 5 June 2007, it plunged to an intra-day trough of around 3200 before it closed at 3767 on the same day. Thereafter, the index was fluctuating around the range of 3700–4200 for the next 7 weeks. While believing that the index was still on the high side, the author had at end May 2007 recommended to reduce the stock market bubble by a few steps, first by keeping the index below the psychological barriers of 4200 with appropriate curbing measures; then push the index further down to the range of 3800–4000 in the month after, and then push the index to the range of 3600–3800 or 3600–4000 in the 1–6 months thereafter. The aims of the 3-step recommendation were (a) to minimize the economic costs of adjustment by avoiding sharp plunges which could affect the normal running of the economy; and (ii) keep the losses and pains of most share investors within bearable levels (see Box 8.2.4).

---

**Box 8.2.4:   A Gradual Correction of Share Price Could Be Less Painful Than a Sharp Plunge of the Same Size**

Unlike the case of a sharp plunge in share price, a gradual correction would allow more shares changing hands during the correction. That is, some over-leveraged share investors would still have the chance to sell their shares before the share price fell below their bearable levels. Thus, a more gradual correction of share price would help keep the losses and pains of more share investors within their bearable levels, although the total monetary loss for all share investors would be the same as the case of a sharp plunge of the same size.

## 8.2.5 *The Surge Since July 2007*

Unfortunately again, because of misleading recommendations by at least two groups of research officials or think tanks, the State Council did not recognize the importance of keeping the psychological barriers,[8] not to mention the need to bring the index down to less risky levels. Meanwhile, the Chinese supervisory body had approved too many mutual funds which were getting extremely popular after the corrections since 30 May 2007.[9]

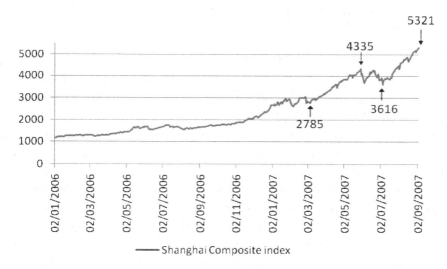

**Figure 8.2.5.** Stock Price Movements in 2007Q3

---

[8] From the news in the media well after the changes, there were some think tanks recommending the government to give up any target on the share index. Another group of officials recommended to keep the stock market boom to allow for more central government enterprises to complete their reform and transformation through IPOs in the stock market. Unfortunately, these recommendations were made without recognizing that (i) the stock market was already at very high and unsustainable levels, and (ii) the stock market could easily resume its dangerous upward momentum.

[9] Before the correction on 30 May 2007, there was a significant portion of individual investors speculating in penny stocks or shares with extremely poor market fundamentals. As the mutual funds were less hurt by the correction due to their focus on blue chips, mutual funds had become very popular thereafter.

Because of these two mistakes, the mutual funds, now with huge amounts of inflows of funds from individual investors, were able to push the index beyond the psychological barriers in an extremely tactful way.[10] As a result, the index shot up from 3616 on 5 July 2007 to 5321 on 3 September 2007 (i.e., by 1705 points, or 47% in less than two months).

## 8.3 The Economic and Political Risks of a Bursting of Asset Bubble: China's Last Chance to Gradually Squeeze the Bubble?

### 8.3.1 *The Risk of Being Kidnapped by the High Share Price*

Upset with the above developments and the potential risk, the author had decided to make his final warning to the Chinese government in early September 2007. In the final warning article,[11] the author first noted that the average PE ratios in the Shanghai and Shenzhen stock markets had already reached 59 and 69, respectively. If share prices continued to rise at the current pace and momentum, the Chinese government would very soon reach the "dead position" (死地) defined in the Chinese military strategy literature. That is, the Chinese government would be "kidnapped" by the very high share price level in the sense that she would no longer dare to implement any curbing measures as this could easily trigger the bursting of the bubble. Even if the government chose to do nothing, a relatively minor shock sometime in the future could be sufficient to trigger the bursting.

---

[10] The mutual funds as a whole had persistently used the following strategy to push the index up from less than 3700 to more than 5300: first pushed the index beyond a whole number barrier (e.g., 3800, 4000, 4200), then took a very brief rest and then pushed the index beyond the next whole number barrier.

[11] The article was directed to the related Chinese authorities through the author's personal communication channels in early September. It was also published in the Hong Kong Economic Journal on 6 September 2007.

---

**Box 8.3.1:   The PE Ratios Could Understate the Stock Market Over-Valuation During the Bubble Period**

Note that during the bubble period, the PE ratio rose less than the rise in share price because of the rise in company earnings. However, as explained in Section 8.4.3, part of the earnings were profits from share and property investment (or revaluation gains), which was less reliable than the core business earnings. Thus, even the high PE ratios of 59 and 69 could have understated the stock market overvaluation at that time.

---

## 8.3.2 *Two Types of Bubble Bursting*

The article then did the following cost and benefit analysis for the Chinese leaders: First, if the Chinese government managed to use sufficient curbing measures to stop the share prices from rising further (or better still, push it lower to less vulnerable levels), China would continue to have a bright prospect of eventually becoming a major world economic power. This would be so even if the curbing measures could result in a fall of GDP growth from the overheated rate of 11.9% to a more sustainable rate of 10% or even a slowdown rate of 9%, simply because 9–10% would still be very high when compared with the world average. By then, the current Chinese leaders would not spoil the trust of the Chinese people and their predecessors including Deng Xiaopeng. On the other hand, if share prices were allowed to rise at the current pace, then a bursting of bubble and a complete destruction of the related leaders' historical status would just be a matter of time. Besides, the more it rose before the bubble burst, the worse the subsequent plunge and economic crisis would be. If the recession were severe enough, it could even trigger political and social turmoil, which would be extremely dangerous for countries like China. As the chance of a bursting of bubble in a particular period will depend on (i) how high the share price level is; and (ii) whether there is a large enough shock to trigger a bursting, nobody can accurately predict when the bursting will occur.

However, what is sure is that, the greater the rise in the share (and property) prices, the greater will be the probability of a bursting. Until the very end, share prices can rise to such a high level that even relatively minor shocks can trigger a collapse.

### 8.3.2.1 *First Type of Bursting: Severe Recession But Not Disastrous Political Instability*

The article then classified the potential bursting into two types. The first type is one in which there is a large enough triggering shock at the early stage. As the cumulated rise in share price before the bursting is still smaller than that of the second type, the bursting will result in only severe economic recession, but not severe political and social instability. Of course, such bursting will still imply enormous economic pains to a huge number of Chinese citizens: In addition to the harms done to hundred millions of share investors and their innocent family members, it will hurt an even greater number of innocent people. For example, many firms may become bankrupt just because they cannot collect the account receivables from those firm owners who follow the stock market speculating herds.[12] Thus, employees of the innocent firms and their family members will also suffer. Even for those firms who are not affected by this, the reduction in aggregate demand arising from the economic recession will still force them to make massive retrenchments. Furthermore, the collapse of the stock market will to certain extent result in a plunge in the already high property price, thus substantially increases the amount of banks' non-performing loans and the number of "property slaves", a very popular nickname in China for those property owners who suffer heavily from the high mortgage repayment burden arising from the high property price. In short, the bursting will affect not only hundred millions of share investors and their family members, but a much greater number of innocent people through direct business and economic relations, indirect multiplier effects and domino effects, such as the triggering of a collapse in property prices, the

---

[12] Note, this had to some extent happened in some crisis-hit economies during the Asian Financial Crisis in 1997–1998.

weakening of the banks' ability and incentive[13] to finance firms' normal business, and etc. With such deep and extensive damages, the related Chinese leader's reputation and historical status will be completely destroyed.

### 8.3.2.2 *Second Type of Bursting: Disastrous Political Instability*

However, perhaps the most disastrous outcome is the second type of bursting in which the bubble has the chance to grow into a huge one before the bursting. In this case, the economic damages would be large enough to cause the resignation of the premier and severely weaken the central government's authority of ruling. By then, there could be struggles for political power among factions within the Communist Party, thus resulting in political instability or even military confrontation. Meanwhile, the severe economic recession could also trigger Chinese peoples' suppressed hatred against corruption, the high degree of income inequality and other unreasonable phenomena, which could result in further social instability or turmoil. If other competing countries at that time try to systematically support the unrest and fuel the conflicts, it is possible for China to be split into a few parts. By then, China would be dragged into endless political and social instability. Economic stability would then be a luxury, not to mention the prospect of developing into a major world economic power.

To convince the Chinese leaders that the chance of the above two outcomes was not as slim as it first appeared, the article quoted the experience of the Asian Financial Crisis during which the political leaders and central bank governors in Indonesia, Thailand and Korea had all lost their power in the crisis or post-crisis periods. Finally, the article warned that, with the share prices already at the vulnerably high levels, the skill required to achieve a soft-landing would be extremely high (i.e., it required fairly accurate choice in the types, doses, sequencing and timing of the curbing measures). Even a moderate misjudgment of the

---

[13] Because of the adverse selection and moral hazard problems have become more severe (e.g., much greater risk and difficulty in identifying the right borrowers and monitoring their behavior), the already hurt banks during that time will usually choose to close their umbrella (i.e., not lending or lending a much smaller amount whenever in doubt).

situation or the extent of the problem could be sufficient to result in either failure to stop the bubble or extremely costly plunges in share prices. For example, it is possible for the authority to underestimate (a) the market's resistance to the curbing measures when share prices are rising; and (b) the market's fragility to the cumulated curbing effect when share prices are starting to correct.

### 8.3.3 *The Curbing Measures Engineered by the Party Leader*

Soon after the submission of the warning article to the Chinese leaders through the Xinhua News Agency, the People's Bank of China, the State Administration of Foreign exchange, the Ministry of Finance, the China Securities Regulatory Commission and other related government bodies had announced a series of curbing measures. These measures included further rises in interest rates and the bank reserve requirement ratio, the Ministry of Finance's issuance of special government bonds on behalf of the newly set up China Investment Corporate Limited (i.e., to offset part of the monetary growth pressure arising from the trade surplus, net FDI inflows and speculative inflows), the extension of the QDII scheme to allow for overseas share investment by Chinese residents through funds managed by qualified brokerage firms or investment banks (i.e., to encourage controllable outflows to offset part of the inflows), a temporary suspension in the approvals of new mutual funds for domestic share investment, and the speeding up of IPOs by Hong Kong listed Chinese enterprises in China's A-share market (i.e., to increase the supply of shares so as to absorb part of the excess liquidity in the share market and to pull down the average PE ratio in China's A-share market).[14] Thereafter, the Central Propaganda

---

[14] In addition to the above measures, the basic infrastructure of the stock futures market was also made ready for the final approval by the top leaders. Without the stock futures market, share investment in China had been skewed to the purchase of shares in the upward direction as there was no major facility for share investors to bet for a fall in share price. The establishment of the stock futures market would allow share investors to bet for either a rise or fall in share price. Nevertheless, the author published two articles highlighting that the timing of such set up and the choice of a low gearing ratio at the initial

Department had published an article warning the risk of share investment, suggesting that the party leader instead of just the State Council could then be in charge of the problem. Yet, because of the established upward inertia and expectation, and more importantly, the resistance of the mutual funds,[15] the Shanghai Composite Index made only a minor correction before it surged to the peak of 6092 on 16 October 2007, with an average PE ratio of 71.

Nevertheless, with persistent waves of curbing measures made by the Chinese government, further corrections in the global market and some fund managers' gradual awareness of the risk of the unsustainably high share price level, the Shanghai Composite index started to correct and reached 5,270 on 19 November 2007.

---

stage would be important. Otherwise, it could cause more problems than benefits. For example, with a vulnerably high share price level, some major fund managers could profit a lot with the following strategy: (i) first quietly build up a huge short position in the stock future market and accumulate huge amount of index component shares in the spot market at the normal price; and (ii) then trigger a panic sales of shares by shorting in the futures market and dumping shares in the spot market in a high profile. When the share prices plunge to low enough levels, they could profit the gains by buying back shares in the spot market and unwinding their short position in the futures market. Thus, a wrong timing in the establishment of the stock futures market could be an event that triggered the bursting of China's stock market bubble. To avoid this and to provide Chinese share investors a facility to hedge or bet for a fall in share price, the author highlighted that it would be better to start with an initial low gearing ratio of no more than 4 times (preferably 2 times). An initially low gearing ratio would also allow China to identify problems and correct mistakes at the early stage. For example, with a high gearing ratio, individual investors may easily get bankrupt if they underestimate the risk of, or become addicted to, gambling in the stock futures market. With a low gearing ratio at the initial stage, some of them may have a chance to learn from a painful, but not yet fatal, mistake. When everything is going well, the Chinese authority can then gradually raise the gearing ratio to higher levels. After the publications of the articles, the Chinese government had opted for a postponed establishment of the stock futures market (until 3 years later) instead of an adoption of a lower gearing ratio.

[15] A survey among the fund managers suggested that 80% of the fund managers at that time believed that Chinese share prices were over-valued. However, because of the influx of money into the funds and absence of any major short selling facilities and performance pressure, many fund managers had no choice but to keep on bidding up share prices.

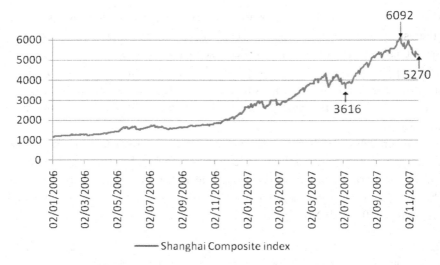

**Figure 8.3.3.** Stock Price Movements in 2007Q4

## 8.4 The Gradual Bubble Squeezing Strategy

### 8.4.1 *Early 2008: Low Risk of Second Type of Bubble Bursting, But Still High Risk of First Type of Bursting*

In a follow-up proposal on the same day, the author first noted that the Chinese government curbing measures were necessary. Otherwise, the Shanghai Composite Index could have surged beyond the 7000, 8000 or even 10000 points. By then, the Chinese government would be kidnapped by the high share price, and the second type of bubble bursting would be just a matter of time (i.e., the irrecoverable political and social chaos triggered by the bursting of the enormous bubble and subsequent depression). However, with the curbing measures and then the correction of the stock index to the less over-valued level of 5270, the risk of the disastrous second type bubble bursting had greatly diminished. After expressing his thanks to the Chinese top leaders and the related government bodies on their correct decision and effort at that very crucial moment, the article stressed that there remained the risk of the first type of bubble bursting. For example, it remained highly likely that the Shanghai Composite Index could fall by more than 50% from the 5270 point at that time, which could still trigger an economic recession. Although the severity of the recession might not be sufficient to permanently stop China from coming back to normal economic development, it could still be sufficient to cause the resignation of some top leaders responsible for macroeconomic management as well as severe economic pains to the huge population.

### 8.4.2 The Strategy: Squeeze Only Part of the Bubble

To avoid such a possibility, the article recommended the Chinese government to squeeze another part of the bubble by taking advantage of the downward trend in the global and domestic market at that time. With such squeezing before the soon arriving global recession (see Chapter 11 for more details), the momentum of the subsequent and unavoidable correction of stock prices could be mitigated to a more manageable level. This could then mitigate the severity of the soon arriving domestic recession, thus help avoiding the top economic leaders from being challenged for not clearing at least part of the bubble before the recession. On the other hand, it is also important not to squeeze the whole bubble. Otherwise, it would immediately lead to the above undesirable result.

### 8.4.3 Stock Price in Early 2008 Was Still Substantially Over-Valued

After spelling out the above strategic direction of gradual bubble squeezing, the article proceeded to explain why China's stock prices at that time were still over-valued and could fall by more than 50% in the forthcoming future. It first noted that the average PE ratios for the listed companies in the Shenzhen and Shanghai stock markets were still 58 and 62 times, respectively. Even if one assumed a rather optimistic profit growth for the listed companies, the PE ratios would still be very high in the next two years. Moreover, it should be noted that a significant portion of the very high profits registered in the previous year was due to *unsustainable non-core business investment profits* (e.g., speculative profits from investments in the stock market and property market, revaluation gains due to the stock and property holdings amid the stock market bubble and rampant property inflation at that time). If we take this into account, the degree of over-valuation could be much higher than that suggested by the above PE ratios.

In addition, *the core business profits could fluctuate substantially with business cycle.* For example, once the economy contracted from the over-heated mode to the soon arriving recession mode, a 10–20% reduction in sales could cause a more than 50% reduction in profit or even turn the profit into a loss (see Box 8.4.3a for the implications of the above discussion on share investments).

---

**Box 8.4.3a:   Firms' Profit Will Exhibit Bigger Cycles Than Sales and GDP: Its Implications on Share Investments**

Combining the above discussions on

(i)  the non-core business earnings (i.e., investment profits and reval-uation gains); and

(ii)  the core business earnings (i.e., the earnings would fluctuate more than sales because of the existence of a relatively large fixed cost in most firms),

firm's reported profit would swing substantially between the trough and the peak of business cycles. This would in turn mean that share prices would exhibit much bigger cycles than sales and GDP. For share investors, this would mean that it could be highly profitable to buy shares during the recession and only start selling the shares when the economy is at the later phase of the upswing (see more discussions in Box 8.4.3c).

---

Thus, once we take into account of the above impacts of business cycle, the actual extent of over-valuation during the normal or downturn phase will be even higher.

Worse still, according to the *asset price overshooting and over-adjusting phenomena* discussed in Box 8.4.3b, once the stock price plunges from an over-valued level, it will fall well beyond the normal equilibrium value before it gradually adjusts back to the equilibrium level in the long run.

Furthermore, herding behaviors (discussed in Section 8.2.1.3) will increase the magnitude of the swings, thus making the plunge or over-correction more severe.

Thus, with the above conceptual discussion, it became apparent why it could be likely that China's stock price could fall more than 50% from the level at that time.

---

**Box 8.4.3b:   The Possibility of Over-Adjustment and Herding Behaviors in Asset Price Movements**

In Box 8.4.3a, I have explained that firms' profits, and hence share prices, would exhibit bigger cycles than sales and GDP. On top of this, the literature on asset price overshooting also suggests that asset price, such as exchange rate and share price, could rise or fall beyond the long run equilibrium path. For example, if exchange rate or share price adjusts faster than the general price level or wage, an unanticipated change in the monetary policy or the money market environment could result in a rise or fall in the asset price beyond the new long run equilibrium.

In addition to the difference in adjustment between the asset price and other variables, there could also be other factors that contributed to the over-adjustment of asset price. For example, a crisis such as the global financial tsunami or the Asian Financial Crisis could force a lot of share investors into a liquidity-constrained position, thus resulting in lack of effective demand even when the share price fell to a substantially under-valued and attractive level. On the other hand, boom in the asset market could induce market participants to increase their financial leverages beyond their usual norms. This could also temporarily push the asset price well beyond the long run equilibrium path.

Finally, development of the vicious cycles discussed in Section 8.2.1.2 and the herding behaviors discussed in Section 8.2.1.3 could also push the asset price well beyond the long run equilibrium path.

**Box 8.4.3c:    An Interesting Share Investment Strategy**

From the discussions in Box 8.4.3a and 8.4.3b, one important implication for share investors is that it could be highly profitable to buy
shares during the recession and only start selling the shares when
the economy is at the later phase of the upswing. In fact, this is the
strategy that the author has been using: buy when the economy is
weak and hold it until the economy is overheated. For example, after
accumulating enough Singapore and Hong Kong shares during the
low period in 2004–2005, the author had been holding the same
amount of shares until 2007. During that period, what he did was
just switching shares (i.e., from the leading shares to the lagging
shares). By 2007H2, the author was convinced that the US sub-prime
crisis would eventually cause a recession in Asia (see Chapter 11
for the rationales), he therefore made the bode, or more correctly
the prudent, decision of selling all his shares, which had in
turn saved him the necessary money to buy shares at extremely
attractive prices in November 2008 and March–April 2009.[16]

*(Continued)*

---

[16] After the sharp plunge in November 2008, there was an "Obama rally" in early 2009.
However, the economic and market environment was so bad that the author believed the rally
could only be short-lived. He therefore sold half of the shares purchased in November 2008,
which had in turn allowed him to purchase more shares during the plunge in March 2009.
Nevertheless, with the policies announced by the Federal Reserve and the US Treasury in
March–April 2009 (e.g., a relaxation of the mark-to-market rule, further quantity easing,
requesting the banks to raise more capital while preparing the stress tests on banks so as to
raise the market confidence on banks), the author was convinced that things could stabilize.
He therefore used his remaining money to buy more shares during the early stage of the
rebound (i.e., mainly in March–April 2009 with the last few batches of purchase left to
May–June 2009 for the sake of greater certainty and safety). Since then, despite substantial
rebound of share prices in subsequent months, he still sticked with the strategy outlined in
Box 8.3.4c, i.e., only do swapping of shares from the leading shares to the lagging shares,
while keeping the substantial holdings of shares until the global economy enter the phase of
overheating (say, 3–5 years from 2009). The above discussion also suggests that ability to
identify whether the economy is in the recession or overheating phase is important to the
strategy. Nevertheless, for most readers of this book, they should have the required ability
although it may not be as good as what the author had acquired over the past thirty years.

---

**Box 8.4.3c:**   (*Continued*)

With the additional ability to pick the right shares at the right time, the return to such a strategy was just enormous.

Another interesting observation from the author's experience is that property shares in Asia could be one of the ideal shares for such a strategy, mainly because

(i)   the relatively high fixed cost in estate development (see Chapter 9 for more detailed discussions);

(ii)   the accounting requirement for listed firms implies that the property development firms have to incorporate the change in valuation of their large holdings of land and (commercial) properties into the profit and loss account; and

(iii)   most property firms in Asia have a certain leverage in their estate development, thus making their profit and hence share price more sensitive to the business cycle.

---

### 8.4.4 *The Danger of Selective Listening and Unrealistic Trusting-To-Luck*

In fact, the author was not the only one with the above views. There was an outstanding minority of stock market strategists or economists in China warning the possibility of about 50% plunge in China's stock index. When the Shanghai Composite Index was around 4,000 points, Alan Greenspan, the former Federal Reserve Chairman in the US, and Li Ka Shing, the richest tycoon in Hong Kong, had already warned that the Chinese stock market was substantially over-valued. Warren Buffett, the well-respected share investor in the US, had also used a very polite tone to say that he could not at that time find any "cheap and investable" share in China. With the extensive and valuable experiences of these heavy-weight people and the above systematic and insightful analysis made by the author, it should be obvious to the Chinese political leaders that the stock market at that time was substantially over-valued.

In the article, the author also highlighted that Greenspan and many other heavy-weight people had more than one time warned about the severity of the US sub-prime problem (see Chapter 11 for details).

Unfortunately, the stock market is a market with quite a large number of greedy participants who do not have the patience, or long enough time horizon, to stay out of the market until the problem is over. As a result, many of them chose to select what they wanted to listen and unrealistically believed that there might not be a recession.

To caution people about this unrealistic hope, the author had bluntly stressed that, barring any unforeseen big shocks, the US economic slowdown or recession would definitely come. In addition, it would definitely affect China's and Asia's exports. The only questions remained were (a) how severe would the soon arriving global recession be; and (b) how long would it take to affect the Chinese and Asian economies. In the past and its subsequent near future, the market had given, and would still be giving, market participants a lot of chance to escape. Of course, the problem was many market participants' selectively listening and unrealistic trusting-to-luck.[17]

For stock investors, unrealistic trusting-to-luck would mean heavy loss to their investments. For policy makers, unrealistic trusting-to-luck could mean the end of their careers and political future.[18]

---

[17] Similarly, for the case of the global stock market, there were already sufficient signs in 2007H2 or even 2007H1 that share investors should be cautious about the subsequent developments of the US sub-prime crisis and hence the global economy as well as the potential plunge in share prices. For example, in February, March and May 2007, Alan Greenspan had come out a few times to use a moderate tone to warn on the US sub-prime crisis and the risk of a US recession (see Chapter 10 for more detailed discussions). The market did fall immediate after some of his comments. However, as the stock markets were dominated by trading activities with short time horizons, bargain hunting activities were able to cause a sharp rebound just a day after the corrections. At that time, if a share investor took a medium- (or long-) term view such as the author, he would have quite a few good chances to escape from the subsequent disaster. Even if he sold the shares during the corrections in early 2008 and stopped buying the shares back, he could still be able to avoid the subsequent disaster. [Of course, if everyone left the market at that time, the market would start the plunge without any rebound at that time. So, the discussion would only be useful to individual investors when most of the market participants fail to anticipate the need to escape.]

[18] In fact, such unrealistic trusting-to-luck occurred not only in China's stock market. For example, in 2007Q2-Q3, despite the overheated GDP growth of over 11%, excessive M2 growth of about 18%, rampant rise in asset price and early signs of a higher and rising CPI inflation since April 2007, many people and even economists were still believing in, or hoping for, no significant rise in general price inflation in the subsequent quarters.

### 8.4.5 *The Need to Squeeze Another Part of the Bubble*

Having explained the importance to squeeze another part of the bubble before the soon arriving global recession, the article recommended the Chinese government to continue the previous curbing measures, with the possibility of varying the strength of the measures with changing market and economic conditions. The government should allow the concurrent and subsequent global stock market correction and the domestic anti-inflation measures at that time to work for an orderly correction of the Chinese stock market. Such arrangement of *"letting (and monitoring) the market force to work"* will save the government from the political trouble of being challenged to be the one triggering the correction of the stock market. Meanwhile, the Chinese government should temporarily suspend the approval of new mutual funds for shares. Such suspension of funds would help avoid further influx of funds into the stock market. The short-term

---

**Box 8.4.5: Suspension of the Straight Through Train to Hong Kong Stock Market**

In that article, the author had also recommended the Chinese government to suspend (i.e., not just delay) the proposed plan of "Straight Through Train to Hong Kong Stock Market", which would allow Chinese residents to buy and sell Hong Kong shares freely. This was necessary because the Straight Through Train would destroy the capital control in China. In addition, given that (i) the global stock market would make deeper corrections; (ii) Chinese investors' psychology was distorted by the bubble; and (iii) individual investors lack the experience and exposure to the Hong Kong stock market, the Straight Through Train could result in heavy losses to the Chinese investors during the soon arriving correction of the global stock market. Even if situation could be better in the more distant future, it might still be better to allow Chinese share investors to invest in Hong Kong shares through the QDII scheme, with which the Chinese government could still control the amount of capital outflows through changes in the permitted amount of QDII investment in each year.

target was to bring the Shanghai Composite Index below the 5000 point, say, to the range of 4500–5000 in the first phase, and then to the range of 4000–4500 in the second phase. If the stock index fell too quickly, the government should use some light measures to softly support the stock market so as to ensure a soft landing. Once the index reached the second phase target or level lower than that, even though the bubble was not entirely squeezed and the share prices remained substantially over-valued, the harm of subsequent corrections during the soon arriving global and domestic recession could be contained to a more bearable level by reversing some of the earlier curbing measures (e.g., gradually bought back some of the government bonds, reduced the required reserve requirement ratio for banks, and cut domestic interest rates).

## 8.5 The Correction in 2008: From Bubble Squeezing to Avoidance of Over-Correction

### 8.5.1 *Further Corrections in 2008Q1 to a Less Vulnerable Level*

With further deterioration of the external economic environment arising from the sub-prime crisis in the US, greater monetary austerity measures

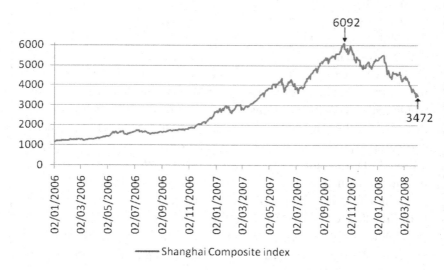

**Figure 8.5.1.** Corrections in Late 2007 & 2008 Q1

arising from rising domestic inflation, market's gradual realization of the over-valuation of Chinese shares, anticipation of weaker domestic economy and other bad news, the Shanghai Composite Index started to make further corrections in early 2008. For example, by end February-2008, the index fell to a less over-valued level of 4348. With the sharp plunge in the US and global stock market in March 2008, the index fell further to a less vulnerable level of 3,472 by 31 March 2008.

### 8.5.2 *The Shift from Bubble Squeezing to Avoidance of Over-Correction*

Nevertheless, with further deterioration of the US property market, the global asset market and then the global economy, it became apparent in 2008Q2 that the Shanghai Composite Index would probably over-correct and fall beyond the 2000 point support. Thus, the mission of the Chinese government at that time had gradually changed from facilitating the correction of the stock market to reducing the over-correction of the share price index.

In fact, in the much earlier policy articles published in February and March 2008, the author had started to explain the reasons for, and discuss the plan of, using various policies to reduce the stock market over-correction during the soon arriving recession. For example, in the policy article published on 6 February 2008, the author had warned that China's export would be severely affected by the soon arriving global recession (see the detailed discussions in Chapter 11). While the article agreed to keep the tight control on money supply and credit growth until the high and rising CPI inflation at that time started to fall to more reasonable levels, it also explained that it would be a better move for China to start following the interest rate cuts in the US. In addition to the reasons listed in Box 11.1b, the sequence of interest rate cuts could reduce the downward momentum and the extent of over-correction during the recession period. The article also recommended the Chinese government to get herself ready to use huge fiscal expansion and to relax the tight monetary policy when China's export and domestic economy started to be weaken by the soon arriving global recession (see the detailed discussion in Chapter 11).

In the two articles published on 18–19 March 2008, the author further explained that the US property market would continue to fall and the US recession will be far more severe than most of the forecasts at that time. The articles also re-iterated that China's export, domestic economy and stock market would be severely affected. In view of the time lags involved in fiscal and monetary expansions, the articles suggested that the Chinese government should start raising the scale of its fiscal expansion (e.g., further increase the construction of public housing, start the construction of the high speed railway between Beijing and Shanghai, and start the infrastructural part of the medical reform and other infrastructural investments such as new underground lines in major cities). It also urged the Chinese government to start reducing the interest rate so as to mitigate the downward momentum of share price in the subsequent months. On the other hand, the Chinese government should reserve the stamp duty reduction and the more powerful policy of quantity easing of money supply for subsequent support of the stock market (see the rationales in Box 8.5.2).

---

**Box 8.5.2:   Effect of Changes in Stamp Duty on the Share Prices in China**

As stamp duty reduction (or increment) would only affect the transaction cost but not the intrinsic value of shares, a change in the stamp duty would in the normal circumstance have little effect on the long term value of shares. However, as stamp duty increments in China had traditional been followed by sharp corrections of the stock market, stamp duty changes could be a powerful policy weapon simply because most market participants believed that it would affect the share price level. Nevertheless, as the impact was mainly through market expectation but not the long-term intrinsic value of shares, it would be better to keep the policy weapon until the last stage, i.e., when it became clear that there would not be any forthcoming events that could cause a substantial reversal of share price to the downward direction. That is, if the authority used the policy at the right time so that the share price would not fall again, the policy would help

*(Continued)*

> **Box 8.5.2:**   (*Continued*)
>
> reducing the over-correction of share prices, and market participants would continue to believe that stamp duty change is a powerful policy on the share price. However, if the authority used the policy too early so that some subsequent events caused a reversal of share price back to the downward direction, the stamp duty reduction could at most cause a temporary rebound of share price and would not be able to help reducing the over-correction of share price. In such a scenario, future reduction in stamp duty might no longer be as powerful a policy as it was in the past.

Unfortunately, because of (i) the difference in views about of the severity of the soon arriving global recession; and (ii) concerns on the high CPI inflation at that time, the then Governor of the People's Bank of China did not agree to reduce the interest rate at that time (see Box 11.1b for more details). As a result, the Shanghai Composite Index continued to fall at a rapid pace (see Figure 8.5.2).

By 18 April 2008, the index was only 95 points above the major psychological barrier of 3,000 points. In an attempt to stop the index from falling further, the Ministry of Finance announced a reduction of share transaction stamp duty from 0.3% to 0.1%. However, because of (a) the reasons outlined in Box 8.5.2; (b) the downward inertia of share price was already established; and (c) concerns about further deterioration of the domestic and global economy, the stamp duty reduction could only caused a temporary spike of the share price index from 3,095 on 18 April 2008 to 3,761 on 5 May 2008 (see Figure 8.5.2). Thereafter, the index softened back to 3,300 on 6 June 2008, and was just waiting for another excuse to continue the correction.

Meanwhile, the higher Chinese-US interest rate differential at that time had caused a reasonably large speculative inflows and hence a speeding up of the M2 growth to 18% in May 2008 (see Chapter 11 for more details). On 7 June 2008, when the People's Bank of China announced another one percentage point rise in the banks' reserve requirement ratio just before the release of the money supply statistics, the announcement triggered a 7.7% correction of the index on the next working day (10 June

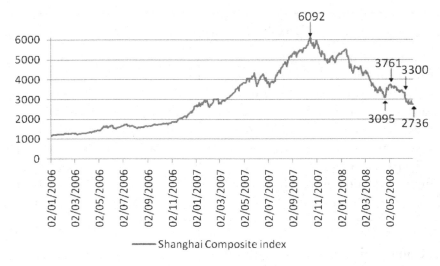

**Figure 8.5.2.**   Further Corrections in 2008Q2

2008) to 3,072. Thereafter, the index broke the 3,000 psychological barrier on 12 June 2008 and reached 2,736 by the end of June 2008.

### 8.5.3 *The Global Recession and Further Plunges in Share Price in 2008H2*

By then, it became apparent to the author that the degree of stock market over-correction would be severe. In response to that, the author had written two policy articles on 23–24 June 2008, to urge the Chinese government to start making drastic cut in interest rates (see Section 11.1 and Box 11.1b on the February 2008 proposal to follow the interest rate cuts in the US), while keeping the monetary growth target amid the high inflation at that time.

Nevertheless, the Chinese central bank did not follow the interest rate cuts in the US until further deterioration of the economic environment prompted the higher authority to urge the central bank to start relatively minor interest rate cuts from September 2008. Meanwhile, the global economy continued to deteriorate. By the end of September 2008, the Shanghai Composite Index fell to a possibly undervalued level of 2,293. During the

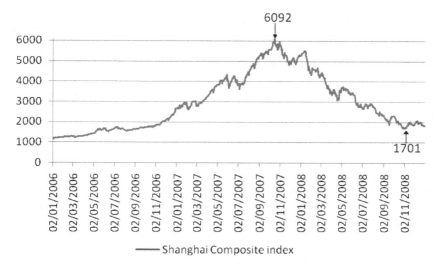

**Figure 8.5.3.** Over-Corrections in 2008H2

global financial tsunami triggered by the collapse of some major US financial institutions, the Shanghai Composite Index fell with the deep plunge of the global stock market. On 4 November 2008, the index fell to the low and obviously undervalued level of 1701 (see Figure 8.5.3).

### 8.5.4 *The Stabilization and Then Gradual Recovery of the Stock Market Since November 2008*

Fortunately, with the adoption of the author's proposal of ultra fiscal expansion by the Chinese government from November 2008 (see the details in Chapter 11), the Chinese stock market started to stabilize and then rebounded from the low. With further reduction in domestic interest rates by the Chinese central bank from December 2008, substantial quantity easing in domestic money supply and credit in early 2009 and rebound of the global stock market from March 2009 (see Chapter 11 for more details), the Shanghai Composite Index recovered further. By 4 May 2009, it recovered above 2,500 and then hovered around the range of 2,500–3,500 during the subsequent year.

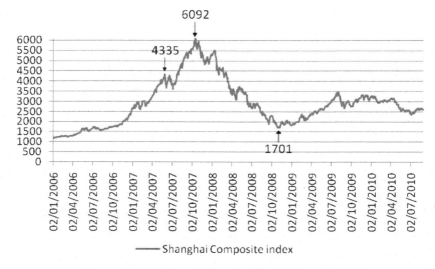

Figure 8.5.4.   Rebound from the Low in November 2008

# Chapter 9

# China's Property Inflation I: Root Causes and Consequences

In this chapter, I will discuss property inflation as a recent phenomenon in China. The substantial surge in property price in recent years had caused enormous economic pains to the low to middle-high income earners and had aggravated income inequality in China. Furthermore, if continued to be unchecked, sustained property inflation could pull up rentals and then wage and CPI, which could make the Chinese economy vulnerable to a plunge in property price and then a crisis similar to that in the US in 2007–2009 and the Asian Financial Crisis in 1997–1998.

In Sections 9.3 and 9.4, I will also explain that sustained rampant property inflation could pull up rentals, wage and general price. Once an upward spiral between excessive rise in property price, wage and costs of livings is established, it could pull China's wage and price from the currently competitive level to highly uncompetitive levels (see Section 9.4 on how the 1986–1997 property inflation in Hong Kong has pulled the economy from a very competitive one to a very expensive one, and how Hong Kong is now locked in the vicious cycle of high property price, high costs of livings and high wage).

Given the above microeconomic pains, macroeconomic costs and systemic risk of high property price, understanding the root causes of excessive property inflation in China and finding the appropriate solution are of utmost importance to the welfare of Chinese citizens and the vision of China to develop as a major economic power in the world. In this chapter, I will discuss the root causes behind, and the severe consequences of, China's property inflation in recent years. In the next chapter, I will recommend a viable solution to the problem. Before doing so, let us first have a look of the movements of property price in China in recent years.

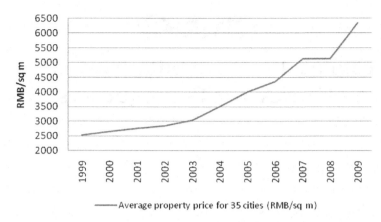

**Figure 9.1a.**   Annual Property Price for 35 Cities

*Source*: CEIC.

## 9.1 Movements of Property Price in Recent Years: The Rapid Rise Since 2004

As shown in Figure 9.1a, average property price for the 35 major cities were rising at a more gradual pace of 4.7% per annum between 1999 and 2003. However, it started to rise at a faster pace of 14% per annum between 2003 and 2007. With

(a)  the plunge in China stock price index (e.g., Shanghai Composite Index fell from the peak of 6092 on 16 Oct 2007 to the low of 1706 on 4 Nov 2008);

(b)  the government's tightening of monetary policy and curbing measures on the property market in 2007Q4; and

(c)  further deterioration of the US sub-prime crisis into a global financial tsunami,

there was a moderate consolidation in China's property market between October 2007 and January 2009, mainly in terms of low transaction volume and only very minor correction in property price (see Figure 9.1b).[1]

---

[1] There were in fact corrections of property price in major cities from the "high level" to "less high level" (see Figure 9.1c for the case of Beijing). However, these were offset by the rise in the second line cities, thus resulting in a virtually flat average for the 35 cities.

**Figure 9.1b.** Monthly Property Price for 35 Cities

*Source*: CEIC.

Nevertheless, with the government's relaxation of monetary policy since February 2009 (i.e., huge increase in bank loans and money supply) to combat the impact of the global recession on the Chinese economy, China's property price started to shoot up again. By July 2010, average property price for 35 major cities in China had reached 8680 RMB/m$^2$, 45% higher than the local minimum in January 2009.

The situation in major cities was even more severe. For example, as shown in Figure 9.1c, the average price in Beijing has reached 25,737 RMB/m$^2$ by June 2010.

Such property price will be unaffordable not only to the low or middle income earners, but also to the middle-high income earners. For example, consider a middle-high income urban family at that time with a monthly income of 12,000 RMBs. If the family bought a 90 m$^2$ flat at the price of 1.8 million RMBs with a 20% down payment and a mortgage loan of 1.44 million RMBs at a mortgage rate of 5–6% for 20 years, the monthly mortgage installment would be 9504–10318 RMBs. That is, the family would have to squeeze 79–86% of its monthly income for the mortgage installment, and the remaining 1682–2496 RMBs per month would not be sufficient to cover the family's normal living expenses.

Source: CEIC.

**Figure 9.1c.** Property Price in Beijing

## 9.2 Microeconomic Reasons: Why It Could Be Disastrous to Let "Free" Market Force to Guide China's Property Market

In view of the potential systemic risk and the economic pains to Chinese residents, the author had written five series of articles on the severe consequences and the root causes of China's property inflation.[2] The first series was on the need to curb property inflation before the formation of property inflation expectation. Once such expectation is established, there will be some important changes in economic behaviors, which will fuel the rise in property price and make it much harder, or almost impossible, for the government to contain the property inflation. The second to fifth series then focused on the root causes, the consequences and then the solution of the housing problem in China. It first explained that, because of the existing imperfect settings in China's property market and income distribution, it

---

[2] The five series of articles were summarized by the Xinhua News Agency as internal reports to the Chinese government. They were also published in the *Hong Kong Economic Journal* between 12 May 2006 and 22 May 2006, between 10 October 2006 and 6 November 2006, between 24 December 2007 and 5 January 2008, between 2 March 2010 and 16 March 2010, and between 17 July 2010 and 24 August 2010 respectively.

could be disastrous to just rely on free market force to do the main allocation and coordination job in China's property market. Thereafter, the article series recommended the appropriate solution to the problem.

In this section and the next section, I will first elaborate the microeconomic reasons (this section) and the macroeconomic reasons (next section) on why it could be disastrous to rely only on "free" market force to guide China's property market under the imperfect settings.

In China, the simple supply and demand analysis, such as that shown in Diagram 9.2.4, is usually used to analyze China's property market and impacts of related policies. In this section, I will explain why it could be misleading to use the supply and demand analysis to evaluate, and make recommendations on, housing policies in China.

### 9.2.1 *High Income Inequality*

Firstly, one important implicit assumption of the supply and demand analysis is a relatively equal distribution of income. As documented in standard microeconomic textbooks, it means that for those who really need or want a particular goods or services, they will be willing to pay a higher price, and hence be allocated with that goods or services at the cost of less budget for other goods and services. In other words, when the income distribution is relatively equal, people's "needs" or preferences will play a dominant role in the allocation of such goods and services.

Nevertheless, as current income distribution in China is highly unequal (e.g., with a Gini coefficient of 0.468 in 2008, much higher than the world average), those who are willing to pay a higher price for a flat are not necessarily those who "need" the flat (e.g., the general public), but those who are "rich" enough to pay for the flat (e.g., the rich people or the speculators in China, or foreign buyers with much higher income than Chinese citizens). As a result, the very limited supply of housing would eventually be allocated to those who are "rich", but not those who "need" the flats. In fact, it is not uncommon that some speculators or rich people in China own more than ten or even tens of properties. In short, because of *severe income inequality* among Chinese residents as well as between foreign buyers and local Chinese, just relying on "free" market force to allocate housings in China could lead to highly undesirable result.

## 9.2.2  *Huge Barriers of Entry*

The second problem is that supply and demand analysis assumes no barrier of entries. The reality is that not every individuals or small enterprises in China could buy a piece of land and build their own houses at a reasonable cost (see Box 9.2.2 for its difference with the western world). This is because the scarcity of land has dictated the building of high rise apartments instead of 2–3 storey houses in the cities in China, and there is an economy of scale in building these high rise apartments. In addition, property development in China involves a very **high fixed development cost** such as the fixed cost in connecting the public water supply, electricity supply and sewage drainage as well as providing common areas, facilities, lifts and security for residents in the whole estate. As a result, estate development in China has to reach a certain scale (i.e., number of flats) before it is economically viable or cost effective. Such barrier of scale could only be overcome by property developers with sufficient financial strength, but not individuals or small enterprises from other industries.

---

**Box 9.2.2:   An Important Difference Between the Property Market in the Asian Cities and That in the Western World**

Unlike the case in the US or other Western countries such as Australia where there are a lot of builders building 2–3 storey houses for home purchasers, the limited space in Hong Kong, Singapore and major cities in China implies these cities have to build high rise apartments to meet the demand for housing. As the building of such high rise apartments involves a very high fixed development cost and substantial economies of scale, only major developers with sufficient financial strength, instead of small sized builders, could overcome the barrier of scale. As a result, there are insufficient competitions in the property market in these Asian cities.

*(Continued)*

**Box 9.2.2:**   (*Continued*)

As will be explained in the subsequent sections, these Asian developers soon, through trial-and-error or learning-by-observation, form some kind of informal cartel through the common adoption of some industrial practices or industrial norms, such as a gross profit margin of at least 40–60% for each housing estate. In China, the developers even establish common industrial practices such as selling the flats with the toothpaste-squeezing strategy (see Section 9.2.5 for more details), hoarding the land for a few years before the formal estate development, and so on.

Thus, unlike the builders in the Western world, these Asian developers do have a relatively strong market or pricing power on their products. In the subsequent sections, I will discuss the severe implications of such a market structure problem to China. Here, I would like to highlight the following difference between the Western world and China: When there is a property boom in the Western world, those who buy the flat before or at the early stage of the boom are probably the group that benefits the most from the boom. Of course, builders will also benefit in terms of greater turnover and slightly higher profit margin, but the major share of gain from property price appreciation will go to property investors. On the other hand, when there is a property boom in Asia, property developers can be the group benefiting the most, not only through a substantially higher gross profit margin, but also the through the appreciation of their hoarded land and properties. Of course, early home buyers will also benefit from the boom, but a significant part of the gain will first be taken off by the developers when they buy the flat at a relatively high price from the developers. In fact, this is why property developers in Hong Kong are so rich that they are the group that owns most of the other companies and assets in Hong Kong. In fact, the richest tycoons in Hong Kong are all developers. If China's property market was allowed to operate in its current form for another one to two decade(s), we would very soon see some Chinese developers emerging as some of the richest tycoons in China.

Meanwhile, there are also **cumulative dynamic efficiencies** in property development in China (see Diagram 9.2.2). That is, through past experience of property development, experienced property developers have accumulated numerous cost savings and revenue enhancement practices or set-ups in marketing and sales, building and designs, financing, purchases and procurements, inventory managements as well as outsourcing and sub-contraction of building works. As a result, large and experienced property developers are usually more efficient than small and less experienced developers, not to mention individuals and inexperienced small enterprises from other industries. Thus, there is in fact a **huge barrier of entry** in China's property development market.

---

**Why the AC curve is downward sloping with respect to experience?**

As developers could accumulate numerous cost saving practices and set-ups through their previous development of housing estates, the average cost (AC) curve would be a downward sloping curve with respect to the cumulated number of flats built by the developers.

**An important source of barrier of entry**

Ceteris paribus, potential developer A with no property development experience would have a far much higher average cost than the experienced developer B. Thus, cumulated dynamic efficiency is an important source of the high barrier of entry in China's property market.

---

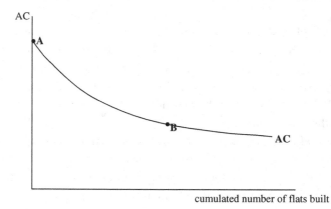

Diagram 9.2.2. Cumulated Dynamic Efficiency

If so, were there any successful new entries into China's property market? The answer is yes. For example, large property developers from overseas, those small developers in less developed areas who manage to use their personal connections (i.e., guang-xi) or illegal means to acquire lands at artificially low price, or even "original rural residents" in the expanded city areas who rebuild their 3–4 storey houses into 8–9 storey buildings are examples of new entries. Nevertheless, these entries are not sufficient to change the overall pattern qualitatively and there remains a huge barrier of entry in China's property market. In the next section, I will explain that it is this barrier of entry that result in housing supply that is less than social optimal, housing price that is uncomfortably high for middle and middle-high income earners, and an era of super abnormal profit for property developers in China.

### 9.2.3   High Fixed Development Cost and Hoarding of Lands

Because of the huge barrier of entry and high fixed development cost in property development, Chinese property developers can, and will, be more cautious in their property developments. With the help of the huge barrier of entry and product differentiations among housing estates, if most property developers are more cautious, they can in effect collectively squeeze the number of available flats so as to attain a higher price that is close to the profit maximizing price. Once the higher gross profit margin or price have become an industrial norm, then effectively all the property developers are collectively choosing the profit maximization price by squeezing the number of flats below the social optimal level.

Worse still, with rising property price, property developers soon find it beneficial to find various ways to hoard the lands for a few years or even more than ten years, delay the starting date of the estate development, develop the estates by phases, and hoard part of the built-up properties for a better price. This will in turn squeeze the number of available flats further and push the property price higher. In the next section, I will explain that higher property price and the enormous profit from hoarding of lands and properties has prompted more property developers bidding for and hoarding lands more aggressively, and finding ways to hoard their lands and properties beyond that permitted by government regulation. This will in turn result in an upward spiral between land price and property price as well as a vicious cycle between rising property price and developers' hoarding of lands and properties.

With developers' hoarding of lands, using supply and demand analysis to make related policy recommendations can be misleading. For example, some not-very-well-trained economists in China had recommended the Chinese government to substantially increase the residential land supply as a tool to curb property inflation in 2006–2007. The problem is that, when the upward inertia of property price was established, an increase in residential land supply would only allow property developers to use various loopholes to hoard lands at low price. The actual medium-term increase in built up flats could only be moderate, not to mention the very minimal effect on the high property price and the high gross profit margin of property development. Worse still, some dogmatic believers of market even concluded that the rise in property price only reflected the forces of supply and demand. The government should not, and could not, stop the market force. Being upset by the misleading conclusion which would put most Chinese citizens in severe economic pains and create greater income inequality in China, my series of articles condemn this group of economists and dogmatic believers of market for their ignorance and poor economics training. In the next few sections, I will explain that one crucial source of problem in China's property market is the problem of its market structure. The problem of high property price cannot be solved unless we address to this market structure problem.

### 9.2.4   *The Market Structure Problem: Asymmetries Between Buyers and Sellers, No Supply Curve in China's Property Market*

According to the supply and demand analysis, the intersection point of the supply and demand curves will give the equilibrium price and quantity (i.e., $P_0$ and $Q_0$) such as that shown in Diagram 9.2.4. In addition, the height of the demand curve will reflect the marginal consumer's perceived marginal benefit. For example, the height of point A will reflect the point-A-consumer's perceived marginal benefit. On the other hand, each consumer could buy the product at the equilibrium price $P_0$, even if his perceived marginal benefit is much higher than $P_0$. As a result, the total consumer surplus will be the area $CS_0$ as shown in Diagram 9.2.4.

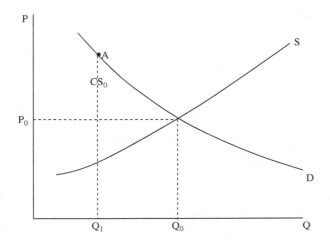

**Diagram 9.2.4.** Traditional Supply & Demand Analysis for the Industry

Nevertheless, one implicit assumption of the supply and demand analysis is that there are numerous sellers and buyers, so that there is no supplier who has the market power to charge a price higher than $P_0$. As a result, the whole group of suppliers cannot collectively reduce the quantity supplied below $Q_0$ so as to achieve a price higher than $P_0$. In addition, the supply and demand analysis also implicitly assumes that there is no significant asymmetry between the sellers and the buyers.

Unfortunately, all these implicit assumptions are unrealistic and inappropriate for China's property market. For example, there are significant *asymmetries in the market power, hoarding power and information between the property developers and home purchasers.* Such asymmetries had enabled developers to use various types of tactics to achieve higher selling price and squeeze out more consumer surplus. Let us see how this could be the case.

As the number of home buyers in China is huge, the implicit assumption on the demand side of the supply and demand analysis is basically justifiable. That is, one is justified to assume the existence of a demand curve such as that shown in Diagram 9.2.4. However, on the supply side, as the location, design and quality of each housing estate could be different from each other, there is a certain degree of **product differentiation** among the housing estates. In addition, as the number of new flats on sales at any single period is limited and developers usually sell their flats by small batches (i.e., the *toothpaste-squeezing selling strategy*), developers usually have a certain degree of market or pricing power on each small batch of new properties on sales. As is well established in economics theory, once the supplier(s) have a certain degree of market or pricing power, there will be no supply curve but only the supply side and the marginal cost curve(s). This is so because the supplier(s) will observe or estimate the demand curve(s), and use the estimated demand and marginal cost curves to decide the profit maximizing prices and quantities. That is, one can no longer draw an independent supply curve, as the quantity supplied and hence the price are no longer independent of the demand curve.

As is well known in economics theory, except in the extreme case of perfect competition or other minor examples, in most models of market structure such as price leadership, monopolistic competition, oligopoly and monopoly, there will be no supply curve but only demand curve; and there will be no supply curve but only the supply side and the cost curves.

As developers have a certain degree of market or pricing power, it is then possible for the developers to collectively squeeze the quantity supplied (through industrial practice, such as at least 40–60% gross profit margin for each estate development) so as to raise their profits through a higher price. In the next section, we will see how they have developed various tactics to achieve very high selling prices for their properties.

### 9.2.5 *Speculative and Panic Demand*

As explained in the previous sections, the high fixed development cost has made the developers more cautious in their estate development, i.e., hoard the lands and build the properties by phases. The high fixed development cost has also created a relatively huge barrier of entry, thus enabling the developers to collectively squeeze the quantity supplied below that under perfect competition, i.e., below $Q_0$ in Diagram 9.2.5a. This in turn enables them to sell their properties at a price at or above $P_1$. Because of the barrier of entry, developers have been able to earn super abnormal profits by squeezing the consumer surplus to $CS_1$ or even lower value (see the subsequent discussion on how developers have used other tactics to further squeeze the consumer surplus below $CS_1$).

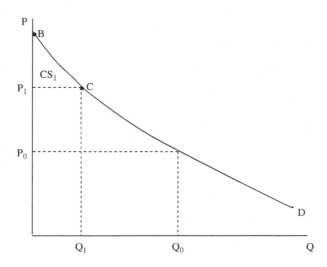

**Diagram 9.2.5a.** Demand and Quantity Supplied for the Industry

In fact, among the home buyers between point B and point C in Diagram 9.2.5a, many are the rich Chinese, speculators, high income earners and foreign buyers with some owning quite a number of properties. The remaining buyers are the middle-high income "property slaves" who use most of their monthly income for the mortgage installment of a 20-year housing loans. For those potential home buyers below point C of the demand curve, many are the general public who has the "need" but not the "money or income" to buy or mortgage a flat.

If it is just a higher price at $P_1$ and a squeeze of consumer surplus to $CS_1$, the pain will still be less unacceptable. Unfortunately, as there are severe asymmetries between the developers and home buyers in market power, holding power and information about the housing estate, developers are able to use the *"toothpaste-squeezing selling strategy"* and other tactics to (a) squeeze out more consumer surplus; and (b) create speculative and panic demand.

To see this, let us first draw in Diagram 9.2.5b the "real" users' demand curve $d_r$ for a representative housing estate over a specific period. If the particular developer sells all the estate's units ($q_1$) in one batch, he will be able to charge the price $P_1$ as shown in the Diagram 9.2.5a (and Diagram 9.2.5b). The home buyers will still be able to get a certain amount of, albeit smaller, consumer surplus.

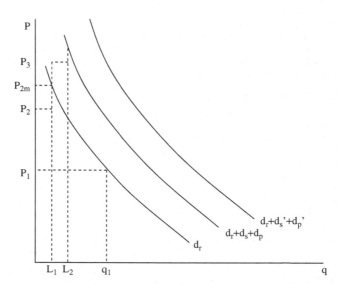

**Diagram 9.2.5b.** Demand and Quantity Supplied for a Representative Housing Estate Over a Specific Period of Time

Unfortunately, the representative developer is not that silly to sell all the units in one batch. Instead, he will sell the units by small batches or lots. That is, by dividing the total number of units into a few phases of development, and subdividing each phase into a number of batches, the developer will be able to use such toothpaste-squeezing selling strategy to achieve a higher profit. For example, the developer can first sell $L_1$ units in the first lot so that he can charge a price higher than $P_1$ (e.g., $P_2$, or even $P_{2m}$, in Diagram 9.2.5b). Usually, the property developer will choose a price $P_2 < P_{2m}$ so that there is an over-subscription for that particular batch. The over-subscription will then enable him to claim that his housing estate is of high quality and very much in demand.

If the property market is already on an upward path,[3] the rising property price will create speculative demand $d_s$ and panic demand $d_p$ for the

---

[3] Usually, the representative property developer will keep the better units in the later batches. If the property market is just stable, he will sell the second lot (of better units) at a higher price or the same price or a slightly higher price. In case the property market is really

particular housing estate (see Section 9.3.1.1 for the discussions on the macroeconomic aspect). As a result, the demand curve in the next period will shift to the $d_r+d_s+d_p$ curve in Diagram 9.2.5b. Thus, when the developer sells the second batch of units $L_2$, he can charge a price much higher than $P_2$ (e.g., $P_3$). This will in turn fuel the overheated property market through the indicator price and expectation channels (see Box 9.2.5). The rise in the overall market will then further raise the speculative demand and panic demand for the representative housing estate, say, to $d_r+d_s'+d_p'$, which will enable the developer to charge an even higher price in the third batch of units.

---

**Box 9.2.5: The Indicator Effect from New Properties to Second Hand Properties**

One interesting phenomenon in the property market in China, Hong Kong, Singapore and some other Asian cities is that the price of new properties set by the developers would become the indicator for the price of second hand properties.[4] That is, because many home purchasers prefer new properties to second-hand properties, developers are able to sell their properties at a price with a 20–50% premium over the price of comparable second hand properties. The higher price of the new properties will in turn raise the expectation and reservation price of potential sellers of second hand properties. The immediate effect will be a rise in the transaction price of these second-hand

*(Continued)*

---

bad, he would either (a) choose to hoard the units if he foresees a recovery in the near future; or (b) cut the selling price if he foresees further weakening of the property market in the near and medium future. Even in case of the latter, he will still be able to extract a significant portion of consumer surplus through the price discrimination implied by the toothpaste-squeezing selling strategy.

[4] Again, this phenomenon might only be popular in Asian cities but not the Western world. If so, the latter would be less prone to the development of property bubbles than some Asian economies.

---

**Box 9.2.5:** *(Continued)*

properties to a level with narrower discount (e.g., 10–25%) to the new properties. As a result, the small amount of new properties can pull up the transaction price of the much bigger pool of second-hand properties market through the indicator effect and expectation channel. To the extent that

(i) developers have the market power to set the price with a premium over the second-hand properties; and

(ii) transaction of second-hand properties at any particular time is only a small percentage of the whole pool of second-hand properties,

ongoing launches of new properties can keep pulling up the overall property price to higher and higher levels. By then, it will be just a matter of time that some negative shocks in the future will trigger a substantial reversal of property price.

---

### 9.2.6    *Other Undesirable Effects*

In addition to the microeconomic pains discussed in the previous section, there are also other undesirable effects if China just relies on the free market force to do the allocation job under the imperfect settings of its property market.

#### 9.2.6.1    *Flat Size Could Become Smaller and Smaller*

One undesirable effect would be the gradual reduction of flat size over time. To achieve a higher selling price per square meter, developers would have the incentives to reduce the sizes of flats so that the total selling prices of the smaller flats will still be within the affordable limit of the potential new home purchasers. However, as the norm of acceptable flat size at any particular point of time will depend on the culture at that time, there is a limit in the pace for developers to reduce the size of flat (i.e., they would have problem selling the flats if they reduce the size of flat well below the acceptable norm at that time). Nevertheless, developers could still reduce the size of flat bit by bit over time. For example, during the property boom, developers building a flat slightly below the acceptable norm with the same total selling price would have little problem selling the flat. If necessary, developers could also (i) temporarily compensate the flat buyers with better decoration when they first reduce the flat size; and (ii) then remove the compensation once the culture starts to be less resistant to the smaller flat size. Over time, with more and more of these smaller-flats produced and purchased, the culture's attitude to these smaller-flats will gradually change from "resistant" to "less resistant" and then to "acceptable" (i.e., the acceptable norm of flat size is reduced).

Thus, although there is a limit in the pace for developers to reduce average flat size, developers would be able to reduce the average flat size by a substantial amount over a long enough time, such as 2–3 decades. In fact, this was what happened in Hong Kong, and there was an emerging tendency of a gradual but sustained shrinkage of flat size in China, Singapore and some other Asian cities. For example, a standard private two-room flat in Hong Kong in the 1970s or 1980s would be about 600–650 square feets. However, after a few property booms over the past three decades, a standard private two-room flat nowadays would only be about 400 square feet. Worse still, the actual built in area of these flats would only be around 250–280 square feet. In many cases, the second room of these two-room flats is not long enough to put in a standard single bed. The home owner would either need to design their own beds so that the small window balcony could make up the remaining part of the bed, or just use the room as a study room. The size of the kitchen is so small that one could touch both sides of the walls by just stretching his or her hands. In fact, the standard two-room flat built by the semigovernment body, once smaller than the private two-room flat in the 1980s, is now larger than the standard private two-room flat by about 100 square feet. Because of the small size of flats, it has become a culture in Hong Kong that many people would invite friends for dinner, or even having their family reunions, in the restaurant instead of their home.

The case of Singapore was better because of its substantial amount of public housing (i.e., HDB flats) had helped stopping the acceptable norm of flat size from going down too fast. Nevertheless, as the Housing

Development Board (HDB) did follow the private developers' action of reducing the flat size during the property boom in the 1990s, the size of Singapore's private and public flats did fall by moderate percentage over the past two decades. For example, the size of a standard private two-room flat had been reduced from around 1100 square feets to about 900 square feet over the past two decades. In view of the dangerous trend, in one of the policy proposal submitted to the Singapore government in 2009, the author highlighted that it would be important for the government to keep the current size of the HDB flats so that it could (i) as an important benchmark, help keeping the acceptable norm of flat size unchanged; and hence (ii) stop the private developers from being able to keep reducing the flat size over time.

The size of flats in China was also reduced by a reasonably large percentage during the property boom over the past decade. For example, a standard private three-room flat in a decade ago would be in the range of 100–110 square meters, while the standard size nowadays would be 90 square meters. Moreover, while two-room flats was not that popular a decade ago, it has become an important type of flats in China and its percentage share in overall supply is still rising.

### 9.2.6.2   *Too Much Effort and Social Resources to Investment of Property*

Another undesirable effect is that too much effort and social resources would be devoted to activities related property investment, which might only have very minor contribution to the productivity and efficiency of the economy. As property investment had turned out to be an important source of wealth accumulation in China, Hong Kong and Singapore, many people had spent most of their time following the news and movements in the property market, and invest their funds on property investment (see Box 9.2.6 on why property investment had turned out to be a successful way of wealth accumulation in China, Hong Kong, Singapore and some other Asian economies). As a result, people's attention, animal spirit and funds were diverted away from the riskier but more growth-enhancing and efficiency-improving activities such as new product and cost saving innovations, or taking the risk to start new businesses with potential positive impacts on the efficiency and productivity of the economy.

Meanwhile, there are too much social resources diverted to investment activities on property. For example, in Singapore (and some other Asian cities such as Hong Kong), advertisement on launches of new properties had occupied most of the weekend advertisement pages in the newspapers. When compared with the launches of the HDB flats by the government, the far bigger scale of newspaper advertisements by the 20% share of private properties had resulted in tons of unnecessary waste of paper (or substantial recycling costs) every day. The high property price and hence the high commission had also supported an unnecessarily large number of property agents in China, Hong Kong and Singapore. More importantly, the high land price and the high property price has resulted in an excessively large property loan businesses for the banks, thus making less bank loans available for other growth-enhancing activities or businesses.

---

**Box 9.2.6: Why Property Investment Had Turned Out to Be a Successful Way of Wealth Accumulation in Some Asian Economies**

In Hong Kong, Singapore and recently in China, as people had made substantial gains from their long-term investment in properties, long-term investment in properties had become the "traditional investment wisdom" in these economies.[5] There are many contributing factors for the substantial capital gains:

(a) Property price would rise with the high real economic growth in these economies;

(b) Urbanization and hence the growing relative scarcity of land had further increase the rise in property price;

(c) Improved infrastructure (such as the latest expansion of underground railways in Singapore and China) and expansion of the cities had substantially raised the underlying values of those

*(Continued)*

---

[5] Of course, for those who were over-leveraged near the peak of the bubble, they could experience substantial loss during the bursting of property bubble. Nevertheless, for those who were not over-leveraged and managed to keep the property for a long enough time for factors (a)-(d) to exert their full effects, they could still make a profit from the invesment.

**Box 9.2.6:**    *(Continued)*

previously remote land the newly developed part of the cities. Thus, people investing in new flats here could still gain even though the developers had taken out a substantial part of the gain at the early stage; and

(d) Most importantly, property price would rise with inflation. In particular, if we look at the record of global inflation, we would found that on-and-off there were episodes that governments in the world fail to keep the inflation rate within their target. That is, even in the case that inflation rate was kept at the 2–3% target rate, property owners could still benefit from the inflation at the expense of people without property. In the episodes that inflation rate was 5–6%, 8–9% or even double digit per annum, every dollar increase in wage would be translated into at least a discounted stream of rental increments over the next few decades. Although the percentage rise in property price, after appropriate adjustments due to reasons (a)-(c), would be similar to the inflation rate over the long run, the rising property price and the fixed debt (i.e., mortgage loan) would mean that those asset owners would benefit substantially from higher inflation rates. Moreover, those capital gains would not be taxed while wage income would be taxed in Asia. Thus, for those who had invested in a lot of properties with mortgage loan, their capital gains would be enormous, and very often greater than their normal income. As a result, the rise in property price had resulted in an increase in inequility of net wealth between property owners and non-property owners.

While long-term property investment had proved to be a good investment wisdom in these economies, it should be noted that it is more a re-distribution of relative wealth and relative income among citizens of the same generation, and between the current generation and the next generation. Other than the re-distribution, property investment activities did not contribute much to the productivities of the economy. In fact, as explained in the main text, it could divert resources, funds and effort away from other more growth-enhancing activities.

## 9.2.7   *Implications of the Above Analysis*

There are many important implications with the above analysis:

A.  Price discrimination and further squeeze of consumer surplus

Firstly, the toothpaste-squeezing selling strategy would enable the developers to squeeze out more consumer surplus through price discrimination, thus allowing property developers to earn super abnormal profit. Meanwhile, total consumer surplus would be further squeezed to a level much lower than the $CS_1$ in Diagram 9.2.5a.

B.  Possibility of negative consumer surplus

Furthermore, if speculative demand and panic demand developed in the later stage, property developers could charge higher price. When the speculative demand and panic demand reach a certain high level, price of the new property could be even higher than that could be afforded by the middle-high income earners, and the "real" consumers' surplus could then be very small or even negative. Unfortunately, only after the property price plunge from the unsustainably high level to a low level, the "real" flat users would then realize that the price they have paid for is unreasonably high, and their consumer surplus at that price is in fact substantially negative (see the explanation in Box 9.2.7).

---

**Box 9.2.7:   Why Home Buyers Might Not Recognize That Their Consumer Surplus Could Be Negative During the Property Boom**

During the property boom, home buyers might not recognize that the high price they are paying for their new flats could imply a forgone satisfaction much greater than the intrinsic satisfaction that could get from the flats, partly because they tend to use the misleading yardstick — the reselling market price of the property — to value the property, and partly because they are misled by the panic created by the property boom. That is, during the property boom, the flat

*(Continued)*

---

---

**Box 9.2.7:** (*Continued*)

purchasers usually found that they could sell their flats at a price higher than the purchase price, i.e., a capital gain. As a result, they have used the higher reselling market price as an "objective" measure of their satisfaction, instead of the "subjective" true feeling on their satisfaction from the flat. Meanwhile, the property boom could have created certain degree of desire or panic to own a flat before it is too late. Buying the flat to remove this panic would imply a short term gain in terms of less anxiety or dissatisfaction. Nevertheless, the removal of the panic could only continue to exist if the property price keeps going up, or at least remain higher than their purchasing price. If the property price ever falls below their purchasing price, the above gain will disappear. Instead, there will be emerging loss due to new panic on the capital loss.

---

That is, they have become a "property slave" and worse still, a property slave who would not be able to sell the property without a substantial loss after the bursting of the bubble, i.e., either being stuck with the heavy mortgage installment for the next 15–20 years or get bankrupt if they do not have enough money to cover the difference between the mortgage debt and the much lower selling price of the property.

## C. Big swings in property price

Nevertheless, such kind of speculative demand and panic demand could not last forever. In Section 9.3, I will explain that when property keep rising beyond that could be supported by market fundamentals, it will then be just a matter of time that the property bubble will burst. By then, the speculative demand and panic demand will suddenly disappear, thus aggravating the plunge in property price. Worse still, the plunge in property price will cause not only the disappearance of the speculative demand and panic demand, but also panic sales by speculators, long-term investors and even real home owners. Seeing the plunge in property price, potential "real" home buyers will also choose a wait-and-see attitude. Thus, in addition to the disappearance of $d_s'+d_p'$ in Diagram 9.2.5b, there will also be a sharp increase in the amount of flats available for sales in the secondary market and a temporary inward shift of $d_r$.

As the cumulated rise in price and the cumulated quantity of speculative demand and panic demand in the past are substantial, it is possible that property price could plunge by a substantial percentage, e.g., about 65% such as that in Hong Kong during the Asian Financial Crisis and more than 80% such as that in Japan in the early 1990s.

### D. Economic incentives behind some established developers' behaviors

Fourthly, there are deep economic incentives behind some established developers' behaviors such as acquiring lands at artificially low price through connections and illegal means, hoarding of lands for a few years or even over ten years, delaying the land and property development beyond that required by the government regulation, selling the properties with the toothpaste-squeezing selling strategy, keeping part of the built up units for later sales, issuing VIP cards (i.e., developers can use a very small discount to group the potential home buyers together so that they can actually count or estimate the demand and the maximum price they can charge) and arrange pre-sales to a privileged group (i.e., developers can use a discount to nurture a group of speculators that buy and sell properties in each of their new projects).

Compared with the huge economic benefits of these behaviors, many of the existing government regulations that penalize the inappropriate behaviors are just too small, thus making them virtually ineffective and meaningless. Thus, from the perspective of the developers, it is not likely that the related government bodies could fine them for the inappropriate behaviors, partly because it is difficult for the central government to check these in all the local areas in a big country like China and partly because local officials in the related government bodies could be bribed. Even in the hard luck case that they are fined, the fine will be just too small when compared with the benefits.

## 9.3   Macroeconomic Costs and Systemic Risk

In addition to the microeconomic problems, there are also systemic risk and macroeconomic costs to let free market force to guide China's property market under the imperfect settings. The major source of such costs and risk is an excessive rise in property price. If continued to be unchecked, the higher property price will pull up rentals and then wage and general price level, which will in turn fuel the rise in property price, thus forming an upward spiral between property price, rentals, wage and general price level. Once such spiral is established, it can

(a) pull China's rentals, wage and general price level from the currently competitive level to highly uncompetitive levels (see Section 9.4 for similar case of significant loss of competitiveness in Hong Kong during the high property and general price inflation in 1986–1997); and

(b) make the economy vulnerable to a plunge in property price and then a crisis similar to that in the US in 2008–2009 and the Asian Financial Crisis in 1997–1998;

Let us see how this can be the case.

### 9.3.1 *Excessive Rise in Property Price*

#### 9.3.1.1 *From Change in Expectation to Changes in Economic Behaviours*

As highlighted in Chapter 8, once an *upward inertia* of asset (property) price is established, such as the case in 2004–2007, there would be an *expectation of asset (property) inflation* (i.e., the seeding stage of a huge rise in property price). This would in turn cause some important *changes in economic behaviours* which will fuel the rise in property price. For example, as noted in Yip (2005), once the upward inertia is established and the property inflation is built into expectation, people will demand more property by increasing their financial leverage (e.g., through more loans). For those who have already owned a flat, their "gains" from the property market will induce them to shift to a bigger flat or buy more flats. Even for those who do not have an urgent need to buy a flat, when they see their peers earning substantially from the property market, they will be under pressure to buy a flat before it is too late. That is, expectation of property inflation can generate speculative demand and panic demand which will fuel the rise in property price. Meanwhile, the greater investment in property or related assets will also induce people to reduce their desired cash-to-deposit ratio, which will in turn increase the money multiplier and fuel the rise in property price (see Box 8.2.1 for the details).

On the credit supply side, banks officers and executives are also under peer pressure to outperform, or at least perform the same as, their peers. Thus, banks will be willing to lend more when the above clients come to the banks. In fact, during the property boom, banks will tend to run down their excess reserve and borrow overseas to outperform, or keep the same performance as, their competitors. Furthermore, with expectation of further rise in property price and share price of property firms, there will also be more inflows of speculative funds (through the illegal channels or the abuse of legal channels in the case of China).

The effect of all these behavioral changes on money supply can be better seen with the help of the following equation:

$$M = m \times \text{MB}$$

where $M$ is money supply, $m$ is money multiplier and MB is monetary base. As explained in Box 8.2.1, when people reduce their desired cash-to-deposit ratio and banks run down their excess reserve ratio, the money multiplier will increase. Even if there is no change in monetary base, the rise in money multiplier by itself is enough to cause a substantial rise in money supply and fuel the rise in property price. Worse still, the substantial overseas borrowings by banks (to meet the higher demand for loans) and the substantial inflows of speculative funds will create either substantial appreciation pressure of the domestic currency or substantial monetary growth pressure for the economy. Thus, unless the central bank is willing to accept a substantial surge in her exchange rate (which could also be highly undesirable) or able to sterilize all these changes, there will be a substantial rise in monetary base which will create a much greater rise in money supply through the money multiplier. As a result, the rise in both MB and $m$ will interact together to cause a substantial increase in money supply which will further fuel the rise in property price and other asset price.

To illustrate the power of these behavioral changes, Table 9.3.1a reports the domestic credit growth of the crisis-hit economies during the asset inflation era before the outbreak of the Asian Financial Crisis in 1997–1998:

As we can see, during the asset inflation era before the financial crisis, the domestic credit growth in these economies was unsustainably high when compared with their GDP growth. In particular, the credit growth in 1997 had reached the high range of 20–44%.[6]

**Table 9.3.1a.**  Domestic Credit Growth in Some Asian Economies in 1991–1997

|             | 91   | 92   | 93    | 94   | 95   | 96   | 97   |
|-------------|------|------|-------|------|------|------|------|
| Thailand    | 15.5 | 18.0 | 22.7  | 29.4 | 23.0 | 14.0 | 34.5 |
| Indonesia   | 18.9 | 14.1 | 21.0  | 22.9 | 21.7 | 22.7 | 25.7 |
| Malaysia    | 18.5 | 16.6 | 12.3  | 14.8 | 29.5 | 31.2 | 29.3 |
| Philippines | 1.7  | 13.2 | 133.4 | 16.9 | 33.6 | 47.2 | 43.6 |
| Korea       | 22.4 | 11.5 | 12.8  | 18.5 | 14.6 | 19.4 | 23.3 |
| Singapore   | 13.9 | 5.5  | 12.0  | 12.8 | 17.5 | 17.3 | 19.5 |

*Source*: East Asian Economic Perspectives, Special Issue, Vol. 11, February 2000.

**Table 9.3.1b.**  China's Loan and Real GDP Growth in 2006–2007

|         | GDP  | Total Credit | Property Loans | Home Loans |
|---------|------|--------------|----------------|------------|
| 2006Q1  | 12.4 | 28.0         | 46.8           | 18.9       |
| 2006Q2  | 13.1 | 30.8         | 53.7           | 19.7       |
| 2006Q3  | 12.8 | 34.3         | 55.7           | 23.8       |
| 2006Q4  | 12.7 | 32.9         | 54.3           | 22.3       |
| 2007Q1  | 14.0 | 25.3         | 33.3           | 20.5       |
| 2007Q2  | 14.5 | 26.5         | 30.8           | 23.8       |
| 2007Q3  | 14.4 | 28.3         | 27.5           | 28.8       |
| 2007Q4  | 14.2 | 30.4         | 27.7           | 32.2       |

*Source*: CEIC.

---

[6] Singapore's credit growth was less rampant. This had in turn contributed to the less severe property inflation during the asset inflation era and less painful corrections during the crisis.

Similarly in China, during the property inflation era period between 2006 and 2007, even though the central banks tried very hard to contain the rise in money supply through sterilization (i.e., sales of central bank notes or government bonds) and substantial rise in banks' reserve requirement ratio (see Figure 4.5.5), China's credit growth in 2006–2007 still exceeded the real GDP growth by a wide margin (see Table 9.3.1b). The higher credit growth had to some extent contributed to the rapid rise in property price in 2006–2007.

---

**Box 9.3.1a:   Experience in the Crisis-Hit Economies During the Asset Inflation Era Before the Asian Financial Crisis**

During the asset inflation era before the Asian Financial Crisis, many banks in the crisis-hit economies, such as Thailand and Malaysia, borrowed huge amount of short-term loans from overseas. Such oversea borrowings, under the quasi-fixed exchange rate system at that time, had created a multiple expansion of money supply through the money multiplier. This in turn enabled them to achieve an excessive credit growth of 20–40% per annum (see Table 9.3.1a). During this asset inflation era, banks' profit growths were impressive. Nevertheless, with the outbreak of the Asian Financial Crisis, foreign lenders' refusal to roll over the short-term loans meant not only abrupt stoppage of capital inflows, but also a huge amount of capital outflows when the Asian banks were forced to pay back the outstanding amount of overseas loans accumulated in the past. The substantial capital outflows would mean a squeeze of domestic monetary base, and worse still, a multiple contraction of domestic money supply and credit. Even if one did not count the other types of capital outflows and other negative changes, the enormous squeeze of domestic credit would be enough to cause a crisis.

---

### 9.3.1.2 *Formation of a Few Vicious Cycles*

Worse still, the rise in money supply and property price will result in the development of a few vicious cycles, which will fuel the rise in property price further beyond the sustainable level. One such vicious cycle is *between property price and share price*. For example, the rise in money supply, the booming economy and the rise in property price will raise the earnings and hence the share price of property firms, banks and other companies. The higher share price will in turn fuel the rise in property price through

(a) direct increase in demand for property (e.g., some share investors might use their profit in share market as a down payment of their new investment in property);
(b) indirect increase in demand for property (e.g., through higher aggregate demand or higher wages during the boom); and
(c) better market sentiment (e.g., sellers in the property can quote a higher selling price when market sentiment in the stock market is good).

Another vicious cycle is *between asset price and aggregate demand*: the rise in property and share price will increase consumption through the wealth effect and investment through the Tobin's q effect and other effects. The rise in consumption and investment will in turn raise the aggregate demand and fuel the rise in asset price.

A third example of vicious cycle is as stated in the previous section: *higher asset price* will induce *greater speculative inflows and more overseas borrowings by banks*, which will in turn fuel the rise in asset price through greater money supply. With the possibility of rising money supply through these two channels and other channels, we have the fourth vicious cycle: the higher property price can pull up rentals and then wages and general price (costs of livings) during the property and economic boom; and the latter will fuel the rise in property price, thus forming an *upward spiral between property price, rentals, wages and general price*. In fact, this is what happened in Hong Kong during the rampant property inflation in 1990–1997 (see Section 9.4 for more details).

### 9.3.1.3 *Herding Behavior and Subsequent Bursting*

Once the economy has gone through the above development stage of rampant property inflation (i.e., with changes in economic behaviors and formation of a few vicious cycles), it is possible to result in the development of herding behavior in the property market. As highlighted in Chapter 8, once the herding behavior is established, more and more people will be attracted, or under pressure, to start investing or raising their investment in the property market. On the credit supply side, banks will be attracted, or under performance pressure, to increase loans to the home buyers and property investors, even if some of them are aware of the risk of an eventual bursting. At this stage, standard curbing measures, such as moderate increase in interest rate, tighter regulation on property development, or moderate tax increment on property transactions, will not be sufficient to stop the property price from surging higher.

However, when the property market enters this final stage of bubble during which close to 100% of the potential property investors and funds has already joined the market, the rise in property price will slow down and then stop. By then, it will be just a matter of time that some negative economic shock in the future would cause a fall in property price and trigger herding behaviors in the downward direction, a reversal of the above vicious cycles and changes in economic behaviors, and expectation of further fall in property price and establishment of downward inertia until the property price plunges to a level well below the normal equilibrium level. In fact, as highlighted in Chapter 8, the later the arrival of the large enough negative economic shock, the smaller the size of the shock is required to trigger the plunge in property price, and the more painful and larger the subsequent plunge in the property price.

### 9.3.2 Macroeconomic Consequences of the Excessive Property Inflation

Thus, given the market structure problem in China's property market and the high income inequality in China, China's property bubble will continue to grow if there are no appropriate policies from the Chinese government. Once the bubble reaches the "dead position" level, it will be just a matter of time in the future that some moderate negative shocks or a good-intention tightening policy will trigger a bursting of the bubble. As the destructive impacts of a bursting of property bubble can be far much greater than that of stock market bubble (see Chapter 11 for the reasons), the Chinese economy will then experienced at least a banking crisis and severe recession. This in turn will trigger social and political instability, which will be extremely dangerous for a country with huge geographical size and internal diversities such as China. In the less severe case, it will result in the resignation of some top officials such as the premier or the ministers. In the more severe case, it can cause the collapse of the government and the Communist Party.

The power of such type of financial crisis should not be underestimated. For example, as noted in Chapter 2, the Suharto government in Indonesia was once perceived as very strong and almost unchallengeable before the Asian Financial Crisis in 1997–1998. However, the very strong Indonesian President did lose his power in 1998. In the subsequent years, Indonesia had gone into a politically chaotic era with very weak leadership and frequent changes in governments until a stronger man, Yudhoyono, won the election. As Indonesia was not a "strategic competitor" of any super power in the world, Indonesians were given the chance to sort out the political chaos among themselves. However, if China ever enters into a similar scenario, China's strategic competitor(s) might find it politically advantageous not to give China any chance to come back.

In addition to the risk of a bursting of property bubble and the subsequent crisis, persistent rise in property price could also transform China from a low-cost, active and vibrant economy into an inactive economy locked by the vicious cycle of high property price, high rental, high wage, high cost and high general price level. One such example is similar transformation in Hong Kong between 1986 and 1997 (see Section 9.4 for more details).[7]

## 9.4 Lessons From Hong Kong

To draw the readers' attention to the plausibility of the scenario discussed in Section 9.3, this section and Box 9.4 will highlight that, similar

---

[7] It should be noted that a bursting of bubble could not guarantee that the economy could be unlocked from the vicious cycle. For example, as noted in Section 9.4, even after the bursting of bubble and then the prolonged recession in 1998–2004, Hong Kong was not able to break the above vicious cycle and regained the economic vibrancy it had between the 1970s and the early 1990s.

to the current situation in China, Hong Kong's wage was in fact highly competitive in the 1980s. However, sustained property inflation and then the above mentioned upward spiral between 1986 and 1997 had pushed Hong Kong's wage, general price and rentals to highly uncompetitive levels. This had not only made the economy vulnerable to the speculative attacks in 1997–1998, the fixed exchange rate system and the downward sluggishness of wage and general price also inhibited its ability to adjust, thus resulting in a seven-year recession between 1998 and 2004. Even by now, Hong Kong's property price, rentals, wage and general price level were interlocked with each other at a highly uncompetitive level, making it (i) an expensive and less vibrant city than that in the 1980s; and (ii) more difficult to benefit from the rapid growth in China.

---

**Box 9.4:  Experience in Hong Kong During the Asset Inflation Era Before the Asian Financial Crisis**

Because of Hong Kong's cultural and geographical proximity to China, Hong Kong was able to benefit a lot from the opening up of China since 1978. This was particularly the case in the more rapid stage of China's opening up between 1986 and 1997. In particular, Hong Kong businessmen (and employees) were able to earn a lot of profits (and much higher wages) between 1986 and 1997. Under the currency board system in Hong Kong, these huge extra foreign exchange earnings had caused substantial rise in money supply and liquidity in Hong Kong. For example, as reported in Table 9.4a, the average M3 and credit growth between 1986 and 1997 were 17.1% and 19.4% per annum, respectively. The latter had in turn made the domestic credit to GDP ratio in 1997 substantially higher than that in 1986.

When these earners repatriated and invested part of these huge extra earnings in properties and shares in Hong Kong, asset price in

*(Continued)*

---

**Box 9.4:** *(Continued)*

Hong Kong started to shoot up (see Table 9.4b and Figure 9.4).[8] The rise in asset price had in turn stimulated consumption (through the wealth effect) and investment (through the Tobin's q effect), and then GDP (through the multiplier effect), investment (through the accelerator effect) and so on. The rise in asset price and the boom in turn caused a substantial rise in rentals, consumer price index and then wage. Soon, an upward spiral between asset price, wage and costs of livings was established. With further earnings from China, and changes in economic behaviors initiated by the asset inflation, wages and prices continued to shoot up from the originally competitive level to highly uncompetitive levels (see Table 9.4c). For example, the average CPI inflation rate between 1985 and 1997 was 9.4% per annum, much higher than the corresponding 3.4% CPI inflation in the US. Within the 12 years, the price and wage indices in 1997 had rose by 2.5–2.9 times that in 1985. Unfortunately, with boom generated by the property bubble, these dangerous movements were not properly recognized until the speculative attacks from October 1997 triggered the bursting of the bubble and the severe post-crisis recession.

---

[8] As shown in Table 9.4b, the repatriation of earnings from China had under the currency board system caused rampant property inflation in Hong Kong since 1986. In particular, after a slower 11% rise of property price in 1990 (due to the Tienenmun incidence in 1989), an upward inertia was built up and started to cause an expectation of higher property inflation from 1991. These had in turned caused the changes in economic behaviors discussed in Section 9.3.1.1, the formation of the vicious cycles discussed in Section 9.3.1.2 and the development of herding behaviors discussed in Section 9.3.1.3. In particular, an upward spiral between property price, wage and costs of livings were established. As a result, Hong Kong's property price surged by the eye-popping rate of 38% and 41% in 1991 and 1992, and continued to rise by 10% and 24% in 1993 and 1994. Despite a moderate correction of −7% in 1995 due to lower global demand for exports, property price made another big surge of 41% in 1997.

**Table 9.4a.**   Money Supply and Domestic Credit Growth in Hong Kong

| Year | M3 Growth[a] | Domestic Credit Growth[b] | Domestic Credit to GDP Ratio |
|------|------|------|------|
| 1986 | 14.3 | 10.6 | 0.81 |
| 1987 | 19.1 | 27.0 | 0.84 |
| 1988 | 17.8 | 26.2 | 0.89 |
| 1989 | 19.0 | 33.9 | 1.04 |
| 1990 | 14.7 | 19.3 | 1.11 |
| 1991 | 13.0 | 17.7 | 1.13 |
| 1992 | 17.8 | 15.3 | 1.12 |
| 1993 | 19.8 | 15.5 | 1.12 |
| 1994 | 20.7 | 17.5 | 1.17 |
| 1995 | 16.3 | 11.8 | 1.23 |
| 1996 | 15.1 | 14.4 | 1.27 |
| 1997 | 19.0 | 26.1 | 1.45 |

*Source*: HKMA Monthly Statistical Bulletin.
a: Adjusted for swap deposit, % growth based on year average; b: Loans and advances in Hong Kong, % growth based on year average.

**Table 9.4b.**   Asset Price Indices in Hong Kong

| Year | Stock Price Index[a] | Property Price Index[b] |
|------|------|------|
| 1986 | 1960 (25.0%) | 113 (12.8%) |
| 1987 | 2885 (47.2%) | 138 (22.6%) |
| 1988 | 2557 (−11.4%) | 168 (21.5%) |
| 1989 | 2781 (8.8%) | 213 (26.6%) |
| 1990 | 3027 (8.9%) | 236 (11.0%) |
| 1991 | 3830 (26.5%) | 326 (37.8%) |
| 1992 | 5546 (44.8%) | 457 (40.5%) |
| 1993 | 7696 (38.8%) | 504 (10.2%) |
| 1994 | 9454 (22.8%) | 623 (23.6%) |
| 1995 | 9098 (−3.8%) | 579 (−7.2%) |
| 1996 | 11647 (28.0%) | 634 (9.6%) |
| 1997[c] | 13295 (14.2%) | 894 (40.9%) |

*Source*: Datastream and Census and Statistics Department, Hong Kong Government.
a: Hang Seng Index, year average; b: Property price index for all private domestic premises; c: Note that the reported price indices for 1997 is an year average. The Hang Seng Index at end July 1997 was 16366, 23% higher than the 1997 average and 10.4 times of the 1985 average. Similarly, the property price index in the third quarter of 1997 was 929, 10% higher than the 1997 average and 9.3 times of the 1985 average.

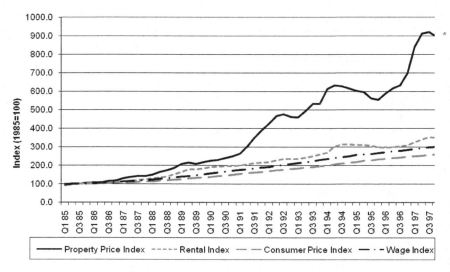

**Figure 9.4.** Property Price, Rental, Consumer Price and Wage Indices in Hong Kong

**Table 9.4c.** Rental, Consumer Price and Wage Indices in Hong Kong

| Year | Rental Index[a] | Wage Index[b] | HK CPI[c] | US CPI[d] |
|------|-----------------|----------------|-----------|-----------|
| 1986 | 108 (8.5%) | 107 (6.6%) | 103 (3.8%) | 102 (1.9%) |
| 1987 | 119 (9.8%) | 116 (8.9%) | 109 (5.7%) | 106 (3.7%) |
| 1988 | 139 (17.0%) | 129 (10.7%) | 118 (7.8%) | 110 (4.1%) |
| 1989 | 177 (27.0%) | 145 (13.0%) | 130 (10.3%) | 115 (4.8%) |
| 1990 | 195 (10.0%) | 163 (12.5%) | 143 (10.2%) | 121 (5.4%) |
| 1991 | 210 (7.7%) | 181 (10.8%) | 159 (11.6%) | 127 (4.3%) |
| 1992 | 230 (9.7%) | 199 (10.1%) | 175 (9.6%) | 130 (3.1%) |
| 1993 | 247 (7.4%) | 220 (10.6%) | 190 (8.8%) | 134 (2.9%) |
| 1994 | 300 (21.4%) | 242 (9.6%) | 207 (8.8%) | 138 (2.6%) |
| 1995 | 307 (2.4%) | 260 (7.6%) | 225 (9.1%) | 142 (2.8%) |
| 1996 | 302 (−1.7%) | 276 (6.3%) | 240 (6.3%) | 146 (2.9%) |
| 1997 | 342 (13.5%) | 294 (6.4%) | 254 (5.8%) | 149 (2.3%) |

*Source*: Datastream and Census and Statistics Department, Hong Kong Government.
a: Rental Index for all private domestic premises, year average; b: Wage index up to the supervisory level (for all included industries), year average; c: Composite consumer price index in Hong Kong, year average; d: Consumer price index in the US, year average.

## 9.5 Summary on the Costs and Risk of Letting "Free" Market Force to Guide China's Property Market Under the Imperfect Settings

As a conclusion, the Chinese government should note that just relying on "free market force" to guide China's property market under the imperfect settings could lead to highly undesirable results. In particular, it will result in

(a) A less than socially optimal quantity of property supplied;

(b) The richer Chinese would own a lot of properties while normal income earners might not be able to afford even one, as market force would only allocate the limited quantity of flats to those who are "rich" instead of those who "need" the flats;

(c) Home buyers have to pay excessively high price and be exploited by property developers;

(d) Size of flats could keep shrinking at a gradual but persistence pace until people are forced to live in very narrow space similar to that in Hong Kong and Japan;

(e) The society's attention and resources would be diverted from other growth enhancing and efficiency-improving economic activities to the less productive investment activities on properties;

(f) There could be big cycles of property price (and painful recession or economic crisis during the plunge).[9] During the upswing, income inequality would be aggravated which could raise social and political dissatisfaction among the general public. When the bubble burst, there would be a financial crisis and severe recession, which could trigger disastrous political and social instability;

(g) Persistent rise in property price could also transform China from a low-cost, active and vibrant economy into an inactive economy locked by

---

[9] Thus, except those minority who manage to buy the property at the early stage of property boom and manage to control themselves not to buy more or bigger properties at the later stage of the boom, most of the property investors and home buyers could be vulnerable to a heavy loss.

the vicious cycle of high property price, high rentals, high wage, high cost and high general price level. One such example was similar transformation in Hong Kong between the mid-1980s and 1997.[10]

In the next chapter, the author will recommend a viable solution to the above problems in China's property market.

---

[10] As noted in Section 9.4, even after the bursting of bubble and the then the prolonged recession in 1998–2004, Hong Kong was not able to break the above vicious cycle and regained the economic vibrancy it had between the 1970s and the early 1990s.

# Chapter 10

# China's Property Inflation II: Recommended Solution

In Chapter 9, the author has explained that because of the high income inequality in China and the market structure problem in China's property market, just relying on the "free market force" to guide China's property market will lead to only a large number of undesirable, painful and hopeless results to Chinese citizens. In this chapter, we will discuss the author's recommended solution to the housing problems in China.

## 10.1 The Recommended Solution

### 10.1.1 *The Basic Structure of the Proposal*

#### 10.1.1.1 *The Initial Proposal and the Government's Response*

In the initial set of proposals published in October–November 2006, it was recommended that the Chinese government should adopt and modify the Singapore housing system by directly supplying a substantial amount of various classes of public housings to the low to middle-high income earners. That is, in addition to sufficient supply of low-rental public housings (i.e., the low-rental flats) to the poor and low-profit public housings (i.e., the economy flats) for sales to the low to middle-low income earners, China should also supply and pre-sell a huge number of public housings to the middle to middle-high income earners at a price that is both affordable to these qualified applicants and profitable to the Chinese government (i.e., the sandwich-class flats or the two-limit flats[1]).

---

[1] The name "two-limit flats" in China means (i) limit on the selling price of these flats; and (ii) income limit on the qualified applicants for these flats.

Since then, the Chinese government had increased the scale of low-rental flats to the poor and economy flats to the low to middle-low income earners. Unfortunately, possibly because of ideological problem (e.g., not good for the government to earn profits from the provision of public flats), the Chinese government had not yet accepted the proposal of huge supply of sandwich-class flats. Instead, it only increased the supply of low-rental flats and economy flats. The trouble was that, once the public housings were non-profitable or non-revenue generating, the size of the supply would be constrained by the state budget. As a result, the total supply of public housings from just the higher supply of low-rental flats and economy flats was just too small when compared with the number of private flats. In view that just the new supply of low-rental flats and economy flats would still be too small to have any meaningful impact on private and hence overall property price (i.e., the "more than 80%" private property market and the "less than 20%" public property market would be two segmented markets), the author published another set of articles between December 2007 and January 2008.

### 10.1.1.2  *The Following-Up Proposals*

The articles first noted that the planned increase in low-rental flats and economy flats was a good policy that would help the poor. Nevertheless, the total number of these flats would still be too small when compared with the number of private flats, and therefore could do little to help containing the surge in property price. The articles also noted that the PBoC's curbing measures on the property market in late 2007 could help cooling the property market for a while (see Box 10.1.1 for more details). However, the deep structural problems discussed in Section 9.2 could not be solved unless one addresses to the market structure problem in China's property market.

The articles then re-iterated and elaborated that the appropriate solution is a substantial supply of various classes of public flats (see Section 10.1.2 on the proposed scale of these public flats). That is, in addition to the planned increase in low-rental flats and economy flats, the Chinese government should also supply and pre-sell substantial amount of sandwich-class flats of higher quality, better design, better location and higher price to the middle to middle-high income earners. The price of the sandwich-class flats should be set somewhere between the construction cost and the private property price so that these flats would on one hand be profitable for the government (see the rationales in Sections in 10.1.3 and 10.1.4), and on the other hand be reasonable and affordable to qualified applicants.

As the prices of these economy flats and sandwich-class flats would be much lower than that of private flats, there should be (i) an income limit for eligible applicants for each class of flats; (ii) each qualified family is only entitled to buy one such public flat; and (iii) there should also be a minimum resident requirement (e.g., at least 5 years) before the owner could sell the public flat in the secondary market.[2]

---

**Box 10.1.1:   The Consolidation from Late 2007, and the Rampant Surge from Early 2009**

With the rampant rise in property price (and share price) in 2007, the People's Bank of China started to impose a quantity restriction on the size and growth of bank loans from late 2007. Meanwhile, further deterioration of the US housing crisis and hence the global economy in 1998 started to affect the asset market in China. Despite the weaker demand between late 2007 and early 2009, developers chose to keep the price unchanged until a change in the economic environment and economic policy. As shown in Figure 9.1b, they managed to keep the average property price in the major 35 cities virtually unchanged between late 2007 and early 2009, although there were reports that the number of transactions fell by a substantial amount during the same period.

*(Continued)*

---

[2] If necessary, the government could require the sellers to pay back part or all of the government subsidies on these public flats.

---

**Box 10.1.1:** *(Continued)*

Nevertheless, with some middle-rank officials' mistaken choice to stimulate the private property from early 2009 (see Section 10.2 for more details), property developers were able to engineer a more rampant rise in property price with the pent-up demand during the consolidation period. Thus, despite of tightening policy and severe economic downturn, property developers could still use their hoarding power and market power to keep the price from falling, and then engineer another surge in the property price when the downturn is over. As a result, they managed to keep expanding the property bubble in the form of *"rapid surge — moderate consolidation — another rapid surge"* in property price.

---

### 10.1.2 *How "Substantial" Is Sufficient?*

Substantial supply here would mean that the supply of public flats could be about **70%** of the total new housing supply. In particular, the share of low-rental flats, economy flats, sandwich-class flats and private flats should be around 10%, 15%, 45% and 30%, respectively. Before explaining the rationales for the apparently high recommended 70% share for public housings, it should be noted that the share of public flats in the total stock in Singapore is 80% (see Box 10.1.3 for more details). Thus, the author had already made appropriate adjustments when making the 70% share of new housings supply recommendation to China. Moreover, as the **stock** of housings in China at that time were mainly private flats, the 70% share of public housings in the *new supply* could at most mean the share of public housings in the total stock of housing supply would rise gradually from less than 20% in the medium future to about 50–60% in the distant future.

Why is it necessary to have such a big share of the sandwich-class flats for the middle to middle-high income earners? The reason is that the middle and middle-high income earners could not afford the private property price at that time. Even if the private property price fell by 20–30%, it was still too expensive for them. On the other hand, if private property price fell by more than 20–30%, it could trigger a severe plunge in consumption and hence recession through the wealth effect, rebounds from existing property owners and other complications. More importantly, as explained in Chapter 9, because of the existing high income inequality in China and the market structure problem in China's property market, relying on free market force to do the allocation job under the imperfect settings will only continue to give the undesirable and hopeless results outlined in Sections 9.2–9.5. In contrast, if the Chinese government could adopt the above recommendations to solve 50–70% of her citizens' housing problem and pull them out of the pain of excessively high property price, Chinese citizens would be extremely grateful to the related leaders. Meanwhile, once the citizens get their own home at an affordable price, the implied political and social stability, and people's gratefulness to the government will enhance the long-term ruling of the Communist Party.

### 10.1.3  *What Price Should the Government Choose?*

If so, what price level the government should choose to make it reasonable to the home buyers and profitable to the government? The recommendation at that time was about 60–70% of private property price (e.g., 60% for the standard quality flats of basic quality and 70% for the better quality flats). For example, the property price in the city and suburb of Shenzhen at that time were about 20,000 RMB/m$^2$ and 10,000 RMB/m$^2$, respectively. So, the recommended price of public flats at that time would be about 12,000–14,000 RMB/m$^2$ and 6,000–7,000 RMB/m$^2$ for the city and suburb, respectively. Because of the income limit for eligible applicants, the resale restriction and a waiting time of at least 2–3 years, these new supply would create a reasonable but not excessive impacts on the private property price in the same district (i.e., it would be a good outcome if the excessively high private property price at that time could fall by about 20% before it stabilize and then pick up a gradual rise that is consistent with economic growth and urbanization).

At the recommended price, the housing development board and the related local government would still have a reasonably high profit margin. To ensure this profit will go into the government budget, the housing development board should act as a leading developer, such as sub-contracting the estate design to academies of architecture and sub-contracting the construction to the builders. As Singapore's Housing Development

Board has a few decades of such experience which should have by now eliminated most of the major loopholes though past learning by doing, the author also recommended the Chinese government to study and learn from the procedures and regulations currently adopted by Singapore.

---

### Box 10.1.3:　Share, Types and Role of Public Housing in Singapore

In Singapore, the stock of public housings forms about 80% of the overall housing stock, while the corresponding shares of private housings is only 20%. Among the public housing supply, there are various classes of flats of different prices and income limits for eligible applicants, i.e., the HDB flats developed by the Housing Development Board for those with monthly income below S$8,000, the DBSS flats designed–built–sell by builders or developers for those with monthly income of S$8,000–10,000 and the Executive Condominium (normally with swimming pools and other private condominium facilities) for those with monthly income of S$8,000–10,000 Singapore dollars. Even among the basic HDB flats, there are 3-room, 4-room and 5-room flats, each with a different discount and hence a different price per square feet.

The coexistence of both public flats and private flats in Singapore had also created some of kind of healthy competition between the two. For example, to convince the Singaporeans to pay for higher prices for the private condominiums, most of the private condominiums in Singapore have swimming pools, fountains, barbecue pits, and gymnastic facilities. The developers also need to make very good housing estate design, use better materials, and provide good internal decoration as well as electrical appliances for the flats to justify the price premium above the HDB flats. On the other hand, the better design of the private flats had also urged the Housing Development Board in Singapore to keep on improving the estate design of HDB flats over the past few decades. To compete with the private properties,

*(Continued)*

---

**Box 10.1.3:** (*Continued*)

the Executive Condominium, the highest class of public flats, had also provided the swimming pool and all the other private condominium facilities as well as private condominium design. As a result, the major difference between private condominium and the Executive Condominium would only be the location and the income and resale restrictions of the latter.

As a "foreign talent" classified by the Singapore government, the author was very impressed by the exchange rate system and the housing system in Singapore. In fact, as illustrated in Chapters 1–7, the author had taken useful elements from Singapore's exchange rate system when designing his exchange rate system reform recommendation to China. The author also believes that one major underlying reason for the political stability in Singapore is its housing system which has helped 80% of its citizens having their own flats at a reasonable and affordable price. Thus, the author believes that appropriate adoption of Singapore's housing system would lay a solid foundation of political stability in China.

---

### 10.1.4 *Why It Has to Be Profitable to the Government?*

Why is it necessary to sell the sandwich-class flats at a price with profit, but not at a price at cost or even with a subsidy? This is so because the proposed number of sandwich-class flats will be enormous, selling them at a subsidized price could create unbearable burden to the government budget. Even if they are sold at cost, a calculation error (e.g., missing the cost of providing the related transport, sewage and other supporting infrastructure), or political barriers for upward revision of selling price with rising costs in the future could still mean enormous fiscal burden. For example, when there is a substantial rise in construction cost, the government could be caught in an embarrassing dilemma of raising the selling price at the cost of losing its popularity, or maintaining the selling price at the cost of operating loss and the risk of accumulating permanent fiscal burden until a budget crisis in the distant future. On the other hand, if the government sells the sandwich-class flats at somewhat higher and profitable price right at the beginning, it would not only help avoiding the above problems, but also have the following advantages.

### 10.1.4.1 *Use the Profit to Support Other Reforms and Reduce other Taxes*

The government could use the huge profit to set up a fund (i.e., the substantial amount of proposed housings over the next few decades could mean enormous and sustained profit to the government), and use the fund to subsidize the medical reform, the education reform, the provision of low-rental flats to the poor. As those who purchase the medium-high quality sandwich-class flats are the middle to middle-high income earners, their average income are usually higher than that of the target groups of the above reforms. It is therefore appropriate to tax the middle to middle-high income earners, and use the proceeds to subsidize the target groups of the above reforms (see Box 10.1.4 on why this type housing or land tax would be one of the least distortive taxes).

---

**Box 10.1.4: The Proposed Profit From Sandwich-Class Flats as One of the Least Distortive Taxes**

Another reason for the proposed profits from the provision of sandwich-class flats is that demand for these flats at the suggested price range would be highly inelastic. This would in turn mean that it will be one of the least distortive taxes. Thus, to minimize the tax distortion effect, the Chinese government could collect the tax (i.e., the profit) here while using the tax receipts to (i) support the expenditure on the medical reform, education reform and provision of low-rental flats to the poor; and/or (ii) reduce other distortive taxes, such as the 17% value-added tax on production.

---

Nevertheless, other direct tax on the middle to middle-high income earners could invite political rebounds from them, and might not be politically right. On the other hand, if the government could supply the housing at a price with a decent profit margin and yet much lower than the private property price, the potential sandwich-class flat buyers would be very willing to pay such type of tax. Thus, the proposal could on one hand solve the housing problem in China and on the other hand allow the government to use the profit to support the medical reform, the education reform and the provision of low-rental flats to the poor.

### 10.1.4.2 *Use the Accumulated Profits to Set Up Useful Funds*

With the above set up funds, the Chinese government could invest part of them overseas and part of them in China. The former, if deemed necessary, would be able to help China mopping up the excess liquidity in the next two decades, thus enabling China to offset the monetary growth pressure arising from the currently persistent and huge trade surplus, and accumulate sufficient overseas assets to match the growing economic status of China (see the detailed discussion in Chapter 7).

Furthermore, when China experience a speculative attack or financial crisis in the future, the Chinese government could repatriate part of the funds, and other overseas assets held by the China Investment Corporation (CIC), the Social Security Fund and other state enterprises or organizations, to help stabilize the financial market and the economy. For the part of funds invested in China, the Chinese government could use part of it for long-term domestic investment and part of it for more liquid domestic investment. Thus, whenever there is an unreasonable plunge (or excessive rise) in stock market price, the government could use part of the liquid domestic assets held by the funds and other government entities to buy in shares during the plunge (or sell out shares during the excessive rise). Such action will at the same time earn extra returns for the government and help the stock market grow along a healthier and less volatile path.

### 10.1.4.3 *Raising the Local Government's Support Through Profit Sharing*

The reasonable profit from the sandwich-class flats could also allow the local government to share part of the profit, thus increasing their incentives to participate in the program and hence increasing the program's chance of success. On the other hand, as the local government could not benefit from the low-rental flats and economy-flats, their incentives to supply just the non-revenue generating public housings are rather weak.

## 10.1.5 *Use the Substantial Public Housing Construction to Offset the Soon Arriving Recession*

The article also noted that the sub-prime crisis in the US at that time would sooner or later cause a global recession and then a substantial fall in China's exports (see Chapter 11 for more details). The latter would in turn affect the Chinese economy through the multiplier effect. Meanwhile, with the expected ending of the Olympic game in August 2008, there could be a moderate decline in domestic demand. To offset these changes and avoid their multiplier effect to trigger a recession in China, there was a need for China to supply a sizable amount of reasonably priced public flats. If the Chinese government start planning the public housings and accept application in early 2008, it would be possible for the Chinese government to use sufficient construction of these public flats to offset the expected decline in aggregate demand. Meanwhile, the provision of low-rental flats to the poor and the sales of economy-flats and sandwich-class flats to the low to middle-high income earners would help contain the rise in rentals through a reduced demand for rented private properties. This would in turn help to contain the CPI inflation in the medium future. With the possibility to queue for the low-rental flats, economy flats and sandwich-class flats, low to middle-high income earners would be less critical to the high CPI inflation at that time.[3]

## 10.1.6 *Impacts of the Proposal*

Since the summary report of the proposal by the Xinhua News Agency in late 2007 and the publication of the articles in the Hong Kong Economic Journal between late 2007 and early 2008, President Hu Jiantao had in early 2008 instructed the related government bodies to start planning a reasonably large supply of two-limit flats for the sandwich-class.

---

[3] Note that the stimulation effect would occur during the construction time, while its curbing effect on rentals would be after the construction. As it would take quite some time to get the construction started, even if the Chinese government started to supply at that time, one could not expect any curbing effect on rentals at least two years after that time. Thus, these measures could only help contain rental inflation and then CPI inflation in the medium future.

Nevertheless, when it came to the detailed planning stage, the related officials had mistakenly deleted the above proposal of having the government taking the role as developer while sub-contracting the construction to the builders so that the related profit could (i) become an important source of revenue for both the local and central governments; (ii) be used to support the medical and education reform. Instead, the development of the two-limit flats was directly given to the developers who successfully bid the project. As a result, the related profit was given to the developers. More importantly, as the local government could not collect their share of revenue from the project, their incentives to support the scheme were very weak. Meanwhile, because of widespread corruption and abuse of power among the low and middle rank local government officials, there were scandals and suspected corruption cases related to the terms offered to the successful bidders of the two-limit flats and the allotment of flats to qualified applicants (e.g., there were news that some high income earners or local government officials drove their expensive Mercedes car to apply for two-limit flats).

---

**Box 10.1.6: Why Some Chinese Citizens Did Not Believe the Singapore Housing System Could Work in China**

While Singapore managed to use substantial supply of public flats to help 80% of its citizens to purchase their own flats at affordable prices and therefore lay a solid foundation for its political stability, the author also asked some Chinese citizens for the feedbacks on having the proposed housing system in China. To the author's surprise, many of them said that it would not work as cheating and corruption would mean that these public flats would be allocated to those who have the connections or power to cheat. The feedbacks aroused the author's interest, and he therefore asked some of them whether the cheating and corruption cases would exceed 10%. Interestingly, the replies were "probably not".

*(Continued)*

---

**Box 10.1.6:** (*Continued*)

While the above sample was small and far from vigorous, it did arouse the author's alert on the general public's perception on the fairness of the government in China. Here, what really matter to the author's concern is not the *actual* percentage but the *perceived* percentage of public flats that would be misallocated. With a perceived percentage of less than 10% abuse, why these people jumped into the conclusion that the Singapore's system would not work in China? Would it be because (i) there were more widespread abuse cases elsewhere in China; and/or (ii) they were "over-attracted" by the abuse cases? Either way, it would be a reflection of their general distrust on the government's ability and determination to tackle widespread abuse and corruption in China. If so, this is something that the Chinese government has to be alerted with. In section 10.5, the author will discuss how the government could eliminate corruption in China through a *sector-by-sector* cum *clean-and-consolidation* strategy, and how further complementary effort on the housing policy would play an important role in the strategy.

---

In view that there were no more announcements of further expansion of the sandwich-class flats since early 2008, and the total announced supply of public flats (i.e., two-limit flats, economy flats and low-rental flats) was still far from sufficient, the author had in September 2008 published another set of articles to urge the Chinese government to start building more public flats to (i) offset the soon arriving recession due to the global financial tsunami; and (ii) help Chinese citizens to purchase their flats at an affordable price.

## 10.2 The Proposal in September 2008

Further to the debate with the then Governor of China's central bank since February 2008 on the potential impacts of the US sub-prime crisis on the Chinese economy, the author had in September 2008 published a following-up set of articles suggesting that the Chinese government needed to use ultra-expansionary fiscal policy to pre-empt China from being pulled into a recession by the spread of the US housing crisis to the global economy (see Chapter 11 for more details). In the articles, the author had proposed to use

(a) substantial construction of inter–city high-speed railways and inner-city underground railways; and
(b) substantial construction of public housings

to offset the anticipated impacts of the deteriorating external demand on the Chinese economy (see Chapter 11 for more details). In addition, the proposed construction of high-speed and underground railways would substantially improve China's infrastructure and productivity in the long run. On the other hand, the proposed construction of public flats would help a lot of Chinese citizens to purchase their own flats at a reasonable and affordable price, and therefore (i) help these people avoiding the microeconomic pains outlined in Section 9.2; (ii) help reducing the macroeconomic and systemic risk of an eventual formation and bursting of property bubble; and (iii) lay a solid foundation of political and social stability in China.

While the first part of the proposal was adopted by the Chinese government in its four-trillion fiscal expansion announced in November 2008, some middle rank officials had mistakenly replaced the proposal of substantial public housing construction by the direct stimulation of the private property market (e.g., through the removal of the central bank's curbing measures on housing loans discussed in Box 10.1.1). Furthermore, with the central bank's substantial quantity easing in money supply since early 2009, China's property price index for the 35 major cities surged by 41% between February 2009 and April 2010 (see Figure 9.1b). In major cities, the corresponding rise was even higher (e.g., 63% surge for the case of Beijing).

## 10.3 The Warning and More Detailed Proposals in March 2010

In view of the mistaken policy and the rampant rise in property price between February 2009 and early 2010, the author published a following-up set of articles in March 2010 to remind the Chinese government the need to tackle the housing problems along the right direction.[4]

### 10.3.1 *A Summary on the Undesirable Consequences of Just Relying on Market Force to Do the Allocation Job in China's Property Market*

The articles first re-iterated that letting the free market force to do the allocation job in China's property market would result in the microeconomic problems and macroeconomic risks outlined in Sections 9.2–9.5. That is:

(a) With the high income inequality in China and the market structure problem in its property market, just relying on the free market force to do the allocation and coordination jobs would result in unnecessarily high property price and a supply of housings well below the social optimal level. In addition, the market force would only allocate the limited supply of flats to the "rich" Chinese and foreign buyers instead of those Chinese citizens who "need" the flats. With the asymmetries on market power, hoard power and information on the housing estate between the developers and the home buyers, developers as a group would be able to use the toothpaste-squeezing selling strategy and other strategies to (i) squeeze most of the consumer surplus out from the home buyers; and (ii) generate speculative demand and panic demand for housings;

(b) Allowing free market force to do the coordination job under the imperfect settings could result in a property inflation era until the eventual formation and bursting of property bubble. The eventual bursting of property bubble would cause a financial crisis and severe economic recession. Even in the less severe case, it would weaken the central government's authority of ruling and invite political instability. If the

---

[4] The first version of the articles was published in the China Securities Journal on 2 March 2010. The second and more detailed version was published in the Hong Kong Economic Journal on 12, 13, 15 and 16 March 2010.

crisis is severe enough, it could even cause the collapse of the government and the Communist Party;

(c) During the property inflation era, the society and many Chinese citizens would be spending too much time and resources on investment activities on property, thus diverting resources and attention away from other more growth-enhancing economic activities, such as technological development and industrial upgrading in China. In addition, developers would have the incentives to keep squeezing the size of flats over time. While each round of reduction would be constrained by the cultural norm of acceptable size at that time, persistent gradual squeeze over one to three decades could result in a substantial reduction in the average flat size. Even if it might not reach the type of "squeezed living" in Hong Kong (and Japan), the resulting small size of flats could be scary and unnecessary; and

(d) Persistent rise in property price could also transform China from a low-cost, active and vibrant economy into an inactive economy locked by the vicious cycle of high property price, high rentals, high wage, high cost and high general price level.

Thus, the Chinese government should first ask itself whether it really likes to accept the above horrible outcomes. If not, it should seriously consider the proposal of substantial supply of public flats to meet the housing needs of the low to middle-high income earners.

### 10.3.2 *Adding the Necessary Competition into China's Property Market*

The articles also highlighted that standard curbing measures could delay the proper curing of the housing problem until it is too late. As explained in Section 9.2, there are strong economic incentives deep behind the developers' behaviors such as hoarding of lands and completed flats, toothpaste-squeezing selling strategy, use of a small VIP discount to count the potential demand for the housing estate, and exaggerating the sales and transaction price of the properties. Thus, if the Chinese government relied only on free market force to do the allocation and coordination jobs, developers would have the incentives to use all available means to resist, counter, or offset the impacts of, standard curbing measures on the property market. Past experience showed that, with the developers' hoarding power, market power and connections with local officials, they could eventually offset or even fully nullify the effect of these curbing policies (see Box 10.1.1 for one such experience between late 2007 and early 2009). Even in the case of very strong curbing measures that managed to result in a substantial reduction in the sales of new properties, they could still resist a meaningful fall in property price until the economic environment or economic policy changed. Thus, standard curing measures did not have a good record of solving the problem. In fact, it had very often diverted attention from the proper curing of the problem.

In fact, it was because of the above considerations of the very complicated nature of the problem, the author had since October 2006 kept on suggesting the Chinese government to directly supply, or directly lead the development of, huge amount of public flats to the low to middle-high income earners in China. Bearing in mind that developers had already formed an informal cartel through the establishment and common adoption of the standard industrial practices outlined in Section 9.2, this could in fact be the only way to add the necessary competition in China's property market. The government's direct supply of public housings would also endow the government a powerful and **direct** policy weapon to influence China's property market, i.e., the government could *directly set the price and decide the number of public flats* to the low to middle-high income earners *instead of waiting for the developers' response to the curbing measures* which could be very different from what the government is hoping for.

Bearing in mind that (i) the amount of public flats had to be large enough to be able to help containing the private property price and create sufficient and healthy competition between the private and public property market (see Box 10.1.3 for the healthy competition in Singapore); and (ii) the need to maintain people's incentives to work hard, the author provided detailed explanations on why the proposed 70% share of public flats in the new supply could only be insufficient instead of too much (see Section 10.1.3 for details), and proposed that the share of low-rental flats, economy flats, sandwich-class flats and private flats in the new housing supply should be around 10%, 15%, 45% and 30%, respectively.

### 10.3.3 *Containing the Potential Correction of Private Property Price: More Classes of Public Flats With Price as the Hard Target*

In view of the rapid surge in property price since February 2009 and hence a substantial enlargement of the property bubble (see Figure 9.1b and 9.1c for the 41% and 63% surge at that time), the articles proposed to have more classes of flats to help achieving a **controllable** correction in private property price. For example, in addition to the original three classes of public flats, the government could add a new class of high-quality public flats whose location and facilities will be similar to private flats while there is still income and resale restrictions. Parallel with this, the discounts for high quality, medium-high quality, medium quality, and standard quality (and less well located) public flats could be 20%, 25%, 30% and 40%, respectively. The aim of the proposed arrangement is to use substantial supply of these public flats to attain a moderate but not excessive correction of private property price (see the later part of this section for more details). For example, as there are still income and resale restrictions for the high-quality public flats, the private property price would at most fall by 20%.[5] [Note: If the government prefers a bigger correction of private property price, it could at the beginning opt for a 25% discount instead of a 20% discount for the high-quality public flats.]

The articles also noted that the proposed discount should only be used to compute the price of public flats at the initial stage. Once the initial price is fixed, subsequent adjustment of price should be based on changes in construction costs, economic growth, scarcity of land and etc. The government

---

[5] This is based on the assumption that, when deemed necessary, the government is willing to adjust the quantity of public flats as described in the subsequent discussion in this section.

should avoid using the change in private property price as a basis of adjustment. Otherwise, this would give the property developers a powerful leverage to influence the price of public flats and hence the overall property price through their market power on private property price (see Box 10.3.3 on similar experience in Singapore during its asset inflation era in 1991–1997).

---

**Box 10.3.3:  Problem of Using Changes in Private Property Price as a Basis for the Increment of Public Flat Price**

During the asset inflation era in 1991–1997 in Singapore, as some individual officials mistakenly believed the free market could give a fair value on property, they had used the rise in private property price as an important indicator for the price adjustment of public flats. This, together with the indicator effect of the price of new private properties on the price of second-hand private and public flats, the developers was able to use the price of a small amount of new private properties to pull up the price of the whole pool of private and public flats (see also the discussions in Box 9.2.5).

---

The articles also highlighted that the proposed 70% share of public flats should be a **soft target** *that could be changed when deemed necessary*. On the other hand, the price of the public flats should be a **hard target** or operating target for the proposed scheme. That is, once the government has decided the prices of the various classes of public flats, it should keep on supplying the flats at these prices until the eligible candidates' demand are met, even though the eventual number of flats is far greater or smaller than the proposed 70% share. The advantage of using the price as a hard target (and the quantity as a soft target) is that the government could have good control on the scheme's impact on private property price.

The above discussion could be better understood with the help of the following diagrams, in which the vertical axis is the average price of the public flats and the horizontal axis is the total quantity of public flats.

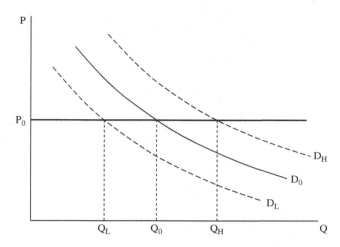

**Diagram 10.3.3a.**   Using Price as the Operating Target

As shown in Diagram 10.3.3a, if $P_0$ is used as the operating target, even if the estimated demand $D_0$ is far greater or smaller than actual demand (e.g., $D_H$ or $D_L$), the final result will at most be a quantity supplied that is far greater or smaller than the initial estimate (i.e., $Q_H$ or $Q_L$ instead of $Q_0$). As it takes times to build the housing estate and the related authority would have a queuing list for the public flats, what the authority has to do is to adjust the planned number of flats in the subsequent years. With the following-up adjustment of the schedule of quantity supplied, the eventual production of public flats will be the same as the actual demand. Thus, the arrangement will not create any problem in the whole process. Meanwhile, the impacts of the chosen price of public flats ($P_0$) on the price of private flats would be as expected, e.g., price of private property would at most fall to that of high-quality public flats, as there are still income and resale restrictions for the latter. In addition, the related authority could at that time and in the future influence the private property price through its choice on the discount on the public flats.

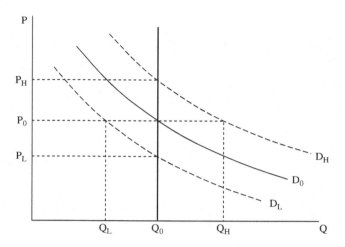

**Diagram 10.3.3b.**   Using Quantity as the Operating Target

On the other hand, if the related authority uses the quantity as the operating target, when the planned quantity $Q_0$ turns out to be far greater or smaller than the actual demand at price $P_0$, there would be substantial excess supply ($Q_0 - Q_L$) or excess demand ($Q_H - Q_0$). Of course, even in such a situation, the related authority would still charge the price $P_0$ instead of $P_H$ or $P_L$. However, as any announced change in the quantity target could be perceived as the related authority's inability to do a proper projection, there could be substantial delay in the adjustment of the quantity target, which could in turn cause serious problems. For example, consider the case in which the quantity target is $Q_0$ while the actual demand is $Q_L$ in Diagram 10.3.3b (i.e., the quantity target $Q_0$ is set at a level much greater than $Q_L$, the quantity demanded at $P_0$). If there is already a bubble in the private property market, the over ambitious target and the delay in adjusting the announced schedule of quantity target to more reasonable level could trigger a bursting of the bubble in the private property market.

In fact, that was what happened in Hong Kong during the Asian Financial Crisis. As the then Chief Executive Officer and his officials of the Hong Kong Special Administrative Region did not understand the difference between using the price and quantity as the operating target, they had come out with a 10-year public flat supply plan with an average quantity supplied of 85,000 flats per annum. As the plan was made even without the very basic estimate of demand (e.g., the actual amount of completed flats before the crisis was only twenty or thirty thousand flats per annum, far lower than the planned eighty five thousand units per annum), it turned out the planned quantity was far much greater than that could be absorbed by the market. Meanwhile, as there was a substantial bubble in the private property market at that time, the emergence of the financial crisis in other economies had therefore had the chance to trigger a bursting of bubble and severe panic in Hong Kong's property market. As the cumulated amount of speculative demand and panic demand before the crisis was enormous, the offloading of these flats (and the temporary disappearance of real demand) had eventually caused a 65% decline in the property price between late 1997 and 2004.

Of course, the above extremely bad outcome for the case of Hong Kong was due to not only the related authority's ignorance in economics, but also mistakes of the previous governments and bad timing of the policy. However, the above discussion does suggest that the mistake of using a hard schedule of quantity target for the public housing plan could lead to disastrous outcomes. On the other hand, if the related authority uses the price of public flats as an operating target and be prepared to adjust the schedule of quantity supplied with the help of a queuing list (i.e., similar to the case of Singapore), the proposed scheme would be able to solve China's housing problem and pre-empt further expansion of the property bubble.

### 10.3.4 *Risk of Just Relying on Standard Tightening Measures*

10.3.4.1 *Developers Have Their Incentives and Hoarding Power to Resist Tightening Measures*

After making the recommended solution to China's housing problems, the articles also urged the Chinese government not to hope that developers would cooperate with, or bow to, any normal tightening measures on the property market. This was so because, as implied by the discussions in Section 9.2, the developers would have the incentives to use all available means to resist, counter, or offset the impacts of, these tightening measures. Even if some of these standard tightening measures, such as the tightening of housing loans, managed to cause a consolidation of the property market, the developers would still try to hold their property price until a change in the economic environment or economic policy. As the developers had a reasonably good hoarding power and the other parts of the economies could also be hurt by the tightening measures, it would usually be possible for developers to resist a meaningful fall in their selling price until a change in the economic environment or economic policy. By then, the pent-up demand accumulated during the consolidation period would cause another surge in property price. As a result, the property bubble could still increase in the form of "*rapid surge — moderate consolidation — another rapid surge*". In fact, that was what happened in China between late 2007 and April 2010 (see Box 10.1.1 for more details).

#### 10.3.4.2 *There Is a Time Limit for the Proper Curing of the Property Bubble*

Once the property bubble reached a certain size, even a moderate reversal of economic conditions or a good-intention curbing policy could trigger a bursting of the bubble and the subsequent crisis as well as political and social instability. While the property bubble in China at that time had not yet reached the "dead position" highlighted by the literature of Chinese military strategy (see Section 8.3 for similar discussion on the stock market), continued dragging around the wrong or ineffective polices (instead of adopting the right and effective policies) would mean that China would sooner or later reached such a dead position.

Thus, instead of just relying on the standard tightening measures and hence the related struggles with the developers which could cause unnecessary delays and even divert attention from the proper curing of China's housing problems, the Chinese government should at the same time announce more plans of public flats for Chinese citizens to queue for.

### 10.4 The Tightening Measures Since April 2010 and the Subsequent Developments

#### 10.4.1 *The Tightening Measures in April 2010*

The article published in the China Securities Journal on 2 March 2010 was just before the National Congress Meeting in China. Meanwhile, many attendants of the Congress had also expressed the dissatisfaction on the surge of property price. In the television news programs, some citizens had even expressed their distrust on the government's ability to contain the property inflation. Some even said that, as a matter of fact, property price had surged more after the tightening measures. Thus, the Chinese government at that time was under enormous pressure to curb the property inflation.

In April 2010, the Chinese government started to announce its "historically most severe" set of curbing measures on the property market. Among these measures, the most important measures were:

(i) For those families who had already owned a flat, no matter the mortgage was fully paid or not, the down payment for their second flats would be raised from 20% to 50%. In addition, the mortgage rate for the second flat was raised to 1.1 times of the base lending rate. However, for first time home buyers, the down payment would remain to be 20% and the discount on the mortgage rate would remain unchanged.

(ii) For those cities with "high property price", banks were discouraged to provide loans for the purchase of the third (or more) residential properties. Banks were not allowed to provide loans to non-residents of the related cities who could not provide evidence of tax payments or social security contributions in the related cities over the past one year.

The aim of the policy was to use the credit restriction to curb short-term speculative demand, long-term investment demand and cross-city demand, while trying not to affect the first time home buyers. While the above nation-wide policies only discouraged the banks to provide loans for the third (or more) residential properties, the local government of Beijing had on 13 April 2010 added an administrative restriction stating that citizens in Beijing would only be allowed to buy one more flats, irrespective of the number of flats that the related families own before the announcement.

Because of the severity of the tight credit policy in recent history, potential home buyers had adopted a wait-and-see approach. Although some speculators had chosen to offload some of their speculative holdings of properties, rich long-term investors with substantial holdings of properties continued to keep their holdings of properties. More importantly, developers had chosen to use their hoarding power to resist any meaningful reduction in the selling price of their properties. As a result, the property market had entered a tug-of-all period, in which the transaction volume in both the new and second-hand properties plunged to historically low levels while the property price was basically unchanged.

### 10.4.2 *The Dangerous Counter-Proposal in July 2010*

By early July 2010, some people in the developer and property agent camp had engineered a campaign emphasizing that the tightening measures had hurt the GDP growth and the decline in private property construction would also affect many other related industries (e.g., the iron and steel industry, the cement industry, and many supplying and servicing industries). They also proposed the Chinese government to remove the curbing measures so as to let the Chinese economy to grow again.

In view of the danger of such a proposal, the author published another article on 17 July 2010. In the article, the author first noted that the tightening measures since April 2010 did manage to stop further rise in the property price, mainly because it had curbed the speculative demand and panic demand. However, if the tightening measures were ever removed, the speculative demand and panic demand would come back. By then, the property price would surge further until the property bubble reached the "dead position" level. Thus, the Chinese government should be cautious that those who recommended the removal of the curbing measures could have their own personal interests, and their proposal was effectively asking the Chinese government to tie up its own hands so that the private property price could continue to surge until the re-emergence of public dissatisfaction and the enlargement of the property bubble to the "dead position" level. Moreover, the curbing measures were only announced in April and most Chinese citizens had put their hope on the curbing measures. If the Chinese government took away these curbing measures just three months after the announcement, the government's reputation and credibility would be seriously damaged. The long-term political consequence of such damage could be very destructive.

### 10.4.3 *The Proper Policy Mix*

The article also expressed the author's appreciation of the designers of the tightening measures which suggested that they had finally recognized that the "*housing need*" of the general public would be far more important than the "*investment demand*" by the richer group. Nevertheless, the article also highlighted that the above tightening measures did not address to the core problem in China's property market. That is, it did not address to the market structure problem outlined in Section 9.2. Without following-up polices along that line, the tightening measures could eventually end up as a failure. Thus, the most appropriate choice for the Chinese government at that time was to start constructing and pre-selling substantial amount of public flats while maintaining the curbing measures at that time. The article also highlighted that the proposed arrangement would keep all the advantages outlined in Sections 10.1 and 10.4.4. For example, one advantage of the arrangement was that people could start queuing for the public flats, and such queuing and the associate change in expectation could help containing the rise in private property price, thus pre-empting further enlargement of the property bubble. The proposal of many classes of public flats would also help to ensure the correction of private property price within the controllable range and help minimizing the cheating and corruption incentives in people's application for public flats (see Section 10.4.4 for more details).

The article also noted that the original proponent of the tightening measures did not recognize the importance of the market structure problem and developers' hoarding and market power outlined in Section 9.2. As a result, it had underestimated the developers' ability to resist, the time required for property price to correct, the extent the economy was hurt by the curbing measures and the accumulation of resistance power by the other camp. More importantly, the housing problem in China was not only one problem, but two problems. That is, in addition to the first well known problem of *excessively high property price*, there was the second problem of a lack of supply of, and hence a *severe shortage in the quantity of, flats that the general public could afford to purchase*. The underlying reason for the second problem was the high income inequality in China, in which the rich could afford to invest in a large number of flats at a price much higher than that could be afforded by the normal income earners. Thus, with the developers' ability to squeeze the quantity supplied and push up the price of private property through hoarding of land, collective choice of a high profit margin and other strategies outlined in Section 9.2, the price and quantity of private flats had adjusted to a "bad" equilibrium in which the total quantity of flats could only satisfy the *"investment demand"* of the rich, but not the *"housing need"* of the normal income earners.[6] Thus, simply using the tightening measures to reduce private property price would not be able to solve the problem. The proper solution should be, in addition to the private property market, the provision of a sufficient supply of affordable flats (by the government) for normal income earners to purchase. That is also why the author has since October 2006 kept suggesting the Chinese government to supply huge amount of affordable public flats to normal income earners.

### 10.4.4 *Other Dimensions of the Proposal*

The article then proceeded to elaborate that every dimensions of the author's proposal were well thought out and organically integrated together with their own significance. For example, the design to maintain the tightening measures on private properties while increasing the public flat construction was to facilitate the correction of private property price while ensuring an increase in the total housing construction and hence the needed stimulation effect to support the economic recovery at that time. When these public flats are completed, it would help to contain the inflation rates in the subsequent years. This would be particularly important if there were severe global asset inflation during the eventual global recovery from the global financial tsunami (see Chapter 11 for more discussions).

---

[6] If there are substantial supply of public flats to normal income earners, investment demand for private flats will decline moderately as there will be less rental demand for private flats. However, it is likely that the rise in quantity of public flats will be much greater than the reduction in the quantity of private flats.

The design to have the price of public flats set somewhere between the private property price and the construction cost was on one hand to help normal Chinese citizens to purchase their own flats at a reasonable price so that they could also enjoy and share the benefit of economic growth which would in turn lay a solid foundation for the long-term ruling of the present government; and on the other hand to use the associate profit to raise the local government's incentives to participate actively in the program, open an important and the least distortive source of central government revenue which could be used to support the medical and education reform as well as reduction of the more distortive taxes such as the 17% value added tax on production.

The design to have a few classes of public flats was to minimize the incentives and consequences of cheating and corruption. Because of the perceived social status of the more expensive class of public flats, most of the higher income earners would prefer paying higher price for their own class of public flats instead of trying to compete for the lower class of public flats through cheating or corruption. Even if some of the very rich ones managed to buy the high-quality public flats through cheating or corruption, the amount of discount they could enjoy would be much smaller than that from the economy flats. The design would also increase the government's control on the potential correction of private property price. That is, price of private property would at most fall to the level of high-quality public flats, as there are income and resale restrictions on the latter.

Most importantly, the design of a substantial amount of public flats was to provide the government a powerful policy weapon that could directly influence the quantity and price of a significant share of flats instead of waiting for the struggling result with the developers whose decision could be very different from what the government was hoping for.

### 10.4.5 *Further Comments in August 2010*

Since the publication of the above article which was relatively critical on the related authority's delay in supplying sufficient number of public flats, Minister Jiang Weixin of the Ministry of Housing, Urban-Rural Development had come out to explain that there were ongoing plans and constructions of six million[7] low-rental flats, economy flats and public-rental flats.[8] Meanwhile, many related ministries also expressed their commitments and determination to continue or strengthen the tightening measures on the private property market.

While glad to hear the plan of six million public flats and the continuation of the tightening measures, the author remained concerned that the six million public flats would not be sufficient to solve the problem. He therefore wrote another policy articles in August 2010. Unfortunately, because of change in staffing position in the Singapore office of the Xinhua News Agency and possibly tightening of media comment on housing issues in China, the article could only be published in a newspaper in Hong Kong and did not have the chance to reach the top leaders and therefore probably had no influence on China's housing policy. Nevertheless, it could still help future policies by summarizing some of the article's arguments as follows:

(a) The article first noted that as the rich Chinese could afford a large number of private flats while the much bigger population of moderately well-off Chinese could afford quite a few private flats, the "investment demand" in Chinese was in fact huge, i.e., huge enough to push the private property price up to the level that quantity of private flats was only enough to meet the "investment demand" by the richer group while not enough to meet the "housing need" of the normal income earners. In fact, even if private property price fall by 20–30% from the level at that time, it would still be unreachably high for the normal income earners. Thus, even if the tightening measures managed to cause a 20–30% correction of private property price, most of these cheaper private properties would still end up in the hand of the rich and existing home owners who could purchase the flats with less than 50% bank loans or even one-off cash payments without bank

---

[7] Out of the plan of the six million public flats, there was substantial delay on the local government side. As a result, the effective supply of public flats at that time was far much smaller than the plan.

[8] Public rental flat is a new class of public flats which allow the sandwich-class to rent the flat until they get the money to buy private flats.

loans. Only a small portion of the cheaper private properties would end up in the hand of middle-high income first time home buyers who have to use most of their next 20-year income to repay the mortgage. For the middle or low income earners, the cheaper private flats would still be unreachably high for them. Moreover, whether the tightening measures could eventually push down the private property price was yet to be seen: While the chance of a correction in first-line cities was higher, the correction, if any, could be much smaller than what most people were hoping for. On the other hand, the chance of a correction in second-line cities was very slim.

(b) As a "foreign talent" who has been observing Singapore over the past fifteen years, the author believed one important underlying reason for the political stability in Singapore was a sufficient supply of various classes of affordable public flats to 80% of its citizens (see Box 10.1.3). Even so, Singapore still have to work very hard to contain the property inflation, as the small percentage of new private property price could affect the whole property market through the indicator effect outlined in Box 9.2.5. Given China's high income inequality and low GDP per capita, China's share of public flats in the total *stock* of housing should not be much lower than that of Singapore. Thus, the 70% proposed share of public flats in the *new housing supply* was in fact a downward adjustment compromise. If the Chinese government eventually opted for a 60% share, the author could still accept it. It was however not possible for any responsible economist to accept a less than 20% share of public flats for only the poor but not the sandwich-class. This was so because such a small share of public flats would not be able to exert the necessary impacts on the private property market (i.e., the bigger private property market and the smaller public property market would end up as two segmented markets).

(c) It should be noted that dissatisfaction among Chinese citizen was already enormous. While some of them might just blamed the developers and the local governments, some of them were also blaming the central government. As the above proposal was crucial to the happiness of half to one billion of Chinese citizens, the related officials should refrain from using excuses or misleading arguments to stop or delay the adoption of the proposal. For example, "insufficient budget" should not be an excuse, as there was substantial profit in the proposed sandwich-class flats. What the government had to do was to draw the plan, pre-sell the flats and then use the ongoing revenue from the pre-sales to complete the construction. The government did not even need to use any extra fiscal budget to do the proposed amount of sandwich-class flats. In fact, the scheme could generate substantial profit and hence fiscal revenue which could be used to reduce other more distortive taxes and increase other useful expenditures. The above discussion also suggested that those who claimed that "the government should not earn profit here" were actually trying to be generous at the cost of the nation. It had not only unnecessarily cut an important and the least distortive source of government revenue, but also cause an unnecessary delay to the proper curing of China's housing problem. Subcontracting the two-limit flats to developers, instead of having the housing development authority leading the estate development by subcontracting the design to academies of architecture and subcontracting the construction to the builders, was also trying to be generous at the cost of the nation. If the government is concerned about the possibility of cheating and corruption in the application process of the public flats, what the government had to do is to pass a law, or issue a policy document, stating that (i) officials involved in such abuse would lost their job; and (ii) applicants involved in such abuse would be prosecuted and the amount of money put in the application for or eventual purchase of the public flats would be confiscated. Of course, at the implementation stage, there would be a lot of emerging problems to be solved, e.g., builders using less material than that stated in the bidding contracts, or very poor design for some public flats. Nevertheless, all these could be removed or avoided over time through ongoing reviews and corrections at the implementation level. As a matter of fact, Singapore had in the past accumulated a very good set of procedures that had basically overcome these problems. What the Chinese government had to do was to adopt these procedures with appropriate modifications.

### 10.4.6 *The Administrative Restriction on Flat Purchase*

While the above article did not have a chance to reach the top leaders, the developers were able to use their market power and hoarding power to resist the tight credit measures from the central government, i.e., they were able to resist a correction of private property price despite a temporary plunge in property sales between April and August in 2010. By September, the peak "golden month" of property purchase in the year, the developers were able to sell a reasonably large number of flats, partly because of the pent-up demand over the past few months and partly because some potential home buyers had lost their confidence on the potential impacts of the government's tightening measures. Thereafter, there were rising dissatisfaction among Chinese citizens as it started to look like that the curbing measures might not be able to bring the private property price down to a more reasonable level. Among the criticizing comments in the internet, an educated person had also rewritten an olden day three-word poem into one that expressing the disappointment on the tightening measures. Because of the quality of the rewritten poem, dissatisfaction among Chinese citizens became more widespread.

In response to the growing dissatisfaction and the pickup of property transactions in September, the State Council announced further tightening measures on 30 September 2010, i.e., just before the week-long National Day vacation which made October nicknamed as the "silver month" of property transaction in the year. The most important measures were:

(a) Banks were not just discouraged, but forbidden, to provide loans for the purchase of the third (or more) residential properties. Banks had the responsibility to make sure that the down payment of the second residential property would be at least 50% and the mortgage rate would be 1.1 times of the base lending rate. Banks also had the responsibility to follow the announced policy of not making mortgage loans to non-residents who could not provide evidence of tax payments or social security contributions in the related cities over the past one year;

(b) Minimum down payment ratio by first-time home buyers were also raised to 30%.

In addition to the above nation-wide measures, the central government also pressurized local governments of major cities to impose their own stricter and city-specific tightening measures.

For example, in the announcement made by the Shenzhen local government on 30 September 2010, local residents were not allowed to buy flats if their family already owned two or more flats in the city. For those who have one or no flat, the maximum number of flats they could own would be two. The power of such administrative restriction was that the richer citizens who had two or more flats would no longer be allowed to buy flats. While these richer Shenzhen citizens would not sell their large holdings of properties, the restriction did mean the developers and the luxurious property market had lost the most important sourse of clients.

In fact, the announcement made by Shenzhen (i.e., the Shenzhen model) was even stricter than that made by Beijing on 30 April 2010, i.e., the Beijing model which allowed its citizens to buy only one more flat, irrespective of the number of flats they owned before the announcement. That is, the richer Beijing citizens with two or more flats could still buy one more flat while the richer Shenzhen citizens with two or more flats would not be allowed to buy anymore. As a result, some property agents were speculating that (i) there could be a correction in the luxurious property market in Shenzhen; (ii) developers in Shenzhen might have to reduce the selling price of their flats; and (iii) the second-hand property market would not correct unless the developers started to sell their property at a lower price.

On 7 October 2010, the Shanghai local government also adopted the Beijing model which only allowed its citizens to buy at most one more flat. In addition, the Shanghai local government also indicated that it would be the first city that pioneers a property tax on property owners. Thereafter, other major cities with "high property price" such as Hangzhou, Ningbo, Fuzhou, Nanjing and Guangzhou also announced their city-specific administrative restrictions. While most of these administrative restrictions were similar to the less strict Beijing model, Nanjing was closer to the Shenzhen model. On the other hand, Guangzhou, while adopting the less strict Beijing model, also added an administrative restriction that forbidden non-residents to purchase properties in Guangzhou even if the non-residents were rich enough to pay for the properties without the help of bank loans.

### 10.4.7 *Remarks on the Administrative Restrictions*

While the impacts of the above administrative restrictions are yet to be seen, it is perhaps more important to note that the central government is now very determined to curb the property price. Thus, even if the above administrative measures do not manage to bring the property price down, the central government could announce even stricter administrative (or economic) measures until the developers conceded. So, the question now is not the central government's **willingness** to curb the property price. Instead, the question is its **ability** to choose the right policy recommendation to keep the property price in check.

Thus, the author would like to highlight that the discussions in this chapter and Chapter 9 could be more important. In particular, because of the high income inequality and market structure problems, provision of sufficient number of affordable public flats could be the only proper solution to China's housing problem. For example, even in the unlikely scenario that the tightening measures manage to bring the private property price down by 20–30%, it would be more likely that the then cheaper private properties being sold to the richer Chinese who are still eligible to buy the second flat instead of being sold to those who need but do not have a flat.

The tightening measures could also create other distortions or problems. For example, because of the administrative restrictions, those richer Chinese with a few or even tens of properties would be more determined to hold their properties. There are also emerging signs that people are shifting funds into business properties and the stock market. If left unchecked, there could be formation of a business property bubble or re-emergence of a stock market bubble in the future. Given that

(i) the US had lately indicated its intention of a second quantity easing in money supply;
(ii) it would be just a matter of time the global economy would recover; and
(iii) the previous cumulated increase in global money supply, unless all mopped up by the related governments, would probably start exerting its inflationary effect during the global recovery,

the chance of an eventual development of the above bubbles in China could be much greater than most people believe.

In addition to the potential distortions, there could also be an exit problem with the above administrative restrictions. That is, if one day these administrative restrictions were removed, pent-up speculative demand and long-term investment demand by the richer Chinese could cause a very rampant surge in property price. Thus, before the removal of the administrative restrictions, it would be important for the Chinese government to provide sufficient number of affordable flats to the low to middle-high income earners in China.

At the time of writing this chapter, there is news that the Chinese government plans to build 6 million public flats per annum in the forthcoming Twelfth Five-Year Plan. If so, 5 years down the road there would be 30 million public flats. Assuming a family size of 3 or slightly more, this would meet the housing need of 90 million, or almost 1 billion, Chinese citizens.[9] While excited with the plan, the author would like to highlight that:

(a) The planned quantity supplied should be a soft target and the price of public flats should be the operating target, i.e., the government should be prepared to revise the plan if the actual demand turned out to exceed or fall short of the planned quantity supplied;

(b) There should also be a plan for the sandwich-class flats, which could help solving the pain of the sandwich-class and minimize the incentives of widespread cheating and corruption in the allocation of public flats;

(c) Quality checking of the public flats is very important.

If the above points are not taken seriously, there is a possibility that the good-intention policy could eventually end up hurting, instead of improving, the citizens' impression on the government.

## 10.5 Continuing the Anti-Corruption Strategy From the Housing Sector

### 10.5.1 *The Strategy of Cleaning Corruption Sector-by-Sector*

In Chapter 5, the author has proposed a strategy to clean the country-wide corruption culture sector by sector. That is, the government should first group and focus most of its resources and effort on a target sector (e.g., the banking industry). After eliminating the corruption culture in that sector, the government could repeat the same procedure to the second sector and then the third sector, until the corruption culture in all sectors were eventually cleaned. The strategy was actually borrowed from the Chinese military wisdom of "*intentionally open an escaping exit to the surrounded enemy*" (围兵必阙) (see Section 5.3.7 for more details). That is, while focusing most

---

[9] At the time of the proof reading of the book, the Chinese government announced another substantial increase in the planned number of public flat construction in 2010 and 2011.

of the resources and effort to clean the corruption in the chosen sector, intentionally leaving an exit for part of the corrupted officials to escape to other sectors would reduce the resources and costs involved in the elimination of corruption in the chosen sector. When the corrupted officials found that the risk and potential penalty of receiving bribe in the target sector would be much higher than those in other sectors, they would whenever possible prefer taking bribes in the other sectors instead of the target sector. This would in turn imply a substantial decline in corruption activities in the target sector to manageable level. The strategy would also substantially reduce the resistance of corrupted officials whose connections should not be underestimated if they were ever forced to group together.

### 10.5.2 *The Strategy of Cleaning-and-Consolidation Followed by Another Cleaning-and-Consolidation*

After eliminating the corruption culture in that sector, the Chinese government should make effort to establish an anti-corruption culture and corruption-reporting channels in that sector. That is, substantial consolidation effort should be made to ensure that the fruit of clean culture has its root in that sector. After completing the cleaning-and-consolidation steps in that sector, the government could then proceed to repeat the same cleaning-and-consolidation strategy in another well chosen sector. If the Chinese government continues this strategy sector by sector, China would one day be able to eliminate most of the corruption in the country.

### 10.5.3 *Why the Banking Sector and Then the Housing Sector*

In Chapter 5, the author also quoted the public high-level examination (i.e., the university entrance examination) in China as an example that the establishment of an anti-corruption culture in a particular area is not as impossible as most people believe. The author also recommended China to choose the banking industry as the next sector for the above anti-corruption strategy, mainly because the WTO commitments and hence the need to clean up the non-performing bank loans in 2005–06 had already put the Chinese government in the *"no-retreat but must-fight-to-survive position"* (绝地一战) (see Box 10.5.3).

**Box 10.5.3:    Why China's Banking Industry Was at the Must-Fight-to-Survive Position**

When China joined the WTO in 2001, it had agreed to gradually open its banking industry to foreign banks over the subsequent 5 years. Given the high non-performing loans in the domestic banks at that time (see Chapter 5 for more details), it was important for China to clean up the non-performing loans in the domestic banks. Otherwise, the subsequent entrance of the foreign banks would cause substantial drainage of deposits from domestic banks to foreign banks, which could in the long run make the domestic banks unable to survive (see Chapter 5 for the detailed discussions). Fortunately, with the strategy of inviting foreign strategic partners and the three-step injections, China was able to establish better internal control within the domestic banks, and divert foreign banks' effort and resources to helping the strengthening China's domestic banks from creating fatal competition to domestic banks.

Because of such a *must-fight-to-survive position*, the Chinese government would have the determination to implement the necessary measures to clean the banking industry. As a matter of fact, this *must-fight-to-survive position* did push the Chinese government to implement the necessary measures to clean the banking industry (see Chapters 3 and 5 for more details on the banking reform). By now, China's banking sector is basically clean in the sense that corruption cases in the banking sector are basically individual behaviors instead of systemic behaviors. There are also signs that a reasonably clean banking culture has had its early root in the sector. To make sure the root would grow stronger, the author believe the Chinese government should do further consolidation works here.

Meanwhile, given that the public high-level examination and the banking industry are now two sectors with a reasonably clean culture, the author would like to recommend the Chinese government to choose the public housing sector as the second target of the above anti-corruption strategy. The reason is that the Chinese government is again at the *no-retreat but must-fight-to-survive position* in public flat provision. As explained in Chapter 9 and this chapter, property price was already at extremely high level. If property price made another one or two rampant surge from the current level, the property bubble could sooner or later reach the *"dead-position level"*. Meanwhile, most Chinese citizens have put their housing hope on the central government. If the government manages to solve their housing need, this would lay a solid foundation for the long-term ruling of the Communist Party. If the government fails to solve their housing need or there are widespread scandal cases on the quality of public flats, the government's image could be seriously hurt. Thus, no matter the Chinese government chooses the tightening measures cum administrative restrictions, the author's proposal of substantial supply of public flats, or a combination of both, the Chinese government would have strong incentives to ensure a clean implementation of the measures.

### 10.5.4 *Importance of Proper Implementation and Counter-Checking*

Of course, the author would recommend grouping most of the resources and effort on the supply of public flats. In particular, the government should make effort to ensure the proper design, construction and allocation of public flats, such as

(a) designing a fair allocation procedure (e.g., balloting) of public flats to eligible applicants. It is also important to have a counter-checking arrangement by an overall supervisory and complaint department to ensure the implementing department is honestly doing its job;

(b) setting up a specialized department which would design and implement checkable procedures to ensure the builders or developers would build the public flats according to the safety and material standards specified in the bidding contracts. Again, it is important to have the overall supervisory and complaint department checking that the implementing department is honestly and diligently doing its job.

(c) having a small public housing design department ensuring the design of the whole public housing estates, which include the flats, the buildings and the common facilities, are of good standard. Again, making the implementing department responsible to the overall supervisory and complaint department is important;

(d) having a few classes of public flats with different prices instead of just once class of economy flats. This is because the very cheap price for economy flats would create very strong incentives for corruption. On the other hand, because of the perceived social status of the more expensive class of public flats under the multi-class public flats system, most of the higher income earners would prefer paying higher price for their own class of public flats instead of trying to compete for the lower class of flats through cheating or corruption.

### 10.5.5 *The Most Capable General Is the One Who Could Make His Army Grow*

Once the corruption culture is cleaned and an anti-corruption culture is firmly established in the housing sector, the government would only need to keep a small amount of army (resources) to maintain the anti-corruption culture there. The success in the banking and housing sectors would also mean that the government could recruit more armies (resources) in its anti-corruption campaign. Thus, the government could use the remaining portion of the old army (resources) plus the newly recruited army (resources) to repeat the same cleaning-and-consolidating procedure in another sector. Through such sector-by-sector strategy of concentrated effort of cleaning, consolidating, and then another concentrated effort of cleaning, the population of corrupted officials would keep falling over time until one day the Chinese economy is much less corrupted.

# Chapter 11

# Fiscal and Monetary Policies During the Global Financial Tsunami

In 2008 and 2009, the US subprime crisis finally triggered off a severe correction of the US property price and the collapse of some major over-leveraged financial institutions, such as Lehman Brothers and Merrill Lynch. These in turn triggered a financial tsunami and global recession in 2008–2009. To pre-empt the Chinese economy from being pulled into a deep recession with severe financial dis-intermediation and financial de-leveraging similar to those happening in the US, the author had recommended the use of ultra expansionary fiscal and monetary policies to contain China's economic slowdown, thus pre-empting an extensive degree of financial dis-intermediation and financial de-leveraging from happening in China at the very first stage. In this chapter, we will see how the time lags in international economic transmissions and China's ultra expansionary fiscal and monetary policies had helped pre-empting the above vicious cycle from happening in China.

Having said that, it should be noted that China had done that in a rather imperfect way and there was an element of luck in the decision process. There were a lot of rooms for further improvements. In this chapter, I will review the decision process in details and point out that China needs to make significant improvements in its macroeconomic policy research. Improvements along this line could in the future ensure China making the right policy decisions without counting on luck.

## 11.1 Signs of an Economic Slowdown in 2007H2 and Early 2008

While the Chinese top leaders had eventually adopted the ultra fiscal expansion in 2008Q4, there was in fact a debate in China between late 2007 and mid 2008 on whether the US sub-prime crisis would eventually cause a significant slowdown of the Chinese economy. As I will explain in this chapter, the debate had to some extent delayed China's adoption of the ultra macroeconomic stimulations, and hence contributed to a *"not-too-bad" but painful* enough slowdown of the Chinese economy in 2008H2 and 2009H1. On the other hand, if the Chinese top leaders did not have the political wisdom to judge that the minority's warning of a severe slowdown was correct, China could have gone into a much deeper recession. Thus, ability to make the correct diagnosis at the early stage is a pre-requisite for good macroeconomic policy decisions.

In this and the next sections, I will explain that there were in fact early signs in 2007H2 and early 2008 that the US sub-prime crisis could trigger off a severe correction of the US property price, a global recession and then a significant slowdown of the Chinese economy, although most of the negative impacts on China's export and GDP could only be felt from 2008Q3. If the related economic policy departments could make the right diagnosis at the early stage, the slowdown of the Chinese economy in 2008H2 and 2009H1 could have been mitigated to a much milder one. Through such discussion, it is hoped that economic policy departments in China could in the future made effort in strengthening their capacities in macroeconomic diagnosis.

As shown in Figure 11.1a, the US home price index rose at the rampant pace of 10.2% per annum between 1997Q3 and 2006Q1, a pace that was unlikely to be sustainable and was much faster than the 3.1% annual rise between 1987Q1 and 1997Q3. With the outbreak of the subprime

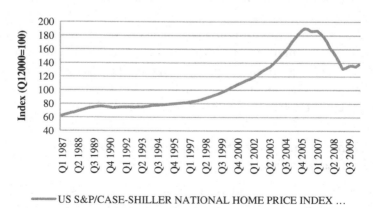

—— US S&P/CASE-SHILLER NATIONAL HOME PRICE INDEX …

**Figure 11.1a.**   US Home Price Index

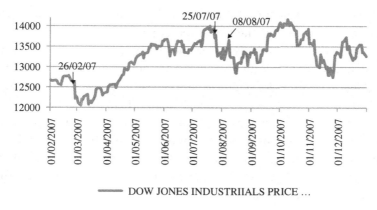

**Figure 11.1b.**  US Stock Price Index

crisis, the US property price index started to fall from the peak of 190 in 2006Q1. By 2007Q4, it had fallen by 10.3% from the peak.

On 26 February 2007 (and then on 6 March 2007 and 11 May 2007), the former US Federal Reserve Chairman, Alan Greenspan, came out to warn that he believed that there was chance that the US economy would slip into a recession (because of the problem of the sub-prime loans). The warnings had resulted in moderate but temporary correction of the US and global stock markets on the next day. For example, as shown in Figure 11.1b, the Dow Jones Industrial Index fell by 3.3% on 27 February 2007. However, as the stock markets were dominated by trading activities with short time horizons, the market soon forgot about the substantial downside risk in the medium future. In fact, after fluctuating within a range in March 2007, the Dow Jones Industrial Index resumed its rising trend from April 2007.

Like many other foreigners, the author was at the beginning ignorant about the sub-prime issue in the US. Nevertheless, with the knowledge on economic crisis and macroeconomic policy management accumulated over the past thirty years, the author was woke up by Greenspan's comments and the corrections in the stock market between late July and early August 2007. Thereafter, he started to follow the sub-prime issue in the US. By 2007H2, he was convinced that the US property price would continue to correct and the size of the potential property price correction would be sufficient to cause a severe recession and trigger a few vicious cycles and other complications. As a result, he sold all his holdings of Singapore shares in 2007H2. In the policy articles published in late 2007, he also suggested the Chinese government to get herself ready for the severe consequences of substantial corrections of the US property price.

From early 2008 onwards, it became even more apparent, or more correctly, crystal clear to the author that the US sub-prime crisis would trigger off a global recession. As such, the author had written two sets of articles in early 2008. The first set was published on 6 February 2008, which used the export growth in previous recessions to warn the Chinese government that the soon arriving global recession would unavoidably cause a substantial fall in China's export growth from the 25.7% in 2007 to a single-digit, or even negative, export growth in China (see Box 11.1a and Table 11.1 for the rationales of such a warning).

---

**Box 11.1a:  Why a Good Economist Should Be Able to Anticipate the Sharp Plunge in China's Export Growth from 2008H2**

As China's export growth before the global financial tsunami was well above 20% for many years, it was hard for Chinese officials to foresee or anticipate that China's export growth could plunge to a single digit or negative rate during the soon arriving global recession. Neverthe-less, if one bothered to check China's export growth for a longer time horizon, such as that shown in Table 11.1, he or she should know that China's export growth did fall from the usual 22–36% to single digit level during the mild global recession years in 1996, 1998, 1999 and 2001.

Given that the US problem would trigger a more severe global recession, it should be quite easy for a good economist to correctly anticipate a sharp plunge in China's export growth during the global recession. Unfortunately, most policy bodies, forecasters and macroeconomic commentators in the media did not even bother to do the very basic job of checking China's export growth beyond the 5–6 year span. As a result, all these people had made very misleading comments on the subsequent state of the Chinese economy. It is the hope of the author that young readers of this book will take a more serious attitude and avoid committing the same type of mistakes in the future.

Table 11.1  China's Export Growth in US$ (%)

| Year | Export Growth |
|------|---------------|
| 1994 | 36.3 |
| 1995 | 23.1 |
| 1996 | *1.6* |
| 1997 | 20.9 |
| 1998 | *0.5* |
| 1999 | *6.2* |
| 2000 | 27.7 |
| 2001 | *7.0* |
| 2002 | 22.1 |
| 2003 | 34.6 |
| 2004 | 35.4 |
| 2005 | 28.4 |
| 2006 | 27.2 |
| 2007 | 25.7 |

With the anticipated deterioration of the global and domestic economy, the article also recommended the People's Bank of China to follow the cuts in US interest rates with reasons stated in Box 11.1b. The article also recommended the Chinese government to get herself ready to use huge fiscal expansion, and to relax the tight monetary policy, when China's export and then GDP started to be weakened by the soon arriving global recession.

---

**Box 11.1b:  Why the Chinese Central Bank Should Have Followed the US Interest Rate Cuts from Early 2008**

The article first noted that, with the 0.75% and then 0.5% reduction of US discount rate in late 2007 and early 2008, the higher renminbi-US dollar interest differential and the anticipated depreciation of the US dollar vis-à-vis renminbi would be sufficient to induce uncovered interest arbitrage and hence substantial capital inflows into China through the illegal channels or the abuse of legal channels.[1] This

*(Continued)*

---

[1] The article also note that, even if the inflows were not yet unmanageable at the beginning, realization of the widely anticipated substantial cuts in US discount rate and substantial depreciation of the US dollar in the subsequent future would soon make it necessary for the Chinese authority to follow the interest rate cuts in the US.

**Box 11.1b:**   (*Continued*)

would in turn substantially increase China's monetary growth pressure. Given the high and rising CPI inflation in China in early 2008, the monetary growth and inflation pressure would be more severe if China did not follow the interest rate cuts in the US.

Next, the article used Diagram 11.1 to explain that, after the very tight credit and monetary growth target announced in late 2007 (see Section 8.3.3 and Box 10.1.1 for more details),

(a) there were in fact credit rationing in China; and
(b) the quantity target on money supply and credit, instead of the central bank's recommended base lending rate and deposit rate, would be the binding constraint on the quantity of money and hence inflation pressure in China.[2]

Thus, even if the Chinese central bank followed the US interest rate cuts, the quantity of credit or money in the economy would still be constrained by the quantity target (i.e., $Q_0$ in Diagram 11.1). Reducing interest rate from $i_0$ to $i_1$ would only mean greater degree of credit rationing (e.g., with the lower base lending rate, bank could charge higher interest premium or tighten their lending criteria). Thus, a moderate reduction of the non-binding interest rate at that time would not severely affect the monetary tightening effort in China. In contrast, not following the interest rate cuts in the US could create enormous capital inflows and monetary growth pressure through uncovered interest arbitrage, thus severely weakening the monetary tightening effort at that time.

(*Continued*)

---

[2] For the sake of presentation simplicity, the Figure was drawn for the case with no credit and monetary growth. With monetary and credit growth, both the $Q_0$ curve and the $D(R_0)$ curve will shift to the right over time by similar magnitude, and the result will be qualitatively the same as the case with no monetary or credit growth.

**Box 11.1b:**   (*Continued*)

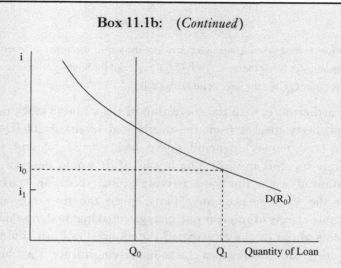

**Diagram 11.1.**   Credit Rationing in China

In the above Diagram, the vertical line $Q_0$ represents the Chinese central bank's quantity target on credit (or money supply), while $i_0$ represents the base lending rate announced by the central bank.[3] $D(R_0)$ is the loan demand from borrowers who could satisfy the risk criterion $R_0$ set by the banks. With the excess demand for credit shown by $Q_1-Q_0$, the commercial banks had rationed $Q_0$ amount of loans by the following methods: (a) raise the interest rate premium for those who could only borrow from the banks at a premium above the base lending rate; and/or (b) tighten the lending criteria

(*Continued*)

---

[3] The tricky part here is how to use the available information to identify the situation at that time (e.g., credit rationing or equilibrium). Knowing that the central bank could not simultaneously target both the price and the quantity, I started to doubt about the usual belief at that time that the Chinese credit market and money market was in equilibrium. Judging from the fact that there were quite some borrowers who could not get their desired credit at the base lending rate plus their usual risk premium at that time, I deduced that there was some kind of credit rationing in China and therefore drew $i_0$ below the intersection point of $Q_0$ and credit (or money) demand curve.

**Box 11.1b:** *(Continued)*

(e.g., refuse to lend to some borrowers or reduce the size of the loans). As a result, the actual quantity of credit (or money) was $Q_0$, not $Q_1$; and the binding constraint was the quantity target $Q_0$, not the interest rate target $i_0$ or $i_1$.[4]

Furthermore, with the correction of the Chinese stock market and property market from the overheated levels in 2007Q4, the credit (and money) demand curve had started to, and would continue to, shift inward. The inward shift would be even more pronounced when the soon arriving global recession started to affect the Chinese economy. Thus, given the time lags in the economic effects of interest rate changes, making moderate interest rate cuts ahead of the anticipated economic slowdown could help mitigating the slowdown in the soon arriving future. Last but not the least, reducing the interest rate would help reducing the downward momentum of Chinese share price at that time and the eventual extent of over-correction thereafter (see Section 8.5 for the more details).

Unfortunately, because of (i) difference in views on the severity of the soon arriving global recession; and (ii) concerns on the high CPI inflation at that time, the then Governor of the Chinese central bank

*(Continued)*

---

[4] Note that the credit rationing at that time could be just a special case at a particular time in China: In order to contain the surge of share price and property price, the Chinese central bank had imposed a very tight credit and monetary growth target in 2007Q4. In normal cases, even if there is a moderate monetary tightening and hence a moderate shortage of credit supply relative to credit demand, the commercial banks could

(a) tighten the risk criteria in loan approval, which could result in a leftward shift of the loan demand curve from $D(R_0)$ to, say, $D(R_1)$ (not shown in the diagram); and/or
(b) raise the risk premium until the credit demand is close or equal to the credit supply $Q_0$.

Given sufficient time, both of these would tend to bring the credit and money markets towards equilibrium.

---

**Box 11.1b:**   (*Continued*)

did not agree to reduce the interest rate. By late 2008, obvious signs of severe slowdown had prompted the higher authority to urge the Chinese central bank to start reducing interest rate.[5]

---

## 11.2 Potential Consequences of the Anticipated Plunge in US Property Prices

The second set of articles was published on 18–19 March 2008. It highlighted that the soon arriving global recession would be more severe than most people believed. The set of articles first criticized the rather popular forecasts on the US economy at that time. It noted that just a few months ago these forecasters had, without providing any sensible supporting reason, misleadingly forecasted that the worst scenario in the US economy would be just a slowdown of growth to 1–2%. After seeing more negative outcomes in the first two months of 2008, they only revised the forecasts to a very minimal negative growth in the US economy. Worse still, they misleadingly forecasted that the US economy could recover in the second half of 2008, and China's export growth would only declined by a few percentage points and could still registered a double digit growth. Being

---

[5] Although Premier Wen Jiabao had thereafter correctly commented that "*the academia was right, the central bank was wrong*" on the related macroeconomic diagnosis, the author would like to highlight that this was just a normal disagreement on the macroeconomic diagnosis. That is, with the high CPI inflation in China at that time, the then central bank governor naturally thought that it was better not to reduce the interest rate. However, through the actual painful experience during the Asian Financial Crisis and subsequent strong desire to draw lessons from the crisis, the author was aware that the economic environment could deteriorate substantially during a crisis like the global financial tsunami or the Asian Financial Crisis. Thus, young readers of this book should bear in mind that even many years of devoted effort on knowledge accumulation could still be insufficient until they are "*baptized*" by a crisis (i.e., have gone through the painful experience of a crisis). That is, there is still a big difference between reading books on a crisis and the actual painful experience during a crisis.

upset by these misleading forecasts, the author highlighted that the forecasts were in fact low-quality forecasts or, more correctly, pure guessing without any good supporting reason or evidence. Before elaborating the author's reasoning for a more severe outcome, the article cautioned the Chinese policy makers not to be misled by this low-quality and unreliable pure guessing. The Chinese policy makers should also avoid taking a simple average of this pure guessing and the author's scenario. Instead, the Chinese leaders had to use their wisdom to judge whether the above pure guessing or the author's analysis would be more trustworthy. Otherwise, it would still cause substantial delay in the use of appropriate economic policies to pre-empt the huge and unnecessary economic losses.

### 11.2.1 *Somebody Had to Absorb the Loss*

The set of the articles then proceeded to spell out the author's reasoning for the possibility of a very severe US recession in the quarters ahead. After noting that the market at that time was still calling the US economic problem as a sub-prime crisis, it first clarified that the sub-prime problem was just a triggering factor and one of the most hurting part of the US housing crisis. With further changes in the economic and market conditions, the problem had already changed to the problem of a bursting of the US property bubble, i.e., the latest and the subsequent deep plunges in property price in the whole US property market and the severe negative financial and economic consequences caused by the deep plunges in property price. As the total value of the whole US property market was enormous, even a 30% decline in the US property price would mean a huge economic loss that could not be easily absorbed by the US home owners, the US financial institutions, the US government or any combinations of the three. While the US government could reduce the correction by printing more money, it could be very risky to use this method to avoid any correction of property price. This was so because the required monetary injection would be so enormous that its effect on subsequent inflation and exchange rate changes would be far more serious than the original problem in the US property market (see Box 11.2.1 on the inflation risk on the subsequent quantity easing by the Federal Reserve, and Box 11.2.2b on the need to accept a necessary correction of property price and the role of the government to minimize the necessary correction).

---

**Box 11.2.1:   The Subsequent Quantity Easing by the Federal Reserve and the Potential Risk of a Global Asset Inflation**

As will be discussed in Section 11.7, when the crisis deepen, the US Federal Reserve did inject enormous monetary base to offset the effect of a plunge in the money multiplier and hence keep the money supply growing, i.e., the Quantity Easing One (QE1) in 2008–2009. This had in turn pre-empted the US economy from entering a great depression similar to that in the 1930s. In addition, as could be seen from Figure 11.1, the quantity easing had avoided an over-correction of the US property price, i.e., it started to stabilize from 2009Q2 after falling 31% from the peak. Nevertheless, as will be explained in Section 11.7, even if the Federal Reserve works very hard to mop up the excess liquidity during the recovery, there will probably be a severe global asset inflation and CPI inflation during the global recovery. While the contribution of the US's QE1 to the global economy is likely to be greater than the potential inflation cost to the global economy, the US's QE2 from November 2009 can at most benefit the US economy at the cost of potential asset bubble and then crisis in other economies.

---

If property price had to correct, there had to be somebody absorbing the implied loss, i.e., the loss would fall on somebody, even though he did not like it. This "somebody" could be

(i)   the property owners (including those who had paid up, and those who had not paid up their mortgage loans);
(ii)  the financial institutions;
(iii) the government,

or any combinations of the three parties. Even if part of the burden or loss fall on the property owner, the implied consequences on the US consumption and hence its multiplier effect on the US GDP would be enormous. For the other parts of the loss that fell on the financial institutions (e.g., when the home owner declare bankruptcy), the implied loss of capital and the surge in lending risk (due to surge in the problems of adverse selection and moral hazard) would result in substantial reduction in bank loans. The latter would result in a credit crunch and severe financial disintermediation, making firms and the whole economy short of funds for the normal operation and investment, which would mean a substantial reduction in aggregate demand and hence output.

## 11.2.2 *No Painless Solution to the Bursting of Property Bubble*

Such problem would be very difficult to solve. Take the Federal Reserve's action to cut the discount rate towards zero and supply huge amount of funds to the banking system in early 2008 as an example. As the banks' interest rate margin between the lending and deposit rates was only a small percentage (e.g., 2–4%) of the total loans. With the recognition of the surge in adverse selection and moral hazard problems (e.g., banks became less certain whether a commercial or individual borrower would declare bankruptcy at a later stage), even if the Federal Reserve could restore the banks' lending capacity through the huge injection of capital or liquidity, bank would not do what the central bank hoped them to do. Instead, the banks would raise the interest rate margin (and cut the loan size) to compensate the higher risk in lending and offset part of their previous loss.

As a result, even if the Federal Reserve made substantial cuts in its discount rates and huge injections of funds to financial institutions, there would still be substantial credit crunch and a very minimal reduction in mortgage rate at least in the early stage. Worse still, the above negative economic consequences had not included the negative impacts due to the collapses of US financial institutions at that time and the subsequent future.

Thus, there is no painless solution to the bursting of the property bubble or other asset bubble (see Box 11.2.2a on similar conclusions on other asset bubbles).

**Box 11.2.2a:   China Could Be in Big Trouble If It Did Not Squeeze Its Stock Market Bubble Before the Global Financial Tsunami**

In fact, there is in general no painless solution to the busting of asset bubble. That was also why the author had over the past one year or so wrote many policy articles advising and helping the Chinese government to (a) gradually squeeze the stock market bubble to less vulnerable level; and (b) supply huge amount of reasonably-priced public housings to low to middle-high income earners so as to constrain the rise in private property price in China, and gradually bring it to more reasonably level in the more distant future.

Fortunately, the Chinese leaders at that time had adopted at least part of these recommendations, thus avoiding China from a big disaster — the worst scenario would be a bursting of China's stock market bubble and property bubble triggered by the bursting of the US property bubble and global recession. Since the Chinese stock market had made a reasonable correction just before the soon arriving property, financial and economic crisis in the US, even if the US problems would be more serious than most people believe, China could still contain the harm to a bearable level if she could use her economic policy tools appropriately. The author also believed that China's gradual squeezing of stock market bubble would be seen as a successful case in the history of economic management, although the actual squeezing was far from perfect and had plenty of rooms for further improvements.

If there was no painless solution, one natural question would be what painful solution the US could choose. One of the traditional solutions was as Greenspan suggested: let the property price fell to a reasonably low level so as to attract bargain hunters and new home purchasers with purchasing power to bottom-fish or bargain hunt the property.[6] For the existing property owners, they only had the following three choices: (a) kept the property and tighten their belt until the recovery of the property market; (b) sold the property and realized the loss; and (c) declared bankruptcy or "walked away from their homes". The first two choices would be a substantial decline in US consumption. The third choice would mean the financial institutions had to absorb part of the loss which would of course weaken their ability and inclination to lend. As said, all these would contribute to a substantial decline in economic activities in the US. Of course, it would always be better to decisively avoid a bubble at its seeding and development stage. If the bubble was already formed and established, the next best solution would be a gradual squeezing of bubble to less vulnerable (but still over-valued) level. Nevertheless, as the US property price had already declined by quite some percentage, it was cleared in early 2008 that the bursting of the US property bubble would be unavoidable. The US government could at most mitigate the subsequent plunges in property prices and the economic consequence of such plunges.

---

[6] Of course, with hindsight from the US experience (see detailed discussions in Section 11.7), the related government could, at the early stage of the correction, make drastic cuts in its discount rate to offset the rise in the risk premium in the market interest rates and hopefully cause a moderate reduction in the market interest rates. During the second stage of the correction, the related government could inject substantial liquidity into the market so as to (i) pre-empt or mitigate financial de-leveraging and over-corrections in the financial and property markets; and (ii) ensure there is sufficient available funds in the market for the bargain hunters and new home purchasers to do bargain hunting at the low enough, but not excessively low, property price levels. To further reduce the necessary correction of property price and the implied short-term economic pains, the related government could choose to inject a bigger amount of liquidity which could cause a bigger immediate depreciation of its currency and a higher inflation in the distant future. Nevertheless, even with these refinements to mitigate the necessary corrections of property price, the related government still has to accept and endure a certain extent of property price correction from the highly over-valued level.

---

**Box 11.2.2b:   There Is Still a Role for the Government to Minimize the Necessary Correction and Offset Its Economic Impacts**

While there is no painless solution, it does not mean that the government could not play a role in minimizing the necessary correction of the asset price and mitigate the economic pain caused by the correction. As explained in Section 11.2.1, printing money to stop the asset price from correcting could cause too high an inflation in the future. However, the government could still choose to have an optimal combination of monetary injection and correction of property price. That is, the government could still minimize the necessary correction of property price by injecting a reasonable amount of liquidity into the economy, i.e., the government could choose to accept a higher inflation risk during the recovery in exchange for a less severe correction of property price and recession during the crisis period. In addition, the government could use fiscal policy or other policies to mitigate the impacts of the necessary correction of property price. In fact, as noted in Box 11.2.1 and shown in Diagram 11.1, the Federal Reserve had managed to use the QE1 to avoid an over-correction of property price in the US at the cost of a higher inflation risk during the recovery period.

---

### 11.2.3 *The Global Economy Was Still at the Beginning and Deepening Stage of the Great Recession*

As (i) the correction of the property price at that time was still far from sufficient (see Box 11.2.3a for the rationales behind such a judgment); and (ii) the effect of the decline in property price had just started to spread to other parts of the economy, the articles highlighted that it was only the beginning of the recession, and more severe and painful economic corrections were yet to come. For example, the not-yet-sufficient decline in property price had only started to affect consumption in 2008Q1. What people were seeing could be only a small part of the total effect. If one added the total effect of further subsequent plunges in property price, the total direct effect would be many times of what people were experiencing at that time. Worse still, the multiplier effect would mean that the total direct and multiplier effects would be *another few times of that "many times of what people were experiencing"*.

---

**Box 11.2.3a:   Why It Could Be Judged That the Correction of Property Price at That Time Was Far From Sufficient**

There were quite a few strong signs for a well-trained macroeconomist to judge that the correction of the US home price at that time was far from sufficient. Firstly, the home price index at that time (i.e., 2007Q4) had only corrected by 10% from the peak in 2006Q1. Such correction was still small when compared with the cumulated rampant rise between 1997Q3 and 2006Q1. Secondly, the volume of property transaction at that time was very light, suggesting that potential buyers still believed the property price was still too high. A third reason for such a judgment was the huge inventory of unsold properties at that time, which suggested that the excess supply in the property market was huge.

---

Furthermore, all these had not yet included the direct and indirect effects of fall in property price on investment, credit card bad debts and so on. Thus, even if one

(a)  assumed the Federal Reserve could avoid or mitigate the impacts of financial institution failures, plunge in share prices and credit crunch to the real economy at that time; and
(b)  included the stimulation effect of the substantial cuts in discount rate, the anticipated tax rebate in May 2008 and the weakening of the US dollar at that time,

the extent of the US recession would be far more severe than most people believed.

It should also be noted that *multiplier effect takes time*, i.e., it would take quite some months or quarters for the initial decline in consumption and investment to exert most of their effects on the real economy through the multiplier effect. In addition, it would take further time for the fall in output to exert its full effect on employment. Even if one did not include the effects of further subsequent fall in US property price, it was easy to judge that the above mentioned forecasts of only another two quarters of mild recession would be seriously wrong. After highlighting that, the articles proceeded to explain that the soon arriving recession would be far more severe than that in 2001 (see Box 11.2.3b for reasons for such a judgment).

---

**Box 11.2.3b:   A Bursting of Property Bubble Would Usually Cause a More Severe Recession Than a Bursting of Stock Market Bubble**

The articles also pointed out that, because of the different characteristics between the property market and the stock market, the bursting of housing bubble in the US at that time would be far more severe than the moderate recession caused by the bursting of the IT bubble in 2001. Firstly, property mortgage means that the leverage for property investment is usually higher than that of stock investment by normal US citizens. Thus, when compared with the fall in share price, a fall in property price of the same percentage would mean greater investment loss and hence greater negative wealth effect on consumption.[7] This would be particularly the case for the US at that time as (i) the recommended 20% down payment ratio in the US was far much smaller than the 30% in Hong Kong; and (ii) the actual down payment ratio for many mortgage loans, especially those done in 2006–2008, was far less than the 20% adopted in China and Singapore. Secondly, the fall and the recovery of share price are usually faster than those of property price. Thus, the impact of a plunge in property price would be more prolonged. Thirdly, after the busting of the IT bubble in 2001, Greenspan had

*(Continued)*

---

[7] Although the rises and falls in share price are usually greater than those of property price, share investors are usually more prepared for a fall than property investors.

---

**Box 11.2.3b:** (*Continued*)

cut the US interest rate by a substantial amount which had in turn helped pushing up the US property price and hence offset the impacts of the plunge in share price. On the other hand, it would be quite unlikely that the drastic cut in interest rates by Bernanke could push up the US share price at that time. In fact, it might not even be able to stop the share price from falling further. Thus, it was impossible at that time to use a rise in share price to offset even part of the effect of the plunge in property price. Finally and most importantly, the total value of the US property market was far much greater than that of the US stock market, and the distribution of properties was also more even than that of shares (i.e., shares tends to be more concentrated in the hands of the rich while properties tends to be more evenly distributed in the hands of US citizens). Thus, a fall in the property price of the same percentage would tend to hurt the US consumption more.

---

Given that China's export growth had declined from the 27.7% in 2000 to only 7% in 2001, the article urged the Chinese policy makers not to underestimate the impacts of the soon arriving global recession on China's exports and GDP.

Noting that it would take months or quarters for fiscal and monetary policies to exert large enough stimulation effects on the economy, the article recommended the Chinese government to

(a) substantially increase the actual construction of the economy-flats and two-limit-flats for the low to middle-high income earners;
(b) approve and start the construction of the planned high speed railway between Beijing and Shanghai;
(c) bring forward and start the building of clinics, hospitals or other related hardware of the planned medical reform; and
(d) speed up other infrastructural constructions (e.g., new and more underground railway lines in major cities).

On the monetary side, while it was necessary to keep the credit and monetary growth target to constrain the rise in CPI inflation at that time, it should start to follow the US's cut in interest rates (see Box 11.1b on why cut in interest rate was not a binding constraint on China's credit tightening policy at that time). When the soon arriving global recession started to influence the Chinese economy and China's CPI inflation started to fall, the Chinese government should consider appropriate relaxation of the restrictive policy on monetary and credit growth.

## 11.3 The Debate With the Central Bank in 2008Q2-Q3

The fiscal part of the above proposals was well received by the Chinese top leaders and the State Council. This had in turn contributed to the sped-up approval and actual implementation of the high-speed railway between Shanghai and Beijing as well as the announcement of more planned supply of public housings at that time.[8]

Nevertheless, the proposal to start cutting interest rate amid the high CPI inflation in early 2008 but ahead of the soon arriving global recession was not that well received by the then Governor of the Chinese central bank. Despite similar view on the need to control asset and CPI inflation in 2007 and early 2008, development in the US property market had changed so fast that the author and the then Governor of the Chinese central bank had very different views about the global and Chinese economic outlooks in 2008. The latter believed that it was still necessary to keep a tight monetary policy because (i) the central bank had just started its tight monetary policy; (ii) the overheated stock and property markets had just started to soften; and (iii) the CPI inflation was still on the high side (i.e., 8.7% in February 2008). While agreeing that the central bank should keep a tight

---

[8] As discussed in Section 11.4.4, with stronger signs of a slowdown in the subsequent quarters, the State Council had planned and started more high-speed railway lines between major cities and more underground railway lines within major cities. The author believes these high-speed inter-cities railways and inner-cities underground railways, if appropriately done, will also generate significant long-term benefits by augmenting China's transportation system, productivity and competitiveness.

target on monetary and credit growth until China's CPI inflation started to fall, the author also foresaw the soon arriving severe global recession. In view of the time lags in monetary and fiscal policies, the author also explained that it was necessary for China to start following the interest rate cuts in the US (see the rationales in Box 11.1b) and to start part of the fiscal stimulation before it was too late.

As a result of such discrepancy in views, China did not follow the interest rate cuts in the US. Meanwhile, because of the heavy costs involved in writing these policy articles (see Box 11.3 for more details), the author had basically stopped writing policy articles in 2008Q2-Q3 with only a few occasional reminders re-iterating that the soon arriving economic slowdown could be severe.

In June 2008, with export orders showing clearer signs of weakening, the Chinese top leaders became more aware of the risk of a severe slowdown. Nevertheless, as the Chinese central bank still insisted on its previous view, the Party and the State Council started to collect more updated information on the economy through study-visits to various types of enterprises as well as various cities and provinces. By September 2008, the Chinese top leaders were convinced by the overwhelming information and leading indicators that the Chinese economy would soon experience a severe economic slowdown. Seeing this, the author started to write a few sets of very influential articles on how to use ultra expansionary fiscal policies and then expansionary monetary policies to mitigate the economic slowdown in the subsequent quarters.

---

### Box 11.3: A Problematic Culture Among Chinese Officials

Because of the macroeconomic policy management skill in China was not yet up to the level that the author had accumulated over the past thirty five years, the author had to write a lot of policy articles to help China avoiding major mistakes in its exchange rate system reform and macroeconomic policies. Nevertheless, writing this large number of

*(Continued)*

**Box 11.3:** *(Continued)*

policy articles had taken away a lot of the author's research time for academic journal paper publications. On the other hand, the author's university at that time could only count journal paper publications, as it was difficult to set up a fair and objective measure on the quality and contribution of policy recommendations by various economists. Meanwhile, as the Chinese official channel was only interested in reporting the author's policy analyses but did not want to report to the higher level that the author needed their help to solve the above problem of mismatch between journal publications and policy articles, the author had no choice but focusing on his journal paper publications and suspending the writing of policy articles.

While this had given him the necessary the necessary time for journal publications in 2008Q2-Q3, some potential policy mistakes in China had on and off "forced" the author to write policy articles to stop the potential mistakes. For example, to help the Chinese people from suffering a more severe recession triggered by the global financial tsunami, the author was once again "forced" to take the pain of squeezing his research and family time in 2008M9-2009M1 to write the series of proposals on the ultra expansionary fiscal and monetary policies outlined in Sections 11.4–11.6. In April 2010, as there was once again proposal to speed up the appreciation rate of renminbi, the author was forced to write another two articles to convince the Chinese leaders not to accept the proposal.

Despite of these hard efforts from the author side, the decision of the Chinese official channel not to report the author's need for support had costed China a lot on the policy front. For example, if there was support from the Chinese government, the author could have written the housing policy recommendations outlined in Section 10.3 in March 2009, i.e., at the early stage of the property price hike and before China's adoption of the less appropriate credit tightening measures (see the detailed discussions in Section 10.4). If not because

*(Continued)*

---

**Box 11.3:** (*Continued*)

of lack of support, the author could have written Section 11.6.3 in May–June 2009, which could have helped the Chinese central bank mopping up the excessive liquidity and hence pre-empted the CPI inflation hike since 2010Q4. This latest trend also suggests that the author would be less and less influential on China's macroeconomic policies. While the Chinese central bank might be able to deal with standard economic problems, the author is worried whether it could solve tough major macroeconomic issues without disastrous mistakes (see the Preface for more detailed discussions).

The fact that the Chinese official channel did not even bother to report the author's need for help also made him aware of the following two problems in China's bureaucracy:

(i)   With so many levels of hierarchy in the bureaucracy, there are many sad things happening that most people (and the top leaders) are not aware of;

(ii)  Chinese officials only care about what their boss thinks, as this is the key to their promotion. That is, if there is anything that can please their boss, they would be very eager to do it, no matter this is good or bad to the society. On the other hand, if there is anything with a risk that their boss might not like, they would choose not to report it or even hide it, even though this could be important to the country or their boss.

While the author has given up his hope asking for support and would only stick with his new practice of writing policy articles only if time allows, he also senses that such type of culture has been hurting a lot of Chinese people, and would one day cost China heavily.

---

## 11.4 The Ultra Expansionary Fiscal Policies

The first set of articles was published between late September 2008 and early October 2008. To convince the Chinese leaders that huge enough fiscal expansion was necessary to contain the slowdown pain within an acceptable level, the article first explained that it was already unavoidable that the Chinese economy would experience a relatively painful slowdown in the subsequent quarters (see the discussions in Box 11.4). The only question remained was on how severe the slowdown would be, and the result would very much depend on how much fiscal and monetary stimulations the government was willing and able to engineer.

---

**Box 11.4:  Why It Was Necessary to Have the Ultra Expansionary Fiscal Policies**

To convince the Chinese top leaders that ultra fiscal stimulation was necessary to mitigate the subsequent economic downturn in China, the articles in late September 2008 first explained that the slowdown at that time was just the very beginning of the downturn. In the subsequent quarters, the downward pressure on the Chinese economy would be greater and greater. The stimulations discussed by economic officials and discussants in the media were too minimal and could not stop China from slipping into a severe recession. To help train some young readers of this book as a good policy maker in the future, let us now review in details the reasons behind the judgment.

As explained in the author's previous articles, the original and difficult-to-solve problem of the US economy was the collapse of the US property price. With the total value of the US property market at an astronomic amount, even a 30% decline in property price would mean an astronomic investment loss. The reality was that somebody had to pay for the loss, which could be the asset owners who had paid up the mortgage, the mortgagees, the banks, the holders of the mortgage back securities (MBS), the insurance companies and public agents who guarantee the MBS, the US government or any combinations of the above. As explained in previous chapters, the banking and financial system is analogous to the heart of a human body and the flow of funds is analogous to the blood of the body. If the heart (the banking and financial system) fails to work, the blood (funds) would

*(Continued)*

**Box 11.4:** (*Continued*)

not be able to flow through the body (economy) and all other organs (industries) would die. As this heart must be rescued, the US government had no choice but to rescue the banking and financial system, such as using the 70 billion US dollar Trouble Asset Relief Program (TARP) funds to save some major financial institutions while searching for more ways to ensure the banking and financial system to function at least in the basic way.

Even if the US government could thereafter do a very god job here, the downturn of the global economy would accelerate in the subsequent quarters. As explained in the previous discussion, the first round of decline of the US consumption at that time had not fully reflected the effect of the fall in property price at that time. Worse still, the subsequent fall in the US property price would still be substantial. It should also be noted that part of the effect of the earlier fall in property price was actually absorbed by the precautionary money, or even the borrowing and credit card limits, held by the US consumers and firms. As most of these precautionary money or borrowing limit had already been used to absorb the impacts of the earlier plunge in property price, the potential harm of the subsequent plunge in property price would be far much greater than that caused by the earlier plunge in property price.

Worse still, the reduction in consumption and investment at that time was actually the first round of decline. Basic macroeconomic theory has told us that this first round decline would, through the multiplier effect, pull the output down by a multiple of the first round decline. In addition, the decline in output would, through the accelerator effect, pull down private investment which would in turn pull down output through the multiplier effect.

Perhaps neglected by the discussants in the media was that it would take quite some time for the multiplier effect and accelerator effect to exert its full impacts on the economy. Thus, the observed

(*Continued*)

**Box 11.4:** (*Continued*)

decline in the US consumption at that time could be just at the stage of somewhere between the first round and the second round of decline. Bearing in mind the US property price would continue to decline and the subsequent multiplier effect and accelerator effect were yet to be seen, it was actually not difficult to judge or perceive that the downturn of the US economy at that time was still at the early stage, and the economic pains of the subsequent quarters would be far more severe.

What would add to the US downturn would be the deterioration of the European and Asian economies in the subsequent quarters. One reason for the less severe downturn of the US economy at that time was that the European and Asian economies were still at the early stage of the downturn. As a result, the cumulated depreciation of the US dollar in the earlier quarters had to some extent help the US export and therefore mitigate the downturn in the US. However, there were more and more signs that the European and Asian economies would unavoidably experience a recession. Given the cumulated appreciation of the Euro over the previous quarters, the downturn could be more severe in Europe. When the European and Asian economies enter the deeper stage of recession in the subsequent quarters, the US export would no longer be able to help the US economy as it did in the previous quarters.

Furthermore, what the Chinese economy had to deal with would not be just the plunge in demand from the US, but also the subsequent widespread decline in demand from Europe and other Asian economies. Thus, the degree of the global recession and downward external demand pressure that China had to encounter would be far much greater than most people perceived at that time.

Another thing that many economic discussants could have underestimated was the following issue. According to the author's accumulated insights on macroeconomic policy management over the past thirty years, the negative effect of accumulated rampant currency

(*Continued*)

**Box 11.4:** (*Continued*)

appreciation and/or wage and price inflation might not be that visible during the boom period. However, these changes could show their full negative effect when the economy started to fall from its peak. The following are two standard examples from Singapore and Hong Kong:

(a) The first example was the currency appreciation and wage increments in Singapore between 1981 and 1984. During that period, the Singapore nominal effective exchange rate was appreciating at 5.4% per annum, making a cumulated appreciation of 21.6%. In addition, nominal wage increments accelerated to 11.2% per annum in 1982–1984 from the high single digit rate in 1981. Since July 1979, the overall CPF contribution rate was raised a few times from 37% of the workers' basic salary to 50% in July 1984. The substantial cumulated currency appreciation and labor cost increments had resulted in a substantial deterioration of Singapore's relative price competitive. However, with the booming economy in 1984, the deterioration of the competitiveness did not appear to have substantial impact on the economy. However, with the internal weak weakness, the reduction in external demand during the moderate global economic slowdown in 1985 was able to trigger a severe recession in Singapore. Thus, unlike the global economy which experienced a relatively severe recession in 1982 but only moderate slowdown in 1985, Singapore only experienced a moderate recession in 1982, mainly because its relative price competitiveness was still sound. However, with the substantial deterioration of relative price competitiveness in the subsequent years, Singapore's recession in 1985 was far more severe than the moderate economic slowdown in the global economy.

(b) Another example was the persistent and rampant rise in asset price, rentals, wage and CPI in Hong Kong between 1990 and 1997 (see Section 9.4 for the reasons for the formation of the asset bubble at that time). The asset bubble had in turn caused a booming economy

(*Continued*)

---

**Box 11.4:**  (*Continued*)

and excessive rise in rentals, wage and CPI (see Chapter 9 on the extent of the rise), which had in turn transform Hong Kong from a highly competitive economy in the 1980s to a highly expensive and uncompetitive economy in 1997. However, during the bubble period, nobody was aware of the enormous deterioration of the relative price competitiveness and its potential harm. Nevertheless, with the internal weakness, the speculative attack during the Asian Financial Crisis was able to trigger a bursting of both the property bubble and stock market bubble. Since then, Hong Kong had entered a severe and prolonged recession between 1998 and 2004. Only after the bursting of the bubbles, people in Hong Kong started to realize their wage and CPI was highly uncompetitive.

Given the substantial accumulated appreciation of renminbi and rampant rise in wage and cost in China over the past few years, it was possible that a negative external demand shock could trigger a severe downturn in China. To pre-empt this, it would be important at that time for China to use ultra fiscal expansion to offset the impact of the negative external demand shock on the Chinese economy.

---

The second part of the article set then provided more details on the ultra expansionary fiscal proposal. It first highlighted that China's tax revenue and other fiscal revenues could shrink substantially during the economic downturn. To pre-empt China from getting into the difficult situation of insufficient fiscal budget for the continuation of the recommended ultra fiscal stimulation at the later stage, the articles emphasized that finding ways to engineer the maximum stimulation effect with limited budget deficit burden was of utmost importance.

### 11.4.1 *Tax Rebate Instead of Tax Reduction*

For example, there were tax reduction recommendations in the form of higher personal tax allowance or cut in tax rates at that time. The articles first highlighted that these tax reductions would be a long-term concept, i.e., a permanent reduction in tax revenue. On the other hand, anti-recession economic stimulation would be a short-term concept, e.g., 2–3 years of recession. Using a permanent tax reduction to achieve a short-term economic stimulation would induce the market to worry about the possible emergence of a structural deficit. When the fiscal revenue started to shrink during the economic downturn, such worry could even grow to irrational extent, which could mean rather large negative impacts, including negative impacts on exchange rate and other asset price through market expectation.

Thus, to achieve the short-term economic stimulation target, it would be better to have a tax rebate. The advantage of a tax rebate or a temporary tax reduction would be the achievement of a short-term economic stimulation without causing a permanent fiscal burden, thus avoiding the above worry of a structural deficit. Moreover, a tax rebate would have a much shorter implementation lag than a temporary or permanent tax reduction: A temporary or permanent tax reduction would imply the taxpayers could pay less tax when the tax bills arrived, which could mean a few to twelve months after the fiscal decision. On the other hand, a tax rebate would mean an immediate hard cash to the taxpayers' hands within 1–2 months of the fiscal decision.

Of course, it might be necessary and worthwhile for China to raise the personal tax allowance over the long-term. However, with the soon arriving economic downturn, it might not be that appropriate to make a permanent increase in personal allowance at that point of time. A safer and more appropriate choice would be a few tax rebates over the subsequent 2 years. When the economy started to stabilize and recover in the subsequent 2–3 years, China could then consider making the long-term adjustment of personal allowance.

Meanwhile, as the low-income taxpayers had a higher marginal propensity to spend than high-income taxpayers, giving each taxpayer a fixed and same amount of tax rebate, irrespective whether they were rich or poor, could produce a bigger stimulation effect than a permanent increase in personal allowance or a permanent reduction in tax rate. Furthermore, as the low-income taxpayers would need the rebate more than the high-income taxpayers during the economic slowdown, there would be additional political popularity and social impression gain on top of the above economic stimulation effect.

---

**Box 11.4.1:   Sign That China Was Still Weak
in Macroeconomic Management**

The article also highlighted that the above argument was in fact a minimum common sense requirement for economic commentators, analysts, think tank or officials. It was surprising that some of the "so-called specialists" in the media were still talking about tax reduction instead of tax rebate at that time. Thus, it would be quite doubtful that these so called specialists could help China to tackle the soon arriving global recession. For those economic officials, they should also be more aware of their limited knowledge on macroeconomic management and theoretical background, and be more ready or willing to seek advice from true specialists.

---

## 11.4.2 *Substantial Public Housing Constructions*

On the expenditure side, following the logics of the above discussion, the use of an once-and-for-all increase in fiscal expenditure (such as once-and-for-all infrastructural constructions) to achieve the short-term stimulation would be preferred to the use of a permanent increase in fiscal burden (such as a permanent increase in the number of government bodies or employees, or a permanent increase in the wage of civil servants). Of course, this did not mean that China had to freeze or cut all the permanent expenditures in the subsequent two years. However, among the planned increase in fiscal expenditures in the subsequent two years, it would be preferable to have a high ratio of once-and-for-all expenditure so as avoid the problem of structural deficit in the future.

After highlighting that the scale of stimulation discussed by other economists at that time would not be sufficient to stop China from entering a relative severe recession and the need to pre-empt a relative severe budget deficit in the subsequent two years, the article recommended ultra fiscal stimulation along two lines: one was huge infrastructural constructions (see Section 11.4.3) and another was a substantial increase in public housing constructions. In fact, the latter recommendation could be seen as a follow-up extension of the author's original proposal made in 2006–07 (see Chapters 9–10 for more details). Thus, adoption of the proposal amid the slowdown would mean the following benefits to the Chinese economy:

(a) As explained in Chapters 9–10, the original proposal of a significant share of public housings to qualified applicants at a reasonable price could on one hand contain further unreasonable surge in private property price, and on another hand help Chinese citizens owning their flat at a reasonable price. [Note: As detailed in Chapters 9–10, the original proposal was a huge supply of public housings until it form a significant portion of the total supply, e.g., about 10% in the form of subsidized low-rental housing for the poor, about 15% in the form of economy-flats to the low income earners, about 45% in the form of sandwich-class flats for the middle to middle-high income earners, and about 30% in the form of private property for the rich and high-income earners.]

(b) Furthermore, the profits from the proposed huge supply of sandwich-class flats could be used to finance the medical reform, education reform and the subsidized low-rental housing with relatively little economic distortion (i.e., as the qualified applicants' housing demand curve is relatively inelastic at the relevant price range, the profit as a form of land or housing tax will create relatively little economic distortion).

(c) The huge amount of public housing construction could more than offset the reduction of private property construction, stimulate the economy, and allow the private property price to continue its correction towards more reasonable and affordable levels.

In early 2008, the author had recommended the Chinese government to start the planning of a huge amount of public housings so that the actual construction could be started promptly when subsequent economic statistics confirmed the anticipated change in the direction of the economy. With economic statistics in September 2008 further confirming the beginning of a severe economic downturn, the article highlighted that it was time to start the construction of these planned public housings as a **mean** to keep the subsequent slowdown within acceptable limit.

The article also elaborated how the proposed public housing constructions could be used to generate a much larger stimulation effect with limited or no extra burden to the fiscal deficit. For example, suppose the Chinese government sells a developer a piece of land to build a certain number of sandwich-class flats or economy-flats. As the capital for the estate development is from the developer, the government's fiscal burden would at most be investment in the supporting infrastructure such as transport and public facilities. Thus, the Chinese government could use a relatively small fiscal expenditure to achieve a much bigger stimulation effect.

Of course, as the downward pressure on the Chinese economy in the subsequent two years could be enormous, the required increase in public housing constructions could be far much greater than that could be absorbed by the number of developers at that time. Thus, China should at the same time adopt the recommended Singapore model. That is, the government's housing development board could act as a developer: keep the control of the estate development, but sub-contracts the building of flats to the builders.[9]

The article also proposed the following arrangement: The housing development board could pre-sell the public housings, collect the payments by installments and use the installments to finance the next stage of the estate construction.[10] With such an arrangement, the Chinese government could use a relatively small amount of fiscal expenditure to start a large number of housing estates and hence achieve a large first round stimulation effect. Through the expenditure multiplier, this bigger first round effect would produce a even bigger stimulation effect on the economy. Thus, the proposed policy would be consistent with the aim of using a relatively moderate amount of fiscal expenditure to achieve a large stimulation effect.

---

[9] This would mean that the government would take the profit (and the limited risk) of the estate development. For design of the housing estate, the housing development board could choose to do its own design or sub-contract it to architecture academies or private architecture firms.

[10] For example, the housing development board could follow the following practice adopted by private developers: request the purchasers of public housings to pay the first installment and do a bank loan for the subsequent installments, use the first installment to finance and complete the first stage of construction and then use it to ask the bank to release the second installment, use the second installment to finance and complete the next stage of construction for further release of installments from banks, and so on.

Of course, as a prudent policy proponent, the author would recommend a lower pre-sales leverage of, say, 3 times at the early stage.[11] Even so, after the multiplier effect, this leverage ratio could still generate a total stimulation effect of at least 10 times of the fiscal expenditure. In addition, in case China's fiscal revenue deteriorate substantially during the recession period, the Chinese government could raise the pre-sales leverage, and hence keep the stimulation going without extra burden on the fiscal side. Another advantage of keeping the control of estate development would be: after the building and sales of the estate, the government could earn a decent profit margin arising from the difference between the construction cost and the selling price of the sandwich-class flats to the middle and middle-high income earners. As the number of those flats would be enormous, the government could use the huge profit to (a) cover some of budget deficit during the recession period; and (b) set up a fund that could support the medical reform, the education reform and the provision of low-rental housings for the poor.

No matter the Chinese government choose to keep the control of estate development or sub-contract it to the developers, using substantial public housing constructions to achieve the economic stimulation would be one of the most fiscal expenditure saving, or even fiscal revenue generating, methods. Furthermore, this could (a) help low to middle-high income earners purchase their own flat at a reasonable price; and (b) offset the anticipated negative effect of a substantial reduction of private property construction during the correction period. Finally, the article re-iterated that the global and domestic economic condition in the subsequent quarters could be

---

[11] If the government was really short of budget, it could even collect the down payments of the pre-sales before they started the construction. As the price of public flats was much cheaper than that of private flats, potential buyers of these public flats would be willing to accept such an arrangement. After using the down payments to do the first stage of construction, the government could then collect the next installment (i.e., buyers' bank will release the mortgage loans in batches according to the progress of the construction) to start the next stage of construction. By doing so, the government would not even need to use any fiscal budget to build a huge amount of public housings. Of course, if the central government is concerned about moral hazard activities in the local government level, it could opt for the arrangement in the main text, i.e., require the local government to use its own budget to start the first stage of construction.

extremely weak. After reading the article, it would be insane if the related economic officials still under-estimated the severity of the soon arriving economic adversity, thus resulting in insufficient public housing constructions and insufficient fiscal stimulation to pre-empt or mitigate the painful downturn.

### 11.4.3 *Huge Infrastructural Constructions*

Finally, following the above logics, the Chinese government could approve a huge number of profitable infra-structural projects for bidding, building and operation by private or state enterprises. One such example was the previously approved high-speed railway between Beijing and Shanghai. In view that the downward pressure on the Chinese economy would be enormous, the articles also recommended the Chinese government to plan, approve and start:

(a) more high-speed intercity railway lines, such as the extension of the high-speed Beijing-Shanghai railway line to Guangzhou, Shenzhen and Hong Kong;
(b) more new underground lines in major cities; and
(c) more toll highways, bridges, and tunnels.

As these projects would be bid and constructed by private, state or foreign enterprises, this arrangement could achieve a significant stimulation effect with little extra fiscal burden.

### 11.4.4 *The Four-Trillion-Yuan Fiscal Expansion*

As Chinese top leaders at that time were already convinced by the overwhelming case reports and leading indicator statistics that the Chinese economy were about to experience a severe slowdown, the above proposal of ultra fiscal expansion was well received, and contributed to the government's announcement of the four-trillion-yuan ultra fiscal expansion in November 2008. In particular, the proposal of huge infrastructural constructions had contributed to the starting of the construction of more high-speed intercity railways and underground railways within major cities. On top of the macroeconomic stimulation during the economic slowdown, the author believes these railway lines, if appropriately done, will also generate significant long-term benefits by augmenting China's transportation system, productivity and competitiveness. If appropriately done, this could in the future end up as an important exporting industry of China, i.e., China could bid for such type of building contracts in other economies in the more distant future. Of course, if the high-speed intercity railways were built without the support of a reasonably cost and benefit analysis (e.g., building a line even though there is insufficient demand to cover the costs), it could end up as a long term fiscal burden to the country. Thus, it might be safer to stick with the author's original choice of asking the private, state and foreign enterprises to bid for a specific line on a BOT (Build-Operate-Transfer) basis.

Meanwhile, follow-up proposals by some other economists and think tanks, such as measures to stimulate rural demand for electrical appliances,[12] were included in the ultra fiscal stimulation package. Nevertheless, unlike the proposals made by the author, these measures would increase China's fiscal deficit. It is thus important for China to remove most of these measures during the recovery period so as to avoid a long-term structural burden to China's fiscal budget.

Given that China's GDP would be about 30 trillion yuans in 2008, the announced four-trillion-yuan fiscal expansion over a two-year span, if all are in the form of additional expenditures on top of the usual annual expenditures, would mean a substantial stimulation through the fiscal multiplier. As we will see, the ultra fiscal stimulation did contributed to a more moderate economic slowdown in the subsequent quarters. In addition, it was in fact the announcement of the ultra fiscal expansion that reversed the downward direction of China's stock market index (see Box 11.4.4 and Chapter 8 for more discussions).

---

[12] Under the scheme, rural residents would be given a government subsidy if they replaced their electrical appliances by new purchases. The aims were to upgrade rural living standard on one hand, and to stimulate the economy on the other hand (i.e., by offsetting the reduction in aggregate demand for electrical appliances during the economic slowdown). Similar subsidies for new car purchases were also given to support the development of China's car industry, stimulate domestic demand and make more cars available to Chinese citizens.

### Box 11.4.4:   It Was the Ultra Fiscal Expansion Announcement That Reversed the Downward Trend of China's Share Prices

As shown in Figure 8.5.4, the Shanghai Composite Index rebounded from the trough of 1701 immediately after the announcement. In the next few days, the market started to doubt whether the announced fiscal expansion would be in the form of additional expenditures on top of the usual annual expenditures, or just a re-packaging of the usual annual expenditure and planned expenditure announced in the past. Such a doubt had contributed to a moderate dip in the stock price index. However, with further confirmation by the government through actual actions and clarifying speeches, stock market participants were eventually convinced that the fiscal expansion would be large enough to ensure the slowdown would not be too painful. As a result, the index started to stabilize and then rebound from the over-corrected trough.

It should be noted that, before the announcement of the ultra fiscal expansion, many think tanks and economists had proposed a lot of market specific measures to stop the stock market index from falling further. However, as the market sentiment had changed and the economic outlook was no good, all these measures did not seem to be able to stop the share price index from over-correcting. On the other hand, once the market was convinced that the ultra fiscal expansion could keep the economic slowdown within acceptable limit, the share price index started to reverse its downward trend.

**Lesson:** The above Chinese experience highlighted that macroeconomic stability is an important determinant of stock market stability. Without a stable macroeconomic environment, it is difficult to have a stable stock market, especially when the stock market has started its correction from an excessively over-valued level. On the other hand, once there was news that the macroeconomic environment would stabilize, the stock market would be able to stabilize around a fair value, or even reverse its trend from the over-corrected level.

Having said that, there could still be risk and cost of the ultra fiscal expansion, not so much on the macroeconomic aspect at the decision stage, but more on potential abuses or mistakes at the implementation stage. For example, local governments were eager to submit huge project applications which could enable them to get a significant amount of funding from the central government budget and a substantial amount of loans from the banks. As

(i)   the construction of the infrastructural project would stimulate the local economy, and
(ii)  local GDP growth and the completion of the project itself could be important performance evaluation criteria for local officials,

local government officials had strong incentives to fight for the project approval even if they knew the project could be economically wasteful. Worse still, corrupted local officials could use the project as a means to receive briberies from contractors. Thus, if the local government projects were not properly screened, it would be possible that quite a number of these projects would eventually end up as loss-making projects, which would mean either

(a)   a huge loss and future burden to the local government budget; and/or
(b)   a rise in non-performing loans in the banking sector in the future.

In case of the latter, it could eventually mean a substantial write-off of the banks' capital. Through the banks' asset-capital leverage ratio (see Section 11.6.2.3), this would at the minimum hurt the banks' ability and willingness to lend, thus resulting in a moderate credit crunch, in the future. In the worst scenario, it could seed a banking crisis in the distant future.

Another problem was that the proposal of huge public housing con-structions was not adopted. One major reason for this was the failure of some middle-rank economic officials and think tanks to appreciate the logics and wisdom behind the author's proposal at that time, i.e., the use of the huge public constructions to

(a) stimulate the economy (and offset the reduction of private property constructions) amid the economic slowdown; and at the same time
(b) allow the high private property price to continue its moderate correction towards more reasonable and affordable levels.

Instead, these officials and think tanks had mistakenly recommended the stimulation of the private property demand as a mean to increase private property constructions. These recommendations had contributed the subsequent removal of the central bank's curbing measures introduced in late 2007 and then excessive increase of bank credits from 2009Q1 (see Chapters 9–10 for more details). Nevertheless, because of the market structure problem of China's private property market discussed in Chapter 9, this type of stimulation would only cause a sharp surge in private property price with at most moderate increase in private property constructions. As a result, previous effort to cool the private property market was completely wiped out. From February 2009 onwards, the already unreasonably high private property price started to rocket up again from its local minimum. The rebound also allowed the private developers to sell a substantial amount of their hoarded properties at a very high profit margin. Nevertheless, there was only moderate increase in private property constructions. By April 2010, the high and unaffordable private property price once again emerged as a major economic, social and political issue in China. In view of this, the Chinese central government started to re-introduce some credit tightening measures on the private property market (see Chapter 10 for more details). Nevertheless, as the private developers' hoarding power was much better due to the enormous profit earned during the private property price rebound, they would be able to resist the economic pressure from these credit tightening measures, and could continue to hoard their properties and lands until a reversal of policy or major change in economic conditions (e.g., a high inflation period during the global recovery, as will be discussed in Section 11.7). Even in the less likely case that they are eventually forced to reduce their selling price, it would be a long struggle with enormous pain to flat purchasers and huge cost to the economy. Besides, because the market structure problem was never touched, the reduction in private property price could be rather minimal. In fact, this was why the author had kept on recommending the huge supply of public housings to bring in sufficient competition and directly tackle the market structure problem in China's property market. Thus, any policy that fails to address the market structure and inequality problems in China is unlikely to be successful.

Through the above discussion, the author hope that young readers of this book could further appreciate the importance of theoretical training in economics, and the danger of dogmatic belief on free market force. For example, if the above officials and think tanks were better trained in economics, they should be able to identify that the assumptions behind the supply and demand analysis did not fit the reality of China's property market, and would not be a good tool to analyze China's property market. If it was not these officials' failure to understand the market structure problem and mistake in identifying the wrong area of stimulation, China would be in a much better position by adopting the proposal of huge public housing constructions instead of stimulating demand for private property.

## 11.5 The Interest Rate Policy

The second and third sets of articles were on the monetary policies and were published between early October 2008 and early January 2009. The two sets of articles suggested that, parallel with the ultra fiscal expansion discussed in the previous section, the Chinese government should also made drastic cuts of her interest rate until very low levels. Thereafter, she should make substantial once-and-for-all increases in money supply at the early stage of the downturn to pre-empt large scale of financial de-leveraging and financial dis-intermediation from happening in China.

### 11.5.1 *Better to Start the Interest Rate Cuts Before the Slowdown*

Let us first discuss the rationales behind the proposal of drastic interest rate cuts towards very low levels. As explained in Box 11.1b, there was in fact credit rationing in China at that time. Thus, quantity target on credit and monetary growth, instead of interest rate, was the binding constraint on China's inflation at that time. Moreover, the traditional interest rate channel is only one of the many transmission mechanisms of monetary policy. Even if interest rate was below the intersection of the supply and demand curves, maintaining the quantity constraint on credit or money supply could still help containing investment and consumption through the credit channel or other channels, thus enabling China's CPI inflation to continue its downward adjustment towards the government target before further economic deterioration in the subsequent quarters dictates a quantity easing.

In addition, as the Federal Reserve of the US had already reduced its discount rate from 5.25% in October 2007 to about 4.5% in January 2008 while the Chinese central bank had instead raise her discount rate by 0.81 percentage point during the same time, the interest rate in China was much higher than that in the US. With the market expectation of further renminbi appreciation, there would be enormous speculative inflow pressure if China did not follow the interest rate cuts in the US. Such speculative inflow would in turn create substantial monetary growth and inflation pressure on China. Thus, the choice of not following the interest rate cuts in the US could in fact weaken the anti-inflation attempts at that time.

More importantly, as warned by the author's previous articles, the credit and money demand in China would make substantial inward shift with further deterioration of domestic demand in subsequent quarters. If one took into account of the time lag of the effect of interest rate cut, it would be better to reduce the China's interest rate before, instead of during, the economic slowdown. Thus, the articles in early 2008 had recommended the related authority to start cutting the interest rate, firstly by 0.27% or 0.54%, and be prepared to use further cuts in interest rate and fiscal stimulation to mitigate the slowdown of the Chinese economy. The articles in early 2008 also explained that further interest rate cuts could mitigate the decline in Chinese share price at that time: Although further deterioration of domestic demand in subsequent quarters would still cause further reduction of share price, the recommended interest rate cuts would still help to slow down the pace and momentum of the fall, thus giving the stock market a longer time to adjust, which could help reducing the pain involved in the unavoidable correction (see Box 8.2.4 on how more transaction among participants could help keeping the losses and pains of more share investors within their bearable level, although the total loss for all share investors would be the same as the case of a sharp plunge of the same size). Moreover, if the cumulated cut in interest rate is sufficient and the timing of interest rate cuts is good enough, it could help reducing the over-correction of the stock market. This would in turn help pre-empting the possibility of another cycle of excessive surge or bubble from the over-corrected level in the more distant future. The articles also emphasized that making the first interest rate cut at that time was in fact a wise and necessary step that would put China in the more secured position and the "*more flexible position for forward advancement or backward defense*" (进可攻, 退可守) emphasized by the literature of Chinese military strategy.

### 11.5.2 *China's Failure to Cut the Interest Rate Before the Slowdown*

Nevertheless, as discussed in Box 11.1b, because of very different views about China's economic outlook at that time, the then Governor of China's central bank refused to reduce China's interest rate until September 2008. On the other hand, the US had reduced its discount rate by another 2.25 percentage points between January 2008 and August 2008. Worse still, without going through the monetary policy committee of the central bank, the then Governor even declared that China's central bank might instead raise China's interest rate and renminbi's appreciation rate. Because of such declaration, he was later impolitely ordered not to raise interest rate. While the author is in favor of central bank independence with check-and-balance through medium-term performance review and renewal every five years and very careful screening in the first appointment, the above Chinese experience also suggests that it is important that major monetary decisions should go through discussion and voting in the monetary policy committee of the central bank.

### 11.5.3 *First Interest Rate Cuts and Fiscal Expansion, Then Quantity Easing*

Whatever, not raising interest rate and the renminbi appreciation rate could at most help avoiding further mistakes. That is, despite the rapid deterioration of the global economy and the 3 percentage points drastic cuts in US discount rates between October 2007 and August 2008, the

Chinese central bank had not yet made the first right step to cut her interest rate. Only until September 2008, the Chinese central bank started to make a very minimal 0.27% cut in the base lending rate with no parallel reduction in the deposit rate. In the article in early October 2008, the author first noted that the above asymmetric interest rate cut was at least the first half step in the right direction. He then clarified that the "*negative interest rate*" consideration discussed by other economists at that time was misleading. Of course, according to this simple and well-known concept, a sustained negative real interest rate would, *during the normal time*, trigger or fuel excessive rise in asset price. Nevertheless, limited by the strength of their foundation in economics training, those who applied the above concept to China's situation had failed to identify a very important and possibly dominating factor on asset price movement at that time: the role of **expectation** during the rapid surge or decline of asset price.

In fact, that was why during China's stock market bubble formation period in 2006–07, the author had kept on iterating that

> "*It is important to curb the expectation and pre-empt the bubble with strong enough curbing measures at the very early stage of a potential bubble. Once the expectation of further rise in asset price is firmly established, even a 3 percentage points rise in interest rate would not be sufficient to stop further surge of asset price towards substantially over-valued levels. Thereafter, a reversal of economic condition could in the future trigger another plunge in asset price to a possibly over-corrected level. During this correction phase, once the expectation of further fall in share price is formed, even a substantial reduction of interest rate could at most mitigate the plunge.*"

The articles in October 2008 then highlighted that the Chinese stock market at that time was in fact at the correction phase of the above scenario. Worse still, as firms' profit would fall by a greater percentage than sales (see Box 8.4.3a),[13] and could even turn negative, with further

---

[13] Because of the existence of a relatively large fixed cost in the operation of modern firms, firms' profits and hence their share prices would usually fall by a greater percentage than sales during the recession. Similarly, firms' profits and share prices would usually rise by a greater percentage than sales during the boom.

deterioration of domestic and global demand in the subsequent quarters, downward pressure on the stock market in the subsequent quarters would be enormous. Thus, the Chinese government should throw away the above misleading application of "negative interest rate", and use series of aggressive cuts in interest rate to slow down the fall in share price and reduce the eventual over-correction of the stock price index.

Regarding to the proposal of direct government purchase in the stock market by some other economists, the articles suggested that the Chinese government should first use interest rate cuts to help supporting the stock market. When the stock market make further plunges to clearly under-valued levels during the subsequent quarters, the government could then start adopting the proposal of buying in shares to support the stock market. Otherwise, the related government bodies or enterprises could be caught into deep trouble. The articles also highlighted that

> *"It does not need a fall from the hill top to kill someone, even a fall from the middle of the hill is sufficient to kill a person."*

After clarifying the mistake of the above misleading discussion in China, the article recommended the Chinese central bank to cut both the lending and deposit rates in the next round of rate cut. In fact, the asymmetric cut in interest rate in September 2008 had caused further plunge in the stock price index by reducing the expected profits of banks. During the next round of interest rate cut, the Chinese central bank should avoid being once again misled by the above misleading discussion on "negative interest rate".

Finally, while the Chinese government could first use ultra fiscal expansion and aggressive cuts in interest rates to stimulate the economy at that moment, it should also make itself prepared to relax the credit and money supply control when deemed necessary. In particular, if there were signs that the soon arriving recession reached the stage that it could affect the normal functioning of the credit market and financial system in China, the government should use substantial quantity easing to pre-empt the emergence of financial de-leveraging, financial dis-intermediation and other vicious cycles.

## 11.6 The Substantial Quantity Easing in Credit and Money Supply

### 11.6.1 *Time for Substantial Quantity Easing*

With the severe plunge in global stock market in November 2008, the author published the third set of policy articles between early December 2008 and early January 2009, suggesting that it was time for China to make a substantial quantity easing in credit and money supply. The articles first explained that in the subsequent quarters, there would only be recession and deflation risk instead of inflation risk. In addition, on top of previously proposed ultra fiscal expansion and drastic cuts in interest rate, it would be better to start the quantity easing before the economy deteriorated further. Such quantity easing could pre-empt changes in economic behaviors and bank behaviors in the unfavorable direction which could trigger more vicious cycles. On the other hand, if China delayed the interest rate cuts and quantity easing beyond the early stage of the slowdown, there could be emergence of a few vicious cycles such as those occurred in the US at that time. In other words, adopting the quantity easing and interest rate cuts before or at the very early stage of the recession would give a result very different from having the same policies during the recession.

### 11.6.2 *Some Preliminary Points Before the Discussion*

Before explaining the reasons and logics behind the above proposals, the articles first elaborated the following preliminary points:

#### 11.6.2.1 *The Importance of the Financial System to the Economy*

The role of the financial system, which includes the banking system and the financial markets (e.g., the stock market and the bond market), is to pool and channel funds from the savers to those borrowers or firms with good investment opportunities. As each individual's savings is rather limited, without the help of the capital raising and pooling function of the financial system, it would be extremely difficult for someone to have enough savings to build or establish a railway line, a car manufacturing plant, an airline company, a telephone company and so on. This would in turn mean that human beings have to live in a relatively primitive level. Thus, it would be fair to say that the banking system and the financial markets are in fact one of the most important innovations in human history. On the other hand, if the banking system and financial markets suddenly collapse or fail to function, our living standard would go backward drastically. In fact, even in the case of a temporary problem in the functioning of the financial system, such as that in Indonesia during the Asian Financial Crisis or that in the US during the financial tsunami, the related economy would at least dip into a severe recession.

Therefore, once the financial system (the heart) has problem, the related government has to act quickly to save the heart so as to ensure the blood (funds) could flow through all the parts of the body (the economy), and hence pre-empt the death of other parts of the body (industries) which could in turn trigger other fatal vicious cycles. Because of that, no matter how many horrible things some CEOs or senior executives in the US financial industry had done, the first thing the US government had to do was to save the financial system so that at least part of the funds could continue to flow through all parts of the economy. Thereafter, the government could then penalize the related companies and executives, revise the regulations to avoid similar mistakes in the future, and ban the malpractices in the finance industry.

For those dogmatic free market believers who only knew how to memorize the concept of moral hazard, but did not understand the above important role of the financial system and the potential domino effect of collapses of major financial institutions, they were effectively using one theory to overshadow the whole issue. If the government did follow their recommendation of letting these financial institutions failed, the world would probably dip into a Great Depression. This would obviously be many times more costly than the benefit of sticking to their dogmatic "principles".

### 11.6.2.2 *The Importance of the Banking System in Asia*

The second preliminary point is that, according to statistics on funds raised by companies, the amount raised from the banking system in China and other Asian economies is much greater than those from the stock market and bond market. Thus, whether the banks as financial intermediaries would function properly or exhibit major changes in behavior could seriously affect the Chinese economy.

### 11.6.2.3 *Financial Institution's High Leverage Level and its Potential Risk*

The third preliminary point is on the high financial leverage in commercial banks, insurance companies, investment banks and hedge funds in the US. With a high asset-to-capital ratio (or capital-asset multiplier), these financial institutions had been using one dollar of capital to do more than ten, or even thirty, dollars of asset investment. As a result, the return on capital (and hence share price) of these financial institutions could be represented by the follow equation:

$$\frac{profit}{capital} = \frac{profit}{asset} \times \frac{asset}{capital}$$

$\Rightarrow$ return on capital = return on asset $\times$ asset-to-capital ratio

During the boom period, even if the return on asset is only 3–5% per annum, an asset-to-capital ratio of 12 times would mean that the return on capital would be 36–60% per annum. [For example, commercial banks' interest margin between lending and deposit rate is usually around 3%; US commercial banks' capital adequacy ratio before the financial tsunami was usually around 8% which would imply a leverage ratio of about 12 times.]

Such high return on capital would naturally mean a high share price. As the incentive scheme in the Wall Street at that time was biased towards short-term profit without dual attention to medium- and long-term risk. Many CEOs and senior executives in those financial institutions had chosen to raise the short term profit by adopting a high asset-to-capital leverage ratio. For some hedge funds and investment banks, the leverage ratio could be easily over thirty times. During the boom period, the choice of raising the leverage ratio would mean higher return on capital, higher share price and higher bonuses to the CEOs and senior executives in the short-term.

Nevertheless, such high leverage ratio without dual attention to the medium- and long-term risk had quietly seeded a crisis for these financial institutions. When the fall in US property price started to pull the economy into a recession, even a 5–10% loss in asset could be sufficient to make these financial institutions insolvent. Even if the government comes into the rescue, its share price still had to plunge towards zero.

### 11.6.2.4 *Bank's Role in Reducing the Adverse Selection and Moral Hazard Problems*

The fourth preliminary point was on the role of banks in reducing the adverse selection and moral hazard problems. After a few centuries of learning by doing, the banking industry had developed many practices to reduce the adverse selection and moral hazard problem. If these practices are properly followed, banks would be able to help the economy to channel funds to those borrowers with a high probability of repaying the loans. On the other hand, this is unlikely to be the case if the funds are allocated by the government, or other organizations assigned by the government in short notice. Thus, no matter how much money the government can print (during the financial tsunami), it does not have the capacity to take up the above role of the banking system, i.e., being relatively effective in selecting the borrowers who would repay the loans and in reducing moral hazard activities by borrowers.

For example, during the financial tsunami, quite a number of European banks were nationalized and many American banks had received huge capital injections by the government. However, as the government could not take up the banks' role in selecting and monitoring borrowers, the European and US government still had to rely on the banks to do the daily operation (i.e., minimizing the adverse selection and moral hazard problems through screening and monitoring) during the financial tsunami. After the financial tsunami, it would still be better for the European and US government to privatize these nationalized banks.

For China, although it was justified to worry that small and medium enterprises may fail because of lack of bank loans, one also need to bear in mind that some of these small and medium enterprises could no longer be viable because of permanent reduction in demand or other permanent reasons. Forcing the banks to make loans to these small and medium enterprises would result in substantial non-performing loans in the future. Thus, a more effective way is to make every effort to use expansionary fiscal, monetary and even exchange rate policy to pre-empt substantial deterioration of the macroeconomic environment faced by the small, medium and large enterprises. Meanwhile, the banking industry should be allowed and encouraged to continue its role in selecting and monitoring borrowers on the basis of business consideration.

### 11.6.3 *Why Necessary to Use Ultra Expansionary Fiscal and Monetary Policies?*

#### 11.6.3.1 *The Theoretical Analysis and Lessons from the US Experience*

Why was it important to make every effort to stimulate and stabilize the macroeconomic environment? Firstly, if the economy deteriorated further to, say, a severe recession or even an economic crisis, the adverse selection and moral hazard problems would surge to the state that the usual effective practices adopted by banks would no longer be effective. For example, borrowers with good past record could be suffering heavy losses or even at the edge bankruptcy during the recession. Examples of these included the three major car manufacturers in the US and the closure of some exporting firms in China at that time.

When the customers, especially those not so well-known small and medium firms, come to the banks to extend the loans or apply for new loans, the bank would now be less sure whether the borrowers could survive through this round of global recession, i.e., the banks were less able to select the right borrowers. In addition, the customers could have become insolvent for reasons unknown to the banks. Their loan applications could be an attempt to make the last bet or to fill another black-hole of loss. The reasons stated in the loan application form might not be the genuine reasons. Bearing in mind that the banks' interest margin between lending and deposit rate could only be 3–5%, the bank could suffer a huge loss if the borrower could not repay the loans or had simply used the loans to fill another black-hole of loss. Thus, choosing not to lend in case of doubt would in fact be the correct choice for banks. In fact, this is why banks usually try to avoid approving new loans during a relatively severe recession. Even for good record customers' extension of loans, banks could choose to reduce the size of the extended loans (i.e., to reduce the risk) and charge a higher interest rate (i.e., a higher interest rate premium). That is, banks would usually choose to "close the umbrella" during the rainy days. Such self-protective actions by banks would mean that private firms as a whole would not be able to get the amount of funds they used to have. This would in turn forced them to cut some less urgent investment and less crucial operating expenditures, which would in turn pull the economy further down through the expenditure multiplier effect.

Furthermore, once there is a relatively severe recession or crisis, the collateral value and the borrowers' net worth could fall substantially, thus making it possible that the bank might not be able to collect all the principals in case of bad debt.

Take the US at that time as an example, as the property price, share price and other asset price had dropped substantially, quite a number of borrowers were unable to repay their loan installments. This had in turn forced the commercial banks to make huge loss provisions and/or actual write-offs. For the not so badly performed banks, the results were a change from profit to loss, a substantial fall in share price and the need to raise funds to keep the capital adequacy ratio above the 8% norm. For the badly performed banks such as some regional banks with heavy exposure to mortgage loans, the results were insolvency and bankruptcy. Of course, as

(a) those mortgage loans before 2005 would be less likely to be underwater (i.e., of negative net asset value);
(b) most of the mortgagees with negative net asset value would still pay the installments as long as they remained employed; and
(c) banks would get back part of their the principals when they auctioned the foreclosed properties,

most of the commercial banks in the US were still in the better scenario with business in red and trying to raise funds everywhere to restore the capital adequacy ratio. In fact, it was the latter that make the US Treasury to inject huge liquidity to these commercial banks through special loans or purchase of their shares at that time. Meanwhile, the Federal Reserve had drastically cut its discount rates towards zero and make huge amount of liquidity available to commercial banks at the close-to-zero discount rate, i.e., the aim was to encourage the banks to start lending and hence avoiding further deepening of the recession (see subsequent discussions on why it could only partially achieve the target at that time).

While the above recue actions had helped reducing the downward momentum of the economy, they were made after the US recession had exceeded the threshold that would trigger a few vicious cycles and some major adverse changes in economic behaviors (see later discussions). As a result, much greater rescue effort was required to achieve the same effect. For example, among the huge liquidity injection by the US Treasury and the Federal Reserve at that time, a very large portion of it was injected into the commercial banks (e.g., Citibank), major investment banks (e.g., Morgan Stanley) and insurance companies (e.g., AIG) to plug the black-hole of capital shortage and financial deleveraging in these institutions. That is, very few of the injected funds were eventually ended up as bank loans to US firms.

Furthermore, although the Federal Reserve had cut the discount rate, the federal fund rate and short-term government bond rates to levels very close to zero, the occurrence of the crisis and recession had already caused a substantial surge in the interest risk premium so that commercial interest rates such as the mortgage rates, the prime lending rates and corporate bond rates continued to stay at relatively high levels (i.e., the rise in the risk premium had offset most of the effects of the cut in the discount rate on commercial interest rates). Given that the expected inflation had changed from a positive number to a negative number, the real commercial interest rates were in fact much higher than that before the crisis. This had in turn helped pulling the economy into a deeper recession.

In the next section, I will use the above theoretical analysis and US experience to highlight that, before or at the early stage of a recession, using fiscal, monetary and exchange rate policies to stimulate the economy could pre-empt a lot of complications such as the emergence of a few vicious cycles and some major adverse changes in economic behaviors. Thus, instead of waiting for further deterioration of the economy, China should cut interest rates aggressively and then use quantity easing to pre-empt the recession from reaching the threshold that could trigger the vicious cycles and changes in economic behaviors, which would in turn pull the economy into a great recession.

### 11.6.3.2 *Lessons for China's Monetary Policy*

After the above theoretical discussions and review of the US experience, the articles proceeded to highlight their potential lessons to China's monetary policy at that time. One of the important lessons is as follows:

*Instead of doing passive interest cuts and then quantity easing after the deterioration of the economy (and hence repeat the painful US experience in China), it would be better to do aggressive interest rate cuts and then quantity easing before further deepening of the recession.*

Why is it necessary to do sufficient monetary (and fiscal) stimulations before, or at the early stage of the recession? In addition to the consideration of time lags in these policies, another important reason for doing sufficient stimulation at the early stage is to keep the deterioration of the economy to the minimum so as to pre-empt some major adverse changes in economic behaviors and the emergence of a few vicious cycles, which could pull the Chinese economy into a great recession. Examples of the major adverse changes in economic behaviors include

(a) changes in bank behaviors that could result in a certain degree of financial dis-intermediation (e.g., banks become more reluctant and less able to lend because the deeper recession had (i) caused a surge in the adverse selection and moral hazard problems; and (ii) weakened the banks' ability to lend due to the loss provisions and/or actual write-offs caused by further deterioration of the economy);
(b) changes in borrower behaviors that could result in financial de-leveraging (e.g., further deterioration of the economy would force or induce many borrowers to deleverage);
(c) a fall in the money multiplier through changes in depositors' behaviors and bank behaviors (e.g., further deterioration of the economy would induce the depositors to raise their cash-to-deposit ratio and the banks to raise their excess reserve ratio);

(d) firms' decision to deleverage, shelf their original investment plan and cut down non-core operations during the deepening of the recession.

Examples of vicious cycles would include those discussed in Sections 8.2.1 and 9.3.1.

In short, these vicious cycles and changes in economic behaviors, if allowed to happen, would pull the economy into an even deeper recession, Therefore, it was important for the Chinese government to use sufficient monetary and fiscal stimulations to pre-empt the recession from reaching the threshold that could trigger these changes in economic behaviors and vicious cycles.

In addition, doing aggressive interest rate cuts before or at the early stage of the recession would immediately cause a reduction in banks' lending rate and other commercial interest rates.[14] On the other hand, delay in the interest rate cuts would allow the recession to raise the interest rate premium between the commercial interest rates and the more secure government interest rates. By then, even if the central bank cut the discount rate or government bond rate aggressively, most of its effect would be offset by the rise in risk premium, thus resulting in very little or no reduction in the nominal commercial interest rates such as the case in the US at that time. Thus, doing aggressive cut in interest rates before or at the early stage of the recession could help China from repeating the US experience in which the commercial and individual borrowing rates did not follow the aggressive cuts in the discount rate. In addition, substantial reduction of interest rate at the early stage could help stimulating the economy, reduce firms' and individuals' economic pains during the recession, and mitigate the fall in property price, share price and the related vicious cycles.

The articles also addressed to some economic and central bank officials' concern that quantity easing at the time would lead to higher inflation in the future. It first noted that the concern would be valid during the normal time. Nevertheless, China was actually in the exceptional case of

---

[14] Even in the adverse case that a deep enough recession had eventually cause a rise in the risk premium, the banks would still have to make a lot of effort to raise the risk premium, and the implied delay in the rise in risk premium would still help the economy. Moreover, as the reduction in the interest rate at the early stage had mitigated the downturn, the rise in the risk premium in this case could be smaller.

encountering a soon arriving severe recession unless sufficient stimulations were made before it was too late. As highlighted in the above theoretical discussion and review of the US experience, once the recession exceeded a certain threshold, it would cause some major adverse changes in economic behaviors and the emergence of a few vicious cycles, which would in turn pull the economy into a deeper recession. In addition, doing the stimulation after the recession exceeding this threshold would require a far much greater quantity easing, as was the case in the US at that time. Thus, when the money multiplier started to rise during the recovery period, the implied pressure on inflation and the exchange rate would be much bigger (see Section 11.7 for more detailed discussions).

### 11.6.3.3  *The Recommended Implementation Guidelines*

Thereafter, the articles recommended the following implementation guidelines on the increase in M2: Firstly, the increase in monetary base should be at sufficient to offset the effect of changes in capital flows and the moderate changes in money multiplier caused by the moderate recession. On top of this, the central bank should make a few rounds of once-and-for-all increase in M2 so as to stimulate the economy and pre-empt the potential emergence of widespread financial deleveraging. In other words, no matter what happen to the capital flows and the money multiplier, what the central had to do was to

(i)   maintain its M2 growth target; and
(ii)  add a few rounds of once-and-for-all increase in M2.

As highlighted in the author's other policy articles (see Boxes 11.4 and 11.4.1), there were very clear signs that China would only have recession and deflation risk, instead of inflation risk, in the subsequent quarters. There were also plenty of past evidences in other economies that, under the weak macroeconomic environment, the above monetary injection would not cause inflation in the subsequent quarters. Of course, when the recession was over and the money multiplier started to rise during the recovery, China had to mop up the injected liquidity to avoid fueling the inflation during the later stage of recovery. However, as explained above, if China did not do any quantity easing at that time, the subsequently worse than expected deepening of recession would eventually forced it to do so. By then, China would have to suffer a more severe recession. Worse still, the required amount of injected liquidity would be far much greater (i.e., to offset the effect of the avoidable changes in economic behaviors and vicious cycles), which would in turn mean a larger cycle of exchange rates and greater inflation risk during the recovery and then overheating phase.

### 11.6.3.4 *Let the Banks Earn Higher Profits Before or at the Early Stage of the Recession*

In addition to the above lessons for China's anti-recession policies, another important lesson from the US experience was to *allow the Chinese banks to earn a higher profit before or at the early stage of the recession*. This would enable the banks to use the higher profits in the subsequent quarters to off-set the necessary loss provisions and/or write-offs during the recession, which would in turn mitigate the decline in banks' capital adequacy ratio, contain the potential decline in bank loans and hence keep the potential scale of financial dis-intermediation to a very low level. Failure to do so would mean that the decline in bank loans and the moderate degree of financial dis-intermediation would to a certain extent affect the normal running of the economy, which would in turn make the recession worse.

Some viable polices for China at that time would include (i) a few temporary exemptions or reductions of profit tax or business tax for the banks over the subsequent 2–3 years; and/or (ii) a reduction in the high bank reserve requirement ratio at that time.

### 11.6.3.5 *China's Quantity Easing Since Early 2009*

After the publication of the above articles in early 2009, the People's Bank of China had started its quantity easing from early 2009.

As we could see from Figure 11.6.3a, China's M2 surged by 14.7% in the five months between end January 2009 and end June 2009. While the delayed increase in M2 still managed to mitigate the subsequent recession, the Chinese central bank should start mopping up the once-and-for-all increase in M2 right after the financial tsunami. That is, by July 2009, it should be relatively clear that the better than expected US rescue package in March–April 2009 had stopped the US and global economy from deteriorating further (see Chapter 12 for more details). Thus, the Chinese central should start mopping up the excess liquidity by choosing either path 1 or path 2 in Diagram 11.6.3a. Unfortunately, the Chinese central bank was unaware of the need to gradually mop up the excess liquidity after the financial tsunami. Such negligence had in turn contributed to a sharp rise of CPI inflation from 2010Q4 (see Figure 11.6.3b).

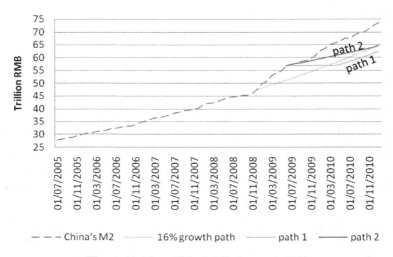

**Figure 11.6.3a.** China's M2 since early 2009

*Source*: Datastream.

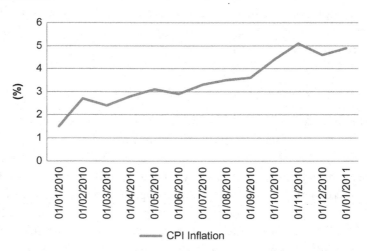

**Figure 11.6.3b.** China's CPI Inflation

*Source*: Datastream.

# Chapter 12

# Macroeconomic Outlook: Risk of Severe Asset and CPI Inflation, Exchange Rate Cycle and Then a Crisis Outside the US After the Recovery

In this chapter, the author will explain that the quantity easing in the US during the global financial tsunami had helped the global economy avoid a great depression similar to that in the 1930s. However, the quantity easing in the US had also increased the risk of a huge global exchange rate cycle, a severe global asset inflation, and a rampant global price and wage inflation. It would also seed the possibility of an asset bubble and then a crisis in economies outside the US at the later phase of the global economic recovery, e.g., at the overheated phase of the economic cycle.

In what follows, the first section will summarize the author's warnings on the above risks even before the ending of the global financial tsunami. With further signs confirming the author's concerns, the remaining sections will spell out the author's subsequent discussions on the risk. The author believes that well-trained economists will share his view that the above risks are very real and the related governments should make every effort to avoid or mitigate the potential disaster.

## 12.1 US's QE1 Helped Avoid a Great Depression, But Raised the Risk of Subsequent Global Asset Inflation and Exchange Rate Cycle

After recommending the Chinese government to use substantial quantity easing to pre-empt major financial de-leveraging and financial dis-intermediation from happening in China during the global financial tsunami, the author published two articles in early January 2009 (i.e., well before the end of global financial tsunami), warning the possibility of a huge global exchange rate cycle and a severe global asset inflation during the global economic recovery from the financial tsunami.

### 12.1.1 *The US's QE1 Had Helped the Global Economy Avoid a Great Depression Similar to That in the 1930s*

The articles first used the following equation to explain how the US's quantity easing at that time, later known as Quantity Easing One (QE1), had helped the global economy avoid a great depression, and how it had raised the risk of a severe global asset inflation and then CPI inflation during the global economic recovery:

$$M = m \times MB$$

where MB is the monetary base, $m$ is the money multiplier, and M is the money supply that will directly affect the economy. Under normal circumstances, the money multiplier $m$ can be assumed to be constant. Nevertheless, as explained in Box 8.2.1, during exceptional times such as an asset inflation era, a severe economic recession or a financial crisis, there are changes in economic behaviors that cause a substantial change in the money multiplier. Failure to be aware of the changes will result in misjudgment on the economic outcomes and insufficient stimulating or curbing policies.

Take the US experience during the financial tsunami as an example. The plunge in property prices and then the financial tsunami had forced many financial institutions (such as investment banks, hedge funds and insurance companies), firms and individuals to deleverage (i.e., reduce borrowings and hold more cash). In addition, there was a certain degree of financial dis-intermediation when commercial banks cut their loans and held more excess reserves (partly because their lending ability was weakened by the loss provisions, and partly because the surge in moral hazard and adverse section problems). As explained in Box 8.2.1, the rise in the cash-to-deposit ratio and the rise in banks' excess reserve ratio would cause a substantial decline in the money multiplier $m$ (see Box 12.1.1a and

Figures 12.1.1a on the subsequent evidence of a substantial plunge in the US's money multiplier during the financial tsunami).

According to the above equation, a substantial decline in $m$ would cause a substantial downward pressure on money supply which would exhibit in the form that many firms and individuals would be short of funds to support the usual economic activities. If the US government did not increase the monetary base by a substantial amount, the US economy would probably go into a great depression similar to that in the 1930s. Fortunately, economists had learnt from the painful experience of the Great Depression in the 1930s. As a result, a properly trained macroeconomist should by now know that the US government had to inject huge amount of liquidity into the economic system in order to pre-empt the collapse of the financial system.

---

**Box 12.1.1a:  Subsequent Data Confirmed that There Was a Plunge in the US's Money Multiplier During the Financial Tsunami**

At the time the articles were written, there were not yet enough data to support the author's argument. However, in a policy workshop in August 2009, the author had provided figures similar to Figures 12.1.1a and 12.1.1b to support the argument. As could be seen from Figure 12.1.1a, the money multiplier in the US fell substantially from around 8.5–9.5 to about 5 during the financial tsunami. Without appropriate actions from the Federal Reserve, this drastic fall in $m$ would cause a substantial reduction in money supply which would trigger more vicious cycles and pull the US economy into a great depression. Fortunately, as shown in Figure 12.1.1b, the Federal Reserve did inject enormous amount of monetary base to ensure that the US money supply could grow at a speed slightly faster than the pre-crisis rate.

---

Let us now use the above equation to explain why it was necessary that, even after the US Treasury's provision of huge amount of loans to the affected financial institutions through the Troubel Asset Relief Program (TARP), the Federal Reserve had to inject even more enormous liquidity into the economic system. As discussed above, the Federal Reserve's injection would mean a substantial rise in monetary base. At the

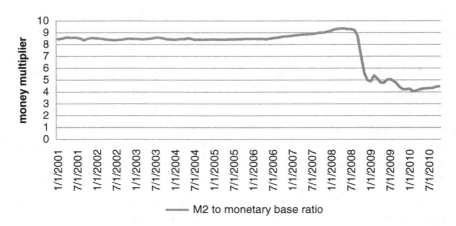

**Figure 12.1.1a.** M2 to Monetary Base Ratio

*Source*: Datastream

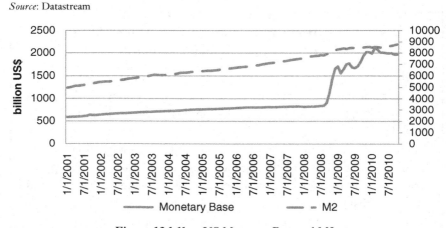

**Figure 12.1.1b.** US Monetary Base and M2

*Source*: Datastream

early stage, it might be the case that the Federal Reserve did not recognize that the initial rise in monetary base MB was not sufficient to offset the effect of a reduction in *m*. However, the Federal Reserve had very soon recognized the need to inject even more MB to keep the M2 growing *at least* at the usual speed. As a result, the subsequent injection made by the Federal Reserve was far much greater and was close to what was required to keep the money supply growing (see further discussions in Box 12.1.1b).

**Box 12.1.1b: Why Did the Federal Reserve Manage to Keep Its Money Supply Rising Without the Help of This Book's Discussion?**

As this book's discussion on the reduction of money multiplier $m$ due to changes in economic behaviors could be something new, it might be the case that the Federal Reserve at that time was not aware of the discussion. Nevertheless, as long as it chose money supply as the intermediate target and was willing to make substantial adjustment of its monetary base to achieve the target, it would be able to keep the money rising at the target rate.

**Lesson:** Central banks should choose money supply but not monetary base as the intermediate target. This is because money supply, instead of monetary base, is the one that affects the level of economic activities. In particular, during exceptional times such as an asset inflation era, a severe recession or an economic crisis, hesitate to make substantial changes in the monetary base to ensure a healthy money supply growth can result in economic disasters.

During the Federal Reserve's search process for the appropriate type and dose of monetary stimulation, there were obviously rooms for further improvements. However, it was undeniable that the Federal Reserve's performance at that time deserved respect and recognition.

**Box 12.1.1c: Implications to China's Macroeconomic Management During the Global Financial Tsunami**

Whatever, the above discussions still implied important potential improvements that the Chinese government at that time could pay attention to. Firstly, as highlighted in the author's previous discussion, if the related government could at the very beginning implement a far much greater and sufficient amount of fiscal and monetary stimulation

*(Continued)*

**Box 12.1.1c:** (*Continued*)

(e.g., the first fiscal stimulation in the US was up to a bigger scale and the monetary injection at the very beginning was at the above revised scale), it would be possible to mitigate the over-correction of the financial markets and the economy at the early stage. When the government began to see that the economy had a severe shortage of funds, the related government had to be aware of the need to do a far more aggressive injection of monetary base so as to offset the effect of the plunge in the money multiplier due to changes in economic behaviors. The article also reminded the Chinese policy makers that past record of the author's policy recommendation had shown that the author was a very prudent and effective policy discussant. If the author insisted that the Chinese government had to be more determined to raise the scale of the stimulation policy, it would most likely reflect that the author recognized that China reached the *"must-fight-to-survive"* position.

## 12.1.2 *The Risk of a Severe Global Asset Inflation and Then CPI Inflation*

In the above discussion, we have explained that the Federal Reserve's huge injection of monetary base at that time was in fact the only choice as the US was already at the *must-fight-to-survive* position. Otherwise, the US economy and hence the global economy would very likely go into a great depression. Nevertheless, after the successful avoidance of a great depression, one point could be certain was that it would be just a matter of time that the great recession would be over. While part of the recorded reduction in $m$ could be permanent (say, due to some permanent financial deleveraging such as lower leverage by investment banks and hedge funds), most of the reduction in $m$ was due to changes in economic behaviors during the recession. When the economy recovers to the pre-crisis level, the money multiplier will surge substantially from the excessively low crisis-level. Worse still, when asset price establishes an upward inertia during the recovery, $m$ can rise beyond the pre-crisis level. By then, if the Federal Reserve does not, or fails to, mop up most of the injected liquidity during the crisis, the rise in money supply implied by the rise in $m$ will be enormous and dangerous. If the then upward inertia in asset price has resulted in an expectation of asset inflation, and the emergence of the few vicious cycles and herding behaviors outlined in Chapters 8 and 9, it can result in rampant asset inflation and CPI inflation. Furthermore, soon after the quantity easing by the US at that time, the European Union, Japan, China and many other economies also injected a substantial amount of monetary base during the financial tsunami. Even if China could, at the later stage, mop up all the injected monetary base, the future challenge of a global asset inflation and CPI inflation could be severe and hard to handle.

Thus, the Federal Reserve and other central banks should be cautious with the above risk of rampant asset inflation and possibility of a subsequent formation of asset bubble during the global recovery. Nevertheless, even if the Federal Reserve and the related central banks would be alerted to the above risk during the global recovery, it could still be difficult for the global economy to avoid a rampant asset inflation and CPI inflation era. This was so because the previous and subsequent amount of monetary base injection would be just too enormous, and was spreading from the US to all other economies through capital flows. Even if the Federal Reserve worked very hard to do the mopping up during the global recovery, at least part of the injected liquidity would not be mopped up. Even if this would be only a few percents of the total injection, the rise in the money multiplier in all the economies during the recovery and the huge size of the injection during the financial tsunami would still mean a huge amount of excessive global money supply (and effective monetary growth with the rise in $m$ during the recovery).[1] This would in turn imply enormous asset inflation and CPI inflation pressure for the global economy. (See Box 12.1.2 for the author's new concern on signs of a change in the dynamics.)

In addition, even if the Federal Reserve at that time made effort to mop up the injected monetary base, its target would still be the money supply in the US instead of the global money supply. As a sizable portion

---

[1] Unless the related central banks know the whole issue and are willing to do the necessary mop-up (which would also mean a risk of excessive mop-up), the rise in money multiplier during the global recovery will probably more than offset the shrinkage of monetary base and result in a relatively large effective money supply growth.

of the US monetary base injection flew into many other economies through capital flows, it would cause a relatively rapid asset inflation in these economies.

In Section 12.3, we will continue to discuss US's Quantity Easing Two (QE2) and its implications to the US and other economies.

---

**Box 12.1.2:   Signs that the Dynamics has Changed**

At the time of adding this discussion box, there were already signs of higher inflation in economies outside the US. Thus, the higher price would mean that the global economy should not mop up all previous injections, i.e., a mop-up of all previous injections could cause a recession as the price level is already higher. If the inflation just means an once-and-for-all rise in price over a certain period, the mop-up job would not be that difficult, and things would still be OK. Unfortunately, the higher inflation would very likely create an expectation of higher inflation. This would in turn induce many governments to accommodate their money supply to the higher inflation. If so, the dynamics and evolution of the subsequent development would be very different from the case of a simple MB injection during the financial tsunami followed by a simple liquidity mop-up during the recovery. Seeing from this perspective, it seems very likely that the global economy would have to say good-bye to its latest 2–3% inflation era. In the very lucky and possibly unlikely case that most of the related governments had done a decent job of in their anti-inflation battle, the global economy might just have a 4–5% inflation for the next few years. In the more likely case that at least some governments have not done their anti-inflation jobs properly, the global economy might have to go through a 5-7% or even higher inflation era.

---

### 12.1.3  *The Possibility of a Huge Exchange Rate Cycle*

The articles also noted that the monetary base injected by the US would be much greater than that made by other economies. Thus, it would be just a matter of time that there would be a huge cycle in the exchange rate between the US dollar and other currencies.[2] That is, the US dollar would first depreciate by a substantial amount. The downward momentum of the US dollar could then trigger herding behaviors and expectation of further depreciation of the US dollar, which would in turn result in an over-depreciation of the US dollar. By then, unless in the unlikely case that the Federal Reserve had given up its discipline on its money supply, it would be just a matter of time that the US dollar would rebound strongly from the over-depreciated level.

Thus, to pre-empt a huge cycle of exchange rate, the Federal Reserve and other central banks should, at the early-middle stage of the global recovery, start mopping up the excess liquidity injected during the financial tsunami. Nevertheless, as noted above, the chance that the Federal Reserve and other central banks could mop up most of the excess liquidity was in fact rather slim. Thus, it would be important for China to plan for appropriate offsetting policies to minimize the impact of such a huge exchange rate cycle in the subsequent future.

## 12.2 The Global Stock Market During and After the Financial Tsunami

In this section, the author will briefly review the developments of the global stock market during and after the financial tsunami. In addition, the author will use his experience to illustrate some important lessons for share investments. While these lessons are less related to the author's vision on macroeconomic policy management, the author has unintentionally acquired this knowledge as understanding of big cycles in the stock market and the property market is an important part of macroeconomic policy management. In fact, ironically, because the author's original intention to study these asset markets is not to make money which has allowed him to observe the characteristics of these asset markets in more objective ways, it

---

[2] At the time the article were written, there was not yet very drastic change in the exchange value of the US dollar. One possible reason was that the money multiplier had plunged to an exceptionally low level so that the effective money supply was growing at the usual speed. Another possible reason was that the market was too busy with the various major developments during the financial tsunami such as the collapses or problems of major financial institutions, i.e., it would be difficult to borrow money and do US dollar carry trade in the middle of the tsunami.

turns out that his acquired knowledge has given him a big windfall before and after the financial tsunami.

On the other hand, for those whose only aim is to earn money from these markets, some might have lose their judgment just because they have taken too big a position right from the beginning (i.e., one might become ultra nervous and might not even be able to sleep properly if he or she over-invests in these markets). For those who manage to avoid that trap, quite a large percentage of participants might be trapped into unnecessarily frequent trading, which can again stop them from identifying major medium-term or long-term changes (see also Box 12.2.1d on how pre-mature profit taking can stop an investor from earning a decent profit from a major rally). Even for those who manage to avoid these and the other traps, the eagerness to making money might shift their attention to just the result of earning or losing money. This can stop them from spending suf-ficient effort to (i) study objectively the underlying reasons for the result; and (ii) draw important lessons objectively from the experience. For exam-ple, once the person earns money because of a change in economic environment or a change in government policy, he will quickly look for other opportunities instead of spending deep enough effort to understand why there is such a change, and under which conditions it can happen again. The eagerness to look for investment opportunities might also stop them from spending sufficient effort to develop and update their theoretic backgrounds, which is in fact one of the most decisive factors on the out-come of the investment. On the other hand, it is just very natural for a devoted economist to ask why there is such a change, and under which con-dition it can happen again. Thus, the desire to help people ironically equips this type of macroeconomists the necessary knowledge to earn from the asset markets.

To reward young readers who have the aspiration and devotion to help the people of their countries, the author will write down some of the lessons he has drawn from the share investment experience during the financial tsunami. Nevertheless, young readers are also warned that they might not be able to achieve much if their only aim is to earn money.

The brief review in this section will also provide a better background for our discussion on US's Quantity Easing Two (QE2) in Section 12.3.

## 12.2.1 *The Plunge and Then the Rebound: Some Lessons for Share Investments*

Because of the judgment that it would be just a matter of time that the global financial tsunami would be over and the anticipation of a severe global asset and CPI inflation thereafter, the author started to accumulate shares during the major plunge of the global stock market in November 2008 (see Figures 12.2.1a–c), thanks to the prudent decision of selling all of his shares in 2007 which gave him the option to use 40% of his cash to buy shares at extremely low price (see Box 12.2.1a on why there were objective measures that supported purchase of shares at that time).

---

**Box 12.2.1a: Objective Measures That Supported Purchase of Shares During the Major Plunge in November 2008**

With the outbreak of the financial tsunami fuelled by enormous short selling in the global stock market, the plunge in November 2008 was extremely sharp (see Figures 12.2.1a–c). One of the conventional wisdom in the stock market is that buying shares during a plunge can be as dangerous as using hand to catch a falling knife, as one will not know how far the stock price can fall. During the accumulation of shares at that time, the author's hand was also shaking, as he could not rule out the possibility of further fall in share price well beyond his purchasing price. However, he also knew that he had to start accumulating shares as there were also objective measures suggesting that the share prices at that time were enormously attractive from the medium-term and long-term perspectives. Thus, while the plunge was scary, objective measures such as the expected PE ratios, the expected dividend yields and the discounts between the firms' share price and net asset value suggested that one could start accumulate shares for medium-term or long-term investments.

Furthermore, with indiscriminating selling and plunges like that, there were in fact a lot of cheap and relatively safe shares. For

*(Continued)*

---

---

**Box 12.2.1a:** (*Continued*)

example, many of the listed shares in Hong Kong, Singapore and other East Asian economies still had high *positive* profits, steady incomes and high net asset valus. Even if one made appropriate downward adjustments of the expected profits and asset values in subsequent quarters, there were still a lot of shares with very low expected PE ratios, high expected dividend yields, and net expected asset values far greater than the share prices. In fact, almost all the shares the author bought at that time had expected PE ratios of only 3–5 times and share prices at 30–50% discount of the net asset values. One of the Hong Kong REITs he bought had even a dividend yield of 22% at the purchasing price.[3] Thus, while the tsunami hurt many investors with over-exposure to assets, it also created a very good buying opportunity for those with cash, the right knowledge, the patience, and the courage to take the opportunity in the very panicking environment.

---

After the major plunge in November 2008, the global stock market sort of stabilized around a low level. By late December 2008, there came the "Obama rally" due to the market's hope of a very different economic environment after the inauguration of the Obama as the US President in 20 January 2009. However, with the financial system and the economy in the US in extremely bad shape, the author judged that the market was over-optimistic as nothing had changed, and it was unlikely that Obama could turn the situation around and clear the financial mess within a short period. He therefore sold half of the shares accumulated in November 2008 (i.e., 20% in shares, and 80% in cash for share purchasing when there are clear sign that the global stock market would rebound).

---

[3] The advantage of buying REITs at that time was that its rental income was already locked by tenancy agreements signed before the financial tsunami. That is, the average rental income would remain unchanged at that year, fell at most a few percent in the next year and then gradually more in the third and fourth year. However, by the time one reached the third or fourth year, the financial tsunami could be over. By then, rentals would pick up, and more importantly, there could be a substantial upward revision of the net asset values of the REITs.

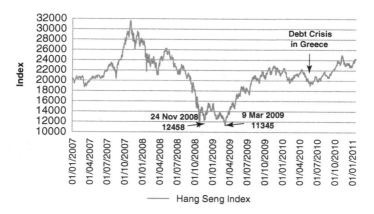

**Figure 12.2.1a.**    Hong Kong's Stock Price Index

*Source*: Datastream

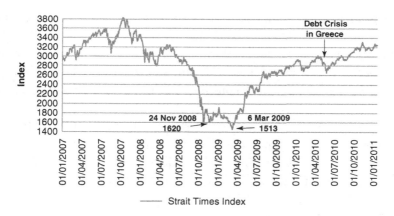

**Figure 12.2.1b.**    Singapore's Stock Price Index

*Source*: Datastream

By early January 2009, the market soon realized that it was over-optimistic and therefore fell back to levels before the Obama rally. In early March 2009, further bad news on some major companies and the financial system in the US had given short sellers another golden chance to push the US and many other stock price indices to new lows (see Figures 12.1.2 a–c). Again, the author started to accumulate shares with shaking hands, thanks

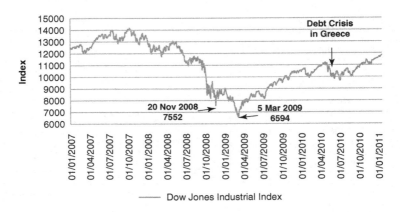

**Figure 12.2.1c.** US's Stock Price Index

*Source*: Datastream

to the prudent and rational decision of keeping substantial cash and taking some profits during the unsustainable Obama rally.

In response to the plunge and the failure of the financial system to function properly, the US government this time started to try all types of effort to stabilize the financial system. Among these, the most important measures were:

(a) Using the TARP funds to support both financial and non-financial companies, plus a much bigger and perhaps more important liquidity facility and quantity easing by the Federal Reserve;

(b) A relaxation of the mark-to-market rule for the listed companies;[4]

---

[4] Before the change, listed companies were required to use market price to value their assets. Such accounting rule had been working reasonably well before the financial tsunami. However, during the financial tsunami, the market failed to give a reasonable price for many assets. This in turn forced many companies (including the banks) to make substantial loss provisions even though the losses were not yet realized and the companies could probably write back some of the loss provisions when the economy and the asset market recover from the extreme lows. Recognizing that the accounting rule was in fact one of the major causes for the excessive panic and plunge in shares prices, the US government had eventually made appropriate relaxation of the accounting rule. Seeing that the relaxation would mean companies no longer need to make huge loss provisions which could by itself cause a strong rebound from the lows, the author rushed to buy more shares at that time.

(c) The US Treasury's announced plan of a stress test for banks while requesting the banks to raise capital from the market before, and after, the stress test (i.e., the capital raising and the stress test would raise market confidence on banks).

By then, the author was convinced that the US financial market could stop deteriorating from here. If so, the stock market could rebound strongly from the extremely under-valued levels, simply because of the disappearance of a huge *fear discount* caused by the financial tsunami (see Section 12.2.2 for more detailed discussions). He therefore sped up the accumulation of shares while watching the stock market for more supporting signs on the above judgment. With more and more supporting signs in the subsequent weeks, he ended up purchasing shares almost every day between early March 2009 and late April 2009. By early May, he had only 5% cash which was reserved for the last few batches of stock purchase when there was very clear sign that the global stock market passed its worst time. With more good news and further strengthening of the global stock market in that month, he was convinced that the global stock market probably passed its worst time and would continue to rally substantially in the subsequent years. He therefore used the remaining 5% cash to make the last few batches of purchase in May 2009.

After completing the accumulation of Hong Kong and Singapore shares and seeing further substantial surges in the two stock markets, the author basically kept the same amount of exposure in these two markets. Meanwhile, he started to pay more attention to the US stock market. Soon, he recognized that the US stock market's rebound lagged behind the two Asian markets, mainly because the economy, the financial system and the companies in the US were serious hurt by the plunge in US property price while these were far less the case in the two Asian economies. Given that the US share prices were at extremely attractive levels and it was just the beginning of a 3–5 year rally, the author judged that it was in fact relatively safe to buy US shares at that time (see Box 12.2.1b for further discussions). He therefore decided to abandon his usual practice of not using margin facilities to buy shares. While controlling the margin ratio at a reasonably safe level, he accumulated a reasonable amount of Citigroup shares at the price range of

US$2.7–US$4.0.[5] A year later, i.e., from late May 2010, after seeing the correction of the share price of Chevron (the second largest oil giant in the US) during the sovereign debt crisis in Greece, he started to cautiously accumulate a reasonable amount of the shares at the price range of US$67–US$73. Thereafter, he kept more or less the same exposure to shares, with the plan of gradually selling the shares during the overheated phase of the global economy recovery (see Chapter 11 on the recommended strategy of accumulating shares during the recession and gradually selling shares during the overheating).

Nevertheless, with some of his holdings of Hong Kong and Singapore shares rising to relatively high and less attractive levels, the author soon recognized it was necessary (i.e., safer and more profitable) to switch from the leading shares to good-quality lagging shares with lower PE ratios, higher dividend yields and/or bigger discounts between the share prices and the net asset values (see Box 12.2.1c for further discussions).

---

**Box 12.2.1b: Why Hong Kong, Then Singapore and Then the US Stock Market**

When the author did his accumulation of shares in the three stock markets, he did it with consideration of only safety and potential profitability. For example, during the plunge in November 2008, he happened to first accumulate shares from the Hong Kong stock market, mainly because the plunge and the short selling in Hong Kong at that time made some Hong Kong shares the most attractive shares (i.e., the cheapest shares, and hence the safest shares with the highest upside potential) in the three markets. However, during the plunge in March–April 2009, he did much bigger accumulation of shares in the Singapore stock market, simply because some of the shares there were the most attractive (i.e., safest and with the highest upside potential).

*(Continued)*

---

[5] To avoid the exchange rate risk arising from the expected cycle of the US dollar, the author was actually using a US dollar margin facility, i.e., borrowing US dollars, to finance the purchase of the US shares.

**Box 12.2.1b:** (*Continued*)

When writing this discussion box, the author begins to recall that investment culture in Hong Kong was more speculative (i.e., with more short selling and more speculating investors) than that in Singapore. This in turn contributed to a bigger plunge, and hence more attractive investment opportunities, in the Hong Kong stock market in November 2008. However, by March 2009, both the Hong Kong and Singapore stock markets had enough time to make the necessary adjustments to the shocks. On the other hand, share investors in the Singapore stock market were more conservative than those in the Hong Kong stock market. The more conservative inclination of Singapore's investors would mean that it required a bigger discount to convince them to hold the shares during the unfavorable market environment. Thus, it was not surprising that Singapore share prices had also to fall to more attractive levels during the plunge in March 2009.

As explained in the main text, the shares in Singapore and Hong Kong were more attractive (i.e., *safer*, and perhaps *more undervalued* with greater upside potential) than the US shares during the plunge in March 2009. For example, the share price of Citigroup plunged to US$1 while the share price of Keppel Land in Singapore plunged to S$1 at that time. However, it was not quite clear whether Citigroup could survive through the financial tsunami, while Keppel Land in Singapore was still having decent profit (and was thereafter able to give an 8% dividend if one purchased the share at S$1). Thus, it was obvious that Keppel Land in Singapore was a safer investment. Subsequent developments had also proved that the upside potential of Keppel Land was also greater. For example, after the 9 right issues for every 10 shares at an exercise price of S$1.03, the closing price of Keppel Land on 26 January was $4.66, i.e., a profit of S$6.93 [= (S$4.66–S$1) + 0.9 × (S$4.66–S$1.03)] plus the dividends in 2009 and 2010 if one purchased the shares at S$1. On the other hand, the profit for Citigroup during the same period was only US$3.82 [= US$4.82–US$1] if one bought the share at US$1.

(*Continued*)

**Box 12.2.1b:** (*Continued*)

While roughly knew that the upside potential of Keppel Land would be much greater, a even stronger reason for the author to accumulate substantial amount of Keppel Land at that time was the safety consideration. That is, if one chose the wrong share and the company got bankrupt, the loss would not be just the amount he invested in, but also the opportunity cost (i.e., investment profit from other shares during that great time for share investment) that the person had forgone. Thus, it was just obvious for the author to choose Keppel Land instead of Citigroup at that time. Nevertheless, the situation was different when Citigroup rose to around US$3 (Keppel Land also rose to around S$3.5, but profit was much higher because of the right issues). Because the US financial system had stabilized, Citigroup once again became a safe investment. As a result, the author started to accumulate a reasonable amount of Citigroup shares in the price range of US$2.7–US$4.0 (see the main text discussion).

One important lesson from the above discussion is that, along with the expected *upside potential*, *safety* is also a very important consideration for share investments during the extreme lows. If one chose a company that eventually went bankrupt, his loss would not be just the amount invested. A more important loss could be the far much greater profit forgone if the money was invested in another shares during that great time for share investments.

**Box 12.2.1c:    The Strategy of Switching from Leading Shares to Lagging Shares, and from Leading Markets to Lagging Markets**

As explained in the main text, with the anticipation of a strong and at least 3–5 year rally of the global stock market after the financial tsunami, it might be better to avoid pre-mature profit taking by

(*Continued*)

---

**Box 12.2.1c:** (*Continued*)

keeping the shares until the overheated phase of the global economic recovery. However, if one had good stock picking ability, some of his shares might rise faster than the other lagging shares during the early phase of the rebound. Under such circumstance, it might be better for him to switch his share holdings from the leading share to good-quality lagging shares with lower PE ratios, higher dividend yields and/or bigger discounts between the share prices and net asset values. Such switching strategy would bring not only greater safety but also greater upside potential. That is, with lower PE ratios, higher dividend yields and/or bigger discounts between the share prices and net asset values, there is less downside risk and bigger upside potential for the portfolio.

In fact, the rapid rise of some of the author's holding of shares had forced or induced him to do so.[6] For example, after the accumulation of Keppel Land at S$1.0–$1.6 and the exercise of the right issues at S$1.03, price of the share rose to $3.6–$3.9 within a year. While knowing the management of the company was excellent and the share would rise further, the author became more concerned that (i) the historical PE ratio had risen to about 15 times (although better expected profit that year would probably bring the PE ratio down to around 10 times); and (ii) the big discount between the share price and net asset value had disappeared. Meanwhile, there were still other lagging property shares with (i) a historical PE ratio of only 3–7 times (and expected PE ratio of only 2–5 times); and (ii) a 25–35% discount between the share price and net asset value. After judging the lagging property shares (e.g., United Overseas Land) had lower downside risk and greater upside potential, the author decided to do the share switching although he knew that Keppel Land would still go further up.

(*Continued*)

---

[6] In fact, the author had done similar switching between 2005 and 2007. While the Strait Times Index rose from around 2000 points to 3700 points during that period, such switching strategy had enabled him to triple the value of his shareholdings during that period.

---

**Box 12.2.1c:  (*Continued*)**

Similar to the above line of thought, one could also do the switching from the leading markets to the lagging markets. In fact, the author's shift of share accumulation focus from the Hong Kong market to the Singapore market and then to the US market (see Box 12.2.1b) was just a modified example of the strategy. Having said that, one had to have the ability to identify a safe enough share (market) with greater upside potential before such a switching strategy could be meaningful.

---

**Box 12.2.1d:   Some Common Mistakes Committed by Some Investors at That Time**

During the financial tsunami and the subsequent rebound of the stock market, the author also observed some common mistakes made by some share investors:

1.  *Trying to catch the bottom*: Quite a lot of share investors missed the chance of buying shares simply because they were trying to catch the bottom. Such intention would very often induce the investors to keep delaying the purchase during the fall. In many cases, the investors kept lowering the target buying price with the fall in share price until they missed the low. In other cases, for those trying to catch the bottom with one big purchase, the big purchase would make them too nervous and hence over-sensitive to subsequent share price movements, i.e., most might end up selling the shares when they saw the share price going down. Thus, very few would end up with the luck of buying some shares at the bottom. Even for these lucky investors, the amount of shares they purchased (and hence the eventual profit) would be far much smaller than those using the strategy below, i.e., the amount of share purchased could matter more

*(Continued)*

**Box 12.2.1d:** *(Continued)*

than the level of purchase price in this golden period of share investment.

On the other hand, if these investors used the objective measures mentioned above, they would have bought a reasonable amount of shares at extremely attractive prices. Unlike those who tried to catch the bottom, the author knew that it could at most be luck for one to catch the bottom. Instead, he chose to do gradual accumulation by batches after the share prices had fallen to extremely attractive levels. This in turn (i) allowed him to accumulate a reasonable amount of shares before the rebound; (ii) made him not so ultra-sensitive to the plunge, i.e., if the fall was more than expected, he could still reduce the target price (and size) of the subsequent batches of purchase; and (iii) made him willing to buy substantial amount of shares just after the share price rebound from the low. In fact, the amount of shares he purchased after the rebound was much greater than the amount he purchased during the plunge. [Note: Given that one would not know the low, wait for early signals of rebound before doing the remaining accumulation would be a safer and more optimal choice.]

2. *Worry about the downside risk but not the upside risk*: After missing the low, most investors hesitated to buy shares during the rebound because they worried that the share price would fall back after the strong rebound, i.e., they worried about the downside risk but did not seem to be aware of the upside risk. With the above mentioned objective measures and concern about a severe asset inflation during the global economic recovery, the author was able to judge that the upside risk at that time was far much greater than the downside risk.

3. *Pre-mature profit taking*: Even for those who managed to buy some shares around the low, they could be trapped by the inclination of trading too often, i.e., they did pre-mature profit taking with the hope of buying back the shares at lower price. However,

*(Continued)*

**Box 12.2.1d:   (*Continued*)**

with strong rebound liked that, chance that they could buy back the share at lower price was rather slim. Thus, there were two main possible outcomes for such pre-mature profit taking: (i) keeping missing the rally while hoping the share price could go down; and/or (ii) buying back the shares, or most likely other shares, at much higher prices. On the other hand, if one used the above objective measures, they would know that the share prices were still very attractive, and might therefore be able to avoid the pre-mature profit taking. With the help of the objective measures and the awareness of severe asset inflation in subsequent years, the author had of course made the right decision to keep the same exposure to share during the first and next few phases of the rally.

4. *Pre-occupied by short selling*: During the financial tsunami, there were also a lot of professional investors shorting the shares during the plunge. Through their comments in the media, the author also found that these people were very smart investors. Nevertheless, one major mistake they had made was being too eager to do the short selling, even when the share prices had fallen to extremely attractive levels. Thus, what they could do during the rebound in March–June 2009 was at most covering their short positions. As a result, while they were earning some money during the plunge, they also missed the golden opportunity of buying huge amount of shares at extremely attractive price. Thus, even for the small portion of short sellers who managed to change their positions from short to long after the first phase of rally in March–June 2009, they did not benefit from what they could have, partly because they had to buy the shares at far less attractive prices and partly because the amount of shares they bought was far less than what they could have if they were not too pre-occupied with the short-selling during the first phase of the rebound. Parallel with the short selling behaviors was little intention to hold the shares for a long enough period (e.g., a few years) to enjoy the sustained rally. On the other

(*Continued*)

## Box 12.2.1d:   (*Continued*)

hand, as the author saw it as an immoral behavior to hurt people through excessive short selling, he just focused his attention on accumulation of shares during the plunges and the early rebound. This in turn allowed him to accumulate a relatively large amount of shares at extremely attractive prices. Moreover, as his intention was for medium-term hold, say, a few years until the overheated phase of the recovery, he was able to enjoy both the first huge rebound and the subsequent phases of rally since March 2009.

In fact, the strategy of buying shares during the recession and selling share during the overheated phase could be very profitable. For example, after buying shares during the low in 2005, switching from leading shares to good-quality lagging shares in 2005–2007, and selling all the shares in 2007, the value of the author's shareholdings had already tripled. After waiting patiently for more than one year and did the share accumulation in November 2008 and March–June 2009, and then repeating the share switching strategy, the author's net value of shareholdings in January 2011 rose to 4–5 times of the net value of the shareholdings in 2007, i.e., 12–15 times of the value of shareholdings in 2005. With the expectation of a severe asset inflation during the global economic recovery, the author is expecting at least another doubling of the net value of his shareholdings, i.e., 24–30 times of the value of shareholdings in 2005. [Note: with the above mentioned share switching strategy, one did not need a doubling of share price indices to double the value of his shareholdings.]

Another important point is that, the amount of gain from the expected doubling in the last stage would be much greater than the double or tripling at the early stage, i.e., the expected doubling would be equivalent to 12–15 times of the holding values in 2005. Of course, it is also important to sell the shares before it is too late. In particular, trying to sell at the peak will mean a reverse mistake of the above common mistakes. Again, a gradual profit taking during the overheated phase can be a better and safer strategy.

Meanwhile, because of the (i) fear of a severe CPI, wage and property inflation in Asia during the global economic recovery; (ii) reluctance to increase his share exposure beyond the safety margin; and (iii) fear of holding too much cash after selling shares during the overheated phase of the global economic recovery, the author rushed out to buy a few properties in Singapore from June 2009 so as to ensure that, during the overheated phase of the global economy, he would only have moderate amount of cash after paying off the property loans with the profits from the shares.

Behind such an *"apparently aggressive move"* was in fact the author's fear on the extent of Asian property inflation in the subsequent years. Diagram 12.2.1 depicts his expected pattern of property price in Singapore and some other East Asian economies:

Point A is where he made his first purchase of property (i.e., June 2009). In the subsequent five years or longer, Asian property price will probably be going up well beyond point A. By then, it would be just a matter of time that property price would collapse from the peak (e.g., point B) to, say, point C. Such a substantial collapse of property price would be sufficient to cause a severe recession or even crisis, with many property owners caught into trouble. Nevertheless, because of rampant rental, CPI and wage inflation during the surge between point

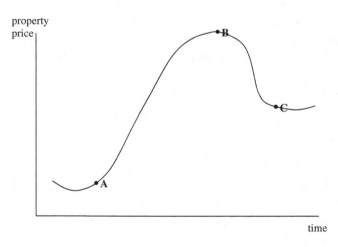

Diagram 12.2.1.    Potential Property Price Pattern in some Asian Economies

A and point C, the property price at point C would still be much higher than that at point A. Thus, only those property owners who bought their property at the early stage of the rise (e.g., around point A) and never buy any more properties, increase their mortgage loans, or switch to bigger and more expensive properties could be immune from the subsequent crash.

While the author has the knowledge to buy what he wants in one goal at the early stage, it is doubtful whether the general public will have the knowledge and self-control to avoid increasing their property investment during the overheated phase of the cycle. In view of that, the author took a chance to provide the necessary warnings to the Singapore government just after his purchase of the properties. In 2009H2, the Singapore government was collecting academia's suggestions on long-term development of Singapore. The author took that chance to write down his concern about rampant property inflation in Singapore and other East Asian economies, although he knew the discussion was a bit off the main theme of long-term development strategy. Fortunately, the ministers in charge were brilliant and experienced enough to appreciate the potential threat. Thereafter, the Singapore government had up to now implemented four rounds of curbing measures to contain the rise of property price in Singapore. With such government determination and awareness, the author believes that, among the Asian economies, Singapore would score very high in containing its property inflation and hence the subsequent harm during the collapse of Asian property price. Having said that, the author would like to highlight that controlling property inflation amid the current global environment and Asian settings (see Chapters 9–10) would be very difficult. Thus, what Singapore can eventually achieve will probably be a smaller over-valuation of property price and hence less severe harm during the collapse. Moreover, even if Singapore does its own job properly, subsequent plunges in asset price in any economy in the region can trigger contagious effects on the whole region. That is, even if an economy started with a fair value of asset price, a crisis in the region could still trigger a plunge in its asset price to a substantially under-valued level. Given that Singapore could at most contain its surge in asset price to less over-valued level, the plunge during the crisis could still be far greater than most people could bear.

**Box 12.2.1e: Another Major Difference between the Property Market in East Asia and that in the Western World**

In Chapter 9, I have discussed some important differences between the property market in East Asia and that in the western world. In Box 9.2.6, I have also explained why property investment has turned out to be a very successful way of wealth accumulation in some East Asian economies. In fact, as explained in the main text above, even the author rushed out to buy *a few* properties at the early stage of the rebound from the global financial tsunami. While such an action was rational from an investor point of view, such a drastic action also made the author as an economist to start thinking on the underlying causes and implications of this widespread phenomenon in many East Asian economies (i.e., many of the rich hold tens or even hundreds of properties and the reasonably well-off hold a few properties, while a significant percentage of the low to middle income earners could not even afford to buy a very small flat).

Thus, when Professor John Williamson of the Peterson Institute visited Singapore and met the author during his leisure time, the author asked him whether he would be interested in having more than one property in the US. To the author's surprise, Professor Williamson gave a very definite answer of "no". When asked why, he highlighted the great trouble of filling in the tax form in the US. Along with the answer could also be the higher margin tax rate for extra rental income in the US and other western economies. On the other hand, as explained in Box 9.2.6, property investment in many East Asian economies has turned out to be a very rewarding investment. In fact, after the initial down payment, it was not uncommon in Singapore and many East Asian economies that the monthly rental income could cover the monthly mortgage installment (i.e., the interest and the principal repayment). Even in the cases that the rental income was less than the mortgage installment, the gap would be small and could be easily absorbed by the property investors. More

*(Continued)*

**Box 12.2.1e:** *(Continued)*

importantly, inflation would very soon push the rental towards, and then beyond, the mortgage installment. By then, the property investor would have a property with (i) a market price well above his purchasing price; and (ii) a rental income not only greater than the mortgage installment but also rising with economic growth, inflation, urbanization, improving infrastructure and growing scarcity of land in the East Asian cities.

Nevertheless, such rationality from an individual investor point of view could also mean a huge *"investment demand"* for property, which could (i) ensure that market force would only allocate the scarce number of flats to those *"have the money"* instead of to those who *"need the flat"*; and (ii) make it very difficult for the government to contain the property inflation. For example, as explained in Section 12.5, the Singapore government was trying very hard to curb the rise of private property price since 2010. One of the measures was to substantially increase the supply of land for private property development, i.e., the amount of land released was rather substantial by historical standard. Nevertheless, the rise of private property price since April 2009 has already induced many existing private property owners in Singapore to start buying more properties. Given that about 20% of Singaporean households are staying in private properties, even if these households would on average be induced to buy only one more private property, the increase in demand would be far much greater than the above increase in supply implied by the government's increase in supply of land.

Thus, the increase in the land supply itself would not be sufficient to contain the rise of property price. In addition, given the time gap of around 3 years between the pre-sale and the completion of private properties, it would not be wise to satisfy all these increase in demand by greater supply of land. That is, such increase in supply of flats could be more than the projected increase in actual "living" demand (i.e., rental demand and owner-occupied demand). Too much increase

*(Continued)*

---

**Box 12.2.1e:** (*Continued*)

in the supply of flats could result in a more severe plunge in private property price when a bursting of asset bubble in other East Asian or developing economies trigger a contagion effect on Singapore. Thus, in addition to an increase in supply to meet the projected increase in actual "living" demand, the Singapore government also need to curb part of the above increased in investment demand. In fact, that was what the Singapore government trying to do during its third and fourth rounds of curbing measures (see Section 12.5 for more details). Having said that, the author believes the Singapore government still has to prepare for more curbing measures as the expected higher price and wage inflation would very soon trigger a second surge of private property price, and then spirals among property price, rental, price and wage. Along with this, the Singapore government also needs to (i) further increase the supply of various types of public housings (e.g., HDB, DBSS and EC) for various classes of low to middle-high income earners; and (ii) ensure that the rise in private property price would not pull up the price of public flats through the indicator effect outlined in Chapter 9 (see Section 12.5 for further discussions).

---

### 12.2.2 *Why It Could Be Judged in March–April 2009 That the Global Financial Market Had Probably Passed Its Worst Time*

After the very powerful rebound of the global stock market, the author, in a policy conference in August 2009, provided a reason for the rebound, and shared his view on the macroeconomic and financial outlook. First, he noted that it was possible in March–April 2009 to foresee that

(a)  the US recession would continue for a while; but
(b)  the stock market had probably passed its worst time.

Thus, in March–April 2009, many well-trained economists were right with the first prediction, but missed the second. On the other hand, some very smart stock participants were right with the second prediction but with the wrong reason. He then explained why very few got both right in March–April 2009.

To explain this, he highlighted that there was in fact a huge *fear discount* in the global stock market during the lows in November 2008 and March 2009. Such fear discount was related to the fear of further failures in the US financial system, or failure of the financial system to function properly. For example, there were substantial financial disintermediation as (i) the banks' lending ability was substantially weakened by the loss provisions; and (ii) the banks' willingness to lend had plunged because of a surge in the adverse selection and moral hazard problems. Meanwhile, most companies, organizations and even local governments had difficulties to raise funds from the financial markets such as the stock market and the debt market. As a result, (i) many companies were forced to postpone most investment plans and cut the non-essential operations; and (ii) many organizations and local governments had to cut their less essential expenditures. All these were by themselves enough to cause a relatively severe recession.

However, after the US government's stabilization effort in March–April 2009 (i.e., appropriate relaxation of the mark-to-market rule, the stress test plan and the banks' capital raising, the Federal Reserve's quantity easing, and the use of TARP funds to support both financial and non-financial companies), the risk of domino failures of US financial institutions, or a collapse of the US financial system, had drastically decline. Thus, the worst scenario at that time would at most be a severe recession, but not a collapse of the financial and economic system. Thus, the strong rebound of the global stock market in March–July 2010 was mainly due to the disappearance of a *fear discount* (on the US financial system failing to function properly). Given that a lot of money was still on the side line at that time, sooner or later there could be a *fear of insufficient holdings of shares and assets* held by fund managers and market participants. When they started to replenish their holdings of shares and assets, one could see further rally of share and asset prices.

In the conference, the author also highlighted two potential investors' mistakes at that time:

(a) Because of the fear discount and the above explanations, the stock market low in March 2009 (and November 2008) was an "exceptional low". Any judgment using the "exceptional low" as a reference point would be misleading. That is, many investors hesitated to buy shares in June–July 2009, simply because the rebound from early March 2009 was "already substantial". However, if they correctly refused to use the "exceptional low" as the reference point, and used objective measures such as the expected PE ratios, the expected dividend yields and the discounts between the share prices and the net asset values to assess the investment potential, they should be able to find that it was still a great time to buy shares and hold it for more than tripling of the share prices within the subsequent 3–5 years. Similarly, some investors who had bought some shares during the low might have taken profit pre-maturely, simply because they thought the rebound from early March 2009 was "already substantial". When the share prices rose beyond their profit taking level, many of them would end up missing the subsequent rally or buying the shares back at a much higher price.

(b) Another potential mistake was that some investors made their decisions based on an extrapolation of the latest trend of the share price. Such extrapolation of trend would on the other hand result in too optimistic prediction on the subsequent rise in share price, simply because the low in March 2009 was an exceptional low and the rise of share price would become slower when share price recovered to less under-valued levels.

Instead of the above misleading rules, share investors could have a better picture of the shares' upside potential if they used the objective measures mentioned above.

### 12.2.3 *Recession but No Great Depression in the Global Economy*

After highlighting that the stock market had probably passed its worst time and would have at least a 3–5 year rally with occasional pullbacks, the author also explained that the US economy was only at the bottoming and stabilization stage. Nevertheless, the author also dismissed any further possibility of a great depression highlighted by some media commentators and discussants at that time. As economists had written down the lessons from the Great Depression in the 1930s and the lost decade from Japan, the substantial fiscal expansion, drastic cuts in discount rates toward zero and then the enormous quantity easing had already helped the global economy avoid a great depression similar to that in the 1930s. Thus, the concern raised by the above media commentators and discussants was just pure guessing, and was not very sensible from a well-trained economist's point of view.

### 12.2.4 *The US Dollar Carry Trade and Early Signs of Asset Inflation in Some Asian Economies*

While agreeing that the US's QE1 had helped the global economy avoid a great depression, the author also repeated the warnings on the risk of global asset inflation and exchange rate cycle highlighted in Section 12.1 He also used Figures 12.1.1a–b to highlight that subsequent data on the money multiplier in the US supported his initial warnings outlined in that section.

After that, he used the same equation to highlight that there were in fact early signs in Hong Kong, Singapore and some other East Asian economies that the US's QE1 would cause severe asset inflation there:

$$M = m \times MB$$

Unlike the US in which the failures in its financial system and the changes in economic behaviors had caused a drastic reduction in the money multiplier ($m$) from the range of 8.5–9.5 time to 4–5 times during the financial tsunami which had forced the Federal Reserve to raise the US monetary base (MB) substantially so as to keep the money supply (M) growing and avoid a great depression, there were not that much disruptions in the financial system and changes in economic behaviors in Hong Kong, Singapore and other East Asian economies. As a result, the money multiplier ($m$) there did not change much during the financial tsunami. However, with the US's QE1 and a close-to-zero US short-term interest rate, part of the US QE1 had ended up as capital flows into these East Asian economies (e.g., through the US dollar carry trade, or simply East Asian banks' US dollar borrowings to finance the property loans in their economies).

With a fixed exchange rate or just moderate appreciation of these currencies,[7] the capital inflows had caused a substantial rise in monetary base (MB) in these economies. With a relative constant $m$, this would mean a substantial increase in money supply through the money multiplier. That was also why the banking system in Hong Kong, Singapore and some other East Asian economies was flooded with liquidity with close to zero interest rates. For example, if one did a mortgage in Singapore at that time, he could easily get a mortgage rate below 1% in the first year, and then 1–2% in the second and third year. Such low mortgage rates and ample supply of bank loans had resulted in a sharp rise in property price in Hong Kong, Singapore and some other East Asian economies. Meanwhile, the capital inflows, and then the low interest rate and ample supply of liquidity in these East Asian economies also contributed to a sharp rise in share price there.

While most of the rise in asset price at that time was just a recovery from the lows, there would be a second round of surge during the economic recovery. For example, during the financial tsunami and early recovery at that time, the ample supply of liquidity and the asset inflation would not be able to trigger much increase in wage and general price, as aggregate demand was still below the potential output. However, with the continuation of the economic recovery, aggregate demand would sooner or later reach the potential output. By then, the ample supply of liquidity and the

---

[7] In Yip (2005), the author has explained that the exchange rate system in Singapore had enabled it to use substantial depreciation against the US dollar to mitigate the speculation pressure during the Asian Financial Crisis and the recession during the post-crisis period. On other hand, this was not possible under the currency board system in Hong Kong. As a result, the outcomes in Singapore was much better, even it was geographically and economically much closer to the centre of the crisis than Hong Kong. However, as the capital inflows due to US's quantity easing this time was just enormous, the relative advantage of Singapore's exchange rate system might not be able to contribute too much a difference in result. Nevertheless, as will be explained in Section 12.4, the better housing system in Singapore might be able to help Singapore reducing the potential disaster.

cumulated rise in property price, rentals and other asset prices would trigger a substantial rise in wage and price. The rise in wage and price would in turn cause a second surge in the property price, rental and other asset price. By then, there would be a few vicious spirals between asset price, rentals, wage and general price.

As explained in Chapters 8 and 9, the asset market could then go from the seeding stage to the development stage, and then the final stage of an asset bubble (see Section 12.4 for further discussions).

## 12.3 The US's QE2 and Its Potential Impacts

In the previous sections, I have explained that the US's QE1 had helped the global economy avoid a great depression, but at the same time raised the risk of a severe global asset inflation, CPI inflation and exchange rate cycle in the subsequent future. In this section, I will first discuss the potential impacts of US's QE2 on US's output and inflation. In the next section, I will discuss the risk of asset bubbles and then crises in economies outside the US in the medium future (e.g., 5–10 years after the US's first quantity easing).

### 12.3.1 *The Debate on the Effect of QE2 on US's Output and Inflation*

After a reasonably strong rebound of the US GDP growth to 4.9% in 2009Q4 and 3.7% in 2010Q1 (see Figure 12.3.1a), the sovereign debt crisis in Greece in 2010Q2 had triggered the fear of a more wide-spread European sovereign debt crisis and hence a moderate correction of the global stock market and the Euro (see Figures 12.1.1a-c and Figure 12.3.1b).

Meanwhile, the austerity measures on the fiscal expenditure in the peripheral economies of the European Union had resulted in a relative severe recession in these economies. In fact, the global stock market only started stabilizing after the European Central Bank (ECB) decided to buy up some of these sovereign debts (see Box 12.3.1a).

After the sovereign debt crisis in Greece, there were signs in the 2010Q2 statistics that the US recovery pace had slowed with a risk

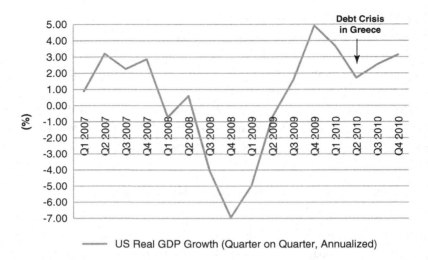

Figure 12.3.1a.   US GDP Growth

*Source*: Datastream

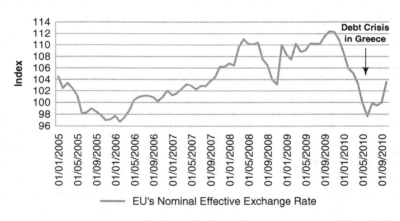

Figure 12.3.1b.   EU's Nominal Effective Exchange Rate

*Source*: Datastream

of insufficient momentum for a full recovery (e.g., see Figure 12.3.1a for the slower US GDP growth in 2010Q2). With the belief that (i) the US economic recovery at that time was too slow; (ii) US's CPI inflation pressure at that time remained tame (see Figure 12.3.1c); and

**Box 12.3.1a:   Who Benefit the Most from the ECB Rescue: The European Banking System or the Crisis-Hit Economies?**

While the media was focusing on the crisis-hit economies as the rescue target of the ECB, it should be noted that a more important rescue target of the ECB was the European banking system. As many of the major banks in Germany, France and other core economies of the EU were also holding a lot of sovereign debt issued by the crisis-hit economies, any default of the sovereign debt of the crisis-hit economies would trigger bank runs or other disastrous effects on these European banks. Once so, the European banking system, debt market and other asset markets could fail to play its usual economic function, which would in turn mean severe recession in all EU economies and then the global economy.

In fact, after his accumulation of shares in November 2008 and March–June 2009, the only time the author got worried and sold some of his "leading shares" was during the debt crisis in Greece. However, once the ECB decided to buy up some of these sovereign debts, the author knew that things would be under control. That is, the European banking system could, and would, continue to play its normal economic function although the crisis-hit economies would experience a severe recession because of their mistakes in the past. Given that the economic size of these peripheral EU economies were relatively small when compared the US or the core EU economies, the author began to buy some good-quality lagging shares that had experienced a substantial fall during the debt crisis in Greece (see Box 12.3.1b for more details). During the Irish debt crisis in 2010Q4, the author was not that worried as he knew that the European banking system would function as usual because of the ECB's purchase of sovereign debts of the peripheral economies.

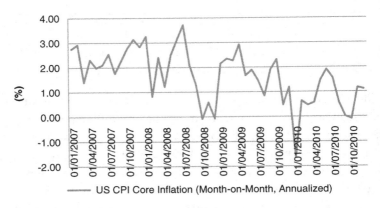

Figure 12.3.1c.  US CPI Inflation

*Source*: Datastream

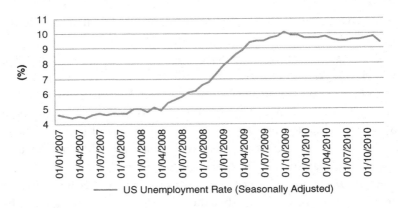

Figure 12.3.1d.  US's Unemployment Rate

*Source*: Datastream

(iii) US's unemployment rate was still high at 9.6% (see Figure 12.3.1d), and would probably stay at high levels for a reasonably long period,[8]

---

[8] The official statement of the Federal Reserve's rationale for QE2 was as followed:

> *"To promote a strong pace of economic recovery and to help ensure that inflation, over time, is at levels consistent with its mandate, the Committee decided to expand its holdings of securities. The Committee will ..."*

Bernanke in early October 2010 hinted the possibility of a second quantity easing, i.e., QE2, when deemed necessary.[9]

However, Bernanke's hint of QE2 invited disagreeing voices from quite a number of famous people in the US. The major arguments of these discussants were:

(a) QE2 would not help stimulate the US economy;
(b) QE2 would cause rampant CPI inflation in the US in the years ahead.

Down below, I will explain that these discussants would probably be wrong, and Bernanke would probably be right on his choice for the US economy. In particular, from the point of view of macroeconomic policy management, the mistake in argument (a) is almost unforgivable. Although the misleading policy implication in argument (b) is more understandable, there is an important lesson that we can draw for future macroeconomic policy management. Nevertheless, while not disagreeing Bernanke's choice for the US economy, I will also highlight in Section 12.4 that the real risk of US's QE2 is the formation of asset bubbles in economies outside the US. As not all the related governments have the knowledge and determination to stop the bubbles growing during the recovery and then the overheated phase of this economic cycle, we will probably see a bursting of bubble and then an economic crisis in some of these economies in the medium future (e.g., 5–10 years after US's first quantity easing).

---

[9] For readers who interested in macroeconomic policy management, the hint (which should be supported by a preliminary plan) can serve two purposes here. Firstly, it can invite feedbacks so that the US central bank could better assess the potential loophole, viability and impacts of the policy. Next, if the US central bank eventually go ahead with its initial plan of QE2, the hint can serve to give the market a chance for the anticipation of QE2, and hence smooth out the substantial impacts of QE2. Unfortunately, the outcome of the first purpose was not that good, simply because of the low quality of the disagreeing voices at that time. Nevertheless, on the second purpose, the hint did give the market the necessary time for anticipation, and hence smoothed out the substantial impact of QE2.

**Box 12.3.1b:   QE2 Provided an Almost Guaranteed Opportunity for Share Investments**

Seeing the above disagreeing voices on the QE2 was not well found, the author judged that it was in fact a good time to buy shares during the anticipation period.[10] Nevertheless, as the author had already purchased, and was still holding, huge amount of shares at very low price during November 2008 and March–June 2009, further purchase of shares would raise his exposure to shares to undesirable levels. Therefore, he decided to modify the switching strategy by taking advantage of a temporary time gap between the purchase and sale of shares. That is, with the anticipated positive impact of QE2 on share price, one could first purchase some good-quality lagging shares and plan to sell the leading shares one or two months later (i.e., after the QE2 effect was priced in the leading shares). For example, with the anticipated rise in oil price and the anticipated QE2 effect, the author first accumulated a reasonably large amount of British Petroleum (ADR) shares at the price range of US$40–42 with a PE ratio of only 5–7 times. After waiting for the anticipated effect of the QE2 and the anticipated change in oil price to exert its effect in the next two months, he started to sell his holdings of China National Ocean Oil accumulated at very cheap price in the past. At that selling price range of HK$17.8–19.5, the historical PE ratio was 22–25 times. Even if one took into account of the

*(Continued)*

---

[10] Bernanke's hint of QE2 when deemed necessary actually acted as a guarantee for share investments (and further rise in the share prices was also what he wanted at that time). That is, no matter the US economy would do well or not in the subsequent months, share investors would still gain. For example, if the US economy was doing well, share prices would rise with the improving economy. Even if the US economy was not doing well, the Federal Reserve would implement QE2 which would push the share prices up through expected inflation. In fact, some analysts had later joked that the situation was equivalent to "*head — shares win, and tail — shares win*".

**Box 12.3.1b:** (*Continued*)

very strong output growth and rise in oil price between 2010 and 2009, the expected PE ratio at that price range would still be 14–15 times, which would be much less attractive than the very low PE ratio of the British Petroleum.[11]

---

[11] After the oil spill in the Gulf of Mexico, the share of the British Petroleum (ADR) had dropped to around US$30 from around US$60 before the spill. As there was insufficient information to judge whether the company could survive after paying the potential damage claims, the author did not have any intention to buy the shares at that time. However, when things stabilized and the share price rose to around US$40 in October 2010, there was more information suggesting that the shares could be a good buy. For example, the 2010Q3 result confirmed that the company's operating profit would continue to be huge at a few billion US dollars per quarter. Thus, even if the $39 billion reserve was not enough to pay all the damage claims due to the spill, what the company has to do is to defer the dividend payments by another few quarters i.e., it was already clear that the company would survive. The only question was how soon it could resume the dividend payment. Moreover, from the author's common knowledge accumulated in the commercial field, firms are usually able to suppress the eventual claim well below what it should be. For example, for those who are eligible to the claims, if the company gives them the choice of either

(a) receiving an a immediate payment of an amount much smaller than the potential claim while giving up the right to sue the company in the future; and

(b) going though the long and tough legal procedure of getting the full damage claim, a reasonably large percentage of people will choose the first option. Thus, it would be very possible that the eventual compensation would turn out to be much smaller than what it should be.

With the anticipation that

[Note: As an academic economist, the author must admit that the above trick used by the company was actually inappropriate.]

(i) it would be just a matter of time that the company's PE ratio will eventually rose from the exceptional 5-7 times to at least 10 times; and

(ii) it would be just a matter of time that the oil price would rise beyond US$100 per barrel,

it would be just a mater of time that the share would rise beyond US$70 from the price of US$40 at that time.

## 12.3.2  *Misconceptions Related to the Liquidity Trap*

Two common, and very often misunderstood, concepts that contributed to the doubt on the effectiveness of quantity easing during a severe recession, an economic crisis or the financial tsunami were

(i)  the argument of *liquidity trap*; and
(ii)  the mis-identification of the traditional *interest rate channel as the only channel* that monetary policy could affect economic activities.

According to the discussion on the interest rate channel, a quantity easing or an increase in money supply ($\uparrow M^s$) would cause a reduction in interest rate ($i$). The reduction in interest rate would in turn increase investment (I), durable consumption ($C_d$) and housing demand ($H_d$), and hence stimulate output through the multiplier effect (see the flow chart below):

$$\uparrow M^s \rightarrow \downarrow i \rightarrow \uparrow I, \uparrow C_d, \uparrow H_d \rightarrow \uparrow Y$$

However, according to the liquidity trap argument, once the government reduces the interest rate to levels close-to-zero, quantity easing would be ineffective as any increase in money supply would only be hoarded by people without any effect on the interest rate. As a result, the traditional interest rate channel depicted in the above flow chart would be blocked in the first step (i.e., without any reduction in interest rate, I, $C_d$, $H_d$ and hence Y would not rise).

The liquidity trap argument could be illustrated Diagram 12.3.1:

---

*The downward sloping section of the money demand curve*

When the economy is in this section (e.g., during the normal period), an increase in money supply would induce people to shift their portfolio from money to bond (i.e., use part of the increased money to buy bonds). The higher demand for bond would push up the bond price and hence cause a reduction in the interest rate until

*(Continued)*

---

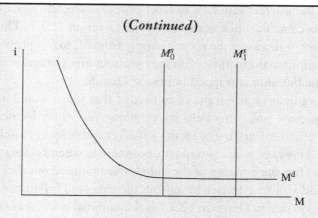

**(Continued)**

Diagram 12.3.1.   Liquidity Trap

the re-establishment of equilibriums in both the bond and money markers.[12]

*The horizontal section of the money demand curve*

When the economy reaches this section (e.g., when the government reduces its interest rate to levels close to zero during a severe recession or a crisis), a quantity easing will not induce people to shift from money to bond, as they are worry about a rise in interest rate from the exceptionally low level, and hence a capital loss in the future. Instead, they will just hoard the extra supply of money. Thus, in this case, a quantity easing could not reduce the interest rate.

---

[12] As is well explained in standard economic textbook, even if people try to use part of the increased money to buy bonds, the total amount of money in the economy (and hence the quantity of money held by the public) would still be the same as the new money supply is fixed by the government. The variable that actually brings the market to equilibrium is not the quantity of money but the interest rate, i.e., the fall in the interest rate will reduce the demand for bond and increase the demand for money until the latter is equal to the new money supply fixed by the government.

When the interest rate falls to level close-to-zero, the money demand curve will become flat such as that shown in Diagram 12.3.1. Thus, even if the government increases the money supply from $M_0^s$ to $M_j^s$, people will just hoard the additional quantity of money without any reduction in interest rate, i.e., the liquidity is trapped in people's hands.

Such argument was once used to predict that Japan would not be able to use monetary policy to help its economy out from its decade-long stagnation after the bursting of its stock market and property bubbles in the late 1980s. However, some prominent economists when reviewing Japan's lost decade after the bursting of the bubbles had pointed out that monetary policy would still be effective by raising the expected inflation ($\pi^e$). That is, the interest rate in Diagram 12.3.1 is the nominal interest rate ($i$), while the interest rate that affects economic activities is the real interest rate ($r$), where

$$r = i - \pi^e$$

Thus, even if the nominal interest rate $i$ can not fall below zero, the related government can still use ultra expansionary quantity easing to increase the expected inflation $\pi^e$, push the real interest rate $r$ to negative levels and hence stimulate the economy. In other words, the inappropriate application of the liquidity trap argument had deprived Japan the chance of using ultra expansionary quantity easing to help its economy out of the lost two decades.[13]

---

[13] Of course, with the hindsight of more than 75% fall in share price and the 80–90% fall in property price in Japan, the stock market and property bubble in Japan in the late 1980s was far much greater than the property bubble in the US before the financial tsunami. With such a huge bubble, one needs to do more thorough thinking on whether it would be appropriate to have a quantity easing that is far much greater than that in the US. Nevertheless, the author believes that it is at least possible to use a reasonably large quantity easing to shorten Japan's lost two decades to less than 5–6 years of stagnation (with a much bigger money supply and lower exchange value of yen, of course). Thus, the different experience in Japan and the US tells us that it is very important to have the right person (with solid economic knowledge) to look after the economy and the central bank. [Note: Japan's problem at that time was not whether there existed good enough economists. The real problem was that its political practice and cronyism had stopped it from getting qualified economists for the post.]

### 12.3.3 *Monetary Policy Has Many Other Transmission Channels*

Another problem of the above discussants in the US media was that they had not even read their second year Money and Banking textbook before they argued that QE2 would not be able to stimulate the economy, thus exposing their ignorance on standard economy theory to the world. As is well documented in standard Money and Banking textbook (e.g., Mishkin, 2009), interest rate is only one of the many channels that monetary policy or quantity easing can affect the economy, i.e., there are many other channels that quantity easing can stimulate the economy even if it cannot push down the close-to-zero nominal interest rate. The following is a summary of what the author explaind to his students during the Money and Banking lectures in October–November 2010 (i.e., just during the anticipation and actual announcement of the QE2 in November 2010).

In addition to the standard interest rate channel, one other channel is the *exchange rate channel*:

$$\uparrow M^s \rightarrow \downarrow ExR \rightarrow \uparrow NX \rightarrow \uparrow Y$$

That is, a substantial quantity easing or increase in the money supply ($\uparrow M^s$) in the US will cause a depreciation of the US dollar. This will in turn stimulate net export (NX) and hence output (Y) through the multiplier effect. In fact, even before the Federal Reserve made the formal announcement of QE2, anticipation of the QE2 in October 2010 had already started to cause a reasonably large depreciation of the US dollar against other currencies. Unfortunately, ignorance about this channel stated in standard economic textbook resulted in the above discussants making the ignorant comments without realizing that the US dollar had already started to depreciate by a substantial amount.

The second channel is the *wealth effect channel*. Although substantial quantity easing during the recession or crisis period will not induce people to use part of the increased quantity of money to buy bonds (thus reducing interest rate) because of the potential risk of a severe capital loss when interest rate rise in the future, substantial quantity easing can induce people to use part of the increased quantity of money to buy shares and other assets. Given that

(i) share price in the US was still substantially under-valued even after the rally between March 2009 and October 2010; and

(ii) QE2 had raised the long run expected value of CPI, wages and asset prices,

the quantity easing would at least induce people to buy more shares and other assets.[14] This would in turn push the share price ($P_s$) and other asset price ($P_{oA}$) up, and hence stimulate the economy through the wealth effect channel:

$$\uparrow M^s \rightarrow \uparrow P_s, \uparrow P_{oA} \rightarrow \uparrow W \rightarrow \uparrow C \rightarrow \uparrow Y$$

That is, the quantity easing will increase the price of shares and other assets, and hence the wealth (W) held by people. This will in turn stimulate consumption (C) and hence output (Y) through the multiplier effect. In fact, even before the Federal Reserve's formal announcement of QE2 in November 2010, anticipation of QE2 in October 2010 had already started to cause a rally in the US and global stock markets. The author believed that stimulated consumption by the asset holders, especially the relative rich in the US. Thus, even though the unemployment rate would remain above 9% in the subsequent months, consumption and retail sales would be much better than that implied by the high unemployment rate.

---

[14] The other assets would include properties: Unlike the undervalued share price at that time, US property price was still correcting from the non-sustainable level in 2006 to more reasonable levels at that time. Even so, the expected inflation created by QE1 and QE2 plus the tax credit for new home purchase did induce quite a lot of Americans to buy properties at that time. This had in turn provided some kind of support against further fall in property price, and hence helped mitigating the eventual correction of property price in the US. In other words, the QE1 and QE2 did help stimulate demand for properties and avoid a bigger negative wealth effect and hence a bigger fall in US's output growth.

The third other channel is the Tobin's q channel. According to standard economic textbook, Tobin's q ratio is defined as

$$q = \frac{\text{market value of firm}}{\text{replacement cost of capital}}$$

As explained in the previous discussion, quantity easing can bid up the share price and hence the market value of firm by (i) inducing people to use part of the increased quantity of money to buy more shares; and (ii) creating an inflation expectation. With the rise in share price ($P_s$) and hence the market value of firm and the Tobin's q ratio to more reasonable levels, the related company will have the incentive to issue new shares so as to earn the difference between the share price (i.e., the market value of firm) and the cost of raising the firm's profit earning capacity (i.e., the replacement cost of capital). That is, the firm will have the incentives and chance to raise capital from the improved stock market. With the capital raised from the stock market, the firm can make real investment (I) which will in turn stimulate output (Y) through the multiplier effect (see the flow chart below):[15]

$$\uparrow M^s \rightarrow \uparrow P_s \rightarrow \uparrow q \rightarrow \text{firms raise capital \& } \uparrow I \rightarrow \uparrow Y$$

Again, the above discussants had missed this channel even though there were more and more companies raising capital from the stock market during the QE1 and QE2. [Note: In Chapter 11, the author said that it was easier for one to use a property boom to offset the negative effect of a collapse of the stock market price, as the size of the property market was usually far much greater than that of the stock market. While the difference in market size would mean that the wealth effect of a booming stock market would not be enough to offset the negative wealth effect of a collapse of property price, sustained rally in the stock market (and private debt market) would enable

---

[15] Even for firms in poor financial shape, the rise in share price would allow them to raise capital from the stock market and hence helped avoiding the firms cutting output or even closing down because of funding problems. Thus, quantity easing would also stimulate the economy by avoiding a reduction of output by firms with funding problems.

companies to raise larger and larger amount of capital from the stock market. If these funds were eventually used for real investment, it would still be possible to use a sustained share market rally to give the economy the necessary momentum to get out from the great recession to an automatic path of self recovery, although the time taken would be much longer than using the property boom to offset the negative effect of a collapse of share prices.]

In addition to the above channels, there are many other channels that quantity easing or expansionary monetary policy could stimulate the economy even in the liquidity trap case. For example, when the Federal Reserve do the quantity easing by purchasing long-term government bonds, even though the long-term government bond rate could not go below a certain level (e.g., 3.5% for 30 years US Treasury bonds) as the increase in central bank's purchase could be offset by the reduction of private sector's holdings when the long term rate reached that unattractive level relative to the risk or the opportunity cost, the private funds forced out from the long term government bond market would eventually end up somewhere (e.g., the share market and private debt market for the case of private investors, the loans market for the case of banks). In fact, one of the aims of the Federal Reserve's purchase was to force the commercial banks to make loans instead of keeping their money in long-term government bonds for a safe and decent return. As being well known, making the commercial banks to go back to normal loan business and the financial market to re-function as usual are crucial to, and perhaps a pre-requisite of, the fully recovery of the US economy.

In short, the above discussants were very wrong in just using the traditional interest rate channel and the liquidity trap argument to argue that QE2 could not stimulate the US economy. Given that

(i) all these discussions were well documented in standard economic textbook, and
(ii) the substantial implications of the misleading argument to the US economy at that time (and to the Japanese economy in the past),

the author believes this kind of mistake is unforgivable. He hopes that young readers of this book could avoid committing this type of mistakes in the future. The discussion also suggests that it is important to have the right person (i.e., well-trained economists) looking after an economy and its central bank. The author also believes that Bernanke will in the future be credited by the Americans for his contribution to the US economy, although he might in the future be condemned by the Asian or other developing economies for the development of an asset bubble there. Should Japan have the right person looking after its economy and central bank in the early 1990s, it could have shortened the stagnation in the lost two decades to just 5–6 years. Should Japan have the right person looking after its economy and central bank in the 1980s, it would have reduced or even avoided the huge bubble right from the beginning.

### 12.3.4 *Potential Impacts of QE2 on US Inflation*

Another argument used against Bernanke's QE2 was that it could cause rampant CPI inflation in the US in the years ahead. While this would be true during the normal time, the sequence of outcomes would be very different when an economy was just at the early stage of recovery from a severe recession, a crisis or the financial tsunami.

One important lesson that the author had learned from his observation over the past thirty five years is as follows:

(a) During the *normal period* (i.e., when aggregate demand is close to potential output), increase in monetary growth will first cause an asset inflation before it causes a rise in wage and CPI inflation, and hence subsequent spirals and vicious cycles between asset price, wage and general price. Thus, the initial asset inflation could be an early sign of more rampant asset inflation and general price inflation. Therefore, it would be important for the related government to substantially curb its monetary growth at the initial stage of the asset inflation.

(b) Nevertheless, the sequence of outcomes could be somewhat different if the related economy's starting point was a *severe recession with a high unemployment rate* (e.g., greater than 9% for the US at that time). In such a case, a substantial quantity easing would help reflate the asset prices that were needed for the re-functioning of the financial system and the initiation of the economy's self recovery (i.e., see the previous sections on how this could help stabilize the property price and cause a rally in the share price and other asset prices in the US; and how these helped the financial system start replaying its usual role in the economic system). Meanwhile, the quantity easing would not be able to cause much wage and CPI inflation in the initial stage of the recovery, simply because aggregate demand was still well below the potential output. That is, if there was plenty of unemployment, it would be difficult for the workers to ask for a higher wage even though some of the asset price had risen a lot. If the demand was still weak with excess production capacity in firms and their competitors, it would also be difficult for firms to raise their prices.

Given that

(i)   the US unemployment rate was still high at 9.6% in September 2010, and it would take years for the unemployment rate to fall to 5–6%;

(ii)  aggregate demand at that time was still well below its potential output so that inflation pressure was low; and

(iii) the US GDP growth was to some extent slowed by the European debt crisis, and it was not clear that the momentum of the US economic recovery at that time was strong enough for a self recovery,

what should the Federal Reserve opt for? If it chose not to do another stimulation, it would definitely be very painful for the American workers (i.e., years of high unemployment rate). Worse still, the economic theory on *hysteresis effect* told us that years of high unemployment would mean that some long-term unemployed could never be able to find a job, i.e., firms would hesitate to employ these workers as firms would see these workers' long unemployment record as a probable sign of some problematic qualities of the workers. Moreover, point (iii) suggested that there is a risk of insufficient momentum of a self recovery (i.e., there could be potential stagnation or double dip, especially if there were other negative shocks in the subsequent future). Points (i) and (ii) also suggested that there could be a substantial time gap between the recovery and the subsequent inflation. If so, it could be better to do another quantity easing at that time, with the plan to do more aggressive liquidity mop-up when the US unemployment rate fell to 7% and then 5–6%.

Based on the above cost and benefit analysis, the author believes that Bernanke has probably made the right choice for his country. If the Federal

Reserve did follow the above discussants' refusal of QE2, American workers would definitely have to suffer more and longer, with a risk of insufficient momentum for a self recovery of the US economy. On the other hand, Bernanke's QE2 would mean less pain for the American workers, faster and more certain recovery for the US, although we have yet to see whether he can control subsequent inflation in the future.

## 12.4 The Risk of a Bubble and Then a Crisis in Economies Outside the US During the Overheated Phase of the Recovery

In the previous sections, the author explained that the US probably needed the QE2. However, many other economies, especially those in Asia and the developing world, could eventually suffer from US's QE2.[16] This is so because before QE1 and QE2, the US property price, share price and other asset price had plunged substantially, the US did need the QE1 and QE2 to stabilize the property price and initiate a rebound of the share price and other asset prices, which would be crucial to the re-functioning of the financial system, and hence the recovery of the US economy. For example, when share prices started to rise, companies would be able to issue more shares for real investment, or at least raise their capital to more healthy levels which would allow them to make investment through bank or debt financing. On the other hand, while the above Asian and developing economies needed US's QE1 to avoid a great global depression which was in fact originated from the mistake of the previous US government, they did not needed QE2 as their share price had rebounded to more normal level while their property price  already became moderately overvalued after the QE1 (see Section 12.2.4 for the discussion of early signs of asset inflation in Hong Kong, Singapore and some other East Asian economies).

---

[16] As the Federal Reserve was also aware of the need to reduce the size of quality easing to a much smaller level at that time, QE2 (600 billion US dollars) was in fact far much smaller that QE1 (1.75 trillion US dollars). Thus, strictly speaking, it was QE2 and at least part of QE1 that had increased the risk of asset buble in some of the Asian and developing economies.

Applying the discussions in Chapters 8 and 9, these markets were already at the seeding stage of a bubble, i.e., an upward inertia of asset price was already established and there were already some changes in economic behaviors (e.g., property investors in many East Asian economies were buying more properties and raising their leverage in the property market; and banks were already aggressively funding their long-term mortgage loans by short-term funding from the US, albeit indirectly). With the aggregate demand rising towards the potential output with the ongoing economic recovery, the ample supply of global liquidity originated from US's quantity easing would soon cause a higher CPI inflation in these economies. In fact, there are early signs of higher CPI inflation in Hong Kong, Singapore and other East Asian economies, and very soon we will see an upward revision of wage in these economies. Once the wage is revised up, it will support further rise in property price. Meanwhile, the rise in price and wage will support further rise in share price and other asset prices.

Thus, unlike the US which will still be at the recovery stage in the next two years, these economies will very soon enter the development stage of a bubble. The eventual outcomes will therefore depend on whether these economies have the knowledge, ability, experience and determination to stop the formation of a bubble before it is too late. As explained in Chapter 8, curbing asset inflation at the development stage is very difficult, i.e., if an expectation of rampant asset inflation is formed, much greater curbing measures will be needed before the asset inflation can be controlled.

Among these economies, some might be able to keep their asset inflation at high but not unreasonably levels, possibly because they have drawn and learned important lessons from their previous painful experience (see Section 12.5 for more discussion on the likely outcomes in Singapore, Hong Kong and China). However, given the large number of Asian and developing economies that are entering the asset inflation and high CPI inflation era, it is likely that some economies will not recognize the need to, or fail to, curb its monetary growth and hence the asset price and general price inflation to sustainable levels. By then, we will gradually see

(i) the establishment of expectation of rampant asset inflation and expectation of higher CPI inflation;

(ii) the formation of upward spirals between asset price, rentals, wage and price; and

(iii) the emergence of the changes in economic behaviors and vicious cycles highlighted in Chapter 8

in these economies. These will in turn push the asset price, rentals, wage and general price further up. The sustained rise in asset price could also trigger herding behaviors which will then push these economies onto an automatic path of growing bubble. By then, it will be just a matter of time that some negative shocks in the future will trigger a bursting of the bubble and then an economic crisis in these economies. As explained in Chapter 8, in the lucky case that there is a large enough negative shock that triggers the bursting at the early stage of the bubble, there will be just a severe recession, but not social and political instability during the crisis. In the unlucky case that the bubble has the chance to grow to a huge one so that even some moderate or minor negative shock can trigger the bursting, there can be enormous social and political instability (e.g., collapse of the government due to protest or riot) during the crisis.

In both cases, even for those economies who manage to keep their asset inflation and CPI inflation at less unreasonable levels, they will still have to go through painful corrections when the crisis elsewhere triggers a contagious correction in the region they belong to. On the other hand, as will still be the US economy (a) at the early and middle stage of the recovery in the next few years; (b) will be more affected by its internal demand, the impacts of the above crises to the US economy could be very limited. In fact, past experience of the Latin American Crisis in the 1980s suggested that one probable triggering cause of the above bubble bursting would be a tightening of money supply or substantial rise in interest rate in the US.[17] Perhaps more frightening is that along with the rise in interest rate and monetary tightening in the US, the US dollar will surge substantially from its exceptional low. Thus, those economies with an asset bubble can also be subjected to a currency attack. The attack can be particularly serious for economies with

---

[17] In the 1980s, the substantial rise in the US interest rate (and surge in the US dollar) triggered the Latin American Crisis. In the 1990s, the rise in German interest rate also caused a recession and then currency attacks in other member countries in the European Union.

(i) free mobility of capital; (ii) an established currency futures market (see Chapter 5); and (iii) a fixed or quasi-fixed exchange rate system.

Ironically, the European Union can be the second safest economy, mainly because (i) the sovereign debt crises there had caused a reasonable correction of the Euro; and (ii) the peripheral EU economies would have to go through a relative severe recession which would mean that there would not be much asset inflation there in the next few years. Thus, the Asian economies or other developing economies can be the most likely group with the above crisis. At the time of writing this section, there is news of political protest in Egypt, and one of the triggering causes is food inflation there. Hence, there is a very real risk in the future that rampant CPI inflation, asset inflation and bursting of bubble could trigger political instability or crises in economies outside the US. However, it should be highlighted that the economic conditions for economies with a bursting of bubble will be far worse than the economic conditions in Egypt today, i.e., Egypt can be lucky to have the protest and political change today instead of in the future.[18] In fact, this is why the author keeps on using the word "*fear*" to describe the share price and property price hike in some East Asian and developing economies.

## 12.5 The Likelihood of a Huge Property Bubble and Then a Crisis in Singapore, Hong Kong and China

After the Asian Financial Crisis, Yip (2005a)[19] had written down the lessons from the crisis; and economic officials in Singapore were very aware of these lessons. Thus, when the author wrote his concern in 2009H2 on the property inflation and then potential property bubble during the global economic recovery, the Singapore government has up to now implemented four rounds of curbing measures on its property market. More importantly, Singapore

---

[18] Note that the case of Egypt was not due to a bursting of asset bubble. Instead, it was due to: (i) long-term political and social problems; and (ii) the latest food inflation and unemployment problems, which allow the development in Tunisia to trigger widespread request for political changes. Thus, the subsequent crisis and recession triggered by the bursting of asset bubble in other Asian and developing economies could be far more severe than that in Egypt.

[19] In addition to the book, see also the journal papers in Tse and Yip (2003 and 2006), Yip (1999, 2002, 2003, 2005b, 2007, 2008) and Yip and Wang (2001 and 2002).

has a huge supply of public housing (i.e., HDB flats), which has met the housing need of 80% of its citizens. Thus, as long as the Singapore government could cut the property price hike transmission channel from the new private property market to the public housing market through the indicator effect outlined in Chapter 9, at least 80% of its citizens would be better immune from the property inflation and then the plunge in the future.

As the Singapore government had in its third round of curbing measures banned property investors with at least one property in Singapore or overseas from buying HDB flats in the secondary market, the above powerful indicator effect channel from new private property market to second hand public housing market has to a certain extent been contained. Nevertheless, there is still a powerful indicator effect from the limited number of new private properties to the larger pool of second hand private properties (i.e., about 20% of the total housing supply stock in Singapore). With second hand private property price following the excessive hike in new private property price, the Singapore government was forced to introduced its fourth round of curbing measures where

(a)  the minimum down payment ratio for property owners with at least one outstanding bank loans was raised to 40%, while the minimum down payment ratio for those without property or outstanding mortgage loans remained unchanged at 20%;
(b)  property investors who sell their flats within 1, 2, 3 and 4 years of their purchase were required to pay heavy stamp duty of 16%, 12%, 8% and 4% of the selling price, respectively.

Despite these heavy curbing measures, property analysts are expecting only drastic decline in property transaction in the short-term with minor or moderate correction of property price. As explained in Chapter 9, unless the shock is extremely big, developers usually have market power and hoarding power to resist any meaningful correction of property price. Meanwhile, the indicator effect from new private property to second hand private property would still work unless the shock is very big. Thus, the author believes the most likely outcome is little change in private property price in the subsequent two quarters.

Meanwhile, the developers' above strategy could allow them to wait until the soon arriving global inflation to spark another hike of private property price in Singapore. That is, when the global CPI inflation, especially the food inflation, started to cause a higher CPI and wage inflation in Singapore, one would probably see another round of private property price hike with (i) higher wage and price supporting higher property price; and (ii) pent-up demand (accumulated during the curbing period) fuelling the second phase of property boom. Worse still, as the US's QE1 and QE2 have resulted in excess liquidity in Singapore's banking system, and Singapore banks' share of property loans in the total loans has reached a dangerously high level, the vulnerability of Singapore's banking system should not be neglected.

Thus, the author believes the Singapore government should make itself ready for the fifth round of curbing measures with

(a)   the minimum down payment ratio for those with at least one out-standing property loans being raised to 50%; and

(b)   a ceiling on the share of property loans in banks' total loans.

Having said that, the Singapore's housing system, exchange rate system (with NEER targeting which would allow it to mitigate the potential impacts of the huge cycle or nominal swings of the US dollar), as well as its economic officials' experience and learning from the Asian Financial Crisis could help Singapore to contain the property inflation and then the subsequent plunge to a more bearable level.

On the other hand, the author is rather pessimistic with his home economy (Hong Kong) as the person in charge is probably a dogmatic market believer. That is, the person in charge does not seem to have the knowledge to understand the disastrous outcome if one just rely on market force to do the property allocation job under the imperfect settings in Hong Kong, such as excessive liquidity in Hong Kong's banking system due to US's QE1 and QE2, the developers' market power and hoarding power, and the high income inequality in Hong Kong. Thus, unlike Mr. Lee Kwan Yew of Singapore who has the devotion and vision to work for his people's benefit by establishing the public housing system when he was young, the corresponding person in Hong Kong does not recognize the need to restart the construction and sales of public housing as a mean to contain the rise in property price and meet the housing need of the low to middle income earners. Worse still, the fixed exchange rate implicit in Hong Kong's currency board system would mean that (i) it could once again invite speculative attacks similar to those in 1997–98 (see the Appendices 5-1 to 5-3 for more details);[20] and (ii) Hong Kong would once again not able to use exchange rate depreciation to facilitate the necessary adjustments and hence mitigate the severe and prolonged recession triggers by the subsequent plunge in property price. In fact, for speculators with political motives to attack China, Hong Kong could be the best starting place of their speculative attack.

---

**Box 12.5:  Why Hong Kong Could be Vulnerable to Speculative Attack During the Overheated Phase of this Recovery**

When one of the reporters of the *Hong Kong Economic Journal* came to interview the author in Singapore during the rebound of Hong Kong's property market in 2009H2, the author had given the warning with a written summary of the issue and the related mechanism. While the reporter was well-trained enough to roughly appreciate the importance of the warning, she was not able to report the core issue and the related mechanism, as the level of understanding required for writing down the whole complicated issue was much higher than that required for a rough understand

*(Continued)*

---

[20] Note, similar to the asset inflation era before the Asian Financial Crisis, there are actually two things happening at the current moment: (i) the peg implies the Hong Kong dollar is currently falling with the US dollar; and (ii) the asset price, CPI and wage in Hong Kong is rising faster than those in the US. As the loss in relative price competitiveness due to (ii) is currently offset by the effect of (i), most people in Hong Kong would not be aware of the risk in the future. However, if one day the US dollar rebounds strongly from its exceptional low, the previous loss of competitiveness due to (ii) will make it difficult and costly for Hong Kong dollar to peg with the rising US dollar. In particular, speculators would find it profitable to repeat the speculative attack in 1997–98 or simply attack the Hong Kong dollar directly.

**Box 12.5:    (*Continued*)**

of the importance of the issue. Thus, it might help the related Hong Kong authority for the author to repeat the warnings and the related mechanism here. To understand the argument, first note that:

(i) Because Hong Kong dollar was pegged to the US dollar, the substantial depreciation of the US dollar since US's QE1 also caused a substantial depreciation of Hong Kong's nominal effective exchange rate (NEER);

(ii) The substantial depreciation of Hong Kong's NEER has offset part of the effect of the surge of Hong Kong's property price since April 2009, i.e., the rise in Hong Kong's property price rentals, CPI and wage, when expressed in the basket of currencies in its NEER, would be much smaller than that expressed in Hong Kong dollar. This has in turn made many people in Hong Kong less alert with the potential loss in relative price competitiveness due to the rise in property price.

(iii) Nevertheless, there was no parallel rise in property price, CPI and wage in the US, which could mean a strong rebound of the US dollar from its over-depreciated level when the Federal Reserve starts to mop up the excess liquidity during the middle or early-middle phase of its economic recovery.

(iv) By then, Hong Kong's currency peg would mean that Hong Kong's NEER would rise substantially with the strong rebound of the US dollar. Together with the substantial rise in property price, rentals, CPI and wage discussed in (ii), Hong Kong's loss of relative price competitiveness would be substantial. That is, the overvaluation of the Hong Kong dollar would then be more apparent to the market, and substantial enough to attract another speculative attack similar to that in 1997–98 (see Appendices 5-1 to 5-3 for further details).

(*Continued*)

**Box 12.5:** (*Continued*)

**Lessons**: Before the Asian Financial Crisis, Mr. Joseph Yam, the then CEO of the Hong Kong Monetary Authority, used to argue (and believe) that, under Hong Kong's currency peg, the Federal Reserve's monetary policy would take care of Hong Kong's economic needs. That is, when the Hong Kong economy is more or less at the same position as the US economy, an overheated (slowing) US economy will induce the Federal Reserve to raise (reduce) US's interest rate, which would in turn raise (reduce) Hong Kong's interest rate and hence help cooling (stimulating) the Hong Kong economy. Nevertheless, what Mr. Joseph Yam was not aware of was the potentially painful consequences when the Hong Kong economy and the US economy were at different positions of the business cycle. For example, during the Asian Financial Crisis and the post-crisis period, the US dollar was appreciating but what Hong Kong needed was a weaker US dollar. Similarly, in 2010 (and perhaps 2011H1), the US still needs the quantity easing but such quantity easing in the US has caused a property inflation and the subsequent spirals in Hong Kong. Even during the time Mr. Joseph Yam made the above comment (i.e., between 1990 and 1997), he actually mis-identified that the Hong Kong economy was at more or less the same position of the business cycle as the US economy. As explained in Section 9.4, the Hong Kong economy was actually in a prolonged overheated phase and asset inflation era because of the huge amount of money earned by its citizens due to the (first and second round of) opening-up in China at that time. Should Hong Kong adopted an exchange rate system similar to that of Singapore instead of the fixed exchange rate implicit in its currency board system, Hong Kong would be able to use a gradual appreciation of the Hong Kong dollar during the overheated phase in 1990–97 and then a major depreciation of the Hong Kong dollar during and after the Asian Financial

(*Continued*)

**Box 12.5:** (*Continued*)

Crisis to mitigate the inflation in 1990–97 and the recession during and after the crisis.[21]

Thus, policy makers and central banks interested in pegging their currency with a major currency should avoid underestimating the likelihood that their economy could sometimes be in a different position as the major economy they are trying to peg to. For example, during the European debt crisis in 2010 (and possibly in 2011 as well), the peripheral EU economies were actually in very different fiscal positions as those in the core EU economies, the adoption of Euro (and the limited mobility of factor of production in reality) has deprived these peripheral EU economies any chance of using a major depreciation or devaluation to mitigate the severe recession in their economies. On the other hand, waiting for the sluggish price and wage to achieve the necessary adjustment would mean a painful recession for many years (e.g., $\geq 5$ years). As explained in an earlier footnote of this chapter, even among the core EU economies, their attempt to peg their currencies with the Deutsche Mark amid major difference in the position between their economies and the German economy in the early 1990s also cost them a lot, i.e., the rise of German's interest rate after Germany's unification in 1990 also caused a severe recession in the other founding members of EU, and speculative attacks on the sterling and other core EU currencies in 1992.

---

[21] Note, what really matters to output and employment is the quantity of export, not the value of exports and current account balance highlighted in the J-curve effect. That is, a major depreciation will not cause any initial deterioration of the quantity of export, output and employment. Thus, the only remaining question is how soon (e.g., 3, 6 or 9 months) the major depreciation could result in a reasonable improvement in the quantity of export and output.

For the case of China,[22] the outcomes would very much depend on what would happen in the next few years. For example, it will very much depend on

(i)    how many public housings that China could supply;
(ii)   how well China could contain its property inflation and pre-empt the formation of other asset bubbles;
(iii)  how well the Chinese central bank could control its monetary growth;
(iv)   how well China could plug its holes on its capital control;
(v)    whether China would monitor its NEER, instead of just the RMB-US$ rate, so as to mitigate the potential impacts of the huge cycle of the US dollar;
(vi)   whether China could contain its NEER appreciation (i.e., failure to do so would attract excessive speculative inflows); and
(vii)  whether China could contain its price and wage inflation, and hence real exchange rate appreciation

in the next few years. If China did badly in some of the above dimensions, there could be a crisis and/or severe recession after the overheated phase of this economic cycle. Even if it made great effort on the above, it is unlikely that China could substantially reduce its current property bubble in the next few years. Thus, it could still be vulnerable to the contagious effect of a crisis or speculative attack in its neighboring economies (e.g., Hong Kong or other Asian economies).

---

[22] Note, if one use affordability as a measure of property bubble, the current property bubble in China is in fact bigger than that in Hong Kong. However, if one use the sustainability concept, China's property price could be more sustainable than that in Hong Kong because (i) the demand by the rich Chinese are still high when compared with the existing stock of properties in China; and (ii) the higher growth in China could help offsetting part of the over-valuation over time.

# References

Buiter, W. H. and Miller, M. H. (1981). Monetary policy and international competitiveness: The problem of adjustment. *Oxford Economic Paper*, 33, 143–75.

——— (1982). Real exchange rate overshooting and the output cost of bringing down inflation. *European Economic Review*, 18(2), 85–123.

Calvo, G. A. and Rodriguez, C. A. (1977). A model of exchange rate determination under currency substitution and rational expectations. *Journal of Political Economy*, 85(3), 617–25.

Chan, A. and Chen, N. F. (1999). An intertemporal currency board. *Pacific Economic Review*, 4, 215–32.

Chang, G. H. and Shao, Q. (2004). How much is the Chinese currency undervalued? A quantity estimation. *China Economic Review*, 15(3), 366–71.

Cheung, Y. W., Chinn, M. D. and Fujii, E. (2003). The Chinese economies in global context: The integration process and its determinants. NBER Working Paper no. 10047.

——— (2007). The overvaluation of renminbi undervaluation. *Journal of International Money and Finance*, 26(5), 762–85.

Dornbusch, R. (1976). Expectations and exchange rate dynamics. *Journal of Political Economy*, 84(6), 1161–1176.

Dornbusch, R. and Fischer, S. (1980). Exchange rates and the current account. *American Economic Review*, 70(5), 960–71.

Eichengreen, B. (2004), Chinese currency controversies. Paper prepared for the Asian economic panel, Hong Kong, www.hiebs.hku.hk/aep/eichengreen.pdf.

Frankel, J. (2005). On the renminbi: The choice between adjustment under a fixed exchange rate and adjustment under a flexible rate. NBER Working Paper no. 11274.

Frankel, J. A. and Froot, K. A. (1986). The dollar as a speculative bubble: A tale of chartist and fundamentalist. NBER Working Paper no. 1534.

——— (1987). Using survey date to test standard propositions regarding exchange rate expectations. *American Economic Review*, 77(1), 133–53.

Friedman, M. (1969). Round table on exchange rate policy. *American Economic Review*, 59(2) 364–66.

Funke, M. and Rahn, J. (2005). Just how undervalued is the Chinese renminbi? *World Economy*, 28(4), 465–89.

Garton, P. and Chang, J. (2005). The Chinese currency: How undervalued and how much does it matters. *Australian Treasury, Economic Roundup*, 2005, 83–109, www.treasury.gov.au/documents/1042/PDF/08_RMBundervaluation.pdf.

Goldstein, M. (2004). Adjusting China's exchange rate policies. Revised version of a paper presented at the *IMF Seminar on China's Foreign Exchange System*, Dalian, May 26–27, www.iie.com/research/topics/renminb-hot.htm.

Johnson, H. G. (1969). The case for flexible exchange rates. *Federal Reserve Bank of St. Louis Review*, 51(6), 12–24.

Krugman, P. and Obstfeld, M. (2009). *International Economics: Theory and Policy*, 8th edn. Addison-Wesley: Boston.

Kouri, P. J. K. (1976). The exchange rate and the balance of payments in the short run and in the long run. *Scandinavian Journal of Economics*, 78(2), 280–304.

MAS (1982/83). Annual report. *Monetary Authority of Singapore*.

McKinnon, R. (2005). China's new exchange rate policy: Will China follow Japan into a liquidity trap? *Singapore Economic Review*, 50(1), 463–74.

————— (2006). China's exchange rate trap: Japan redux? *American Economic Association Meetings*, Boston, 7 January 2006.

Miller, M. (1998). The current Southeast Asia financial crisis. *Pacific-Basin Finance Journal*, 6, 225–33.

Mishkin, F. S. (2009). *The Economics of Money. Banking Financial Markets*, 8th edn. Addison-Wesley: Boston.

Mundell, R. (2004). China's exchange rate: The case for the status quo. Paper presented at *IMF Seminar on the China's Foreign Exchange System*, Dalian, China, May 26–27.

Mussa, M. (1982). A model of exchange rate dynamics. *Journal of Political Economy*, 90(1), 74–104.

Rodriguez, C. A. (1980). The role of trade flows in exchange rate determination: A rational expectations approach. *Journal of Political Economy*, 88, 1148–58.

Tsang, S. K. (1998). Currency board complications: The AEL model for Hong Kong. The proposal was later included in Tsang (1999).

Tsang, S. K. (1999). Fixing the exchange rate through a currency board arrangement: Efficiency risk, systemic risk and exit cost. *Asian Economic Journal*, 13, 239–66.

Teh, K. P. and Shanmugaratnam, T. (1992). Exchange rate policy: Philosophy and conduct over the past decade. In Low, L. and Toh, M.H. (eds.), *Public Policies in Singapore: Changes in the 1980s and the Future Signposts*, Singapore: Times Academic Press, 285–314.

Tse, Y. K. and Yip, P. S. L. (2003). The impacts of Hong Kong's currency board reforms on the interbank market. *Journal of Banking and Finance* (Netherlands), 27(12), 2273–96.

Tse, Y. K. and Yip, P. S. L. (2006). Exchange rate systems and interest rate behavior: The experience of Hong Kong and Singapore. *International Review of Economics and Finance*, 15(2), 212–27.

Williamson, J. (2007). The case for an intermediate exchange rate regime. *Singapore Economic Review*, 52(3), 295–307.

Yam, J. (1998). *Review of Currency Board Arrangements in Hong Kong*. Hong Kong Monetary Authority.

Yip, P. S. L. (1999). The speculative attack in Hong Kong amid the Asian financial crisis. *Asian Pacific Journal of Finance*, 2(1), 79–92.

——— (2002). A note on Singapore's exchange rate policy: Empirical foundations, past performance and outlook. *Singapore Economic Review*, 47(1), 173–82.

——— (2003). A restatement of Singapore's monetary and exchange rate policies. *Singapore Economic Review*, 48(2), 201–12.

——— (2005a). *The Exchange Rate Systems in Hong Kong and Singapore: Currency board vs Monitoring Band*. Singapore: Prentice Hall.

——— (2005b). On the maintenance costs and exit costs of the peg in Hong Kong. *Review of Pacific Basin Financial Markets and Policies*, 8(3), 377–403.

——— (2007a). Editorial overview: Important lessons from some major exchange rate and monetary experiences in Asia. *Singapore Economic Review*, 52(3), 269–83.

——— (2007b). China's exchange rate system reform. *Singapore Economic Review*, 52(3), 363–402.

Yip, P. S. L. and Tan, K. C. (2008). Impacts of ageing population on monetary and exchange rate management in Singapore. *Singapore Economic Review*, 53(3), 245–59.

Yip, P. S. L. and Wang, R. F. (2001). On the neutrality of exchange rate policy in Singapore. *ASEAN Economic Bulletin*, 18(2), 251–62.

——— (2002). Is price in Hong Kong that flexible? Evidence from the export sector. *Asian Economic Journal*, 16(2), 193–208.

Zhang, J. (2004). The debate on China's exchange rate — Should or will it be revalued? Stanford University, *Hoover Institution, Essays in Public Policy*, 2004, no. 112.

# Index